Ecofeminist Philosophy

Studies in Social, Political, and Legal Philosophy
Series Editor: James P. Sterba, University of Notre Dame

This series analyzes and evaluates critically the major political, social, and legal ideals, institutions, and practices of our time. The analysis may be historical or problem-centered; the evaluation may focus on theoretical underpinnings or practical implications. Among the recent titles in the series are:

Ecofeminist Philosophy

A Western Perspective on What It Is and Why It Matters

Karen J. Warren

ROWMAN & LITTLEFIELD PUBLISHERS, INC.
Lanham • Boulder • New York • Oxford

ROWMAN & LITTLEFIELD PUBLISHERS, INC.

Published in the United States of America
by Rowman & Littlefield Publishers, Inc.
4720 Boston Way, Lanham, Maryland 20706
http://www.rowmanlittlefield.com

12 Hid's Copse Road
Cumnor Hill, Oxford OX2 9JJ, England

British Cataloging in Publication Information Available

Library of Congress Cataloging-in-Publication Data

Warren, Karen, 1947–
    Ecofeminist philosophy : a western perspective on what it is and why it matters /
Karen J. Warren.
        p. cm. — (Studies in social, political, and legal philosophy)
    Includes bibliographical references and index.
    ISBN 0-8476-9298-1 (alk. paper) — ISBN 0-8476-9299-X (paper : alk. paper)
        1. Ecofeminism.   I. Title. II. Series.

HQ1233 .W297 2000
305.42'01—dc21   99-087025

Printed in the United States of America

∞™ The paper used in this publication meets the minimum requirements of American
National Standard for Information Sciences—Permanence of Paper for Printed Library
Materials, ANSI/NISO Z39.48-1992.

*Dedicated to
my daughter Cortney Warren,
and my friend Bruce Nordstrom-Loeb,
who have supported this project since its inception*

Contents

Preface

This book has been more than one decade in the making. It began as a single-authored book, started shortly after I had begun to publish material on ecofeminism. I invited philosopher Jim Cheney to co-author a book on ecofeminism with me, and we spent several years, some productive and others not, engaged in research, writing, and co-authoring two articles for eventual inclusion in our book. But the book didn't materialize, in part because I could not see clearly enough what substantive contributions I could offer as a philosopher in a full-length book on ecofeminism. At the time, the nascent field of ecofeminist scholarship included only a handful of philosophical essays, some written by us; I was not then up to the task of thinking through how to develop a distinctive ecofeminist philosophy. Although Jim and I abandoned our book project, I held on to the idea of someday writing a book on ecofeminist philosophy. This book is that book, and several chapters reflect ideas developed while Jim and I were collaborating as co-authors on ecofeminism. I thank Jim for permitting me to use some of that material here and for encouraging me to continue to work solo on a full-length manuscript written in my own voice.

The second phase in writing this book came during 1995, when I was the Ecofeminist Scholar-in-Residence at Murdoch University in Perth, Western Australia. Invited to Murdoch by philosopher Patsy Hallen, I taught—for the first time—a seminar exclusively devoted to ecofeminism. This classroom opportunity provided me with the time, environment, and opportunity to think through much of what appears in this book by prompting me to deliver weekly lectures on ecofeminism from a philosophical perspective. For the opportunity to be the Ecofeminist Scholar-in-Residence I express my gratitude to the Snailwood Fund (and its anonymous patron) for bringing me to Australia, and to Patsy Hallen, who has become a dear friend. I also thank my Australian students and colleagues at the Institute for Science & Technology Policy (ISTP, or, as it is known affectionately on the Murdoch campus, the "Institute for Saving the Planet") for providing me with the personal and institutional support to understand more clearly what I might contribute to a discussion of the nature and direction of ecofeminist philosophy.

The final impetus to complete this book was made possible by a full-year sabbatical during 1998–1999 from my professional responsibilities at Macalester

College in St. Paul, Minnesota. I am grateful to Macalester for granting me the sabbatical and for continuing to provide the institutional support (travel grants, summer grants, faculty development opportunities) necessary for its faculty to be productive teacher-scholars.

The long gestation period of this book has been an important process. Moving from feminism to ecofeminism to ecofeminist philosophy, especially when scholarship in the latter area was virtually nonexistent, has been both exciting and taxing. I eventually came to realize that what I really wanted to do was write a straightforward, nontechnical, but nonetheless philosophical book on ecofeminism for a reflective lay audience. From my experiences as a public speaker and author, I knew that both lay audiences and academics were interested in ecofeminist philosophy, but it was in speaking with nonacademics that my passion for speaking about ecofeminism came alive. I kept remembering the advice given to me by feminist philosopher Iris Marion Young after I had given a presentation at the Eastern Division of the American Philosophical Association of my as-yet unpublished paper, "The Power and the Promise of Ecological Feminism." Iris took me aside after my speech and, in a very sisterly way, said to me, "Karen, you need to write in the way that you speak!" That was 1987. I wanted to heed her advice, but I lacked then both the clarity about what it is I wanted to say and the courage to say it simply, positively, and with the conviction that so often infuses my speaking style.

More than a decade later, this book is an attempt to do that: to simply say what I understand ecofeminist philosophy to be and why I think it matters. I self-consciously chose not to write in a style familiar to mainstream academic philosophy journals (and in which I was expertly trained): narrowly focused analytical argumentation, active defense of one's position against real or imagined critics, exclusive attention to abstract concepts, hypothetical examples and counterexamples, and "grand theorizing." Consequently, the reader will not find in this book some of the issues (e.g., various feminisms as a theoretical grounding for ecofeminist philosophy) and in-house debates (e.g., the "ecofeminism–deep ecology debate") one might find in a philosophy book intended for an audience of professional philosophers and scholars.[1]

Rather, this book is written primarily for an audience of thoughtful readers who may or may not have any philosophical training or background. This includes undergraduate and graduate students, lay readers, and academics who are interested in contemporary issues in women's and feminist studies, environmental studies, and environmental philosophy. The intended audience is not primarily professional philosophers, though I hope they will find material of interest here.

During the ten-year gestation of this project, several people encouraged me to keep the project in sight, to continue to push the limits of what I knew, and to write in my own voice. I want to begin by thanking the two people to whom this book is dedicated: my wonderful daughter, Cortney Warren, and my dear friend, Bruce Nordstrom-Loeb. Their love and support have sustained me in invaluable ways. For years both Cortney and Bruce witnessed my struggle with this book project. Cortney always encouraged me with kudos like, "Keep at it, Mom. You can do it!" I am eternally grateful for Cortney's care, sacrifices, and support of my process. Bruce read each chapter carefully and gave me the sort of constructive feedback that only someone who knows a person well and for a long time can give. Bruce's scholarly insights and emotional support have been a continuous source of nourishment.

Second, I want to acknowledge my gratitude to other family and friends, who sometimes wanted me to complete this book more than I did. Included among them are Clifford Arnold, Peta Bowden, Duane Cady, Adrienne Christiansen, G. Anton Christiansen, Jane Hallas, Patsy Hallen, Pernilla Lembke, Erik Mykletun, Steve Ness, Bill Percy, Jim Radde, Steve Webb, Henry West, my sisters Jan Tull and Barbara Warren, my brother-in-law Tom Loney, my mother Marge Bails, and my feline companions, Anna and Dugan. I thank Laura Christoph-Doyle, artist, quilter, and landscape gardener, for the beautiful "ecofeminist quilt" cover art that she created to capture my ideas about ecofeminism. The actual quilt hangs in my office at Macalester College. It is a visual treat to behold each day as I begin and finish my work.

Third, several friends and colleagues read earlier versions of the manuscript and provided invaluable critical feedback: Charme Davidson, Jennifer Everett, Kim Kilde, Kristin Larsen, Bruce Nordstom-Loeb, Barbara Warren, and Henry West. I especially want to express my gratitude to my writing partner, Kim Kilde, whose thoughtful and multiple readings of the manuscript provided insightful and invaluable suggestions for improvement. I thank Kim for her friendship, enthusiasm, and thoughtful attention to my book project.

Fourth, I want to acknowledge my students, both at Macalester College and elsewhere, whose curiosity, reflection, and criticisms have fueled my energies and challenged my thinking throughout the writing of this book. Noteworthy among these students are Alison Altschuller, Rob Brault, Nisvan Erkal, Vanessa Fjuentes, Karen Fox, Emily Jamison Gromark, Nicholas Herman, Carey Levitt, Ryan Long, Michael Mason, John Millspaugh, Christie Neuman, Kirstin Nystrom, Sarah Peterson, Carolyn Strand, Freya Thimsen, Jake Tobias, Carrie Turnham, Arpana Vidyarthi, and Nicole Weiss. Your interests in my work and philosophical contributions into what needed to be said were helpful to me as I undertook writing specific chapters.

Fifth, I am grateful to several people for editorial assistance. Barbara Wells-Howe, administrative assistant in the Philosophy Department at Macalester College, provided valuable secretarial assistance in producing the final manuscript, and Spencer Carr, formerly of Westview Press, gave me editorial nudging and encouragement early on in the book-writing process, Lynn Gemmell, production editor at Rowman & Littlefield, provided meticulous, prompt, and caring assistance and suggestions for editing and revising the final manuscript, and Matthew Loughran, editorial assistant, provided generous patience and encouragement as the book preparation came to a close. Two students, Paul Pellouski and Jennie Whitehouse, gave tireless and timely help in preparing the book's index. Lastly, I especially want to thank Jim Sterba, editor of the series in which this book appears, for inviting me to submit the book proposal for *Ecofeminist Philosophy: A Western Perspective on What It Is and Why It Matters* to Rowman & Littlefield. Jim assured me from the outset that a book on ecofeminist philosophy that blended my public speaking and written philosophical styles was exactly what he wanted. Thankfully for me, Rowman & Littlefield agreed.

Many people who helped me along the way did so simply by caring about the issues raised in this book—fellow ecofeminist theorists and feminist philosophers, critics of ecofeminism, environmental organizations, citizen groups, book groups, and faith communities. By engaging with me during the past fifteen years over issues raised in this book, you have nourished many of the ideas expressed here. Your conversations, books, articles, reviews, conference presentations, letters, e-mails, and phone calls have helped shape what I do and think about as a woman, teacher, philosopher, feminist, and author.

Finally, I want to thank "Pepindigs" for providing me the housing, space, and the peacefulness of the natural environment of Maple Springs, Minnesota, where I wrote segments of this manuscript. Pepindigs was the bioregional escape I needed at the time I needed it. Engagement with the nonhuman natural environment, particularly with a pod of wild bottlenose dolphins off the coast of Key West, Florida, continues to remind me of what is truly important, what it is to be a human self, and why humans need to care about the ecological community of which we are, in Aldo Leopold's words, "co-members." I thank you all, persons and nonpersons alike, for the roles you have played in my completing this book.

NOTES

1. I have written on these issues elsewhere. See my articles, "Deep Ecology and Ecofeminism," in *Philosophical Dialogues: Arne Naess and the Progress of Ecophilosophy,* ed. Nina Witoszek and Andrew Brennan (Lanham, Md.: Rowman & Littlefield, 1999), 255–69; and "Feminism and Ecology: Making Connections," *Environmental Ethics* 9, no. 1 (Spring 1987), 3–20.

Introduction

In 1975, in her book *New Woman, New Earth,* theologian Rosemary Radford Ruether wrote:

> Women must see that there can be no liberation for them and no solution to the ecological crisis within a society whose fundamental model of relationships continues to be one of domination. They must unite the demands of the women's movement with those of the ecological movement to envision a radical reshaping of the basic socioeconomic relations and the underlying values of this society.[1]

According to Ruether, the women's movement and the ecology (or environmental) movement are intimately connected. The demands of both require "transforming that worldview which underlies domination and replacing it with an alternative value system."[2]

The thoughts expressed by Ruether in this passage changed my scholarly orientation as a graduate student in philosophy beginning to write a doctoral dissertation in 1975. Ruether's book, and subsequent readings of works by Susan Griffin, Carolyn Merchant, and Ynestra King, provided not only the "relevance" piece I needed (which was lacking from my graduate training in philosophy); it also provided the feminist piece I thirsted for in both philosophy and the environmental movement. Through the eyes of these scholars, I gradually came to see myself as an ecofeminist philosopher.

Historically, ecofeminism grew out of grassroots political actions initiated by women; it has found diverse expression in the arts, literature and language, science and technology, philosophy and religion, and nongovernmental organizations (NGOs). Ecofeminism has been advocated by scholars and practitioners across academic disciplines, from all walks of life, from all parts of the globe.

As a professional philosopher, my primary interest is in ecofeminism as a philosophical position. This book is an outgrowth of that interest. It is premised on the conviction that ecofeminist philosophy has enormous potential and power to generate insights and recommendations for any theory, practice, or policy that is feminist, ecofeminist, or environmental. My main goal in this book is to present and defend a particular version of ecofeminist philosophy, one that is grounded in my own Western historical experience and academic feminist perspective as a Euro-American woman living in the United States.

The distinctively Western philosophical perspective on ecofeminism provided in this book is just one of many possible perspectives. In this vein, I do not assume that a philosophical approach to ecofeminism is better than non-philosophical approaches (e.g., to grassroots ecofeminist organizing, or to ecofeminist art, music, literature, or spirituality). Nor do I assume that this Western perspective is a genuinely inclusive perspective—one that captures the diversity of multicultural perspectives on issues of interest to ecofeminists. I am not claiming that the perspective offered in this book is *the only* or *the definitive* or *the best* perspective among ecofeminist philosophical perspectives. It is simply one perspective—the perspective of someone who thinks philosophically about ecofeminism.

Conceptual issues are at the heart of Western ecofeminist philosophy. Not surprisingly, then, a good portion of the content of this book focuses on conceptual issues. One central conceptual issue concerns the nature of the interconnections, at least in Western societies, between the unjustified domination of women and "other human Others," on the one hand, and the unjustified domination of non-human nature, on the other hand. Throughout this book, I refer to these unjustifiably dominated groups as "Others." Reference to "Others" (or "other Others") is to those who are excluded, marginalized, devalued, pathologized, or naturalized—who become "Others"—in Western systems of unjustified domination-subordination relationships. In Western, Euro-American cultures, "Others" includes both "human Others," such as women, people of color, children, and the poor, and "earth Others," such as animals, forests, the land.

"Ecological feminism" (or "ecofeminism") is an umbrella term for a variety of different positions concerned with these connections, what I call women–other human Others–nature interconnections. The reference to "Others" highlights issues of domination, exploitation, and colonization of certain groups ("Others") who have subordinate status in institutions and relationships of domination and subordination. As I will show, a central project of ecofeminist philosophy from a Western perspective is an exploration of conceptual aspects of women–other human Others–nature interconnections.

ORGANIZATION OF THE BOOK

In chapter 1, "Nature Is a Feminist Issue," I motivate ecofeminist concerns by focusing on empirical examples of women–other human Others–nature interconnections. Appeal to this data suggests why any adequate analysis and resolution of such environmental issues as deforestation, water pollution, farming and food production, and toxins and hazardous waste location must be integrally connected to an understanding of the plight and status of women, people of color, the poor, and children. Explication of such empirical data early-on is also meant to suggest one crucial reason ecofeminist philosophy matters: it helps one understand how mainstream environmental practices and policies often reflect, reinforce, or create practices and policies that devalue, subvert, or make invisible the actual needs and contributions of women, people of color, the underclass, and children.

In chapter 2, "What Are Ecofeminists Saying?" I provide an overview of a variety of ecofeminist perspectives on women–other human Others–nature interconnections. Ten such types of interconnections are discussed: historical and causal, conceptual, empirical, socioeconomic, linguistic, symbolic and literary, spiritual and religious, epistemological, ethical, and political interconnections. Through this overview, I familiarize the reader with the range of different, sometimes competing, perspectives that have been advanced in the name of ecofeminism, especially since issues in ecofeminist philosophy arise with regard to each type of connection.

In chapter 3, "Quilting Ecofeminist Philosophy," I offer my version of ecofeminist philosophy. I begin by characterizing the version of ecofeminist philosophy I am defending, providing a visual representation of it as centrally concerned with issues that arise out of the intersection of three distinct but overlapping spheres: (1) feminism; (2) science (including the science of ecology), development, technology, and "nature"; and (3) local or indigenous perspectives. In the remainder of the chapter, I provide conceptual clarification and argumentation for the version of ecofeminist philosophy I defend in this book. I end the chapter with a discussion of ecofeminist philosophical theorizing as quilting.

Chapter 3 is not a quick read. The conceptual analysis and argumentation requires thoughtful engagement with the text on the reader's part. But it is a pivotal chapter of the book since it provides the conceptual props and argumentation on which much of the rest of the book relies.

In chapter 4, "How Should We Treat Nature?" I turn to a discussion of "environmental ethics," the arena in which much of the scholarship of ecofeminist philosophy has taken place. "Environmental ethics" is concerned with human ethical responsibilities toward nonhuman nature. I describe a range of positions in contemporary Western environmental ethics—from mainstream, "canonical" positions in Western philosophy to more radical positions. Although the version of ecofeminist philosophy I defend shares important concerns with several of these positions, I argue that an ecofeminist perspective is a distinctively feminist and potentially transformative perspective in environmental ethics.

Two sorts of worries about the nature and plausibility of an ecofeminist ethic frequently surface in discussions of ecofeminist philosophy. In fact, sometimes these worries have the effect of eliminating ecofeminist ethics from any serious consideration as an environmental ethic. The first sort of worry is raised by critics who subscribe to the view that a universal ethic is both possible and desirable. Given the centrality of issues of cultural diversity and context to ecofeminist philosophy, they worry that, from an ecofeminist philosophical perspective, a universal ethic is neither possible nor desirable. If this is true, they suggest, it is not a plausible position. The second sort of worry is from critics who claim that ecofeminist ethics is at best a set of loosely organized claims—that it is both not a theory and anti-theory. As such, it does not constitute a bona fide ethic.

I address these two worries in chapter 5, "Ethics in a Fruit Bowl." I argue that, properly understood, a universal ethic is both possible and desirable, and that the version of ecofeminist ethics I defend is such an ethic. Using the metaphor of a fruit bowl, I defend my answer by arguing for three features of what I call "care-sensitive ethics." First, an essential aspect of moral reasoning and moral motivation is the ability to care about oneself and others. I call this the "ability to care" condition. Second, the universality of ethical principles is as "situated universals," in contrast to the traditional notion of universals as ahistorical, transcendent, absolute universals. I call this the condition of "situated universalism." Third, the appropriateness or suitability of any ethical principle in a given context is determined by considerations of care. I call this the "care practices condition." I argue that care-sensitive ethics honors traditional values such as utility, self-interest, duty, and rights, to be morally salient, even if not overriding, features of ethical situations. I end the chapter by showing how an ecofeminist ethic can be helpful in understanding and resolving ethical issues in environmental contexts, and why the versions of ecofeminist ethics and ecofeminist philosophy I defend constitute bona fide theoretical positions.

In chapter 6, "Must Everyone Be Vegetarian?" I consider the issue, controversial among ecofeminists, of universal moral vegetarianism. Some ecofeminists argue that moral vegetarianism is a necessary condition of any ecofeminist practice and philosophy. Others either are not so sure or disagree. I argue for a version of what I (along with a few other ecofeminist philosophers) call "contextual moral vegetarianism," showing the significance of a care-sensitive approach to issues of hunting and vegetarianism.

Some critics worry that ecofeminist philosophy is not sufficiently ecological to be a bona fide basis for environmental (read: ecological) ethics. I address this worry in chapter 7, "What Is Ecological about Ecofeminist Philosophy?" I answer the question in two distinct but related ways: First, I discuss the leading position to date in ecosystem ecology known as "hierarchy theory." I argue that there are six key features of hierarchy theory that make it both compatible with and a theoretical ecological grounding for ecofeminist philosophy. Second, I discuss what is probably the most widely known and popular text in environmental ethics among naturalists, foresters, fish and wildlife managers, parks and recreation ecologists, and field ecologists—the late Aldo Leopold's 1949 essay, "The Land Ethic," from his collection of essays *The Sand County Almanac and Sketches Here and There.* I argue for an updated interpretation of Leopold's land ethic that makes its basic ecological claims compatible with a hierarchy theorist's perspective on ecosystems and its basic ethical claims compatible with the version of ecofeminist philosophy I am defending. I argue that, taken together, these two different ecological starting points—hierarchy theory and an updated version of Leopoldian land ethics—provide independent and sufficient evidence of the ecological grounding of ecofeminist philosophy. Stated differently, together they show the respects in which ecofeminist philosophy is sufficiently "ecological."

But the argument of chapter 7 does not stop there. I also argue that there are important contributions ecofeminist philosophy can make to both the theory and practice of the discipline of ecology. After saying what these contributions are, I end the chapter by arguing for the potential fruitfulness of coalition-building and ongoing dialogue among ecosystem ecologists (especially hierarchy theorists), Leopoldian land ethicists, and ecofeminist philosophers like myself.

Throughout the book evidence is offered about the disproportionate and unjustified environmental harms to women, other human Others, and nonhuman nature. This evidence raises issues about "environmental justice." In chapter 8, "With Justice for All," I argue for an inclusive concept of justice that has three features. First, it retains aspects of the familiar, distributive model of social justice, while revising that model to accommodate feminist critiques. Second, it incorporates nondistributive aspects of social justice overlooked or improperly construed by a distributive model of justice. Third, it shows why an adequate concept of social justice includes issues of environmental justice. I conclude that a reconceived and transformed concept of justice takes women–other human Others–nature interconnections seriously and ensures that the moral considerability of nonhuman nature is included in conceptions and practices of social justice.

I end the discussion of ecofeminist philosophy by discussing the importance of spirituality to ecofeminist philosophy in chapter 9, "Surviving Patriarchy." Discussions of spirituality do not figure prominently in ecofeminist philosophical accounts. Issues about spirituality are either dismissed out of hand as outside the province of philosophy or declared to be sufficiently muddled or conceptually problematic as to not warrant serious philosophical attention.

The view advanced in chapter 9 is different. I begin the chapter by offering philosophical reasons for exploring the potential of ecofeminist spiritualities to intervene in and creatively change patriarchal (and other) systems of domination. I then describe what I understand to be the nature of ecofeminist spirituality and connections between ecofeminist spirituality and power, nonviolence, and care. I then turn to a discussion of a model of patriarchy as an unhealthy human social system, showing that ecofeminist spiritualities do (or could) play important interventionist and creative roles in dismantling patriarchy as a social system.

CLOSING REMARKS

This book is the book I wanted to write about ecofeminist philosophy for a reflective audience. My hope is that you, the reader, will find in these pages ideas and arguments that are interesting, engaging, and useful. Perhaps you will be motivated to engage in dialogue with others about some of the issues raised here. It is my hope that this book stimulates such conversation.

NOTES

1. Rosemary Radford Ruether, *New Woman, New Earth: Sexist Ideologies and Human Liberation* (New York: Seabury Press, 1975), 204.

2. Ruether, *New Woman,* 204.

Chapter One

Nature Is a Feminist Issue

Motivating Ecofeminism by Taking Empirical Data Seriously

Trees, forests, and deforestation. Water, drought, and desertification. Food production, poverty, and toxic wastes. The biodiversity crisis, wildlife, and maltreatment of animals. What do such environmental issues have to do with women, people of color, the poor, and children?

Ecological feminists ("ecofeminists") claim that there are important connections between the unjustified dominations of women, people of color, children, and the poor and the unjustified domination of nature. Throughout this book, I refer to unjustifiably dominated groups as "Others," both "human Others" (such as women, people of color, children, and the poor) and "earth Others" (such as animals, forests, the land). The reference to "Others" is intended to highlight the status of those subordinate groups in unjustifiable relationships and systems of domination and subordination. According to ecofeminists, "nature" (referring to nonhuman animals, plants, and ecosystems) is included among those Others who/that have been unjustifiably exploited and dominated. "Nature is a feminist issue" might well be called the slogan of ecofeminism.

What does it mean to say "nature is a feminist issue"? Minimally, something is a "feminist issue" if an understanding of it helps one understand the oppression, subordination, or domination of women. Equal rights, comparable pay for comparable work, and day care centers are feminist issues because understanding them sheds light on the subordination or inferior status of women cross-culturally. Racism, classism, ableism, ageism, heterosexism, anti-Semitism, and colonialism are feminist issues because understanding them helps one understand the subordination of women. (More is said about this in chapter 3.) According to ecofeminists, trees, water, food production, animals, toxins, and, more generally, naturism (i.e., the unjustified domination of nonhuman nature) are feminist issues because understanding them helps one understand the interconnections among

1

the dominations of women and other subordinated groups of humans ("other human Others"), on the one hand, and the domination of nonhuman nature, on the other hand. I call these interconnections women–other human Others–nature interconnections.

What does it mean to take a *feminist approach* to untangling these interconnections? A feminist approach uses gender analysis as the starting point; gender is the *lens* through which the initial description and analysis occur. Ecofeminism uses a feminist approach when exploring women–other human Others–nature interconnections.

If ecofeminism is about interconnections among *all* systems of unjustified human domination, why is special attention given to women—only one of many groups of humans who are unjustifiably dominated? Ecofeminists begin with gender as a category of analysis. As such, ecofeminists highlight claims about women *as* women in their discussions of interconnected systems of unjustified domination (rather than, for example, on women *as* humans, *as* mothers, *as* wives, *as* daughters, *as* sisters).[1] But this is not because gender oppression is more important than other forms of oppression; it is not. It is because a focus on "women" reveals important features of interconnected systems of human domination: First, among white people, people of color, poor people, children, the elderly, colonized peoples, so-called Third World people, and other human groups harmed by environmental destruction, it is often women who suffer disproportionately higher risks and harms than men. Second, often female-gender roles (e.g., as managers of domestic economies) overlap with a particular environmental issue in a way that male-gender roles do not. Third, some of the Western ideologies that underlie the conception and domination of "nature" are male-gender biased in ways that are distinct from other sorts of bias (a topic discussed in chapter 3). So, in order to unpack specific gender features of human systems of domination, ecofeminists often (but not exclusively) focus on "women."

This chapter uses a feminist approach to discuss *empirical* women–other human Others–nature interconnections. These empirical considerations set the stage for subsequent considerations of a variety of ecofeminist positions (given in chapter 2) and the particular version of ecofeminist philosophy (given in chapter 3) I defend throughout this book.

WOMEN AND TREES, FORESTS, AND FORESTRY

In 1974, twenty-seven women of Reni in northern India took simple but effective action to stop tree felling. They threatened to hug the trees if the lumberjacks attempted to cut them down. The women's protest, known as the Chipko movement ("chipko" in Hindi means "to embrace" or "hug"), saved 12,000 square kilometers of sensitive watershed. The Chipko movement also gave visibility to two basic complaints of local people: commercial felling by contractors damages

a large number of other trees, and the teak and eucalyptus monoculture plantations are replacing valuable indigenous forests.[2]

Forests have been central to the evolution of Indian civilization, India being
known in ancient times as "Aranya Sanskriti" or a "forest culture."[3] The com-
mercialization of forestry under British rule, however, restricted the access of
local Indians to forests, and management practices that aimed at maximizing timber output for a cash economy were introduced. This led to widespread Gandhian
satyagrahas—campaigns of nonviolent civil disobedience by local Indian
women. The Chipko movement is "historically, philosophically and organisa-
tionally, an extension of traditional Gandhian *satyagrahas*."[4]

Both the earlier forest satyagrahas and their contemporary expression in the
Chipko movement are responses to conflicts over forest resource use and degradation. According to Jayanta Bandyopadhyay and Vandana Shiva, what distinguishes Chipko from the earlier struggles is its ecological basis:

> The new concern to save and protect forests through Chipko satyagraha did not arise
> from resentment against further encroachment on the people's access to forest resources.
> It arose from the alarming signals of rapid ecological destabilisation in the hills. . . . It
> has now evolved to the demand for ecological rehabilitation. Since the Chipko move-
> ment is based upon the perception of forests in their ecological context, it exposes the
> social and ecological costs of short term growth-oriented forest management. This is
> clearly seen in the slogan of the Chipko movement which claims that the main products
> of the forests are not timber or resin, but "soil, water, and oxygen."[5]

"Soil, water, and oxygen." The Chipko women understand the ecological significance of forests.

The Chipko movement—a grassroots, women-initiated, ecologically aware,
nonviolent protest movement—is ostensibly about trees. But it is also about
women–other human Others–nature interconnections. This is because, in India
(as in many countries of the Southern Hemisphere, hereafter referred to as the
South), forests are inextricably connected to rural and household economies governed by women. Tree shortages in India pose significant problems for rural
Indian women. The "eucalyptus controversy" illustrates why this is so.

As a result of First World development decisions, indigenous, multispecies forests
have been replaced in India by monoculture tree plantations, most notably eucalyptus plantations. The replacement of natural forests in India with eucalyptus plantations typically is justified by outside development theoreticians on the grounds of
increased productivity. While eucalyptus covers nearly half a million hectares, it is
very unpopular among local women. According to Bandyopadhyay and Shiva:

> What has been called the "eucalyptus controversy" is in reality a conflict of para-
> digms, between an ecological approach to forestry on the one hand, and a reduction-
> ist, partisan approach which only responds to industrial requirements on the other.
> While the former views natural forests and many indigenous tree species as more

productive than eucalyptus, the reverse is true according to the paradigm of Commercial Forestry. The scientific conflict is in fact an economic conflict over *which* needs and *whose needs are important.*[6]

Which needs and whose needs *are* important? Ecofeminists insist that the needs of women as primary managers of household economies are important for at least three reasons.

First, in the South women are typically more dependent than men on tree and forest products,[7] and they are the primary sufferers of forest resource depletion.[8] Trees provide five essential elements in these household economies: food, fuel, fodder, products for the home (including building materials, household utensils, gardens, dyes, medicines), and income-generating activities.[9] As trees become scarce, it is women who must walk farther for fuelwood and fodder and who must carry it all back themselves (e.g., without the help of animals). As men increasingly seek employment in towns and cities, especially to work in eucalyptus plantations, it is women who must carry out men's former jobs plus the laborious tasks of collecting and processing forest products on degraded soils. As new technologies targeted at cash economies are introduced, it is women who have decreased opportunities to use trees as a source of income (e.g., by making objects that can be sold at market). As development projects that fail to address women's specific needs are introduced, it is women who are confronted with the challenges of cooking with inferior fuelwood. Because of their gendered responsibilities for maintaining domestic households, tree shortages have a significant, direct, and disproportionate impact on women. As the U.N. publication *The World's Women, 1995* states:

> Rough estimates of the proportion of rural women affected by fuelwood scarcity—based on estimates by the Food and Agriculture Organization of the United Nations of the percentage of household energy provided by fuelwood—are 60 percent in 32 African countries, nearly 80 percent in 18 Asian countries, and nearly 40 percent in 14 Latin American and Caribbean countries.[10]

In highly deforested areas, the situation for women is the worst, since women must devote more time to collecting fuelwood, thereby reducing the time available to do other activities.

Second, there are customs, taboos, and legal and time constraints that women face that men do not face. As the United Nations documents:

> Economic productivity and development in rural areas of developing regions are low, and women in poor rural regions are overwhelmingly disadvantaged in dealing with their environment. They have less education and training than urban women or rural men, and they are excluded from traditional rural development programmes that might provide such training—and from the credit and other institutional support needed for rural development.[11]

Men and women often have different access to credit and land. The rights of men and women regarding trees often differ significantly. In the United Republic of Tanzania, for example, women (who may be one of several wives of one man) often are permitted to stay on land they do not and cannot own at the discretion of their husbands or fathers.[12] Women in rural areas of developing countries are largely without access to the sort of institutional support needed to participate in and control local development:

> In rural areas, women's roles are those of the poorest-paid labourers—weeding, hoeing and carrying water and wood, combined with the traditional family roles of cooking, child care, health care and reproduction—without even the pay that a labourer expects. While consciousness of these traditional roles has fostered the idea that women are in some sense natural custodians of the environment in rural areas, there is no evidence of this notion and women in rural areas are largely ill-equipped for it. They are without training, status, access to community-based organizations and cooperatives, land and property rights, capital, or environmental institutions that make up the dense fabric of rural life and control its development.[13]

Third, key assumptions of commercial Western forestry work to women's disadvantage. One such assumption is that *the outsider knows best*—that the First World forester (an "outsider") has the requisite technical expertise to solve the problem of the lack of trees in Third World countries. But this assumption is false or problematic. Sometimes it is "the insider" (i.e., the local people most inside the culture)—the Chipko women of India, for example—who are the experts, who have what feminist foresters call "indigenous technical knowledge" about forestry production.[14] Because local women are the primary users of forest commodities in most developing countries, their "day-to-day, hands-on involvement with forestry goes far beyond that of many professionally trained foresters."[15] For example, in a Sierra Leone village, women were able to identify thirty-one products from nearby bushes and trees while men could identify only eight.[16] Women's indigenous technical knowledge grows out of their daily, felt, lived experiences as managers of trees and tree products.

A second assumption of commercial Western forestry is that activities that fall outside the boundaries of commercial fiber production are less important.[17] Yet these activities are precisely those that women engage in on a daily basis. Conceptually, the "invisibility" of what women do accounts for the mistaken assumption that management and production policies of orthodox forestry are not gender-biased. It also explains why many foresters "literally do not see trees that are used as hedgerows or living fence poles; trees that provide materials for basketry, dyes, medicines, or decorations; trees that provide sites for honey barrels; trees that provide shade; or trees that provide human food."[18] Because these foresters literally do not *see* these multiple uses of trees, they also often do not see a lot more, for example, that a diversity of tree species is useful, that men and women may have very different uses for the same tree or may use different trees for different purposes.

A third assumption of orthodox Western forestry concerns efficiency: it usually is better to have large-scale production using a small number of species than small-scale, community-based forestry using a wide variety of species. Again, the Chipko movement challenges this assumption. Since small-scale production reflects local priorities, involves multiple uses of many species of trees, and is responsive to the social reality of women's importance in agriculture and forest production, to threaten small-scale production is to threaten the livelihood and well-being of women.

The empirical data about women and trees in India remind us to notice that other issues usually raised outside an ecofeminist context, such as the loss of old-growth temperate and rainforest trees and the effects of deforestation on indigenous cultures, can usefully become part of an ecofeminist discussion as well. Consider, for example, the impact of the destruction of native forests—those never logged or planted by humans—on indigenous and land-based peoples in Brazil. In the northwest Amazon, an invasion of gold miners has "wrecked devastation on the Yanomami—one of the largest and most culturally intact indigenous groups in the Amazon."[19] Despite current action by the Brazilian government, the destruction of Yanomami culture and livelihood has continued: Yanomami gardens have been destroyed; streams have been polluted with deadly mercury; malaria and other illnesses contribute to the death, starvation, and malnutrition that plagues these native peoples. Between 1987 and 1990, nearly 13 percent of the Yanomami population (about 1,300 people) died as a result of the miners' actions.[20] The military governments that ruled Brazil from 1964 to 1985 viewed indigenous people as "ethnic cysts" to be "excised" from or assimilated into the body politic.[21] Blatant disregard for the culture and health of indigenous peoples is intimately connected with the destruction of the forests and land that constitute their homes.

WOMEN, WATER, AND DROUGHT

The demand for water for agricultural irrigation in developing countries accounted for 30 percent of the growth in water consumption in 1990. World water use is divided among irrigation uses (73 percent), industry uses (22 percent), and domestic uses (5 percent). But less than 3 percent of all water on earth is fresh. The atmosphere, rivers, streams, lakes, and underground stores hold less than 1 percent of the earth's water.

Furthermore, millions of humans have difficulty getting sufficient water necessary for survival, about 5 liters per day. In more than half of the developing countries, less than 50 percent of the population has a source of potable water or facilities for sewage disposal. The World Health Organization estimates that approximately 85 percent of all sicknesses and diseases in developing countries, including diarrhea, trachoma, parasitic worms, and malaria, are attributable to inadequate potable water or sanitation. It also estimates that as many as 25 million deaths a year are due to water-related illnesses. The United Nations International Children's Emergency Fund (UNICEF) estimates that 15 million children die every year before they are five; half of them could be saved if they had access to safe drinking water.[22]

Water scarcity is of special concern for women and children. According to *The World's Women, 1995,* the majority of countries in Africa and many countries of Asia and Latin America are considered water-scarcity countries.[23] In these countries, women and children perform most of the water collection work. Small-scale studies in Africa and Asia indicate that women and girls spend up to forty-three hours per week collecting and carrying water (e.g., in Africa, approximately seventeen hours in Senegal, five hours in rural areas of Botswana, and forty-three hours on northern farms in Ghana; in Asia, seven hours in the Baroda region of India, one to five hours in Nepalese villages, depending on the ages of the girls, and three hours in Pakistan).[24] Because of natural resource depletion, women also must walk farther for water (e.g., up to fifteen kilometers daily through rough terrain in Uttarakhand, India). The effects on women in these countries is significant:

> The proportion of rural women affected by water scarcity is estimated at 55 per cent in Africa, 32 per cent in Asia and 45 per cent in Latin America. Even where water is abundant overall in countries, there still are significant parts of many countries where at least seasonal water scarcity burdens women with added time for water collection.[25]

According to Joni Seager, approximately half the population in the Third World is still without safe drinking water.[26] There are 250 million cases of water-related diseases, resulting in ten million deaths, reported each year.[27] Drinking water is often drawn from public bathing and laundering places, and the same water is frequently used as a public toilet. Lack of sanitary water is of special concern for women and children since, as the primary providers of household water, they experience disproportionately higher health risks in the presence of unsanitary water.

Contaminated water and its disproportionate effects on women, particularly among people of color and the poor, is not just a problem in developing countries. In 1980, the United States produced 125 billion pounds of hazardous waste, enough to fill approximately 3,000 Love Canals. By the mid-1990s, 38 percent of the rivers in the United States were too polluted to swim in. Groundwater, the drinking water source for nearly half of the population of the United States, is contaminated by leaking chemical wastes and other substances.[28]

As an example, in Hardeman County, Tennessee, in 1964, the Velsicol Chemical Company dumped 300,000 fifty-five gallon barrels of unknown chemicals on their 242-acre farm. Some of the barrels burst open, and their contents seeped into the soil. In 1967 a U.S. Geological Survey report showed that the chemicals from the dump site were reaching local water wells. No action was taken. By 1977 residents noticed that their drinking water had a foul odor and taste. Nell Grantham, a licensed practical nurse, took samples of their water for testing. The results confirmed their suspicions: Their water contained harmful chemicals, twelve clearly identified. Local residents were told the water was not safe to drink, cook with, bathe in; vegetables and animals could not be raised on their land. Residents experienced a host of health problems: skin rashes, liver damage, birth defects.[29]

A different sort of water issue that affects women, people of color, the poor, and children are the so-called natural disasters of droughts and floods. A drought is too little water; a flood is too much water. Traditionally, droughts and floods are considered "disasters" only when humans, human communities, and property have been seriously affected. Humans make land more drought-prone and more flood-prone (and, hence, more disaster-prone) by removing the vegetation and soil systems that absorb and store water. As Anders Wijkman and Lloyd Timberlake claim about droughts, "reduced rainfall may trigger a drought, but human pressure on the land is the primary cause."[30]

Wijkman and Timberlake argue that forces of nature ("natural events") trigger disaster events, but they are not the main cause. In the developing world, they identify three main causes of "natural disasters": human vulnerability resulting from poverty and inequality; environmental degradation owing to poor land use; and rapid population growth, especially among the poor.[31] But these three main causes involve a complex set of institutional, economic, cultural, and political factors. According to Wijkman and Timberlake, these complex factors bear an important and typically undernoticed causal role in the occurrence of "natural disasters," such as droughts and floods, that affect millions of humans and animals.

Economic or class interests head the list of human-induced factors that affect the occurrences and locations of droughts as "natural disasters." Wijkman and Timberlake poignantly express this point when they claim that "no wealthy person ever died in a drought," "no relief worker has starved to death during a drought," and "no journalist has died of hunger while covering a drought."[32]

Are droughts and floods—obvious environmental issues with class implications—also gender and age issues? Yes, especially considering that it is poor women and children who are most significantly affected. This is due to a constellation of interconnected factors—with poverty a major factor. No matter how poverty is measured, the poor population is largely and increasingly comprised of women and children. Poverty differentials among both groups are magnified by race, ethnicity, and age.[33] For example, cross-culturally, women are paid less than men, and women in most regions spend as much or more time working than men when unpaid housework is taken into account.[34] Women everywhere control fewer resources and reap a lesser share of the world's wealth than men: Women do more than one-half of the world's work, but receive only 10 percent of the world's income and own only 1 percent of the world's property.[35] Women-headed households are a growing worldwide phenomenon, with between 80 and 90 percent of poor families headed by women.[36] When one remembers that the three elements that make up the major part of Third World disasters are deforestation, desertification, and soil erosion, and that, among humans, it is the poor who are most significantly affected by them, one can then understand why women and children will be disproportionately victims of these disasters.

WOMEN, FOOD, AND FARMING

It is estimated that women farmers grow at least half of the world's food. According to Mayra Buvinic and Sally Yudelman, between one-third and one-half of the agricultural laborers in the Third World are women.[37] They claim that:

> As a rule, women farmers work longer hours, have fewer assets and lower incomes than men farmers do, and have almost as many dependents to support. The disparity is not due to lack of education or competence. Women farmers are poorer because their access to credit is limited. Without credit they cannot acquire productive assets, such as cattle, fertilizer or improved seeds, to improve the productivity of their labor.[38]

Women's share in farming varies widely cross-culturally, but in general men do more of the actual fieldwork when access to machinery or large farm animals is involved (such as in the United States or India), and women do more when the work is done by hand (such as in Amazonia and sub-Saharan Africa).

Women in Africa produce more than 70 percent of Africa's food, typically without tractors, oxen, or even plows.[39] "When one speaks today of 'the African farmer,' one is talking about a woman."[40] The Ugandan poet Okot p'Bitek poignantly expresses this view in his "Song of Ocol."

> Woman of Africa
> Sweeper
> Smearing floors and walls
> With cow dung and black soil
> Cook, ayah, the baby on your back
> Washer of dishes,
> Planting, weeding, harvesting
> Store-keeper, builder
> Runner of errands,
> Cart, lorry, donkey . . .
> Woman of Africa
> What are you not?[41]

To illustrate the plight of women farmers in Africa, consider the root crop cassava. Women do 70 to 80 percent of the growing and harvesting of cassava, and 100 percent of the processing, which includes washing out the natural cyanide found in it (a process that takes eighteen five-hour days). Yet little money has been devoted to research on cassava and the development of processing technologies that would increase both the productivity of women farmers and the demand and price for cassava.[42]

The so-called feminization of agriculture refers to the increasing proportion of women in the agricultural labor force. Women are farm owners and farm managers, with major decision-making responsibilities about production and most agricultural tasks. Women are farm partners, sharing responsibility for agricultural production, typically with another household member. Women are farm workers, either as unpaid family laborers or as wage laborers.[43] The number of women for each 100 men working in agriculture is seventy-one in Africa, fifty-four in Western Europe, forty-seven in Asia and the Pacific, and eighty-four in Eastern Europe.[44]

However, a failure to realize the extent of women's contribution to agriculture (e.g., by First World development policies and practices) has contributed historically to the invisibility of women in all aspects of agricultural work: in ploughing, planting, caring for farm animals, harvesting, weeding, processing, and the storing of crops. It also has contributed to a failure to see ways in which women and their families have been deeply affected by development decisions and projects that have depleted the resource bases on which their productive activities depend (e.g., subsistence agriculture, food processing). This is exacerbated by the fact that women historically have often had little input into those decisions and projects.[45]

Chris Cuomo argues that farms are sites of human oppression in the United States as well:

> Eighty to ninety percent of the approximately two million hired farmworkers are Latino, followed by African-Americans, Caribbeans, Puerto Ricans, Filipinos, Vietnamese, Koreans, and Jamaicans. It is estimated that as many as 313,000 farmworkers experience pesticide-related illnesses each year. Not surprisingly, Hispanic women generally show higher levels of pesticides in their milk than white women do.[46]

Although it is not known how many of the agricultural workforce in the United States, including the percentage of migrant and seasonal farmworkers, are women, the U.S. Department of Agriculture (USDA) has determined that 22 percent of all hired farmworkers in the United States are women. Of this 22 percent, 9 percent are classified as migrant workers, and 45 percent of migrant farmworking women were Hispanic, 45 percent were white, and 6 percent were classified by the USDA as "Black and Other."[47] This sort of empirical data shows why farming, agriculture, and food are important to ecofeminist philosophers.

WOMEN, PEOPLE OF COLOR, CHILDREN, AND HEALTH

The health of women and children, particularly in poor communities of color, is adversely and disproportionately affected by harmful human environmental practices. For example, in some developing countries, women spend much of their time cooking with biomass—wood, straw, or dung—in poorly ventilated areas. They are thereby exposed to high levels of indoor pollution. As the United Nations reports in *The World's Women, 1995,* significant health risks are experienced by women who cook indoors in developing countries.

> One study in Nepal found that women cook for about five hours a day, with indoor particulate concentrations in rural areas as high as 20,000 micrograms per cubic meter. As a result, acute respiratory infections and bronchitis are said to be very common in rural areas.
>
> Nonsmoking women in India and Nepal exposed to biomass smoke have been found to have abnormally high levels of chronic respiratory diseases—with mortality rates comparable to that of heavy male smokers. The enormously high levels of women's exposure to indoor air pollution during cooking found in 15 countries of Africa and Asia indicate very significant health risks to the many women who cook indoors in developing countries.[48]

Health issues in Western countries around chemical sensitivity also affect women. There are three main ways in which chemicals can enter the body: through inhalation, ingestion, or absorption through the skin.[49] In the United States and Canada, the chemical sensitivity literature shows that human sensitivities to substances like formaldehyde are strongly gender related (two to three times the number of cases among women than men) and age dependent (children and older women are the most vulnerable). In the Great Lakes Basin ecosystem, pesticides, heavy metals, PCBs (polychlorinated biphenyls), and dioxins have been shown not only to produce reproductive impairments, cancers, and tumors in fish and mammals and deformities in insect larvae, but in human tissue as well. PCBs have contributed to adverse reproductive outcomes (including decreased sperm count in males), low birth weight, infants born with smaller head circumferences, increased rates of cancer of all types, and circulatory and immune system diseases.[50] Similarly, pesticides and industrial pollutants contribute to many types of reproductive impairment in humans, for example, difficulty conceiving, miscarriages and spontaneous abortions, sperm toxicity, and fetal/infant related health problems.[51] Due largely to their ability to cross the placenta, to bioaccumulate, and to occur as mixtures, persistent toxic chemicals pose disproportionate serious health threats to infants, mothers, and the elderly.

There are important psychosocial aspects of exposure to environmental toxins. Studies in the United States of people exposed to relatively high levels of hazardous substances in Love Canal, New York, and Three Mile Island, Pennsylvania, show the prevalence of fear and anxieties about the future health impacts of such exposure.[52] According to Tom Muir and Anne Sudar, "These impacts are exacerbated by the people's feelings that they have no control over the situation."[53] They live in homes and communities from which no escape seems financially possible. This high level of distress has been shown to be associated with significantly poorer DNA repair in lymphocytes, as compared to low-distress subjects.[54]

Take, for example, the Exxon *Valdez* case. On March 24, 1989, the Exxon *Valdez* ran aground in Prince William Sound, Alaska, spilling 11 million gallons of oil, wiping out countless numbers of birds and sea otters, and drastically affecting ecosystem function in the region. The toll on human lives has also been great. Aleut Indian villages of Chenega Bay and Tatilek and the cities of Valdez and Cordova face increased depression and alcoholism. According to Paul Koberstein:

> In Valdez, records show the divorce rate is four times higher than before the spill. In Cordova, a state survey indicates that nearly two-thirds of the population suffers from post-traumatic stress syndrome, an emotional breakdown that typically occurs after a catastrophe or war. In Homer, demand for substance abuse programs doubled. In Kodiak, admissions to the local mental health centers increased by nearly 50 percent. In many communities, health officials are seeing increases in child abuse and neglect.[55]

Like other indigenous populations, the seventy villagers of Chenega Bay "face the paradox of good money for ruined lives. Many of them earned $2,000 a week on the spill, but the tribe lost an entire year of subsistence fishing" and untold disruptions to their traditional way of life.

While environmental disasters such as those caused by the Exxon *Valdez* affect both men and women, some environmental problems affect women more harshly. In the United States, American Indian women historically have faced unique health risks.

> A survey of households and hospitals on the Pine Ridge Reservation in South Dakota revealed that in one month in 1979, 38 percent of the pregnant women on the reservation suffered miscarriages, compared to the normal rate of between 10 and 20 percent . . . [there were] extremely high rates of cleft palate and other birth defects, as well as hepatitis, jaundice, and serious diarrhea. Health officials confirmed that their reservation had higher than average rates of bone and gynecological cancers.[56]

Inadequate sewage treatment facilities have led to fecal contamination of drinking and bathing water. "Tests done by government officials also showed high levels of radioactivity in the water. The reservation is downwind from old mines surrounded by uranium trailings."[57]

Children are also particularly vulnerable to toxins. According to "What's Gotten Into Our Children," published by Children Now, a California-based children's advocacy organization, some characteristics unique to children make them particularly vulnerable to environmental hazards. Children Now cites four specific areas in which children are physically more vulnerable than adults: food and water, home, schools, and outdoor play areas. Children tend to consume greater amounts of food that contain toxins, thereby multiplying the potential risk.[58] In the United States, the National Resources Defense Council (NRDC) estimates that more than half of the lifetime risk of cancer associated with pesticides on fruit is incurred before the age of six.[59] In homes and schools, hazardous products (e.g., cleaning products), and exposure to lead, radon, asbestos, and indoor air pollution (e.g., tobacco smoke, formaldehyde found in some carpeting, wall-board, and insulation) are thought to be particularly harmful to children since the same amount of exposure to children and adults is believed to produce higher concentrations in the smaller bodies of children. Outdoors, pesticides, harmful sun exposure (due to depletion of the ozone layer), air pollution, and unsafe play areas can result in serious health conditions in children (e.g., breathing certain kinds of asbestos fibers can increase the chance of developing chronic diseases, ground level ozone-caused air pollution can cause respiratory problems such as shortness of breath, coughing).

Furthermore, in the United States, over 700,000 inner-city children are suffer-ing from lead poisoning (and the learning disabilities that result), 50 percent of whom are African, Hispanic, and Asian American.[60] While all children are at risk, poor children are at greater risk: they are more likely to live in neighborhoods with environmental hazards; poor families lack the financial resources to remove hazards from their home or purchase alternative, nonhazardous products; poor children are less likely to have access to health care for treatment; the families of poor children often lack the necessary political clout to insist on the cleanup of hazards in the neighborhood.[61] Furthermore, in Third World countries, usually over half the people are under fifteen years old. So children are a majority of any group. In increasing numbers, children are developing environmental sensitivi-ties, allergies, and asthma (the study and treatment of which is developing into a field of its own, clinical ecology).[62]

WOMEN AND ENVIRONMENTAL JUSTICE

In 1987, the United Church of Christ Commission for Racial Justice published a stunning and now-classic report entitled "Toxic Waste and Race in the United States." Using sophisticated statistical analysis, the report indicated that race (not class) is the primary factor in the location of hazardous waste in the United States: Three out of every five African and Hispanic Americans (more than 15 million of the nation's 26 million African Americans, and over 8 million of the 15 million Hispanics), and over half of all Asian Pacific Islanders and American Indians, live in communities with one or more uncontrolled toxic waste sites. The nation's largest hazardous waste landfill, receiving toxins from forty-five states, is in Emelle, Alabama, which is 79.9 percent African American. Probably the greatest concentration of hazardous waste sites in the United States is on the pre-dominately African American and Hispanic South Side of Chicago. In Houston, Texas, six of eight municipal incinerators, and all five city landfills, are located in predominately African American neighborhoods.[63]

The federal Centers for Disease Control in Atlanta, Georgia, documents that lead poisoning endangers the health of nearly 8 million inner-city, largely African American and Hispanic, children. Countless more live with crumbling asbestos in housing projects and schools. Seventy-five percent of the residents in rural areas of the southwestern United States, mainly Hispanic Americans, are drinking pesticide-contaminated water. Yet Hispanics hold only 1 percent of substantive policy-making positions at the United States Environmental Protection Agency (EPA).[64] Hispanics thereby have limited institutional input at policy-making levels to the plights of Hispanic communities affected by lead poisoning.

Women, especially poor women of color, are organizing throughout the world to fight environmental contaminations of all kinds in their communities. For example, in the United States, Mothers of East Los Angeles (MELA), founded in 1985, protested a hazardous-waste incinerator in the small city of Vernon, California. According to Dick Russell:

> Even in state-of-the-art hazardous-waste incinerators, pollutants escape through the stacks. In Vernon, the burning of an estimated 225,000 tons a year of solvents, pesticides, alcohols, oil and paint sludges, heavy metal residues, industrial liquids, and infectious wastes from hospitals would also leave some 19,000 tons of highly toxic ash, dust, and other by-products to dispose of. All this in close proximity not only to twenty-six schools, but also dozens of food-related industries.[65]

Time magazine reported the outcome of MELA's activities:

> Last week, after six years of agitation marked by four lawsuits, 16 hearings and six mile-long protest marches, the 400-strong Mothers of East L.A. passed around cookies to celebrate a major victory: cancellation of a proposed commercial incinerator they claimed could spew cancer-causing particles over the community by burning 22,500 tons of used motor oil and industrial sludge annually. Citing "political pressure" and the prospect of "interminable litigation," attorneys for Security Environmental Systems, which was to build the facility, ruefully announced "abandonment" of the project.[66]

Women often play a primary role in community environmental activism because environmental ills touch their lives in direct, immediate ways.[67] As Cynthia Hamilton writes:

> Women often play a primary role in community action because it is about things they know best. They also tend to use organizing strategies and methods that are the antithesis of those of the traditional environmental movement. Minority women in several urban areas [of the United States] have found themselves part of a new radical core of environmental activists, motivated by the irrationalities of capital-intensive growth. These individuals are responding not to "nature" in the abstract but to their homes and the health of their children. . . . Women are more likely to take on these issues than men precisely because the home has been defined as a woman's domain.[68]

Because of the direct impact of environmental degradation on their lives, working-class minority women organize around "very pragmatic environmental issues."[69]

The early roots of the upsurge of minority environmental activism in the United States can be found in Warren County, North Carolina, where, in 1982, the state decided to build a PCB disposal site with $2.5 million in federal monies. The EPA modified the permit to locate the site only fifteen feet above the water table (normally fifty feet is required for PCBs).[70] The area's 16,000 residents—60 percent African American and 4 percent Native American—organized a series of marches and protests involving "a cross-section of religious leaders, farmers, educators, citizens of all races" because they felt the decision was racially motivated. The residents lost. Shortly thereafter, the U.S. General Accounting Office reported "on racial and socioeconomic characteristics of communities surrounding hazardous waste landfills in the Southeast [United States]. It found that three out of four were predominantly black and poor."[71]

Citizens for a Better Environment (CBE) released a report in 1989 on the Richmond, California, area, located sixteen miles across the bay from San Francisco and home to about 100,000 residents, about half of whom are African American. Richmond has more than 350 industrial facilities that handle hazardous chemicals, and 210 toxins are routinely emitted into the air, water, as solid waste or in industrial storage sites. According to CBE, "All of the lower income, minority neighborhoods are in the western and southern parts of Richmond where the highest concentration of petrochemical facilities are also located."[72]

Navajo Indians are the primary workforce in the mining of uranium in the United States. According to a 1986 report, "Toxics and Minority Communities" by the Center for Third World Organizing (Oakland, California), 2 million tons of radioactive uranium tailings have been dumped on Native American lands. Reproductive organ cancer among Navajo teenagers is seventeen times the national average. Indian reservations of the Kaibab Paiutes (northern Arizona) and other tribes across the United States are targeted sites for hazardous waste incinerators, disposal, and storage facilities.[73] On July 4, 1990, the *Minneapolis Star Tribune* reported that members of the Kaibab Paiute reservation in northern Arizona were negotiating to bring about 70,000 tons of hazardous waste each year to the Kaibab Paiute reservation in Northern Arizona. An incinerator would burn the waste, and the ash would be buried on tribal land. The Paiutes stand to reap $1 million a year from the waste-burning operation. The Kaibab Paiutes and other tribes are torn between the economic gains and the integrity of their land and traditional ways. "The plans are seductive on reservations where unemployment averages 40 percent."[74]

Garbage and hazardous waste firms are well aware that the majority of reservations, governed by tribal leaders, do not have strict environmental regulations. "On self-governing Indian lands, where tribal councils are the authority, waste companies can avoid tough state laws and the prying eyes of county and local governments."[75]As reported by the *Christian Science Monitor:*

> Recently, over the objection of tribal members, the Rosebud Sioux Tribal Council in South Dakota signed a contract with a Connecticut-based waste disposal firm to

develop a 5,000-acre garbage dump that will accept wastes from Minneapolis, Denver, and beyond. The proposed dump, located on what is thought to be an ancient Indian burial ground, is 70 miles from the site of the massacre at Wounded Knee and in the heart of the unspoiled prairie [North] Americans recently viewed in [Kevin Costner's epic drama] "Dances with Wolves." The contract states that not any existing environmental regulations of South Dakota are applicable and forbids the Sioux from enacting any laws to govern the waste project. What will the Sioux receive in return for receiving this waste? A little more than $1 per ton for the garbage they will be host to forever.[76]

In Canada, much of the land being proposed for parks is already claimed by original peoples. For example, Auyuittuq National Park Reserve, located on Cumerland Peninsula, Baffin Island, established as a park in 1972, was probably first inhabited about 4,000 years ago by Inuit.[77] While several native groups have proposed "joint native-government management regimes," no joint management regimes now exist in the Canadian national park system.[78] Furthermore, subjecting such land to be used as parks and a government-run management scheme raises significant concerns about whether national parks established on lands claimed by aboriginal peoples legally prejudice future land claim settlements by natives.

CONCLUSION

This chapter uses a feminist approach to discuss empirical women–other human Others–nature interconnections. While all humans are affected by environmental degradation, women, people of color, children, and the poor throughout the world experience environmental harms disproportionately. Nature is, indeed, a feminist issue. I turn to a discussion of other sorts of reasons why nature is a feminist issue in chapter 2.

NOTES

1. As I discuss in chapter 3, the category "women" is philosophically problematic. However, for practical and strategic purposes of exploring empirical generalizations that can truthfully be made regarding sex/gendered females, I use the term "women."

2. *The State of India's Environment, 1983–84: The Second Citizen's Report* (New Delhi: Center for Science and Environment, 1985), 94.

3. Jayanta Bandyopadhyay and Vandana Shiva, "Chipko: Rekindling India's Forest Culture," *The Ecologist* 17, no. 1 (1987), 26.

4. *State of India's Environment,* 28.

5. Bandyopadhyay and Shiva, "Chipko," 3, 5.

6. Bandyopadhyay and Shiva, "Chipko," 33, italics in original.

7. *Restoring the Balance: Women and Forest Resources* (Rome: Food and Culture Organization and Swedish International Development Authority, 1987), 4.

8. Louise P. Fortmann and Dianne Rocheleau, "Women and Agroforestry: Four Myths and Three Case Studies," *Agroforestry Systems* 9, no. 2 (1985), 256.

9. *Restoring the Balance,* 104.

10. *The World's Women, 1995: Trends and Statistics* (New York: United Nations, 1995), 48.

11. *World's Women, 1995,* 48.

12. From Sun Up, video (Maryknoll, N.Y.: Maryknoll World Productions, 1987).

13. *World's Women, 1995,* 48.

14. See, e.g., Louise P. Fortmann and Sally K. Fairfax, "American Forestry Professionalism in the Third World: Some Preliminary Observations on Effects," in *Women Creating Wealth: Transforming Economic Development,* Selected Papers and Speeches from the Association of Women in Development Conference (Washington, D.C., 1988), 105–8; Fortmann and Rocheleau, "Women and Agroforestry"; *Linking Energy with Survival: A Guide to Energy, Environment, and Rural Women's Work* (Geneva: International Labour Office, 1987); *Restoring the Balance*; Irene Tinker, "Women and Energy: Program Implications" (Washington, D.C.: Equity Policy Center, 1980); *Women and the World Conservation Strategy* (Gland: International Union for the Conservancy of Nature, 1987).

15. Fortmann and Fairfax, "American Forestry Professionalism," 105.

16. Marilyn Hoskins, "Observations on Indigenous and Modern Agroforestry Activities in West Africa," in *Problems of Agroforestry* (Freiburg: University of Freiburg, 1982); cited in Fortmann and Fairfax, "American Forestry Professionalism," 105.

17. Fortmann and Fairfax, "American Forestry Professionalism," 106.

18. Fortmann and Fairfax, "American Forestry Professionalism," 106.

19. David Moberg, "In the Amazon, An Epidemic of Greed," *In These Times,* 1–7 May 1991, 3.

20. Moberg, "In the Amazon," 3.

21. Moberg, "In the Amazon," 3.

22. Cited in Waring, "Your Economic Theory," 257.

23. *World's Women, 1995,* 49.

24. *The World's Women, 1970–1990, Trends and Statistics* (New York: United Nations, 1990), 75.

25. *World's Women, 1995,* 49–50.

26. Joni Seager, *The New State of the Earth Atlas,* 2nd edition (New York: Simon and Schuster, 1995), 104.

27. Seager, *New State of the Earth Atlas,* 19.

28. Waring, "Your Economic Theory," 259.

29. Nicholas Freudenberg and Ellen Zaltzberg, "From Grassroots Activism to Political Power: Women Organizing Against Environmental Hazards," in *Double Exposure: Women's Health Hazards on the Job and at Home,* ed. Wendy Chavkin (New York: Monthly Review Press, 1984), 246–47.

30. Anders Wijkman and Lloyd Timberlake, *Natural Disasters: Acts of God or Acts of Man?* (Philadelphia: New Society Publishers, 1988), 6. To emphasize the causal role human-induced factors play in so-called natural disasters, Wijkman and Timberlake urge a conceptual change in the common view of natural disasters. They urge a distinction between the trigger events of a nature disaster—too little rain, too much rain, earthshocks, hurricanes, typically "natural events"—and the associated disasters that affect humans and other animals and that are largely human-made. A strong earthquake in an unoccupied

desert area that affects no human or animal populations, then, would be a natural event, but not a natural disaster.

31. Wijkman and Timberlake, *Natural Disasters*, 27.

32. Wijkman and Timberlake, *Natural Disasters,* 49.

33. Seager, *New State of the Earth Atlas,* 121.

34. *World's Women, 1970–1990,* 88, 82, respectively.

35. Seager, *New State of the Earth Atlas,* 120.

36. Seager, *New State of the Earth Atlas,* 21.

37. Mayra Buvinic and Sally W. Yudelman, *Women, Poverty, and Progress in the Third World* (New York: Foreign Policy Association, 1989), 22.

38. Buvinic and Yudelman, *Women, Poverty,* 24.

39. Jane Perlez, "Inequalities Plague African Women," *Minneapolis Star/Tribune,* 4 March 1991, 4A.

40. Quoted in Lloyd Timberlake, *Africa in Crisis: The Causes, the Cures of Environmental Bankruptcy* (Philadelphia: New Society Publishers, 1986), 144.

41. Cited in Timberlake, *Africa in Crisis,* 145.

42. Timberlake, *Africa in Crisis,* 30.

43. Buvinic and Yudelman, *Women, Poverty,* 24–26.

44. Seager, *New State of the Earth Atlas,* 62.

45. *World's Women, 1970–1990,* 75.

46. Chris J. Cuomo, *Feminism and Ecological Communities: An Ethic of Flourishing* (London: Routledge, 1998), 20. The quote is from Beverly White, "Environmental Equity Justice Centers: A Response to Inequity," in *Environmental Justice: Issues, Policies, and Solutions,* ed. Bunyan Bryant (Washington, D.C.: Island Press, 1995), 60.

47. Sonia Jasso and Maria Mazorra, "Following the Harvest: The Health Hazards of Migrant and Seasonal Farmworking Women," in *Double Exposure: Women's Health Hazards on the Job and at Home,* ed. Wendy Chavkin (New York: Monthly Review Press, 1984), 87.

48. *World's Women, 1995,* 49.

49. Jasso and Mazorra, "Following the Harvest," 94.

50. See Tom Muir and Anne Sudar, "Toxic Chemicals in the Great Lakes Basin Ecosystem: Some Observations" (Burlington, Ont.: Environment Canada, 1988; unpublished).

51. Muir and Sudar, "Toxic Chemicals," 61.

52. Muir and Sudar, "Toxic Chemicals," 82.

53. Muir and Sudar, "Toxic Chemicals," 82.

54. Muir and Sudar, "Toxic Chemicals," 82.

55. Paul Koberstein, "Exxon Oil Spill Taints Lives of Aleut Indian Villagers," *The Sunday Oregonian,* 24 September 1989, A2.

56. Freudenberg and Zaltzberg, "From Grassroots Activism," 249.

57. Freudenberg and Zaltzberg, "From Grassroots Activism," 249.

58. Dana Hughes, "What's Gotten Into Our Children" (Los Angeles: Children Now, 1990), 6. (Children Now can be reached at 10951 West Pico Boulevard, Los Angeles, CA 90064.)

59. Hughes, "What's Gotten Into Our Children," 6.

60. Cynthia Hamilton, "Women, Home, and Community," *woman of power: a magazine of feminism, spirituality, and politics,* 20 (Spring 1991), 42.

61. Hughes, "What's Gotten Into Our Children," 35.

62. Muir and Sudar, "Toxic Chemicals," 78–9.

63. "Toxic Waste and Race in the United States: A National Report on the Racial and Socioeconomic Characteristics of Communities with Hazardous Waste Sites," 1987,

Commission for Racial Justice, United Church of Christ, 105 Madison Avenue, New York, NY 10016.

64. Centers for Disease Control, Atlanta, Georgia, cited in Dick Russell, "Environmental Racism," *The Amicus Journal* (Spring 1989), 24.

65. Dick Russell, "Environmental Racism," 29.

66. "Mothers of Prevention," *Time,* 10 June 1991, 25.

67. For example, the South West Organizing Project (SWOP) has been actively involved in protesting and publicizing acts of environmental racism. (SWOP can be reached at 211 10th St. S.W., Albuquerque, NM 87102.)

68. Hamilton, "Women, Home," 43.

69. Hamilton, "Women, Home," 42.

70. Russell, "Environmental Racism," 24.

71. Russell, "Environmental Racism," 24.

72. Cited in Russell, "Environmental Racism," 25.

73. "Toxics and Minority Communities," the Center for Third World Organizing (Oakland, California), 1986.

74. "The Indian and Toxic Waste," *Minneapolis Star/ Tribune,* 4 July 1990.

75. "The Indian and Toxic Waste," *Minneapolis Star/ Tribune,* 4 July 1990.

76. Thomas A. Daschle, "Dances with Garbage," *Christian Science Monitor,* 14 February 1991, 18.

77. Nicholas Lawson, "Where Whitemen Come to Play," *Cultural Survival Quarterly* 13, no. 2 (1989), 54.

78. Lawson, "Where Whitemen," 56.

Chapter Two

What Are Ecofeminists Saying?

An Overview of Ecofeminist Positions

As a political movement, ecological feminism began in the 1970s. French feminist Françoise d'Eaubonne coined the term "ecological feminisme" in 1974 to call attention to women's potential to bring about an ecological revolution.[1] Since then, ecofeminist political events, conferences, and publications aimed at showing important connections among the dominations of women, other subordinated human groups, and nonhuman nature have surfaced throughout the world.

All ecofeminists agree that there are important connections between the unjustified dominations of women and nature, but they disagree about both the nature of those connections and whether some of the connections are potentially liberating or grounds for reinforcing harmful stereotypes about women.

This disagreement among ecofeminists is to be expected. Just as there is not one version of feminism, there also is not one version of ecofeminism. The umbrella term "ecofeminism" refers to a plurality of positions, some of which are mutually compatible and some of which are not. Since ecofeminism grows out of and reflects different and distinct feminisms (e.g., liberal feminism, Marxist feminism, radical feminism, socialist feminism), ecofeminist positions are as diverse as the feminisms from which they gain their strength and meaning.

In the literature on ecofeminism, ten types of women–other human Others–nature interconnections tend to be discussed: historical (typically causal), conceptual, empirical, socioeconomic, linguistic, symbolic and literary, spiritual and religious, epistemological, political, and ethical interconnections. While not all of these positions are themselves *philosophical* positions, each raises interesting philosophical issues.

21

HISTORICAL (TYPICALLY CAUSAL) INTERCONNECTIONS

Historical data and causal explanations are used to generate theories concerning the sources of the dominations of women, other human Others, and nonhuman nature. The historical pervasiveness of patriarchal domination of women and nature has led some ecofeminists to suggest that androcentrism (male-centered thinking) is the root cause of environmental destruction—a claim critics of ecofeminism love to hate.[2]

What are the bases of these alleged historical-causal connections? Again, ecofeminists disagree. Some ecofeminists trace these connections to prototypical patterns of domination that began with the invasion of Indo-European societies by nomadic tribes from Eurasia between the sixth and third millennia B.C.E. For example, Riane Eisler argues:

> The archaeological evidence thus supports the conclusion that it was not metals per se, but rather their use in developing ever more effective technologies of destruction, that played such a critical part in what Engels termed "the world historical defeat of the female sex." Nor did male dominance become the norm in Western prehistory, as Engels implies, when gathering-hunting peoples first begin to domesticate and breed animals (in other words, when herding became their main technology of production). Rather, it happened much later, during the millennia-long incursions of pastoral hordes into the more fertile lands where farming had become the main technology of production.[3]

In her book *The Chalice and the Blade,* Eisler describes the time before these invasions by pastoral patriarchs as a peaceful agrarian era, as a partnership society ruled by "the chalice, not the blade." "The chalice" symbolizes a cooperative, peaceful, egalitarian, partnership society characterized by nurturing relationships among humans and with nonhuman nature; "the blade" symbolizes an aggressive, violent, war-prone, male-dominated society characterized by unequal power relationships and militaristic domination. Eisler then claims that "the root of the problem lies in a social system in which the power of the Blade is idealized—in which both men and women are taught to equate true masculinity with violence and dominance and to see men who do not conform to this ideal as 'too soft' or 'effeminate'."[4]

Other ecofeminists locate the historical-causal explanations of the interconnected dominations of women and nature in cultural and scientific changes that occurred more recently. In her 1980 book, *The Death of Nature,* environmental historian Carolyn Merchant identifies the scientific revolution of the sixteenth and seventeenth centuries as the key turning point in "the death of nature." She observes that as late as 1500 "the daily interaction with nature was still structured for most Europeans, as it was for other peoples, by close-knit, cooperative, organic communities." She goes on to claim that "central to the organic theory was the identification of nature, especially the earth, with a nurturing mother: a kindly beneficent female who provided for the needs of mankind in an ordered, planned universe."[5]

Merchant argues that another opposing image of nature as female was also present though not prevalent: wild and uncontrollable nature that could render violence, storms, droughts, and general chaos. According to Merchant, between 1500 and 1700 the older, organic worldview was replaced by a reductionist, "mechanistic world view of modern science"—one that sanctioned the exploitation of nature, unchecked commercial and industrial expansion, and the subordination of women:

> The metaphor of the earth as a nurturing mother was gradually to vanish as a dominant image as the Scientific Revolution proceeded to mechanize and to rationalize the world view. The second image, nature as disorder, called forth an important modern idea, that of power over nature. Two new ideas, those of mechanism and of the domination and mastery of nature, became core concepts of the modern world.[6]

The Death of Nature weaves together scholarly material from politics, art, literature, physics, technology, philosophy, and popular culture to show how this mechanistic worldview replaced an older, organic worldview, which provided gendered moral restraints on how one treated nature. Merchant writes:

> The change in controlling imagery was directly related to changes in human attitudes and behavior toward the earth. Whereas the nurturing earth image can be viewed as a cultural constraint restricting the types of socially and morally sanctioned human actions allowable with respect to the earth, the new images of mastery and domination functioned as cultural sanctions for the denudation of nature. Society needed these new images as it continued the processes of commercialism and industrialization.[7]

Like Eisler's *The Chalice and the Blade,* Merchant's *The Death of Nature* is not without critics. Some ecofeminist philosophers such as Val Plumwood argue that the historical roots of the unjustified domination of nature originated in classical Greek philosophy and the rationalist tradition. For Plumwood, the culprit is "rationalism," that long-standing philosophical tradition that both defines rationality as the hallmark of humanness and elevates humans over nonhuman animals and nature on grounds of humans' superior abilities to reason. Plumwood argues that the human/nature value dualism at the heart of rationalism has spawned other harmful value dualisms (e.g., masculine/feminine, reason/emotion, spirit/body).[8] She argues that these dualisms have not only been human-centered (or anthropocentric) but also male-centered (or androcentric). Plumwood criticizes environmental philosophy generally for its failure "to engage properly various positions within the rationalist tradition, which has been inimical to both women and nature":

> The failure to observe such connections is the result of an inadequate historical analysis and understanding of the way in which the inferiorization of both women and nature is grounded in rationalism, and the connections of both to the inferioriz-

ing of the body, hierarchical concepts of labor, and disembedded and individualist accounts of the self.[9]

Plumwood urges environmental philosophers to see important connections between anthropocentrism and androcentrism: while anthropocentrism (i.e., human-centered thinking that assumes the superiority of humans over nature) is objectionable, historically anthropocentrism is intimately connected with andro-centrism (i.e., male-centered thinking that assumes the superiority of men over women). Within the Western philosophical tradition, anthropocentrism has often taken the form of androcentrism. As such, Plumwood argues, "the effect of ecofeminism is not to absorb or sacrifice the critique of anthropocentrism, but to deepen and enrich it."[10]

It is unlikely that ecofeminist philosophers will resolve historical questions about the onset of patriarchy and the "twin dominations of women and nature." In fact, claims about the origins of patriarchy may never be resolved. However, as I show in chapter 3, to establish harmful women–other human Others–nature interconnections, one need only show that, at least in Western societies, whenever there has been a historical identification of women and other human Others with inferior nature, the domination of women and other human Others has been explained and "justified" by their connection with nonhuman nature.

CONCEPTUAL INTERCONNECTIONS

Conceptual interconnections are at the heart of ecofeminist philosophy. Since the primary focus in chapter 3 is on such conceptual connections, I offer only brief remarks about conceptual interconnections here.

Plumwood's account of the historical role rationalism plays in the dominations of women and nonhuman nature is also a conceptual account: Plumwood locates the conceptual basis of structures of domination in hierarchically organized value dualisms (such as reason/emotion, mind/body, culture/nature, human/nature, and man/woman) and an exaggerated focus on reason and rationality divorced from the realm of the body, nature, and the physical. The account I offer (in chapter 3) is similar, locating the conceptual connections in an oppressive and patriarchal conceptual framework, mediated by what I call "a logic of domination." But some ecofeminists offer a different sort of account altogether. Some locate the conceptual connections in sex-gender differences, particularly in differentiated personality formation or consciousness.[11] Typically, the claim is that socially con-structed female bodily experiences (e.g., of childbearing and child rearing), situate women differently with respect to nonhuman nature than men. These sex-gender differences are subsequently manifested in different sorts of conscious-ness in women and men, different "ways of knowing" for women than for men.

The work of ecofeminist sociologist Ariel Salleh is a good example of this approach. Salleh criticizes the position in the field of environmental ethics known as "deep ecology" (described in chapter 4) for its failure to "recognize the primal source of the destructive [man/nature] dualism . . . or the deeply ingrained motivational complexes which grow out of it."[12] According to Salleh, this "primal source" is "a distinctly masculine sensibility," the result of "the self-estranged male reaching for the original androgynous natural unity within himself." Salleh criticizes deep ecology's desire for transcendence as a masculinist, "supremely rationalist and technicist" way of thinking. According to Salleh, a preferable approach is based on "women's lived experience." She claims that deep ecology

> overlooks the point that if women's lived experience were recognized as meaningful and were given legitimation in our culture, it could provide an immediate 'living' social basis for the alternative consciousness which the deep ecologist is trying to formulate and introduce as an abstract ethical construct.[13]

According to Salleh, "the unconscious connection between women and nature needs to be made conscious" if there is to be "any real growth towards a sane, humane, ecological future."[14]

EMPIRICAL INTERCONNECTIONS

Many ecofeminists focus on the sort of empirical evidence offered in chapter 1 — data that link women, people of color, the underclass, and children with environmental destruction. As we have seen, some ecofeminists point to various health and risk factors borne disproportionately by these human subordinate groups by the presence of low-level radiation, pesticides, toxins, and other pollutants. Some ecofeminists provide data to show how First World development policies result in policies and practices that directly contribute to the inability of women to provide adequately for themselves and their families. Ecofeminist animal rights welfarists (discussed in chapter 6) argue that factory farming, animal experimentation, hunting, and meat-eating are tied to patriarchal concepts and practices. Some ecofeminists connect violence against women through rape and pornography to violence against nature. Such empirical data document the very real, felt, lived "experiential" interconnections among the dominations of women, other human Others, and nature.

SOCIOECONOMIC INTERCONNECTIONS

One sort of empirical interconnection is sufficiently distinct to warrant separate mention: socioeconomic interconnections. Physicist and Chipko movement activist Vandana Shiva is an internationally renowned ecofeminist who defends socioeconomical interconnections between the exploitation of women, women's bodies, and women's labor, and the exploitation of nature. After conducting a thorough empirical study of the effects of Western agricultural development strategies in India, Shiva argues that Western development is really "maldevelopment," a development "bereft of the feminine" (which Shiva identifies as a conservation or ecological principle). Shiva argues that maldevelopment rests on several false, male-biased assumptions:

> The assumptions are evident: nature is unproductive; organic agriculture based on nature's cycles of renewability spells poverty; women and tribal and peasant societies embedded in nature are similarly unproductive, not because it has been demonstrated that in cooperation they produce *less* goods and services for needs, but because it is assumed that "production" takes place only when mediated by technologies for commodity production, even when such technologies destroy life. A stable and clean river is not a productive resource in this view; it needs to be 'developed' with dams in order to become so. Women, sharing the river as a commons to satisfy the water needs of their families and society, are not involved in productive labour: when substituted by the engineering man, water management and water use become productive activities. Natural forests remain unproductive till they are developed into monoculture plantations of commercial species.[15]

According to Shiva, "maldevelopment" is a paradigm that sees all work that does not produce profits and capital as non- or unproductive work. The neglect of nature's work "in renewing herself" and of women's work in producing sustenance in the form of basic, vital needs is an essential part of the paradigm of maldevelopment fostered by industrial capitalism.

Maria Mies agrees. Using a Marxist-feminist perspective, Mies argues that just as women's bodies and labor are colonized by a combination of capitalism and patriarchy (or capitalist patriarchy), so is nature.[16] The term capitalist patriarchy stresses the ways in which capitalism, as one version of the gender division of labor, gives men control over, and access to, resources not given to women. Mies argues that under capitalist patriarchy, both women and nature function as exploited resources, without which the wealth of ruling-class men cannot be created. Other ecofeminists argue that a socioeconomic analysis of women–nature interconnections links patterns of domination in "an ideological superstructure by which the system of economic and legal domination of women, land, and animals is justified and made to appear 'natural' and inevitable within the total patriarchal cosmovision."[17] Included in this "ideological superstructure" are religions and philosophical perspectives that reinforce the domination of women, people of color, animals, and land as reflecting the will of a supreme, deified, patriarchal male God.

Mary Mellor also uses a historical materialist approach to criticize capitalist patriarchy. Mellor argues that although both men and women mediate between culture and nature, they do not do so equally.[18] This is because the conditions of exploitation and domination affect women and nature differently than they affect men and culture. Although all human beings, as animals themselves, are embodied and embedded in a natural environment, men and women stand in a different relationship to the natural world. The difference in human embodiment is a gendered, material, and historical phenomenon—one involving power relations around the allocation of resources.[19] Mellor defends what she calls "materialist ecofeminism," which is premised on "the fact that the boundaries of women's lives are not defined by capitalist patriarchal economic relations."[20] By naming her version of ecofeminism "materialist ecofeminism," Mellor shows that patriarchy is not simply cultural domination; it is importantly also a material or economic domination.

LINGUISTIC INTERCONNECTIONS

Many philosophers (e.g., Ludwig Wittgenstein) have argued that the language one uses mirrors and reflects one's concept of oneself and one's world. As such, language plays a crucial role in concept formation. Ecofeminists argue that it also plays a crucial role in keeping intact mutually reinforcing sexist, racist, and naturist views of women, people of color, and nonhuman nature.

Euro-American language is riddled with examples of "sexist-naturist language," that is, language that depicts women, animals, and nonhuman nature as inferior to (having less status, value, or prestige than) men and male-identified culture. Women routinely are described in pejorative animal terms: Women are dogs, cats, catty, pussycats, pussies, pets, bunnies, dumb bunnies, cows, sows, foxes, chicks, bitches, beavers, old bats, old hens, old crows, queen bees, cheetahs, vixen, serpents, bird-brains, hare-brains, elephants, and whales. Women cackle, go to hen parties, henpeck their husbands, become old biddies (old hens no longer sexually attractive or able to reproduce) and social butterflies.[21] Animalizing women *in a patriarchal culture* where animals are seen as inferior to humans, thereby reinforces and authorizes women's inferior status.

Similarly, language that feminizes nature *in a patriarchal culture,* where women are viewed as subordinate and inferior, reinforces and authorizes the domination of nature. Mother Nature (not Father Nature) is raped, mastered, controlled, conquered, mined. Her (not his) secrets are penetrated, and her womb (men don't have one) is put into the service of the man of science (not woman of science, or simply scientist). Virgin timber is felled, cut down. Fertile (not potent) soil is tilled, and land that lies fallow is useless or barren, like a woman unable to conceive a child.

In these cases, the exploitation of nature and animals is justified by feminizing (not masculinizing) them; the exploitation of women is justified by naturalizing or animalizing (not masculinizing or culturalizing) them. As Carol Adams argues in *The Sexual Politics of Meat,* language that feminizes nature and naturalizes women describes, reflects, and perpetuates unjustified patriarchal domination by failing to see the extent to which the dominations of women and nature, especially animals, are culturally analogous and not metaphorically analogous.[22]

This brief discussion of sexist-naturist language deserves two clarifications. First, the point of these examples of sexist-naturist language is not to claim that only female humans are denigrated by the use of animal language. That would be false; some nonhuman animal terms are used pejoratively against men and boys. For example, men and boys are called studs, wolves, sharks, skunks, snakes, toads, jackasses, weasels, old buzzards, and goats.[23] Nor is it to claim that all uses of animal or nature language to describe humans is derogatory. That would also be false; some nonhuman animal terms are complimentary. For example, in Western culture, it generally is complimentary to describe someone as busy as a bee, eagle-eyed, lion-hearted, or brave as a lion.[24] Rather, the point is that, *within patriarchal contexts*, the vast majority of animal terms used to denigrate women, and the vast majority of female terms used to describe animals and nature, function differently from those animal terms used to denigrate men. And (as I show in chapter 3) that functional difference is significant: The majority of animal terms used to describe women identify women with (inferior) bodies, sexual objects, domesticated pets or playthings, man's property, spiritually sinful or sin-prone (temptress) creatures vis-à-vis (at least ruling-class) men; the majority of animal terms used to describe (at least ruling-class) men identify men with (superior) intellects or minds, agency, sexual subjects, spirits, rulers, and sovereigns who have power over both women and nature. This is an important cultural difference that occurs within a historical, material context which sees women, animals, and nature as inferior to (at least ruling-class) men.

There is a second reason the cultural context in which animal language is used is important: all uses of derogatory animal language function to denigrate, inferiorize, and reinforce the exploitation of nonhuman animals. As Joan Dunayer claims, "While only some nonhuman animal pejoratives denigrate women, *all* denigrate nonhuman animals."[25] Dunayer argues that this basic distinction, human versus animal, is "the essence of speciesism," the view that nonhuman animals are inferior to (the species) human animals.[26]

SYMBOLIC AND LITERARY INTERCONNECTIONS

We have already seen how Merchant's discussion of two images of nature—an older Greek notion of nature as a benevolent female and a nurturing mother, and a newer, modern image of nature as a (mere) machine, inert, dead—is central to her argument that the move from an organic to a mechanistic model conceptually sanctioned and ethically justified the exploitation of the (female) earth. It did so by removing the sorts of moral barriers to such treatment that the metaphor of nature as alive previously prevented. As Merchant claims:

> One does not readily slay a mother, dig into her entrails for gold or mutilate her body, although commercial mining would soon require that. As long as the earth was con-

sidered alive and sensitive, it could be considered a breach of human ethical behavior to carry out such destructive acts against it.[27]

A discussion of images of women and nonhuman nature, then, raises larger issues about symbolic patterns linking women and nature. Some ecofeminists explore these symbolic patterns in literature and popular culture.

Many ecofeminists draw on "women's nature writing" to unpack the nature of the women–other human Others–nature interconnections.[28] One of the first to do so is Susan Griffin. In the prologue to the epic poem that is her book *Woman and Nature: The Roaring Inside Her,* Griffin writes,

> He says that woman speaks with nature. That she hears voices from under the earth. That wind blows in her ears and trees whisper to her. That the dead sing through her mouth and the cries of infants are clear to her. But for him this dialogue is over. He says he is not part of this world, that he was set on this world as a stranger. He sets himself apart from woman and nature.
>
> And so it is Goldilocks who goes to the home of the three bears, Little Red Riding Hood who converses with the wolf, Dorothy who befriends a lion, Snow White who talks to the birds, Cinderella with mice as her allies, the Mermaid who is half fish, Thumbelina courted by a mole. (And when we hear in the Navajo chant of the mountain that a grown man sits and smokes with bears and follows directions given to him by squirrels, we are surprised. We had thought only little girls spoke with animals.)
>
> We are the bird's eggs. Bird's eggs, flowers, butterflies, rabbits, cows, sheep; we are caterpillars; we are leaves of ivy and sprigs of wallflower. We are women. We rise from the wave. We are gazelle and doe, elephant and whale, lilies and roses and peach, we are air, we are flame, we are oyster and pearl, we are girls. We are women and nature. And he says he cannot hear us speak.
>
> But we hear.[29]

Griffin's writing is impactive. Her writing is testimony to the power of literature and language to convey basic attitudes about women and nature.

A new genre of literary analysis called ecofeminist literary criticism has emerged. According to one of its main proponents, Patrick Murphy, this approach to literary criticism uses

> ecofeminism as a ground for critiquing all the literature that one reads. For literary critics in particular this would mean reevaluating the canon that constitutes the list of major works and texts, and calling for a dialogue between critical evaluations based on humanistic criteria and those based on de-homocentric criteria. This would require, for instance, reevaluating the poetic tradition of the "pastoral," which tends to be based on an idealization of nature rather than a genuine encounter with it.[30]

Ecofeminist literary criticism does not seek only "a literature that meets equally the criteria of ecological and feminist sophistication," but work "that to some extent embody both dimensions."[31]

SPIRITUAL AND RELIGIOUS INTERCONNECTIONS

Ecofeminist theologian Elizabeth Dodson Gray was among the first ecofeminists to examine the roles that religious and sexual imagery play in the patriarchal heritage of the Judeo-Christian and Western intellectual traditions. In her book *Green Paradise Lost,* first published in 1979, Gray claims that a destructive hierarchy of beings is at the heart of biblical accounts of creation:

> In this biblical view of the nature of things woman comes after and also below man. Woman was created (according to this chronologically earliest account of the creation of the world in Gen. 2) out of man's body (rather than from a woman's body as happens naturally). . . . Then come children, so derivative that they are not even in the Creation story. . . . Then come animals, who do not have the unique human spirit at all. . . . Thus animals are below. Further down are plants, which do not even move about. Below them is the ground of nature itself—the hills and mountains, streams and valleys—which is the bottom of everything just as the heavens, the moon and the stars are close to God at the top of everything.[32]

In this hierarchical "pyramid of dominance and status," the higher up one goes, the closer one is to all that is spiritual and superior. Gray claims that "even women, whom today we might view as equally human, are subordinate and inferior precisely on the ground of 'spirit'."[33] She argues:

> Women are not stepping back from these ancient religious myths, so basic to our Judeo-Christian and Western tradition. They are looking at these myths from the newly found perspective of a feminist consciousness and realizing that these myths are patriarchal—i.e., they rationalize and justify a society that puts men "up" and women "down."
>
> But the creation myth also puts down children, animals, plants—and Nature itself. . . . What is clearly articulated here is a hierarchical order of *being* in which the lower orders—whether female or child or animal or plant—can be treated, mistreated, violated, sold, sacrificed, or killed at the convenience of the higher states of spiritual being found in males and in God. Nature, being not only at the bottom of this pyramid but being the most full of dirt, blood and such nasty natural surprises as earthquakes, floods and bad storms, is obviously a prize candidate for the most ruthless "mastering" of all.[34]

Given Gray's account, it is not surprising that the symbols, images, and stories of traditional patriarchal religions receive the attention they do from ecofeminists. Among theologians, it has fueled the debate over "reform or revolution" in traditional religions: Can patriarchal religions be reformed from within to eliminate the harmful patriarchal biases, or are new or prepatriarchal religions required in their place?

Western theologian Rosemary Radford Ruether argues that ecofeminism sounds significantly different when contextualized by women from the Third

World. This is because, for women in countries struggling against the effects of Western colonialism, both the religions of colonizing powers and the religious traditions within their own cultures have complex and historically specific dominating and liberating roles. Ruether cites two important differences:

> First, women from Asia, Africa, and Latin America are much less likely to forget, unlike Northern women, that the base line of domination of women and of nature is impoverishment: the impoverishment of the majority of their people, particularly women and children, and the impoverishment of the land. . . . Second, although many women of Asia, Africa, and Latin America are deeply interested in recovering patterns of spirituality from a pre-Christian past, these spiritualities are those of their own indigenous roots. They are not fetched in as an idealized story from long ago and far away with which one has no cultural experience, but rather this pre-Christian indigenous past is still present. It has been broken and silenced by colonialism and Christianization, but it is still present in the contemporary indigenous people of one's own land, descendants of one's own indigenous ancestors, or even as customs with which the woman writer herself grew up in her earlier years.[35]

Ruether encourages Northern women to "free ourselves from both our chauvinism and our escapism" by playing creatively with what is liberating in our own heritages, including religious and spiritual heritages, while also "letting go of both the urge to inflate our identity as the one true way or to repudiate it as total toxic waste." Ruether also argues that Northern women must become "more truthful and responsible," dealing transformatively with who we are, culturally and economically, rather than appropriating the ideas and practices of indigenous peoples of other worlds. She concludes, "Only in this way can we [Northern women] begin to find how to be true friends and sisters with women—with people—of other worlds, no longer as oppressors trying to suppress other people's identities but also not as 'white blanks' seeking to fill our own emptiness at the expense of others."[36]

Spiritual ecofeminists were among the first ecofeminists in the United States. However, like ecofeminism generally, there is no one version of "spiritual ecofeminism." Spiritual ecofeminists disagree about such basic issues as whether mainstream religious traditions (e.g., Christianity) can be reformed (reconceived, reinterpreted) to provide environmentally responsible and nonsexist practices and theologies; whether any specific environmental practice (e.g., vegetarianism, bans on hunting and animal experimentation, organic farming, population control) is mandated by ecofeminist spirituality; and whether some ecofeminist spiritualities inappropriately mystify and romanticize nature, or coopt indigenous cultural beliefs and practices.

Nonetheless, spiritual ecofeminists agree that earth-based, feminist spiritualities and symbols (such as Gaia and Goddess) are essential to ecofeminism. The works of Starhawk, Charlene Spretnak, Joanna Macy, and Carol Christ are examples of spiritual ecofeminist positions. Consider what they say about ecofeminism.

Starhawk defines "ecofeminism" as a spiritual movement:

> Ecofeminism is a movement with an implicit and sometimes explicit spiritual base. . . . To say that ecofeminism is a spiritual movement, in an earth-rooted sense, means that it encompasses a dimension that profoundly challenges our ordinary sense of value, that counters the root stories of our culture and attempts to shift them.[37]

Like other spiritual ecofeminists, Starhawk insists that women's spirituality is also political.[38] Carol Christ agrees. She claims spirituality is central to ecofeminist politics:

> With many spiritual feminists, ecofeminists, ecologists, antinuclear activists, and others, I share the conviction that the crisis that threatens the destruction of the Earth is not only social, political, economic, and technological, but is at root spiritual. We have lost the sense that this Earth is our true home. . . . The preservation of the Earth requires a profound shift in consciousness: a recovery of more ancient and traditional views that revere the profound connection of all beings in the web of life and a rethinking of the relation of both humanity and divinity in nature.[39]

Spretnak describes the path she took into ecofeminism as involving the embrace of ancient, prepatriarchal, nature-based religion:

> In the mid-1970s many radical/cultural feminists experienced the exhilarating discovery, through historic and archaeological sources, of a religion that honored the female and seemed to have as its "good book" nature itself. We were drawn to it like a magnet, but only, I feel, because both of those features were central. We would not have been interested in "Yahweh in a skirt," a distant, detached, domineering godhead who happened to be female. What was cosmologically wholesome and healing was the discovery of the Divine as immanent in and around us. What was intriguing was the sacred link between the Goddess in her many guises and totemic animals and plants, sacred groves, and womblike caves, in the moon-rhythm blood of menses, the ecstatic dance—the experience of *knowing* Gaia, her voluptuous contours and fertile plains, her flowing waters that give life, her animal teachers.[40]

Spretnak claims that the ecofeminist sense of the spiritual emerges through experiences of ecocommunion with nature—an experience of grace whereby one experiences oneself as a particular expression of the sacred cosmic body.[41]

Like Starhawk and Spretnak, Macy claims that the "ecological self" is a spiritual self:

> There is the experience of being acted 'through' and sustained by something greater than oneself. It is close to the religious concept of grace, but, as distinct from the traditional Western understanding of grace, it does not require belief in God or supernatural agency. One simply finds oneself empowered to act on behalf of other beings—or on behalf of the larger whole—and the empowerment itself seems to come 'through' that or those for whose sake one acts.[42]

For Macy, a requisite condition for awakening to "our ecological selves" is to find new spiritual selves and powers.

Many spiritual ecofeminists invoke the notion of "the Goddess" to capture the sacredness of both nonhuman nature and the human body. Goddess worship has no hierarchy, no centralized institutions, no monumental structures, no liturgy. Carol Christ claims that the symbol of the Goddess "aids the process of naming and reclaiming the female body and its cycles and processes."[43]

What is the Goddess? According to Christ, "the Goddess" is three things. First, the Goddess is divine female, a personification who can be invoked in prayer and ritual. Second, the Goddess is a symbol of life, death, and rebirth—encouraging us to see the changing phases of our lives as holy. Third, the Goddess is a symbol of the legitimacy and beauty of women's power to nurture and create but also to limit and destroy when necessary.

For all spiritual ecofeminists, Goddess worship brings about a shift in the sense of self which is important for both men and women. The shift is allegedly from an atomistic, purely self-interested, egoistic self to an ecological and spiritual self. As Starhawk claims, the Goddess is not for women only: "The Goddess is also important for men. The oppression of men in Father God-ruled patriarchy is perhaps less obvious but no less tragic than that of women . . . men are encouraged to identify with a model no human being can successfully emulate . . . they are at war with themselves."[44]

EPISTEMOLOGICAL INTERCONNECTIONS

Many ecofeminists address epistemological dimensions of women–other human Other–nature interconnections. Epistemological concerns are concerns about knowledge. Ecofeminists interested in epistemology challenge some trademark Western views about knowledge: for example, that knowledge is objective; that the "knower" is an objective, detached, independent, and rational observer; and that nonhuman nature is a passive object of knowledge. To build their case, they often turn to recent work in epistemology by feminist philosophers of science such as Sandra Harding.

Harding argues that the social location of the knower is crucial to understanding and assessing epistemological claims.

> The activities of those at the bottom of . . . social hierarchies can provide starting points for thought—for *everyone's* research and scholarship—from which humans' relations with each other and the natural world can become visible. This is because the experience and lives of marginalized peoples, as they understand them, provide particularly significant *problems to be explained*, or research agendas.[45]

Many ecofeminists agree. They argue that only by listening to the perspectives of "those at the bottom of social hierarchies" can one begin to see alternative ways of viewing an environmental problem, analyzing data, or theorizing about women–other human Others–nature interconnections. The Chipko movement illustrates that often local women foresters "on the bottom" have indigenous technical knowledge based on their hands-on, daily, lived experience as forest managers. This knowledge provides an invaluable perspective on what it is like to live the lives they live—information and perspectives not readily accessible to those who live outside the culture.

Ecofeminist philosopher Lori Gruen builds on the work in feminist philosophy of science in developing an ecofeminist moral epistemology. She argues that ecofeminist theory always grows out of and examines the social context in which moral and epistemological claims are generated. Recognition of the interdependence of science and society, facts and values, reason and emotion "is the first step towards any legitimate knowledge."[46] Gruen writes:

> Ecofeminists recognize that claims to knowledge are always influenced by the values of the culture in which they are generated. Following the arguments made by feminist philosophers of science, Marxists, cultural critics, and others, ecofeminists believe that facts are theory-laden, theories are value-laden, and values are molded by historical and philosophical ideologies, social norms, and individual processes of categorization.[47]

Ecofeminist epistemologies often critique Western notions of objectivity and conceptions of nature as a passive object of study. Probably the most radical critique was initially given by Donna Haraway who claimed that modern Western conceptions of objectivity and nature-as-object are patriarchal ideologies of domination and control. Haraway argues for an alternative, pluralistic, context-dependent view of knowledge, what she calls "situated knowledges":

> Situated knowledges require that the object of knowledge be pictured as an actor and agent, not as a screen or a ground or a resource, never finally as slave to the master that closes off the dialectic in his unique agency and his authorship of "objective" knowledge. . . . A corollary of the insistence that ethics and politics covertly or overtly provide the bases for objectivity . . . is granting the status of agent/actor to the "objects" of the world.[48]

On this view, nature is an active subject—not a mere object or resource to be studied. Nature actively contributes to what humans know about nature. The job of the scientist, philosopher, and theorist is not to try to give accounts that "mirror nature," since mirroring assumes that nature is an unconstructed "given." Nor is it to act as if one "discovers" nature, since claims to discovery (like "Columbus discovered America") mistakenly assume that there isn't anything (or anything important) that already exists and that has agency. Rather, the job of the scientist, philosopher, and theorist is to provide knowledge claims and accounts that are relationally "situated" in important social and material contexts.

According to Haraway, the notion of nature as active subject is something stressed by ecofeminists. She stresses that "ecofeminists have perhaps been most insistent on some version of the world as active subject, not as resource to be mapped and appropriated in bourgeois, Marxist, or masculinist projects. Acknowledging the agency of the world in knowledge makes room for some unsettling possibilities."[49] Haraway says that when one acknowledges "nature as subject."

> Accounts of a "real" world do not, then, depend on a logic of "discovery" but on a power-charged social relation of "conversation." Acknowledging the agency of the world in knowledge makes room for some unsettling possibilities, including a sense of the world's independent sense of humor. . . . Perhaps our hopes for accountability, for politics, for ecofeminism, turn on revisioning the world as coding trickster with whom we must learn to converse.[50]

Haraway argues for a reconception of the practice of science as a socially and politically charged "conversation" with nature, reconceived as active agent. The image of nature as a "coding trickster" conveys the sense of play, interaction, and agency Haraway imputes to all epistemic relationships.

Some ecofeminists who discuss epistemological connections appeal, instead, to the critical theory of such authors as Horkheimer, Adorno, Balbus, and the Frankfurt circle. Salleh, for instance, claims that "their epistemological and substantive analysis both point to a convergence of feminist and ecological concerns, anticipating the more recent arrival of ecofeminism."[51] Patricia Jagentowicz Mills agrees. She argues that "critical theory" provides a critique of the "nature versus culture" dichotomy and an epistemological structure for critiquing the relationships between the domination of women and the domination of nature.[52]

POLITICAL INTERCONNECTIONS

Ecofeminism has always been a grassroots political movement motivated by pressing pragmatic concerns.[53] These include issues of women's and environmental health, to science, development and technology, the treatment of animals, and peace, anti-nuclear, anti-militarism activism. The varieties of ecofeminist perspectives on the environment are properly seen as an attempt to take seriously such grassroots activism and political concerns by developing analyses of domination that explain, clarify, and guide that praxis.

Stephanie Lahar states this point well. Lahar concludes her analysis of the links between ecofeminist theory and grassroots political activism as follows:

> Ecofeminism's political goals include the deconstruction of oppressive social, economic, and political systems and the reconstruction of more viable social and political forms. No version of ecofeminist theory dictates exactly what people should do

in the face of situations they encounter in personal and public life, nor is it a single political platform. The relation of ecofeminist theory to political activism is ideally informative and generative and not one of either prescribing or "owning" particular actions. Ecofeminist theory advocates a combined politics of resistance and creative projects, but the specific enactment of these is a result of dialogue between the individuals involved and the actual situation or issue.

Lahar goes on to claim that ecofeminism "contributes an overall framework and conceptual links to the political understanding of the interplay between social and environmental issues, and routes to political empowerment through understanding the effects of one's actions extended through multiple human and nonhuman communities."[54]

Plumwood agrees with Lahar. Plumwood argues that if one mistakenly construes environmental philosophy as only or primarily concerned with ethics, one will neglect "a key aspect of the overall problem which is concerned with the definition of the human self as separate from nature, the connection between this and the instrumental view of nature, and broader *political* aspects of the critique of instrumentalism."[55]

The political aspects of ecofeminist critiques of ethics and knowledge are explicitly addressed by political scientist Noël Sturgeon in her book *Ecofeminist Natures.* Sturgeon argues for a conception of ecofeminism as an "oppositional political discourse and set of practices imbedded in particular historical, material, and political contexts." Sturgeon interprets ecofeminism as "a fractured, contested, discontinuous entity that constitutes itself as a social movement." Sturgeon's characterization of ecofeminism as a social movement is based on her understanding of social movements as:

> contestants in hegemonic power relations, through which change is produced by numerous kinds of "action," including that of the deployment of symbolic resources, shifts in identity construction, and the production of both popular and scholarly knowledge—as well as direct action, civil disobedience, strikes, boycotts, demonstrations, lobbying, and other more traditionally recognized forms of political action.[56]

According to Sturgeon, ecofeminism is a social movement involved in both the deployment of and theorizing about concepts (e.g., of nature, women, race)— what she calls the "direct theory" aspect of a social movement. Sturgeon's book is a critique of ecofeminist theory and practice "with the goal of making suggestions for the formation of a more inclusive, more politically engaged ecofeminist movement."[57]

Much of the debate among ecofeminists about politics turns on the type of feminism that underlies a particular ecofeminist position. Different ecofeminist politics finds roots in liberal feminism, Marxist feminism, radical feminism, socialist feminism, psychoanalytic feminism, and postcolonial feminisms. What is accepted as an appropriate ecofeminist action, then, will reflect the different and differing perspectives of these feminisms.

ETHICAL INTERCONNECTIONS

Much of the scholarly literature of ecofeminist philosophy has focused on environmental ethics. Ecofeminist philosophers argue that the interconnections among the conceptualizations and treatment of women, other subordinated humans, animals, and (the rest of) nature require a feminist ethical analysis and response. Minimally, the goal of ecofeminist environmental ethics is to develop theories and practices concerning humans and the natural environment that are not male-biased and that provide a guide to action in the prefeminist present.

Ecofeminist philosopher Chris Cuomo argues for "ethics at the crossroads of ethical and political theory and practice" in the form of an "ethic of flourishing." An ethic of flourishing draws on Aristotelian concepts of *eudaimonia* (translated variously as happiness, the good life, living well, excellence, and flourishing) and the *polis* (or, community),[58] as well as a commitment to the value of flourishing, or well-being, of individuals, species, and communities. According to Cuomo:

> in ecological feminism, it is an entity's *dynamic charm*—its diffuse, 'internal' ability to adapt to or resist change, and its unique causal and motivational patterns and character—that renders it morally considerable, and that serves as a primary site for determining what is good for that being or thing.[59]

Cuomo's conception of the flourishing of living things and the "dynamic charm" of systems presumes a degree of physical health and self-directedness that is achievable by both individuals in communities (both social and ecological) and communities themselves.

Ynestra King is among the first North American theorists to defend an ecofeminist ethic based in socialist feminism. King calls for a *rapprochement* between cultural (or spiritual ecofeminism) and socialist feminism within ecofeminism:

> Both feminism and ecology embody the revolt of nature against human domination. They demand that we rethink the relationship between humanity and the rest of nature, including our natural, embodied selves. In ecofeminism, nature is the central category of analysis. An analysis of the interrelated dominations of nature—psyche and sexuality, human oppression, and nonhuman nature—and the historic position of women in relation to those forms of domination is the starting point of ecofeminist theory. We share with cultural feminism the necessity of a politics with heart and a beloved community, recognizing our connection with each other, and nonhuman nature. Socialist feminism has given us a powerful critical perspective with which to understand and transform history. Separately, they perpetuate the dualism of "mind" and "nature." Together they make possible a new ecological relationship between nature and culture, in which mind and nature, heart and reason, join forces to transform the internal and external systems of domination that threaten the existence of life on Earth.[60]

King's view of ecofeminism recommends that ecofeminist ethics dismantle dualisms of mind and body, reason and emotion by finding a place "in which mind and nature, heart and reason, join forces to transform the internal and external systems of domination that threaten the existence of life on earth."[61] (The version of ecofeminist ethics I defend in chapter 5 attempts to do just that.)

CONCLUSION

In this chapter I have provided an overview of the literature on ecofeminism by describing ten types of women–other human Other–nature interconnections discussed by ecofeminists. I turn now, in chapters 3 through 9, to a description and defense of the version of ecofeminist philosophy I am defending. It is one that addresses key issues raised within each of these ten types of positions.

NOTES

1. Françoise d'Eaubonne, *Le Feminisme ou La Mort* (Paris: Pierre Horay, 1974), 213–52.
2. For many environmental ethicists, it is anthropocentrism (human-centeredness) that is the problem, not androcentrism (male-centeredness). For ecofeminists, the historical manifestation of anthropocentrism, at least in Western societies, has been androcentric.
3. Riane Eisler, *The Chalice and the Blade: Our History, Our Future* (San Francisco: Harper and Row, 1988), 46. The quote by Engels is from *The Origins of the Family, Private Property, and the State* (New York: International Publishers, 1972).
4. Eisler, *The Chalice*, xviii.
5. Carolyn Merchant, *The Death of Nature: Women, Ecology and the Scientific Revolution* (San Francisco: Harper and Row, 1980), 1, 2.
6. Merchant, *Death of Nature*, 2.
7. Merchant, *Death of Nature*, 2.
8. Val Plumwood, "Nature, Self, and Gender: Feminism, Environmental Philosophy, and the Critique of Rationalism," in *Ecological Feminist Philosophies*, ed. Karen J. Warren (Bloomington: Indiana University Press, 1996), 155–80.
9. Plumwood, "Nature, Self, and Gender," 22.
10. Plumwood, "Nature, Self, and Gender," 22.
11. See, e.g., Jim Cheney, "Eco-Feminism and Deep Ecology," *Environmental Ethics* 9, no. 2 (Summer 1987), 115–45; Elizabeth Dodson Gray, *Green Paradise Lost* (Wellesley, Mass.: Roundtable Press, 1981); Stephanie Leland, "Feminism and Ecology: Theoretical Connections," in *Reclaim the Earth: Women Speak Out for Life on Earth,* ed. Leonie Caldecott and Stephanie Leland (London: Women's Press, 1983), 67–72; Ariel Kay Salleh, "Deeper than Deep Ecology: The Eco-Feminist Connection," *Environmental Ethics* 6, no. 4 (Winter 1984), 339–45.
12. Salleh, "Deeper than Deep Ecology," 340.
13. Salleh, "Deeper than Deep Ecology," 340.
14. Ariel Kay Salleh, "Working with Nature: Reciprocity or Control?" in *Environmental Philosophy: From Animal Rights to Radical Ecology,* 2nd edition, ed. Michael E. Zimmerman, J. Baird Callicott, George Sessions, Karen J. Warren, and John Clark (Upper Saddle River, N.J.: Prentice-Hall, 1998), 323.

15. Vandana Shiva, *Staying Alive: Women, Ecology and Development* (London: Zed Books Ltd., 1988), 4.

16. Maria Mies, *Patriarchy and Accumulation on a World Scale: Women in the International Division of Labor* (Atlantic Highlands, N.J.: Zed Books, 1986).

17. Rosemary Radford Ruether, "Introduction," in *Women Healing Earth: Third World Women on Ecology, Feminism, and Religion* (Maryknoll, N.Y.: Orbis Books, 1996), 3.

18. Mary Mellor, *Feminism and Ecology* (New York: New York University Press, 1997), 86.

19. Mellor, *Feminism and Ecology,* 58.

20. Mellor, *Feminism and Ecology,* 177.

21. See Joan Dunayer, "Sexist Words, Speciesist Roots," in *Animals and Women: Feminist Theoretical Explorations,* ed. Carol J. Adams and Josephine Donovan (Durham, N.C.: Duke University Press, 1995), 13.

22. Carol J. Adams, *The Sexual Politics of Meat: A Feminist-Vegetarian Critical Theory* (New York: Continuum Company, 1990), 61.

23. Dunayer, "Sexist Words," 16.

24. Dunayer, "Sexist Words," 17.

25. Dunayer, "Sexist Words," 16.

26. Dunayer, "Sexist Words," 17.

27. Merchant, *Death of Nature,* 3.

28. Paula Gunn Allen, *The Sacred Hoop: Recovering the Feminine in American Indian Traditions* (Boston: Beacon Press, 1986); Allen, "The Woman I Love Is a Planet; The Planet I Love Is a Tree," in *Reweaving the World: The Emergence of Ecofeminism,* ed. Irene Diamond and Gloria Feman Orenstein (San Francisco: Sierra Club Books, 1990), 52–57; Lorraine Anderson, ed., *Sisters of the Earth: Women's Prose and Poetry About Nature* (New York: Vintage Books, 1991); Margaret Atwood, *The Handmaid's Tale* (New York: Seabury Press, 1985); Rachel L. Bagby, "Daughters of Growing Things," in *Reweaving the World: The Emergence of Ecofeminism,* ed. Irene Diamond and Gloria Feman Orenstein (San Francisco: Sierra Club Books, 1990), 231–48; Susy McKee Charnas, *Walk to the End of the World* (New York: Ballantine Books, 1974); Charnas, *Motherlines* (New York: Berkley, 1979); Theresa Corrigan and Stephanie Hoppe, *With a Fly's Eye, Whale's Wit, and Woman's Heart: Animals and Women* (San Francisco: Cleis Press, 1989); Corrigan and Hoppe, *And a Deer's Ear, Eagle's Song and Bear's Grace* (San Francisco: Cleis Press, 1990); Annie Dillard, *Teaching a Stone to Talk* (New York: Harper and Row, 1982); Sally Miller Gearhart, *The Wanderground: Stories of the Hill Women* (Boston: Alyson Publications, 1984); Susan Griffin, *Woman and Nature: The Roaring Inside Her* (New York: Harper and Row, 1978); Joy Harjo, *What Moon Drove Me to This?* (New York: I. Reed Books, 1979); Harjo, *She Had Some Horses* (New York: Thunder's Mouth, 1983); Harjo, *In Mad Love and War* (Middleton, Conn.: Wesleyan University Press, 1990); Linda Hogan, *Daughters, I Love You* (Denver: Loretto Heights College Publications, 1981); Annette Kolodny, *The Lay of the Land: Metaphor as Experience and History in American Life and Letters* (Chapel Hill: University of North Carolina Press, 1975); Ursula K. LeGuin, *Always Coming Home* (New York: Bantam Books, 1985); LeGuin, *Buffalo Gals and Other Animal Presences* (Santa Barbara, Calif.: Capra Press, 1987); LeGuin, *Wild Oats and Fireweed* (New York: Harper and Row, 1988); LeGuin, *At The Edge of the World: Thoughts of Words, Women, Places* (New York: Harper and Row, 1989); Patrick D. Murphy, "Introduction: Feminism, Ecology, and the Future of the Humanities," *Studies in the*

Humanities (Special issue on Feminism, Ecology, and the Future of the Humanities, ed. Patrick D. Murphy), 15, no. 2 (1988), 85–89; Murphy, "Ground, Pivot, Motion: Ecofeminist Theory, Dialogics, and Literary Practice," in *Ecological Feminist Philosophies*, ed. Karen J. Warren (Bloomington: Indiana University Press, 1996), 228–43; Mary Oliver, *American Primitive* (Boston: Little, Brown, 1983); Marge Piercy, *Women on the Edge of Time* (New York: Fawcett Crest, 1976); Adrienne Rich, *Your Native Land, Your Life* (New York: Norton, 1986); Leslie Marmon Silko, *Ceremony* (New York: New American Library, 1977); Silko, "Landscape, History and the Pueblo Imagination," in *On Nature: Nature, Landscape, and Natural History,* ed. Daniel Halpern (San Francisco: North Point, 1987), 83–94; Silko, *Almanac of the Dead: A Novel* (New York: Penguin, 1991); Luci Tapahonso, *A Breeze Swept Through* (Albuquerque, N. Mex.: West End Press, 1987); Sheri Tepper, *The Gate to Women's Country* (New York: Bantam Books, 1989); Alice Walker, *Living by the Word: Selected Writings, 1973–1987* (New York: Harcourt, Brace, Jovanovich, 1988); Walker, *The Temple of My Familiar* (New York: Pocket Books, 1990); Kate Wilhelm, *Juniper Time* (New York: Pocket Books, 1980); Terry Tempest Williams, "The Wild Card," *Wilderness* (Summer 1993): 26–29; Irene Zahava, *Through Other Eyes: Animal Stories by Women* (Freedom, Calif.: Crossing Press, 1988).

29. Griffin, *Woman and Nature,* 1 (emphases in the original removed).

30. Patrick D. Murphy, *Literature, Nature, and Other: Ecofeminist Critiques* (Albany: State University of New York Press, 1995), 25.

31. Murphy, *Literature, Nature,* 29.

32. Gray, *Green Paradise Lost,* 3.

33. Gray, *Green Paradise Lost,* 5.

34. Gray, *Green Paradise Lost,* 6–7.

35. Ruether, *Women Healing Earth,* 6.

36. Ruether, *Women Healing Earth,* 8.

37. Starhawk, "Feminist, Earth-Based Spirituality and Ecofeminism," in *Healing the Wounds: The Promise of Ecological Feminism,* ed. Judith Plant (Santa Cruz, Calif.: New Society Publishers, 1989), 174–85.

38. See Charlene Spretnak, ed., *The Politics of Women's Spirituality: Essays on the Rise of Spiritual Power Within the Feminist Movement* (Garden City, N.Y.: Anchor Books, 1982).

39. Carol Christ, "Rethinking Theology and Nature," in *Reweaving the World: The Emergence of Ecofeminism,* ed. Irene Diamond and Gloria Feman Orenstein (San Francisco: Sierra Club Books, 1990), 58.

40. Charlene Spretnak, "Ecofeminism: Our Roots and Flowering," in *Reweaving the World: The Emergence of Ecofeminism,* ed. Irene Diamond and Gloria Feman Orenstein (San Francisco: Sierra Club Books, 1990), 5.

41. Charlene Spretnak, "States of Grace," in *Environmental Ethics: Convergence and Divergence,* ed. Susan J. Armstrong and Richard G. Botzler (New York: McGraw-Hill, 1993), 466–74.

42. Joanna Macy, "Awakening to the Ecological Self," in *Healing the Wounds: The Promise of Ecological Feminism,* ed. Judith Plant (Santa Cruz, Calif.: New Society Publishers, 1989), 210.

43. Carol Christ, "Why Women Need the Goddess: Phenomenological, Psychological, and Political Reflections," in *Womanspirit Rising,* ed. Judith Plaskow and Carol Christ (New York: Harper and Row, 1979), 76.

44. Starhawk, *The Spiral Dance: A Rebirth of the Ancient Religion of the Great Goddess* (New York: Harper and Row, 1979), 9.

45. Sandra Harding, "Rethinking Standpoint Epistemology: What Is 'Strong Objectivity?'" in *Feminist Epistemologies,* ed. Linda Alcoff and Elizabeth Potter (New York: Routledge, 1993), 54.

46. Lori Gruen, "Toward an Ecofeminist Moral Epistemology," in *Ecological Feminism,* ed. Karen J. Warren (New York: Routledge, 1994), 134.

47. Gruen, "Toward an Ecofeminist Moral Epistemology," 124.

48. Donna Haraway, "Situated Knowledges: The Science Question in Feminism and the Privilege of Partial Perspective," *Feminist Studies* 14, no. 3 (Fall 1988), 592–93.

49. Haraway, "Situated Knowledges," 592–93.

50. Haraway, "Situated Knowledges," 593.

51. Ariel Kay Salleh, "Epistemology and the Metaphors of Production: An Eco-Feminist Reading of Critical Theory," *Studies in the Humanities* (Special issue on Feminism, Ecology, and the Future of the Humanities, ed. Patrick D. Murphy) 15, no. 2 (1988), 131.

52. Patricia Jagentowicz Mills, *Women, Nature and Psyche* (New Haven, Conn.: Yale University Press, 1987).

53. See Stephanie Lahar, "Ecofeminist Theory and Grassroots Politics," in *Ecological Feminist Philosophies,* ed. Karen J. Warren (Bloomington: Indiana University Press, 1996), 1–18.

54. Lahar, "Ecofeminist Theory," 15.

55. Plumwood, "Nature, Self, and Gender," 162.

56. Noël Sturgeon, *Ecofeminist Natures: Race, Gender, Feminist Theory and Political Action* (New York: Routledge, 1997), 3, 4.

57. Sturgeon, *Ecofeminist Natures,* 19.

58. Cuomo, *Feminism and Ecological Communities: An Ethic of Flourishing* (London: Routledge, 1998), 70.

59. Cuomo, *Feminism and Ecological Communities,* 71.

60. Ynestra King, "Healing the Wounds: Feminism, Ecology, and the Nature/Culture Dualism," in *Reweaving the World: The Emergence of Ecofeminism,* ed. Irene Diamond and Gloria Feman Orenstein (San Francisco: Sierra Club Books, 1990), 106–21.

61. King, "Healing the Wounds," 117–18.

Chapter Three

Quilting Ecofeminist Philosophy

A Western Perspective on What
Ecofeminist Philosophy Is

Ecofeminist philosophy draws on feminism, ecology and environmentalism, and philosophy in its analyses of human systems of unjustified domination ("isms of domination"). It assumes that such domination is neither justified nor inevitable. As a *feminism* (what I take to be an "ism of liberation"), ecofeminist philosophy uses sex/gender analysis as the starting point for critiquing "isms of domination." As an *ecological* and *environmental* position, ecofeminist philosophy uses ecological and environmental insights about the nonhuman world and human–nature interactions in its theory and practice. As a *philosophy*, ecofeminist philosophy uses *conceptual analysis* (e.g., What do the key concepts of interest to ecofeminism mean?) and *argumentative justification* (e.g., What are the arguments for the interconnected dominations of women, other human Others, and nature, and are they sound arguments?). Ecofeminist philosophy is not, is not intended to be, and should not be limited to "describing" reality or reporting "facts"; it involves advancing positions, advocating strategies, and recommending solutions.[1] This prescriptive aspect of ecofeminist philosophy is central to *doing* philosophy.

Five basic claims characterize the version of ecofeminist philosophy I am defending in this book: (1) there are important interconnections among the unjustified dominations of women, other human Others, and nonhuman nature; (2) understanding the nature of these interconnections is important to an adequate understanding of and solutions to these unjustified dominations; (3) feminist philosophy should include ecofeminist insights into women–other human Others–nature interconnections; (4) solutions to gender issues should include ecofeminist insights into women–other human Others–nature connections; and, (5) solutions to environmental problems should include ecofeminist insights into women–other human Others–nature interconnections.

The version of ecofeminist philosophy I defend grows out of and is responsive to the intersection of three overlapping areas of concern: feminism (and all the issues feminism raises concerning women and other human Others); nature (the natural environment), science (especially scientific ecology), development, and technology; and local or indigenous perspectives.[2] It might be visualized as in diagram 3.1. This Venn diagram provides a broad-stroke picture of the kinds of overlapping factors that are important as input and solution to interconnecting women–other human Others–nature issues. It does so by showing that any policies or practices that fall outside the overlapping three areas demarcated by the asterisk will be prima facie ("other things being equal") inadequate or unacceptable from the ecofeminist philosophical perspective I am defending.

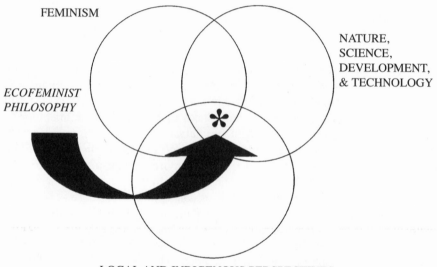

FEMINISM

NATURE, SCIENCE, DEVELOPMENT, & TECHNOLOGY

ECOFEMINIST
PHILOSOPHY

LOCAL AND INDIGENOUS PERSPECTIVES

Diagram 3.1. A Visualization of Ecofeminist Philosophy

A casual perusal of this diagram serves as a visual suggestion of the sorts of policies and practices that will be prima facie unacceptable from the ecofeminist philosophical perspective I am defending. For example, policies or practices that destroy the current ability of rural women in India to maintain domestic economies by replacing indigenous forests with monoculture eucalyptus plantations falls outside the asterisk area: they fail to sufficiently accommodate the concerns of feminist or local Indian women who, as managers of domestic economies, rely on indigenous forests for survival. Or, any First World development and technology projects imposed on Third World communities that make it difficult for local communities to maintain sustain-

able agricultural practices will fall outside the asterisk area: they fail to sufficiently include local perspectives and expertise in the decision-making or to
accommodate feminist and local concerns about the continued survival of
those communities. Or, any policy or practice which causes or permits clear-
cutting in the Amazonian rainforest will fall outside the asterisk area: it fails
to sufficiently accommodate ecological and environmental concerns about the
destruction of the rainforest ecosystem.

The qualification "prima facie" here is important. Appeal to the diagram suggests that patriarchal domination, opposed in principle by any feminism, will fall
outside the asterisk area and, thus, will not be supported by ecofeminist philosophy. But sometimes the present-day socioeconomic realities of patriarchal domination are such that a decision one makes to ensure the survival of women (which
has ecofeminist support) may also keep intact patriarchal structures (which, in
principle, does not have ecofeminist support). For example, a decision to provide
women with the means to maintain domestic economies may ensure the survival
of women and women-headed households while also contributing to the survival
of domestic economies, which are themselves patriarchal and exploitative of the
labor of women. Other things are *not* equal in such a case.

What should one do in such cases? Given the current socioeconomic realities
of patriarchy, often the best a person currently can do is not a perfect or ideal
solution. Often other things simply are *not* equal. Within contemporary patriarchal structures, there will be very real trade-offs between values one holds dear.
For example, one may actively lobby for mass transit even though one currently
drives a car to work. One may support organic farming even though one cannot
currently afford organically raised foods. One may argue for decreased levels of
energy consumption by North Americans even though one currently enjoys the
benefits of airconditioned buildings. One may argue against the replacement of
indigenous forests by eucalyptus plantations on the grounds that the eucalyptus
plantations exacerbate the daily difficulties women in the Southern Hemisphere
face in managing domestic economies, even though those domestic economies
are themselves patriarchal.

My point is this: One simply cannot make ecologically perfect decisions or
lead an ecologically perfect lifestyle within current institutional structures characterized by unequal distributions of wealth, consumption of energy, and gendered divisions of labor. When institutional structures themselves are unjust, it is
often difficult to make truly just decisions within them. (I address this point again
later in this chapter, as well as in chapters 6, 8, and 9.) Sometimes, the best one
can do in the prefeminist present is to support policies and practices that ensure
that present-day women are able to maintain a daily livelihood, while also challenging the very structures that keep intact the unjustified domination of women
by men. The diagram of ecofeminist philosophy (above) shows *what to aim for*
in one's ecofeminist philosophical understanding of and solutions to a gender or
an environmental issue.

THE IMPORTANCE OF OPPRESSIVE
CONCEPTUAL FRAMEWORKS

I have characterized ecofeminist philosophy as being concerned with *conceptual analysis* and *argumentative proof* about women–other human Others–nature interconnections. There is no more basic place to start to understand and appreciate this dimension of ecofeminist philosophy than with an analysis of the "conceptual frameworks" that have functioned historically to maintain, perpetuate, and "justify" the dominations of women, other subordinated humans, and nonhuman nature.

A *conceptual framework* is a set of basic beliefs, values, attitudes, and assumptions which shape and reflect how one views oneself and one's world. A conceptual framework functions as a socially constructed *lens* through which one perceives reality. It is affected and shaped by such factors as sex-gender, race/ethnicity, class, age, affectional orientation, marital status, religion, nationality, colonial influences, and culture.

Some conceptual frameworks are *oppressive*. An oppressive conceptual framework is one that functions to explain, maintain, and "justify" relationships of unjustified domination and subordination. When an oppressive conceptual framework is *patriarchal*, it functions to justify the subordination of women by men.

There are five common features of an oppressive conceptual framework. First, an oppressive conceptual framework involves *value-hierarchical thinking*, that is, "Up-Down" thinking, which attributes greater value to that which is higher, or Up, than to that which is lower, or Down. It may put men Up and women Down, whites Up and people of color Down, culture Up and nature Down, minds Up and bodies Down. By attributing greater value to that which is higher, the Up-Down organization of reality serves to legitimate inequality "when, in fact, prior to the metaphor of Up-Down one would have said only that there existed diversity."[3]

Second, an oppressive conceptual framework encourages *oppositional value dualisms,* that is, disjunctive pairs in which the disjuncts are seen as exclusive (rather than inclusive) and oppositional (rather than complementary) and that places higher value (status, prestige) on one disjunct than the other. Examples include value dualisms that give higher status to that which has historically been identified as "male," "white," "rational," and "culture" than to that which has historically been identified as "female," "black," "emotional," and "nature" (or "natural"). According to these value dualisms, it is better to be male, white, or rational, than female, black, or emotional.

The third characteristic of an oppressive conceptual framework is that *power* is conceived (and exercised) as "power-over" power. There are many types of power (as I clarify in chapter 9). In oppressive systems, power typically is conceived and exercised as power of Ups over Downs. The power of parents over their young children, of judges over defendants, of tyrants over citizens, of rapists over their victims are all examples of power-over. Some of these are justified cases of power-over power; others are not. When power-over power serves to reinforce the power of Ups as Ups in ways that keep Downs unjustifiably subordinated (which not all cases of power-over do), such conceptions and practices of power are unjustified.

The fourth characteristic of an oppressive conceptual framework is that it creates, maintains, or perpetuates a conception and practice of *privilege* as belonging to Ups and not to Downs. The privileges of driving a car, taking out a home equity loan, living in high-income housing areas, or attending a college of one's choice should belong to those who qualify. Sometimes small privileges are given to Downs (e.g., to house slaves or middle-class housewives) to keep them from challenging the power and privilege of Ups.[4] When the privilege of Ups functions to keep intact dominant-subordinate Up-Down relationships which systematically advantage Ups over Downs, they are part of an oppressive conceptual framework and set of practices.

The fifth and philosophically most important characteristic of an oppressive conceptual framework is that it sanctions a *logic of domination*, that is, a logical structure of argumentation that "justifies" domination and subordination. A logic of domination assumes that superiority justifies subordination. A logic of domination is offered as the moral stamp of approval for subordination, since, if accepted, it provides a justification for keeping Downs down. Typically this justification takes the form that the Up has some characteristic (e.g., in the Western philosophical tradition, the favored trait is "mind," reason, or rationality) that the Down lacks and by virtue of which the subordination of the Down by the Up is justified.

Contrary to what many feminists and ecofeminists have claimed, there may be nothing inherently problematic about hierarchical thinking (even value-hierarchical thinking), value dualisms, and conceptions and relations of power and privilege, which advantage the Ups, *in contexts other than oppression*. Hierarchical thinking is important for classifying data, comparing information, and organizing material. Taxonomies (e.g., plant taxonomies) and biological nomenclature seem to require some form of hierarchical thinking. Even value-hierarchical thinking may be quite acceptable in some contexts (e.g., in assessing the qualities of contestants or in rank-ordering participants in a contest). Responsible parents may exercise legitimate power and privilege (as Ups) over their infants (as Downs), be assigned higher prestige or value than their infants for some purposes (e.g., as logical reasoners), and yet not thereby be involved in any type of oppressive parent-child relationship. Up-Down parent-child relationships are only oppressive if the all-important logic of domination is in place; it is what "justifies" the unjustified domination of children by parents. The problem with value-hierarchical thinking, value dualisms, and conceptions of power and privilege that systematically advantage Ups over Downs, is the way in which each of these has functioned historically in oppressive conceptual frameworks to establish the inferiority of Downs and to justify the subordination of Downs by Ups. The logic of domination is what provides that alleged justification of subordination.

This last point raises the issue of justified and unjustified domination. If one describes healthy, morally permissible relationships (say between parents and infants) as relationships of domination, then unjustified domination occurs only where the logic of domination is in place. That is, the logic of domination falsely justifies the power and privilege of Ups over Downs in a way which keeps intact unjustified domination-subordination relationships. Child abuse is a case of unjustified domination; a parent exercising her power and privilege by forcibly removing a child's hand from a hot burning stove is not. So, if one claims that domination can be either justified or unjustified, then it is cases of unjustified domination that are of interest to ecofeminist philosophy. For purposes of this book, my discussion of domination refers to "unjustified domination."

WHY THE LOGIC OF DOMINATION IS EXPLANATORILY BASIC

Since it is the logic of domination that provides the moral premise for ethically justifying the subordination of Downs by Ups in Up-Down relationships of domination and subordination, the logic of domination is explanatorily basic to oppression and oppressive conceptual frameworks. That a logic of domination is explanatorily basic is important for four reasons.

First, since a logic of domination functions both to explain and to justify domination-subordination relationships, it is more than simply a logical structure; it also involves a substantive value system. This value system is what is needed to generate an allegedly morally relevant distinction between Ups and Downs (e.g., that Ups are rational and Downs are not), which, in turn, is used to sanction the justified subordination of what is Down. That value system is embedded in the logic of domination in the form of a moral premise—*Superiority justifies subordination* (or Whatever is Up is justified in being Up and in dominating whatever is Down). The logic of domination thereby operates both as a premise and as a process whereby others are constructed (or thought of) as inferior—that is, as Others. As Lori Gruen claims, in white patriarchal culture, the logic of domination "constructs inferior others and uses this inferiority to justify their oppression."[5]

This construction of inferiority can take many forms, depending on historical and social contexts. It may not be consciously, knowingly, or even intentionally maintained. Habit, custom, and prejudice (and not just consciously developed and endorsed ideologies) affect the social constructions of inferiority. Familiar expressions of these claims of inferiority are that the Ups are better than, stronger than, more powerful than, smarter than, older than, wiser than, more rational than, closer to the divine than, Downs. The logic of domination then functions to sanction the conclusion that Ups are justified in subordinating (dominating, treating as inferior, enslaving) Downs.

The second reason a logic of domination is explanatorily basic is that without it, a description of similarities and differences would be just that—a description of similarities and differences. In order for differences to make a moral difference in how a group is treated or in the opportunities available to it, other moral premises (such as the logic of domination) must be accepted. The logic of domination is necessary both to turn diversity (or difference) into domination and to justify that domination.

To illustrate how differences are turned into justified domination by a logic of domination, let us suppose (even if it turns out to be contrary to fact) that what is unique about humans is our conscious capacity to radically reshape our social environments to meet self-determined ends, as Murray Bookchin suggests.[6] Then one could claim that humans are better equipped to radically reshape their environments in consciously self-determined ways than are rocks or plants—a value-hierarchical way of speaking—without thereby sanctioning any domination or exploitation of the nonhuman environment. To justify such domination, one needs a *logic of domination*—a moral premise that specifies that the superiority of humans as Ups (here, their superior ability to radically alter their environment in consciously self-determined ways) justifies the domination of nonhuman natural others as Others, as Downs (here, rocks or plants that do not have this ability).

It is helpful to formalize such reasoning, so that we can see clearly how the derivation of the conclusion about the justified domination of nonhuman nature rests on acceptance of two important claims: a claim about the moral superiority of humans over nonhuman entities on the basis of some ability humans have that nonhuman entities lack (premise 2 below), and the claim that superiority justifies subordination—the "logic of domination" (premise 4 below):

(A)   (1) Humans do, and plants and rocks do not, have the capacity to consciously and radically change the communities in which they live in self-determined ways.

        (2) Whatever has the capacity to consciously and radically change the community in which it lives in self-determined ways is morally superior to whatever lacks this capacity.

Thus,   (3) Humans are morally superior to plants and rocks.

        (4) For any X and Y, if X is morally superior to Y, then X is morally justified in subordinating (dominating) Y.

Thus,   (5) Humans are morally justified in subordinating (dominating) plants and rocks.

Notice that premise 2 might well be true; that is a topic debated in environmental philosophy. But even if 2 is true, without the logic of domination, 4, all one has are differences (even if morally relevant differences) between humans and some nonhumans. The moral superiority of humans over nonhuman natural beings, if it exists, does not *by itself* justify domination. In fact, one could argue that such moral superiority imposes on humans extraordinary responsibilities toward (rather than unjustified domination over) others less capable. (As we shall see in chapter 4, a "stewardship ethic" does this.) So, it is the logic of domination, 4, that is the bottom-line (necessary but not sufficient condition) in justifications of domination.

A third reason the logic of domination is so important is that historically, at least in Western societies, the oppressive conceptual frameworks that have justified the dominations of women and nonhuman nature have been patriarchal. Environmental historian Carolyn Merchant was among the first to argue for these historical interconnections between the twin dominations of women and nature in her book *The Death of Nature*. Merchant argues that historically, at least in Western societies, women have been identified in art, literature, and philosophy with nature, body, and the realm of the physical, while men have been identified with culture, reason, and the realm of the mental. These associations occur within a patriarchal conceptual framework that then functions to justify the subordination of women. It does so, for example, by associating the "public" realm of culture, politics, and business with the activities associated with men, and the inferior "private" realm of the home, the family, and personal relationships with women (e.g., childbearing and child rearing), and then justifying the unequal and inferior status of women in terms of women's "natural" childbearing and child raising roles.

Historically in Western culture, the justified inferiority of women and other inferiorized groups (other Others) often turns on claims that women and Others were not rational. Ecofeminist philosophers show how an exaggerated emphasis on reason and rationality, and the attendant "hyperseparation" of reason from emotion,[7] has functioned historically to sanction both the feminization of nature and the naturalization of women in ways that make women and nature inferior to male-gender identified culture. If this is correct, then both traditional feminism (concerned with eliminating sexism) and environmental ethics (concerned with eliminating the unjustified domination of nonhuman nature, or "naturism") ought to incorporate these ecofeminist philosophical insights into their analyses and practices.

Again, by formalizing such reasoning, we can see clearly through argument B how patriarchal conceptual frameworks have functioned historically to sanction sexism and naturism.[8]

(B)   (1) At least in Western societies, whenever a group is historically identified with nonhuman nature and the realm of the physical, it is conceptualized as morally inferior to whatever group is historically identified with culture and the realm of the mental.

(2) At least in Western societies, women as a group historically have been identified with nonhuman nature and the realm of the physical, while at least dominant men have been historically identified with culture and the realm of the mental.

Thus, (3) At least in Western societies, women as a group are conceptualized as morally inferior to at least dominant men.

(4) For any X and Y, if X is conceptualized as morally inferior to Y, then Y is justified in subordinating (or dominating) X.

Thus, (5) At least in Western societies, dominant men are justified in subordinating (or dominating) both women and nonhuman nature.

Argument B represents the historically favored position, at least in Western societies, on the justified dominations of women and nonhuman nature. But argument B is unsound, since premise 4—the logic of domination—is false as a prescriptive claim. (It may be true as a descriptive claim about how women, men, and nonhuman nature have been conceptualized and treated historically in Western cultures.) So, one ought to reject argument B.

Are there other premises of argument B besides (4) that are false or problematic? Ecofeminist philosophers argue that 1 and 2 are true—where 1 and 2 are properly understood as *historical* claims (i.e., as claims about how women, nature, and men historically have been viewed in the Western tradition), though not as claims about how women, nature, and men ought to be viewed. Establishing their truths as historical facts is, as Merchant has stated, an important ecofeminist project.

It is important to be clear about what is *not* asserted by premises 1 and 2. They do not assert that women are, in fact, closer to nature than men or that all women and all men are always and everywhere associated with inferior nature (in the case of women) and superior culture (in the case of men). The issue of women's closeness with nature was addressed by Sherry Ortner in her essay, "Is Female to Male as Nature Is to Culture?" Ortner claims that women are universally devalued and subordinated because they are "seen as closer to nature than men, men being seen as more unequivocally occupying the high ground of culture." According to Ortner, because "culture's job is to control nature," men are accorded the right to control women.[9]

But anthropologist Peggy Sanday disagrees with Ortner. Sanday argues that women's subordination is neither universal nor always associated with an inferior nature. Sanday's evidence is based on her studies of 150 tribal societies. She states:

> In societies where the forces of nature are sacralized, . . . there is a reciprocal flow between the power of nature and the power inherent in women. The control and manipulation of these forces is left to women and to sacred natural symbols; men are largely extraneous to this domain and must be careful lest they antagonize earthly representatives of nature's power (namely, women).

Sanday concludes that,

> Men are not universally aligned so unequivocally with the realm Ortner calls culture, "culture being minimally defined as the transcendence, by means of systems of thought and technology, of the natural givens of existence." On the contrary, in many cases men are inextricably locked into such natural givens as death, destruction, and animality.[10]

According to Sanday, "generally speaking, when men dominate, women play an inconsequential role in the sacred and secular domains. Almost always in male-dominated societies, the godhead is defined in exclusively masculine terms."[11] If Sanday is correct, then the truth of premises 1 and 2 turns on their being claims about Up men in nonprimal (e.g., Western) societies. That is why premises 1 and 2 are stated as they are in argument B (i.e., as claims about Western societies).

But there is another reason for stating premises 1 and 2 as they are stated in argument B. Historically, just as not all groups of men have occupied Up positions of power and privilege (e.g., African American men in the United States), some groups of women have occupied Up positions, especially vis-à-vis other women. In Europe and North America, for example, white, wealthy, aristocratic women (e.g., Rose Kennedy) and women heads of state (e.g., Margaret Thatcher) sometimes have been in uncontested Up positions or in Up positions relative to other women (e.g., white women-headed households that employ women of color as domestic servants). These differences among women are reflected in the way premises 1 and 2 are stated: 1 is a historical claim about those societies *in which* and *when* there is a marked separation between the realms of culture and nature (e.g., Western societies), and 2 is a historical claim about those societies *in which* and *when* there is an association of "Up" men with superior culture and women as a group with inferior nature.

However, even Western women who seem to be an exception by occupying Up positions of power and privilege in male-dominated Up-Down societies are often portrayed in ambiguous gender terms: They tended to be seen either as not really women (they "think like a man," have "masculine" characteristics, or "are manly") or as women who have higher status or value relative to other women but lower status or value relative to dominant men (e.g., "pure," "chaste," "untainted," white "virgins" who are placed precariously "on a pedestal"; "exceptional women" who have superior—because man-like—intelligence and reasoning powers, ambition and fortitude, courage and conviction). In such cases, their status as Ups is achieved by varying degrees of separation (or distancing) both from other groups of women and from the inferior realm of contaminated body, the physical and nonhuman nature.

The classic Broverman study in 1970 illustrates this point for U.S. women. One hundred psychiatrists, psychiatric social workers, and psychologists were asked to describe a normal man, a normal woman, and a normal human. The normal man and the normal human turned out to be the same; only the normal woman was different. As philosopher Elizabeth Minnick puts it, "That means that a woman can be *either* a 'normal' human and an 'abnormal' woman *or* a 'normal' woman and an 'abnormal' human—not both. Man is what human IS; woman is deviant."[12]

What about the status of premise 3, namely, the premise that at least in Western societies, women as a group are conceptualized as morally inferior to at least dominant men? All ecofeminist philosophers to date agree that women have been falsely *conceptualized* as inferior to men. This historical conceptualization of women as inferior has been based on any of three faulty assumptions: *biological determinism, conceptual essentialism,* and *universalism.* Biological determinism (popularized by the slogan "biology is destiny") incorrectly locates women as biologically "closer to nature than men" (typically because of women's reproductive capacities) or assumes a biological essence to women (a biological "women's nature"). Conceptual essentialism incorrectly assumes that the concept of women is a univocal, meaningful concept that captures some cross-culturally valid or essential (i.e., necessary and sufficient) conditions of women, womanhood, or femaleness.[13] Universalism incorrectly assumes that, as women, all women share a set of experiences in virtue of the fact that we are women.

Of course, even if all ecofeminist philosophers to date have been unanimous in a rejection of these three assumptions, it does not follow that all ecofeminist philosophers agree about what such a rejection means or implies. Some ecofeminist philosophers have argued, for example, that a rejection of biological determinism and universalism also involves a rejection of notions of "the female" or "the feminine." For example, in her article "Is Ecofeminism Feminist?" Victoria Davion argues that appeals to "the female" or "the feminine" are anti-feminist, since they uncritically valorize women's experiences and present them as universal and biologically grounded. Davion calls such positions *ecofeminine,* not *ecofeminist.* She states that "views which uncritically embrace unified or one-stance views of feminine sides of gender dichotomies are not feminist; they are better understood as ecofeminine than ecofeminist. They are, in fact, dangerous views from a genuinely feminist perspective."[14]

Ecofeminist philosopher Chris Cuomo agrees with Davion's distinction between ecofeminine and ecofeminist. Because ecofeminism sometimes includes positions that Davion and Cuomo see as ecofeminine (not properly ecofeminist), Cuomo introduces a further distinction between *ecofeminism* and *ecological feminism,* identifying ecofeminist philosophy with ecological feminism. In this way Cuomo attempts to distance ecological feminist philosophy from spiritual approaches to ecofeminism ("which zoom in on women") and from ecofeminist approaches that appeal to problematic notions of the female and femininity, construe women's corporeality as naturally or essentially linked to nature, or which characterize women as radically separate from culture.[15] (Note that, unlike Cuomo, I have chosen throughout this book to use the expressions ecofeminist philosophy and ecological feminist philosophy interchangeably.)

Similarly, ecofeminist philosopher Val Plumwood criticizes ecofeminists who assert, on biologically determinist grounds, that women are naturally closer to nature and are "earth mothers":

This type of ecofeminism should be clearly distinguished from other types, and is open to serious objection. . . . Such a position is difficult to sustain in any thorough way, because it depends upon not really examining the polarities or the reasons why a hierarchical and sexist division of labour is established to begin with.[16]

So, it is an important project of ecofeminist philosophy to determine which ecofeminist positions presuppose biological determinism, conceptual essentialism, or universalism, and which do not.

Having clarified what the logic of domination asserts, it is important to clarify what the logic of domination does *not* assert. It does not assert that there are no relevant differences between groups (whether between or among groups of humans or nonhumans) that may make some groups superior or inferior in some relevant respect. Race-car drivers *as* race-car drivers may be superior to ordinary drivers with regard to their ability to drive cars, but nothing follows morally from that fact about who deserves what sort of treatment. Rational humans *as* rational beings may be superior, even morally superior, to any nonrational animals without that by itself implying anything about what humans are morally permitted to do with regard to nonhuman animals. To get such implications, one needs the logic of domination.

A rejection of the logic of domination also does not specify what Downs may be justified in doing to end their domination by Ups (e.g., whether Downs are justified in using violence to end their oppression by Ups). Additional premises are need to justify exercises of power by Downs against Ups.[17]

To summarize what has been said so far, the logic of domination is explanatorily basic and ought to be rejected for three reasons: First, a rejection of the logic of domination asserts that superiority, even moral superiority, does not by itself justify subordination; second, difference by itself does not justify domination; and third, historically, at least in Western societies, the oppressive conceptual frameworks that have justified the dominations of women and nonhuman nature have been patriarchal. A rejection of the logic of domination thereby challenges the historically favored view in Western societies (at least) that an identification of a human group with the realm of the physical and nonhuman nature justifies dominating both that human group and nonhuman nature. It also rules out a moral justification of relationships of domination and subordination on grounds of the alleged superiority of the Ups over the Downs.

But there is an additional, fourth reason the "logic of domination" is explanatorily basic, one that turns on an important distinction between "oppression" and "domination." This reason is that premise 4, the logic of domination, links the *dominations* of women, other human Others, and nature, even if it also links the *oppression* of women, other human Others, and (some) nonhuman animals. That is, the logic of domination is about "domination"; its role in linking oppressions is unspecified. What does this mean, and why is this distinction between domination and oppression important?

Oppression consists in institutional structures, strategies, and processes whereby some groups (Downs) are limited, inhibited, coerced, or prevented from mobilizing resources for self-determined goals by limiting their choices and options. Oppressive institutions use various tools of subjugation (e.g., violence, threats, exploitation, colonization, exclusion) to reinforce the power and privilege of Ups in oppressive systems and to enforce the subordination or domination of Downs.[18] Domination is one such tool of subjugation: it reinforces the power and privileges of Ups over Downs in Up-Down relationships of domination and subordination. All oppression involves domination.

By contrast, not all domination involves oppression. This is basically because oppression limits choices and options. So it is only beings who can meaningfully be spoken of as "having options" who also can meaningfully be said to be oppressed. Since I assume that from a Western philosophical perspective trees, rivers, mountains, communities of flora and fauna, species, and ecosystems are not the sort of things that make choices or have options, I assume that they cannot be oppressed. But they can be dominated.

This terminological distinction between oppression and domination is important in other ways to the particular ecofeminist philosophy I defend in this book. I have defined an oppressive conceptual framework as a set of basic beliefs, values, attitudes, and assumptions that explains, justifies, and maintains relationships of domination and subordination. These conceptual frameworks are oppressive, not dominating conceptual frameworks; they maintain relationships of domination and subordination, not relationships of oppression.[19] The unjustified domination of nonhuman animals and nature is described in terms of relationships of domination and subordination, not in terms of relationships of oppression. I have argued that oppressive conceptual frameworks turn on a logic of domination, not a logic of oppression.

The choice of these terms was deliberate.[20] Persons have conceptual frameworks. In Western contexts, nonhuman natural entities such as rocks, plants, and rivers typically are not considered persons. Conceptual frameworks can and do function in ways that reflect, maintain, and reinforce both the *oppression* and *domination* of others. One can meaningfully speak of the historical, economic, social, legal, political, and psychological causes of oppression, domination, exploitation, and violence. And one can meaningfully speak of the conceptual links between "isms of domination," whether or not those "isms" are also "isms of oppression." But because oppression is linked to oppressive (not simply dominating) conceptual frameworks, it is entities who have conceptual frameworks who can be oppressors and oppressed. In at least Western contexts, this typically is a smaller group than the potential group of entities who/that can be dominated.

This brings us to the fourth reason the logic of domination is explanatorily basic to ecofeminist philosophy. The logic of domination links the *dominations* of women, other human Others, and nature, even if, in addition, it links the *oppression* of women, other human Others, and (some) nonhuman animals. Since, in Western cultural contexts, it is presumed that rocks and rivers do not have the capacity to make choices or entertain options, in these contexts it is a logic of domination, not a logic of oppression, that is key.

Ecofeminist philosophy is more concerned with conceptual analysis than ecofeminist social scientists, say, might be. As a person who thinks philosophically about ecofeminism, I focus my discussion on concepts and arguments, placing them at the center of my contributions to ecofeminist scholarship. But this is not to privilege them over other methods of analysis or styles of presentation (e.g., experiential learning, ethnographic research, data gathering, and processing). It is just what makes what I write distinctively philosophical.

Furthermore, my focus on conceptual frameworks assumes that conceptual frameworks are learned and can be changed; they are not genetically programmed. One of the strengths of experiential learning, for example, is that it often puts a person in a position to act in ways that create "cognitive dissonance." Such cognitive dissonance often helps to motivate one to reexamine one's basic beliefs, values, attitudes, and assumptions—one's conceptual framework. But since actually changing one's conceptual framework often involves an alteration of deeply cherished, clung-to beliefs, it may be "simple but not easy" to do. Changing or abandoning a familiar, and, in that sense, comfortable belief system, as well as dismantling the institutions and behaviors they justify, may involve intense soul-searching. But, according to the version of ecofeminist philosophy I defend, that is both possible and desirable if "isms of domination" are to be eliminated.

RECONCEIVING FEMINISM

My analysis of the five common features of oppressive conceptual frameworks provides a *conceptual* basis for reconceiving feminism, feminist philosophy, and environmental ethics. Again, by formalizing each argument, one can see just why these reconceptualizations must occur.

Consider first an ecofeminist philosophical argument for reconceiving feminism, argument C:

(C)   (1) Feminism is, minimally, a movement to end sexism.
But   (2) Sexism is conceptually linked with naturism.
Thus,   (3) Feminism is (also) a movement to end naturism.

Argument C turns on the claim that sexism is conceptually linked with naturism, premise 2. The primary way to understand the conceptual nature of this link is through the notion of an oppressive conceptual framework, mediated by a logic of domination. So understood, argument C presumes that in their opposition to sexism and patriarchy, all feminists must oppose the logic of domination (required by patriarchal arguments for sexism). Furthermore, since the arguments for the domination of nonhuman nature presuppose the same logic of domination, all feminists must oppose the arguments for the domination of nonhuman nature. On this understanding, acceptance of argument C implies that traditional feminism should be reconceived to include a concern with nonhuman nature. Stated differently, naturism must be included among the systems of domination that feminism opposes.

Should argument C be accepted? One might object to (C) on the grounds that feminists must oppose the logic of domination *only* when it applies to humans. Invoking the distinction between domination and oppression, one might argue as follows: All cases of oppression are unjustified, but not all cases of domination are unjustified. Only those cases of domination that involve oppression are unjustified. Since the domination of nonhuman nature is not a case of oppression, it is justified. Since the domination of humans by gender, race/ethnicity, socioeconomic status, affectional orientation, religion, geographic location, and nationality are cases of oppression, they are not justified. Consequently, the logic of domination *is* justified in the case of nonhuman nature. This establishes that premise 2 is false: sexism is not conceptually linked to naturism. Feminists (and others) ought to reject argument C.

This is a very powerful objection. How might an ecofeminist philosopher like myself respond? My basic response to this objection is that it really is an objection to the plausibility of environmental ethics per se—not to an ecofeminist version of environmental ethics. This is because the organizing principle of environmental ethics (as I show in chapter 4) is that nonhuman nature deserves human moral consideration. That is what makes an ethic an "environmental" ethic. Although environmental ethicists disagree among themselves about why nonhuman nature deserves human moral consideration, what makes them "environmental ethicists" is that they assert that it does. It is an organizing precept and starting point of environmental ethics that there are contexts, at least, in which the human domination of nonhuman nature (and/or nonhuman animals) is unjustified. Insofar as the objection disallows application of the concept of unjustified domination to nonhuman nature, it does so as a blanket claim against the plausibility of environmental ethics, not as a specific claim about an ecofeminist environmental ethic.

Suppose, however, one objects to argument C on slightly different grounds. One might object to the claim that the link between sexism and naturism is "conceptual." The objection might go like this: What these connections between sexism and naturism literally show is that, at least in Western culture, the concept of "nature" has female-gender connotations and the concept of "women" has natural or "nature" connotations. But why should anyone take these connections seriously? After all, it is not as if the subordination of women literally *is* the subordination of nature (or the rape of women literally *is* the rape of nature).[21]

My response to this second objection is that the deep historical enmeshment of the concepts of women and nature, in at least the Western intellectual and cultural tradition, is not something that can be dismissed easily or taken lightly. Both concepts are deeply grounded in social, historical, and material realities. Maybe we *ought* not negatively associate women with nature and nature with women; but if we do not take seriously the negative associations of women with nature, and nature with women, we will not understand how these associations continue to permeate, reinforce, and "justify" behaviors, policies, theories, institutions, and systems of domination. This book is largely about just how those associations continue to fuel unjustified domination.

What does it mean, then, to claim (as I do) that the concepts of women and nature are socially constructed and intersecting? It means that the meanings of these concepts include and reflect such factors as race/ethnicity, class, age, affectional orientation, ability, geographic location, and religion. Consider the concept of women. There is no woman *simpliciter.* To be a woman is to be a woman of a certain race/ethnic, class, age, affectional orientation, ability, religion (or lack thereof), geographic location, and nationality. There is no pure gender; gender always occurs in conjunction with race, class, age, affectional orientation, ability, religion, geographic location, and nationality.

Similarly, the concept of nature is socially, historically, and materially constructed. It is not a fixed, static, self-evident, given, or absolute (nonnegotiable, noncontestable) concept. What is meant by "nature," and even what counts as a "natural object," is constructed from and reflects such factors as the race/ethnicity, class, age, affectional orientation, geographic location, and religion of humans who name, describe, judge, understand, and interact with "nature." The meanings of "nature" are constructed out of human values, beliefs, attitudes and assumptions—different and differing human conceptual frameworks.

Obviously, the claim that "women" and "nature" are social constructions does not deny that there are actual humans and actual nonhuman natural entities. One can hug a human, climb a tree, swim a river, cultivate a plant, destroy an ecosystem, or enjoy being in nature. These entities (e.g., humans, trees, nature) are "physical realities." But what is meant by "human," "tree," or "nature," and what constitutes the identities of "humans" and "nature" are "social realities"—social constructions—as well.

Consider the concept of "country" for Australian aboriginal peoples. What is "country" for them is not what Europeans and Euro-Americans mean by "country," "land," "landscape," "property," or "wilderness." In the words of anthropologist Deborah Bird Rose, the closest European and American-derived expression for "country" (as used by Australian aboriginal peoples) is "nourishing terrain"—a "place that gives and receives life."[22] For Australian aboriginal peoples, country is sacred, alive, conscious, the law, place, managed, owned, land. Country knows, hears, smells, takes notice, takes care, is quiet, dangerous, lonely, sorry or happy or sad, is healthy, sick, or not so good. Country is criss-crossed with "songlines"[23] and "the tracks of the Dreamings: walking, slithering, crawling, flying, chasing, hunting, weeping, dying, giving birth."[24] The relationships between people and their country is a "a kinship relationship, and like relations among kin, there are obligations of nurturence. People and country take care of each other."[25]

Such linguistic differences about what something is called are philosophically important. As we saw in chapter 2, sexist-naturist language constructs concepts of women and nature in historically and culturally specific ways. Sexist-naturist language in Western contexts illustrates the concept of nature is gendered, just as the concept of women is animalized and naturalized, in ways that reinforce and perpetuate the unjustified domination of both. That is something a philosopher needs to take seriously.

Similarly, in Western and colonial cultures, historically the concept of race is animalized and naturalized. In the United States, for instance, the historical justification for dominating African American men was bolstered by language and images of African American men as children, animals, and nature. During slavery African Americans were described as "mere brutes," "animals," "dogs," "coons," "apes," "gorillas." The U.S. Supreme Court decision in *Dred Scott v. Sandford* announced in 1856 that African American men were denied the rights of citizenship "as a subordinate and inferior class of beings, who had been subjugated by the dominant race."[26] As Christopher Stone claims, two years later, in *Bailey v. Poindexter's Ex'r*, the legal status of slaves as things, mere property, or "chattel" was made law:

> [The] fundamental idea [of chattel slavery] is that, in the eye of the law, so far certainly as civil rights and relations are concerned, the slave is not a person, but a thing. The investiture of a chattel with civil rights or legal capacity is indeed a legal solecism and absurdity. The attribution of legal personality to a chattel slave,—legal conscience, legal intellect, legal freedom, or liberty and power of free choice and action, and corresponding legal obligations growing out of such qualities, faculties and action—implies a palpable contradiction in terms.[27]

As "chattel," African American men were not fully persons and could not meaningfully be said to have legal rights.

The importance of the language and imagery describing African American men as a subordinate group is clearly illustrated in the antebellum and postbellum years in the United States. Before the Civil War, the justification of slavery went hand-in-hand with the image of slaves as "imbeciles," "child-like," "childish," "shiftless," "idle" creatures who wiled away the hours in song and daydream. Like a benevolent parent-child relationship, the master-slave relationship was one of the "good master" looking after "child-like" humans who could not care for themselves. In *The Souls of Black Folk,* W. E. B. Du Bois describes this popular and prevalent view of African Americans as inferior, child-like beings: "The older South [held] the sincere and passionate belief that somewhere between men and cattle, God created a *tertium quid*, and called it a Negro—a clownish, simple creature, at times even lovable within its limitations, but straitly foreordained to walk within the Veil."[28] Such views of African Americans functioned ideologically to justify slavery.

However, after the Civil War, when slaves were allegedly "free men," the image of black man-as-child, especially of the black man-as-simple-lovable-child, could no longer function ideologically to justify the domination of African American men. Instead, their continued domination required language and images of African American men as dangerous animals ("coons," "brutes") and "rapists" whose lust and sexual instincts threatened the safety and sanctity of "pure" white women. The continued domination of African American men in the postbellum United States required the use of language, image, and myths of the black rapist, more animal and natural than human and cultured—i.e., racist-naturist language.

Similar racist-naturist language operates with other subdominant ethnic groups in the United States as well. For example, Native American men were routinely described by whites as "uncivilized," "primitive," "savages," "uncultivated," "heathens," whose elimination or conversion to Christianity was a God-given right of white settlers. And Chinese did not have the right to testify against white men in criminal matters because they were "a race of people whom nature has marked as inferior, and who are incapable of progress or intellectual development beyond a certain point . . . between whom and ourselves nature has placed an impassable difference."[29]

Sexist-racist-naturist language is a language of domination. Languages of domination are crucial to effective implementations of the logic of domination by colonizers. As Deborah Bird Rose argues, standard European and Anglo-American land-use attitudes and descriptions of wilderness involve "the peculiar notion that if one cannot see traces of one's own culture in the land, then the land must be 'natural' or empty of culture."[30] So it is that "terra nullius" (land that was not owned) was the official doctrine of (white) Australia until overturned by the High Court's Mabo Decision in 1995. That decision marks the first time Australian aboriginal and Islander people's occupation and ownership of "country" was formally and publically acknowledged.[31] This is an astonishing example of a colonizer worldview, especially since aboriginal Australians have a continuous, uninterrupted history dating back between 40,000 and 60,000 years!

The view that land with no ownership or property is "uninhabited" wilderness is familiar in the United States as well. Wilderness is often conceived as "wild," "idle," worthless "frontier" until "tamed" and "cultivated" through the white settler's agriculture. Land that just lies there, "barren," "useless," "uncultivated" (for example, "untouched" "virgin prairie"), has no value until "domesticated" by the white man's plow. Daniel Spencer describes the attitudes toward weeds, defined as "problem plants," within the framework of agriculture:

A culture and science of weed control developed with western agriculture which has three primary objectives of combating weeds: prevention, eradication, and control. . . . In examining the attitudes of white settlers toward nonwhite inhabitants of the land, it becomes clear that the same logic and strategies that has shaped response to weeds as a perceived threat to civilization is operative in relations to nonwhite. Just as anthropomorphized language used to describe weeds as aggressive, pioneering and colonizing, so nonwhites were naturalized and viewed as human weeds that must be removed, domesticated, or improved.[32]

Spencer argues that by examining the "logic of agriculture as colonization" among white settler communities (the community he discusses is Iowa), one can see "the ways race and place were constructed."[33] White racism is not just a social construct around skin color and ethnicity; it is also an ecological construct, one which reflects and reinforces ecological as well as social factors.

One place one might expect gender-neutral language is in Western philosophy, with its historical focus on reason, truth, objectivity, and impartiality. Yet this is not the case. As Vance Kope-Kasten shows, descriptions of good reasoning, good reasoners, and good arguments abound with sexist domination metaphors: Good reasoners knock down arguments. They tear, rip, chew, and cut them up. They attack them, try to beat, destroy, or annihilate them, preferably by "nailing them to the wall." Good reasoners (typically, men) are sharp, incisive, cutting, relentless, intimidating, brutal. Those not good at reasoning (typically, women) are wimpy, touchy, quarrelsome, irritable, nagging. Good arguments have a thrust to them: they are compelling, binding, air-tight, steel-trap, knock-down, dynamite, smashing, and devastating bits of reasoning that lay things out and pin them down, overcoming any resistance. Bad arguments are described in metaphors of the dominated and powerless: they "fall flat on their face," are limp, lame, soft, fuzzy, silly, and "full of holes."[34] Such language suggests that philosophy is modeled not on peacemaking and nonviolent conflict resolution but on war and adversarial combat: "winners" are male-identified combatants who strike, destroy, kill, humiliate, maim, or otherwise defeat their opponents.[35]

To summarize: Linguistic differences in the construction of concepts for Ups and Downs (e.g., men and women, whites and people of color), or Up and Down traits (e.g., reason and emotion) are philosophically important. As some philosophers (e.g., Wittgenstein) have argued, the language one uses mirrors and reflects one's concept of oneself and one's world—one's conceptual framework. Language use is part of the social construction of concepts. When that language is sexist or racist or naturist, it mirrors and reflects conceptions of women, or people of color, or nonhuman nature as inferior to, having less status, value, or prestige than, that which is identified as male, masculine, white, or "human" (i.e., male). In this respect, the language one uses to construct concepts not only links concepts linguistically, it also can link concepts conceptually. This is why linguistic connections have conceptual significance. As a consequence, the objection to argument C that linguistic connections between sexism and naturism should not be taken seriously fails.

By clarifying well-entrenched, historically favored, and socially constructed linguistic connections between sexism—traditionally the special turf of feminist theory and practice—and naturism, as argument C does, one provides an important way of understanding why, according to ecofeminist philosophy, feminist projects to eliminate sexism should be expanded and reconceived to include the elimination of naturism as well. It is how these linguistic connections function conceptually that provides the basis of my reply to those who would object that the connections between sexism and naturism, at least in Western culture, are not conceptual.

But my argument about conceptual connections between sexism and naturism, argument C, does not stop here. The same sort of reasoning connects sexism with *all* systems of unjustified domination (e.g., racism, classism, heterosexism, ableism, ageism, anti-Semitism, colonialism). At the level of material reality, the reason for this is straightforward: "Women" are white, women of color, poor, lesbian, young, physically and mentally challenged, Jewish, Indian, African, and colonized peoples. If feminism is a movement to liberate all women, it must liberate women from the multiple oppressions that constitute their gendered identities—oppressions based on race/ethnicity, class, affectional orientation, age, ability, geographic location, anti-Semitism, and colonialism. At the level of theory, the reason for this is also straightforward: The conceptual framework used to justify the domination of humans by gender has five basic features: Up-Down thinking, oppositional value dualisms, conceptions of power and privilege that systematically advantage Ups over Downs, and a logic of domination. This is the same basic conceptual framework that is used to justify the domination of humans by race/ethnicity, class, age, affectional orientation, ability, religion, marital status, geographic location, or nationality. And it is the same basic conceptual framework used to justify the domination of nonhuman nature (and/or animals) by humans. Thus, there are good theoretical reasons for requiring that the projects of feminism be expanded and reconceived to include the elimination of all systems of domination.

One might object that if feminism is reconceived to be a movement against all systems of domination, why call it feminist? Why not call it anti-dominationism, or equalism, or something more obviously universal in scope and not feminist, such as humanism? My brief two-part answer is this: First, the starting point of feminism is "women," where "women" is understood as a strategic, organizing concept (not as an essentializing concept about "all women"). What makes a feminist starting point "feminist" rather than, say, environmental, is that it starts with "women," not "nature." Even though it immediately draws in interlocking systems of domination (e.g., racism, classism, heterosexism, ageism, ableism, ethnocentrism, anti-Semitism, colonialism), its starting point is women. By calling the position feminist, one identifies gender as the launching point for the analysis that follows. Second, as I argue at the end of chapter 4, the term feminist continues to have a critical bite in contemporary contexts. To assert that one is a feminist, that one's perspective is feminist, or that one's practices are feminist is to put issues of gender immediately, clearly, irrevocably, perhaps uncomfortably and annoyingly, on the table, where they belong (not under the table or out of the room). Such critical bite is not accomplished in present contexts by terms like anti-dominationism or equalism or (if nonhuman nature were excluded from consideration) humanism.

RECONCEIVING FEMINIST PHILOSOPHY
AND ENVIRONMENTAL ETHICS

The conception of ecofeminist philosophy that I defend in this book involves a rethinking of the projects of both feminist philosophy and environmental ethics.

The argument for reconceiving feminist philosophy is this:

(D)   (1) Minimally, feminist philosophy is a commitment to the elimination of sexism and male-gender bias in philosophy and to put in its place philosophical positions and practices that are not sexist and male-gender biased.

But,   (2) Male-gender bias in philosophy is conceptually linked with naturism and naturist bias.

Thus,   (3) Feminist philosophy must (also) involve a commitment to the elimination of naturism and naturist bias in philosophy and to put in its place philosophical positions and practices that are not naturist and naturist-biased.

Feminist (including ecofeminist) philosophers disagree about what counts as sexism and male-bias, what the elimination of sexism and male-bias in philosophy requires, and what the appropriate feminist replacements for male-biased positions and practices in philosophy should be.[36] In addition, ecofeminist philosophers disagree about what counts as naturism and nature-bias, what the elimination of naturism and nature-bias in philosophy requires, and what the appropriate feminist replacements for the naturist positions and practices in philosophy should be. Nonetheless, according to argument D, feminist philosophy must extend its sex/gender analysis to detect, critique, and eliminate naturism and naturist-bias in the language, concepts, positions, and practices of philosophy, *whenever* and *wherever* such biases occur. The justification for this reconceptualization is that both sexism (and male-gender bias) and naturism (and naturist bias) are conceptually linked through an oppressive and patriarchal conceptual framework mediated by a logic of domination.

A similar ecofeminist philosophical argument concerns "environmental ethics":

(E)   (1) Minimally, environmental ethics is a twofold commitment to the moral considerability of nonhuman nature and to the elimination of naturism in ethical theory and practice.

But,   (2) Naturism is conceptually linked with sexism.

Thus,   (3) Environmental ethics must (also) involve a commitment to the elimination of sexism in environmental theory and practice.

Since a significant portion of this book is devoted to topics in environmental ethics, a full defense of argument E, particularly premise 2, is laced throughout the book. But what has been said so far is adequate to show the plausibility of E: Like arguments C and D, the ecofeminist justification for reconceiving environmental ethics is that naturism (which all environmental ethicists oppose) is conceptually linked with sexism through an oppressive and patriarchal conceptual framework mediated by a logic of domination.

CONCEPT OF PATRIARCHY

Ecofeminist philosophy is often focused on claims about patriarchy. As I use the term, "patriarchy" is the systematic domination of women by men through *institutions* (including policies, practices, offices, positions, roles), *behaviors,* and *ways of thinking* (conceptual frameworks), which assign higher value, privilege, and power to men (or to what historically is male-gender identified) than to that given to women (or to what historically is female-gender identified). I have already described five features of patriarchal conceptual frameworks.

Anthropologist Ernestine Friedl claims that patriarchy (or, male dominance) is "a situation in which men have highly preferential access, although not always exclusive rights, to those activities to which the society accords the greatest value, and the exercise of which permits a measure of control over others."[37] Anthropologist Peggy Sanday agrees, arguing further that male dominance consists in two general types of behaviors:

> First, there is the exclusion of women from political and economic decision making. Second, there is male aggression against women, which is measured here by the following five traits: the expectations that males should be tough, brave, and aggressive; the presence of men's houses or specific places where only men congregate; frequent quarreling, fighting, or wife beating; the institutionalisation or regular occurrence of rape; and raiding other groups for wives. The presense of all five in a society indicates a high degree of male aggression; the absense of all five indicates that male aggression is weakly developed.[38]

What characterizes the position of women under patriarchy is not that women have no power, valued status, prestige, or privilege; they do. Women in India who have responsibilities for water collection and distribution have some power and privilege, and lack other power and privilege. What characterizes women's position is the varying degrees and ways women, as a group, are excluded from political and economic institutions of power and privilege. While the specific forms that male dominance takes will vary, depending largely on the different material realities of women located in historically specific contexts, what women under patriarchy have in common, as a group, is less institutional power and privilege than men.

This focus on "institutional power and privilege" is relevant to a proper understanding of my ecofeminist philosophical critique of patriarchy and "isms of domination." The expression "white skin power and privilege" emphasizes that the benefits white people receive in a white racist society are inherited at birth by virtue of their having white skin or being white. Analogously, the expression "male power and privilege" emphasizes that the benefits males receive in a patriarchal society are inherited at birth by virtue of their being male. Because these benefits are received at birth, the sort of power and privilege that whites or males receive in such societies is not based on individual merit, ability, effort, or need; hence, they are not something for which individuals deserve praise or blame.

Rather, these benefits are institutionally created, maintained, and sanctioned; they reflect the power and privilege of Ups in unjustified Up-Down systems. And such Up-Down systems create, maintain, or perpetuate unjustified "isms of domination" such as sexism, racism, classism, heterosexism, ethnocentrism, and colonialism.

This focus on institutional (rather than individual or personal) power and privilege is important here for three reasons. First, it provides a way of understanding why ecofeminist philosophy is neither inherently anti-male nor inherently pro-female. Ecofeminist philosophy is about institutional structures of power and privilege, not about praise or blame for what individuals (e.g., individual men, women, white people, upper-class people) do or do not do. It does not assume that all and only males are "the problem," or that all and only females are "the solution." The focus of ecofeminist philosophy is unjustified Up-Down systems of power and privilege, particularly patriarchal Up-Down systems, as well as on the actual social contexts in which Ups are beneficiaries of such unjustified Up-Down systems.

Second, although Ups cannot help receiving whatever institutional power and privilege benefits they receive as Ups in unjustified Up-Down social systems, nonetheless Ups are accountable for perpetuating unjustified Up-Down systems through their behaviors (including language) and thought-worlds. This is true even if individual Ups do not want the power and privilege they receive as Ups. That is why ecofeminist philosophy is about both theory and practice,[39] about not only understanding and analyzing but also about both Ups and Downs taking personal and political action against Up-Down systems of domination.

Third, since systems of domination are interrelated, the institutional power and privileges Ups receive will differ depending on the racial/ethnic, class, sexual orientation, age, ability, geographic location, religion, and nationality of those Ups. Different groups of Ups have different degrees of power and privilege in different cultural contexts. Ecofeminist philosophy recognizes these important differences among Ups and Downs in Up-Down systems, while also recognizing commonalities among Ups and Downs where those commonalities exist.

THEORIZING AS QUILTING

As I conceive ecofeminist philosophy, it rejects conceptions of theory in terms of necessary and sufficient conditions. In philosophical usage, "necessary and sufficient" conditions are "if and only if" conditions. To say something, y, is a necessary condition for something else, x, is to say that one cannot have (get, obtain, accomplish) x without y. For example, in gas-run vehicles, having gas in the tank, y, is a necessary condition of the car's running, x. To say that something, x, is a sufficient condition for something else, y, is to say that if x obtains (happens, occurs), y obtains (happens, occurs). To continue with the car example, having gas in the tank is not a sufficient condition for a gas-run car to operate; other conditions must also be met (e.g., a key is turned to the start position in the ignition, the transmission works).

So, a conception of theory as providing a set of necessary and sufficient ("if and only if") conditions for whatever is being theorized about, assumes that such conditions can or ought to be specified in order for a particular account to count as a "theory." This is the conception of theory in traditional Western philosophy and ethics.

For example, in Western philosophical ethics, the position known as ethical egoism asserts that an act is right if and only if it is in the agent's self-interest. Utilitarianism asserts that an act is right if and only if it maximizes "utility" (for society). Kantian ethics asserts that an act is right if and only if the act is done in accordance with a principle ("a maxim") which any rational agent could will to be a universal law. Divine command theory asserts that an act is right if and only if it is commanded by God.

The version of ecofeminist philosophy I defend rejects this notion of theory as a set of necessary and sufficient conditions. This means that I assume that "ethical theory," for example, is not about specifying a set of necessary and sufficient conditions that all and only right acts share in common. Nonetheless, I consider myself and other ecofeminist philosophers theorists. I assume that ecofeminist philosophy is engaged in theorizing, and that the theorizing it engages in is "feminist." How can that be?

The conception of theory that I propose is this: There are some necessary conditions of feminist theory. If there were not, there would be no grounds for calling the theory "a theory," for calling a feminist theory "feminist," or for calling an ecofeminist theory "ecofeminist." But one cannot specify, ahead of time, so to speak, what the "sufficient conditions" of right acts or morally acceptable human conduct is. For that one needs to know things about the historical, material, and social contexts. That is why, on my view of theory, theorizing is not about identifying a set of essential properties—necessary and sufficient conditions.

The metaphor I use for the conception of theory I endorse is that of a quilt: Theories are like quilts. The "necessary conditions" of a theory (say, ecofeminist philosophical theory) are like the borders of a quilt: They delimit the boundary conditions of the theory without dictating beforehand what the interior (the design, the actual patterns) of the quilt does or must look like. The actual design of the quilt will emerge from the diversity of perspectives of quilters who contribute, over time, to the making of the quilt. Theory is not something static, preordained, or carved in stone; it is always *theory-in-process.*

The theorizing-as-quilting metaphor initially came to me as I reflected on the Names Project Quilt. This quilt is a patchwork of 10,500 panels of individual quilt-patches that record and commemorate human lives lost to AIDS—lives that collectively represent different ages, ethnicities, affectional orientations, race and gender identities, and class backgrounds. While each patch is unique, what the patches have in common is what constitutes the necessary condition for inclusion on the Names Project Quilt—each patch commemorates a life lost to AIDS. This necessary condition of having a patch qualify for the Names Project Quilt was clearly identified before the quilt was begun. What was not and could not be known at that time was what the interior design of the completed quilt would look like.

It seems to me that the same is true of ecofeminist philosophical theory and theorizing. Given the characterization of ecofeminist philosophy provided in this chapter, nothing that is knowingly, intentionally, or consciously naturist, sexist, racist, or classist—which reinforces or maintains "isms of domination"—belongs on the quilt. Nor does anything that is not, in some way, about nonhuman nature or human-nature relationships. An ecofeminist philosophical quilt will be made up of different "patches," constructed by quilters in particular social, historical, and material contexts, which express some aspect of that quilter's perspective on women–other human Others–nature interconnections. One cannot know, beforehand, what the actual interior of the quilt will look like.

Since theory is always in-process in a self-critical and self-reflective way, a patch that becomes part of the quilt in one historical time period or setting may be discerned at some later date to fail to satisfy the requisite border condition that no "ism of domination" become part of the quilt (e.g., by being, in fact, naturist, sexist, racist, or classist). If so, then, like a tattered patch on an antique quilt, it is repaired, replaced, or removed. Such adjustments to the quilt do not ruin the quilt or decrease its value, since it is part of the nature of quilting to welcome alterations to the quilt as time or circumstance or wear-and-tear dictate. Rather, such adjustments preserve the value of the quilt as something that is useful over time and that can be altered by future quilters to reflect their insights and perspectives in ways that build upon the work of previous quilters—both the strengths and weaknesses of that work.

For me, there are three features of quilts and quilting that make it an especially apt metaphor for theory and theorizing. First, quilts are highly contextual; they grow out of and reflect specific historical, social, economic, and political influences. A Hmong quilt may reflect important cultural influences not captured on a Texan or Iowan farm woman's quilt in the United States. The Pentagon Peace Quilt, Judy Chicago's "The Birth Project," Jesse Jackson's Rainbow Coalition Quilt, North American slave quilts, and the millions of quilts that serve as a repository of "women's history" are also highly contextual. What makes them the quilts they are is that they satisfy some necessary (border) conditions, typically articulated in terms of some shared experience, beliefs, vision, or purposes known to the quilters. The point of these quilts is not to have one image or one story, based on one and only one view of reality; it is to have a *variety of images or stories.* There images/stories emerge out of the life experiences and visions of people located in different historical circumstances. So, too, with ecofeminist philosophical theory and theorizing as I understand each.

Second, the quilt metaphor helps one visualize the role of generalizations in theory. Like any theory, ecofeminist theory is based on some generalizations. For example, it is a generalization to say that U.S. women, on the average, earn less than men for comparable work. This generalization about commonalities among U.S. women is true, even though it is also true that there are striking differences between what white Anglo-European women, African American women, and American Indian women earn. The quilt metaphor helps illustrate the role these generalizations play in theory in a way traditional theory (as a set of necessary and sufficient conditions) does not: The border conditions of the quilt, which express generalizations based on commonalities, provide the necessary conditions for a patch to become part of the quilt (theory). But they do not specify the sufficient conditions (what the interior looks like); that is provided by the diversity of quilt patches made by different quilters (theorists and practitioners) over time.

Third, quilting is historically a women-identified activity. Dismissed in the nineteenth century as a "minor art" (largely because quilt-making was practiced by women), quilting has reemerged in the latter part of the twentieth century as an important art form that has several functions. Quilts are a form of discourse: they tell stories, record people's lives, provide portraits of the quilters who make them, and often give shape and form to the experiences of those whose stories are not told in literal discourse. Quilts are practical; they are "comforters" that provide warmth, are an integral part of domestic production, and often provide an important source of income for the women who quilt them. Quilts are historical records; they capture diverse or distinct cultural traditions and thereby serve collectively to help preserve the past and create the future. Quilts are aesthetic; they can be very exciting visually, with precise, varied, and vibrant designs, bold color combinations, and exuberant displays of individual and community identities. Quilts are political statements; they can tell the story of the history of a people's migration (e.g., Hmong quilts), raise awareness about politically sensitive issues (e.g., the Names Project Quilt), or promote a particular vision or point of view (e.g., the Pentagon Peace Quilt). Ecofeminist philosophy grows out of and reflects just such forms of discourse.

CONCLUSION

In this chapter I have characterized the version of ecofeminist philosophy I defend throughout the book, emphasizing the importance of understanding oppressive conceptual frameworks. I have argued that ecofeminist philosophy is opposed not only to sexism and naturism, but also to racism, classism, ageism, anti-Semitism, heterosexism, and any other social systems of domination ("isms of domination"). As a feminism, ecofeminist philosophy is a commitment to critique male bias wherever it occurs and to develop a theory and practice that is not male-biased. As an environmentalism, it is a commitment to critique environmental policies and decision-making structures that continue the dominations of women, other human

Others, and nature, and to develop a theory and practice which do not perpetuate interlocking "isms of domination." And, as a distinctively feminist environmentalism and environmental feminism, ecofeminist philosophy moves beyond current feminisms and environmentalisms by incorporating woman–other human Others–nature interconnections in its analysis. According to the version of ecofeminist philosophy offered in this book, any feminism, feminist philosophy, environmentalism, or environmental philosophy that fails to take seriously women–other human Others–nature interconnections is simply inadequate.

NOTES

1. Julie Cook argues that the "colonizing strategy" of philosophical ecofeminism occurs because philosophical ecofeminism plays a *prescriptive*, rather than merely *descriptive*, role in defining what ecofeminism ought to be ("The Philosophical Colonization of Ecofeminism," *Environmental Ethics* 20, no. 3 [Fall 1998], 229). Cook claims that philosophical ecofeminism does this, for example, by not offering "some explanation of the authority that lies behind these prescriptive claims" (229–30). I think Cook misunderstands both what makes ecofeminist philosophy philosophy and what ecofeminist philosophers offer as the "authority" behind the positions they defend. Philosophy is both descriptive and prescriptive. It is not simply, or even primarily, interested in reporting "facts," or describing who says what. It is interested in providing analyses and arguments designed to establish claims and positions that its authors or proponents find helpful, plausible, correct, or "true"—clearly a prescriptive role. The "authority" of a philosophical position that is advanced or advocated is based on the plausibility of the arguments presented by a historically located presenter.

2. "Local" perspectives may or may not be those of indigenous peoples in a community. Inclusion of local perspectives is intended to ensure that grassroots and citizen input be considered in the analysis of and solutions to environmental and gender issues.

3. Elizabeth Dodson Gray, *Green Paradise Lost* (Wellesley, Mass.: Roundtable Press, 1981), 20.

4. Bruce Nordstrom-Loeb made these comments on an earlier draft of this manuscript.

5. Lori Gruen, "On the Oppression of Women and Animals," *Environmental Ethics* 18, no. 4 (Winter 1996), 442.

6. Murray Bookchin, "Social Ecology versus 'Deep Ecology,'" in *Green Perspectives: Newsletter of the Green Program Project* (Summer 1987), 9.

7. See Val Plumwood, *Feminism and the Mastery of Nature* (New York: Routledge, 1993).

8. See Gray, *Green Paradise Lost*; Susan Griffin, *Woman and Nature: The Roaring Inside Her* (New York: Harper and Row, 1978); Carolyn Merchant, *The Death of Nature: Women, Ecology, and the Scientific Revolution* (San Francisco: Harper and Row, 1980); Rosemary Radford Ruether, *Women Healing Earth: Third World Women on Ecology, Feminism, and Religion* (Maryknoll, N.Y.: Orbis, 1996); Val Plumwood, "Ecofeminism: An Overview and Discussion of Positions and Arguments," *Australasian Journal of Philosophy* 64, Supplement on Women and Philosophy (June 1986), 120–39.

9. Sherry B. Ortner, "Is Female to Male as Nature Is to Culture?" in *Women, Culture, and Society,* ed. M. Z. Rosaldo and L. Lamphere (Stanford, Calif.: Stanford University

Press, 1974), 83–84. It may be that in contemporary Western society, which is so thoroughly structured by categories of gender, race, class, age, and affectional preference, there simply is no meaningful notion of "value-hierarchical thinking" that does not function in an oppressive context. For purposes of this book, I leave that question open.

10. Peggy Sanday, *Female Power and Male Dominance: On the Origins of Sexual Inequality* (New York: Cambridge University Press, 1981), 5.

11. Sanday, *Female Power,* 6.

12. Elizabeth Minnick, *Conceptual Errors Across the Curriculum: Toward a Transformation of the Curriculum* (Memphis: Research Clearinghouse and Curriculum Integration Project, at the Center for Research on Women, Memphis State University, 1986), 5.

13. I am making a distinction here between what I call "conceptual essentialism" and "strategic essentialism," understood as the claim that there are some material realities that form commonalities among women. Even with noteworthy differences among women, for reasons of political action and accurate descriptive theory, feminists are correct to call attention to these commonalities.

14. Victoria Davion, "Is Ecofeminism Feminist?" in *Ecological Feminism,* ed. Karen J. Warren (New York: Routledge, 1994), 17.

15. Chris Cuomo, *Feminism and Ecological Communities: An Ethic of Flourishing* (London: Routledge, 1998), 6.

16. Plumwood, "Ecofeminism: An Overview," 133–34.

17. I discuss "power against"—power of Downs against Ups—in chapter 9. One might argue, for example, that Downs in an Up-Down hierarchy of power and privilege are justified in using whatever means are necessary to get their legitimate needs met (a twist on the familiar "just war" doctrine).

18. In her book *Justice and the Politics of Difference* (Princeton, N.J.: Princeton University Press, 1990), Iris Marion Young identifies exploitation, marginalization, powerlessness, cultural imperialism, and violence as five "faces" or "correlates of oppression."

19. Of course, for some dominated beings, relationships of domination and subordination may also be relationships of oppression.

20. Chris Crittenden has articulated and defended my position on the "logic of domination" and the underlying distinction between oppression and domination in his article, "Subordinate and Oppressive Conceptual Frameworks: A Defense of Ecofeminist Perspectives," *Environmental Ethics* 20, no. 3 (Fall 1998), 247–63.

21. Jennifer Everett raised this as a possible objection in an earlier version of this manuscript.

22. Deborah Bird Rose, *Nourishing Terrains: Australian Aboriginal Views of Landscape and Wilderness* (Canberra: Australian Heritage Commission, 1996), 7.

23. See Bruce Chatwin's *The Songlines* (New York: Penguin Books, 1987).

24. Rose, *Nourishing Terrains,* 35.

25. Rose, *Nourishing Terrains,* 49.

26. *Dred Scott v. Sandford,* 60 U.S. (19 How.) 396, 404–5 (1856); cited in Christopher D. Stone, *Should Trees Have Standing? Toward a Theory of Legal Rights for Natural Objects* (Los Altos, Calif.: William Kaufmann, 1974), 6, n. 19.

27. *Bailey v. Poindexter's Ex'r,* 56 Va. (14 Gratt.) 132, 142–3 (1858); cited in Stone, *Should Trees?,* 7, n. 19.

28. W. E. B. Du Bois, *The Souls of Black Folk* (New York: Random House, 1990), 68.

29. *People v. Hall,* 4 Cal. 399, 405 (1854); cited in Stone, *Should Trees?,* 7.

30. Rose, *Nourishing Terrains,* 17.

31. Rose, *Nourishing Terrains,* 19.

32. Daniel T. Spencer, "Ecological and Social Transformations and the Construction of Race and Place: A View From Iowa," unpublished paper, 13.

33. Spencer, "Ecological and Social," 14.

34. Vance Cope-Kasten, "A Portrait of Dominating Rationality," *American Philosophical Association Newsletter on Feminism and Philosophy* 88, no. 2 (March 1989), 29–34.

35. For a discussion of similarities between argument and war, see Edwin Burtt, "Philosophers as Warriors," in *The Critique of War,* ed. Robert Ginsberg (Chicago: Henry Regnery, 1969), 30–42; Duane L. Cady, *From Warism to Pacifism: A Moral Continuum,* (Philadelphia: Temple University Press, 1989), 3–19; Jim Sterba, *Justice for Here and Now* (New York: Cambridge University Press, 1998), 1–13; and George Lakoff and Mark Johnson, *Metaphors We Live By* (Chicago: University of Chicago Press, 1980), 4–6, 77–86.

36. For a discussion of the notion of male-bias in philosophical conceptions of reason and rationality, see my article, "Male-Gender Bias and Western Conceptions of Reason and Rationality," *American Philosophical Association Newsletter on Feminism and Philosophy* 88, no. 2 (March 1989), 48–53.

37. Ernestine Friedl, *Women and Men: An Anthropologist's View* (New York: Holt, Rinehart and Winston, 1975), 7.

38. Sanday, *Female Power,* 164.

39. The reference to "theory and practice" is not intended to suggest that theorizing is not a practice or that engaging in practice is somehow "opposed" to theorizing.

Chapter Four

How Should We Treat Nature?

Ecofeminist Philosophy and Environmental Ethics

For the most part, contemporary environmental philosophy has been "environmental ethics." Environmental ethics focuses on questions about how humans ought to treat nonhuman nature: for example, What is the nature of our responsibility to the natural environment? When and why are we obligated to preserve wilderness areas, protect endangered species, engage in sustainable development and appropriate technology? Are some theoretical approaches to resolving environmental problems more fruitful than others?

There are two primary goals of this chapter: to introduce the reader to the field of environmental ethics, and to situate the version of ecofeminist philosophy I am defending within environmental ethics. I begin with a brief discussion of the concept of "moral considerability." I then provide an overview of the variety of theories in environmental ethics, followed by a sketch of some ecofeminist philosophical worries about key assumptions underlying many of these theories. I end with a discussion of ways in which my version of ecofeminist philosophy does and does not fit into the spectrum of theories in environmental ethics. I conclude that an ecofeminist philosophical perspective is not only a distinctive but a transformative perspective on human-nature relationships.

A word to the reader unfamiliar with the field of environmental ethics in Western contexts: This chapter covers a lot of material. It surveys the field of Western environmental ethics by condensing a large amount of information into a relatively small space and by omitting the particular positions of many environmental ethicists. The rationale in presenting this information is to acquaint the reader with the sorts of issues ecofeminist philosophers like myself grapple with in formulating our perspectives in environmental ethics. I encourage the reader unfamiliar with the material in environmental ethics to read this chapter with an eye toward simply becoming familiar with the main ideas and concepts presented.

MORAL CONSIDERABILITY

Environmental ethicists distinguish between an ethic *of* the environment and an ethic *concerning* the environment. An ethic of the environment asserts that the nonhuman natural environment itself (and/or its nonhuman members) is deserving of moral consideration ("morally considerable"). An ethic concerning the environment denies that the nonhuman environment itself (and/or its nonhuman members) is morally considerable, although there are constraints (moral and other) on how humans may treat the environment. Only an ethic *of* the environment generates a bona fide environmental ethic.

Notice that the distinction between an ethic of and an ethic concerning the natural environment turns on the notion of "moral considerability." It is a basic assumption of environmental ethics that nonhuman animals and/or nature are "morally considerable"; that is they deserve moral consideration by humans.[1] Commitment to the moral considerability of nonhuman animals and/or nature is what makes an environmental ethic an *environmental* ethic.

Nonetheless, there is considerable disagreement and, I think, confusion among environmental ethicists about both the basis of moral considerability and how to prove that nonhuman nature is morally considerable. Typically, one of two related strategies is offered to prove the moral considerability of "nature."

The first strategy is to argue that what makes "nature" morally considerable is that nature has certain properties that make it morally considerable—properties that are shared by all and only morally considerable entities. The properties commonly argued for include: rationality, sentiency, the ability to use a language, possession of a soul, possession of morally relevant interests, being "the subject of a life," and simply being alive. When asked why any of these properties is sufficient to establish moral considerability, the answer often reduces to the claim that these properties are those on which moral considerability rests.

The second and related strategy is to begin with a distinction between *intrinsic* and *extrinsic* (or instrumental) value and then to claim that the moral considerability of the nonhuman natural environment (and/or its members) lies in its having intrinsic value: Nature is intrinsically valuable—a "good in itself" (or an "end-in-itself")—because of its own intrinsic properties and not because of its usefulness for some (human) purpose or end. When asked, "What are these intrinsic properties?" typically the answer refers back to a set of properties nonhuman nature or its members has (e.g., rationality, sentiency, being the subject of a life). We are then back to where we started: If nature has intrinsic worth by virtue of some other traits it has (e.g., rationality, sentiency, being the subject of a life), then what is the moral basis for valuing these other traits as those which warrant recognition or ascription of moral considerability? It seems that both strategies for explaining and establishing moral considerability reduce to just renaming that which is to be explained.[2]

Such difficulties in establishing which properties make something morally considerable lead me to wonder whether the moral considerability of nonhuman nature may be "groundless." I think the moral considerability of nature may be groundless in the same way in which, according to Joel Feinberg, the moral worth of humans is groundless: it may express a "kind of attitude not itself justifiable in more ultimate terms." In the case of respect for human beings, Feinberg argues:

> It may well be that universal "respect" for human beings is, in a sense, "ground-less"—a kind of ultimate attitude not itself justifiable in more ultimate terms. This is what might be said, after all, about parental (and other) love. [In the case of] the parent's unshaken love for the child who has gone bad . . . no quality of the child can be cited as a "reason" in justification of the parent's love. "I am his father after all" might be said to *explain* to others an affection that might otherwise seem wholly unintelligible, but that does not state a *ground* for the affection so much as indicate that it is "groundless" (but not irrational or mysterious for that).[3]

The analogy Feinberg gives to "loving one's child" is key. According to Feinberg, we may *explain* various reasons that we love our children, but there may be no way to *justify* (to prove) that love. In a very important sense, we love our children because we love them. They may or may not be smart, or attractive, or talented, or successful, or have any other praiseworthy traits. Nonetheless, we may love them. Ultimately there is no "ground" or "justification" for our loving them other than the fact that we do.

Feinberg argues that the inability to justify the "equal human worth" of humans is like the inability to justify one's love for one's child:

> "Human worth" itself is best understood to name no property in the way that "strength" names strength and "redness" redness. In attributing human worth to everyone we may be ascribing no property or set of qualities, but rather expressing an attitude—the attitude of respect—toward the humanity in each man's person . . . it is not grounded on anything more ultimate than itself, and it is not demonstrably justifiable.[4]

On Feinberg's view, the claim that all humans deserve respect because all humans have equal human worth is really the expression of an attitude of respect toward the humanity in each human person. Like love for one's child, there is no further "ground" or "justification."

Is the claim that nature is morally considerable really the expression of an *attitude* that is neither grounded in anything more basic than itself nor demonstrably justifiable? Are nonhuman animals and nature regarded as "morally considerable" and "deserving of respect" to the extent that people have such an attitude? I think the answer to these questions is yes. My reluctance to talk about the "intrinsic value of nature" or to identify any one set of properties that nonhuman nature or its members has that makes "nature" morally considerable is that I doubt that there is any one set of necessary and sufficient condition properties that makes all entities—humans, nonhuman animals, or the rest of nature—morally considerable. Furthermore, I doubt that one could prove (justify) judgments about them true even if there were some such identifiable properties. As such, I find appeals by environmental ethicists to such proper-

ties as the ground or basis for justifying claims about the moral considerability of nonhuman nature problematic.

For these reasons, I think that in a very real and important sense, having an attitude of respect for nature or for viewing nature as morally considerable is like
loving one's child. It expresses a groundless attitude—a willingness on our part
to see nonhuman animals and nature as subjects, as active participants in our
worlds, as not mere things (mere resources, properties, or commodities), as
deserving of our care and attention. I suspect that the moral considerability of
nature can be explained but not ultimately proven. It is itself *groundless.*

Even so, it does not follow, and I do not think it is true, that we cannot offer
well-supported, conceptually clear reasons for claiming that humans ought to
treat others, including nonhuman animals and nature, with care, or respect, or as
deserving of moral consideration. In fact, as an environmental ethicist, I assume
we can and should. This book is an attempt to provide what I take to be well-
supported, conceptually clear reasons for claiming that humans, as relational and
ecological selves who are capable of caring about those with whom we relate, can
and ought to care about nonhuman animals and nature. The book also provides
ecological reasons for claiming that both our own health and the health of the
nonhuman environment depend on our caring about nonhuman animals and
nature. In this book I argue, as Feinberg does about "equal human worth," that a
world where humans respect nature is a more just world. But, having said all that,
I suspect that beyond these sorts of reasons for treating nature as morally considerable, no additional "proof"—no attempts to "ground" claims about moral considerability of the nonhuman natural environment (or its members)—is possible.[5]

If the skeptic pushes an environmental ethicist like myself further, demanding
proof beyond well-supported, conceptually clear reasons for viewing nature as
morally considerable, I propose we do what Feinberg suggests we do regarding
the ethical sceptic about "equal human worth": "We should turn our backs on him
to examine more important problems."[6] If all attempts to give reasons for regarding nature as morally considerable fail to convince the skeptic, I suggest we say,
simply and respectfully, that we disagree about this. By respectfully acknowledging that nothing else can be said to convince the skeptic otherwise, we are free
to turn our attention to discussing environmental ethics with those who are
(unlike the skeptic) willing to entertain the possibility that the nonhuman nature
is morally considerable.

OVERVIEW OF POSITIONS IN
WESTERN ENVIRONMENTAL ETHICS

Western environmental ethics is about how humans should treat nonhuman
nature. Four types of positions along a continuum tend to emerge. I say "continuum" because these four types should not be viewed as boxed categories that are

fixed and rigid. Rather, they represent ethical tendencies in ways of thinking about environmental concerns. Visually, these four types of positions may be represented in relation to each other in the following way:

"HOUSE"   "REFORMIST"   "MIXED REFORM   "RADICAL"
                                  AND RADICAL"
_____/_____/_____/_____/_____

Consider examples of each type of position.

The most conservative of ethical positions are what I am calling mainstream positions of *"the house."* I call them "house" positions because they are a diversity of alternative, competing positions in mainstream Western philosophical ethics that are "housed" under the same roof and built on a very similar foundation of shared assumptions. One way they are all alike is that they view the nonhuman environment itself as outside the realm of moral considerability. As such, house positions do not generate an environmental ethic.

House positions are of two main types: *consequentialist theories,* which assess human conduct in terms of the consequences of that conduct, and *nonconsequentialist theories,* which assess human conduct in terms other than consequences (e.g., in terms of motive, duty, rights, intrinsic value, what an all-good, all-knowing, all-powerful God commands or forbids, or what virtue requires).[7] House positions have had very little to say about moral responsibilities of humans toward nonhuman animals and the natural environment. When they do provide arguments (e.g., Kant's arguments against cruelty to animals), those arguments are based on moral obligations humans have *to* other humans where animals are *concerned.* They are not moral obligations humans have directly to animals themselves.

A familiar house position is Garrett Hardin's "Lifeboat Ethics."[8] In lifeboat ethics, the issue is whether so-called First World countries have any moral obligation to help rescue or preserve the lives of people dying in overpopulated Third World countries. (Hardin's answer is no.) Part of what makes lifeboat ethics a house position is that it is wholly *anthropocentric* (human-centered) in what values are deemed relevant and in who or what is "morally considerable."[9]

Each of the remaining three types of positions generates an environmental ethic. *"Reformist"* positions are those that revise house accounts in ways that make the nonhuman natural environment, or at least some members of it, morally considerable, but do so without introducing relatively new and different ways of thinking about humans and ethics. They are "moral extensionist" positions. As such, reformist environmental ethics fall into the traditional house division of consequentialist and nonconsequentialist theories.

Two of the most popular Western reformist positions are consequentialist and nonconsequentialist versions of "animal welfarism" (sometimes called "animal liberationism"). Peter Singer's utilitarian-based animal welfarism asserts that sentiency, not rationality (Aristotle) or ability to use a language (Descartes), is what qualifies a being for moral considerability. Singer's account draws on the work of utilitarian Jeremy Bentham who "was well aware that the logic of the demand for racial equality did not stop at the equality of humans."[10] Singer cites this crucial passage from Bentham:

> The day *may* come when the rest of the animal creation may acquire those rights which never could have been withholden from them but by the hand of tyranny . . . a full-grown horse or dog is beyond comparison a more rational, as well as a more conversable animal, than an infant of a day, or a week, or even a month old. But suppose they were otherwise, what would it avail? The question is not, Can they *reason*? Nor, Can they *talk*? But, Can they *suffer*?

Singer agrees with Bentham that the ability to suffer is what makes a being morally considerable:

> Surely Bentham was right. If a being suffers, there can be no moral justification for refusing to take that suffering into consideration, and, indeed, to count it equally with the like suffering (if rough comparisons can be made) of any other being.[11]

Singer claims that anyone who fails to realize that animals deserve moral consideration is simply being "speciesist": "Speciesism—the word is not an attractive one, but I can think of no better term—is a prejudice or attitude or bias towards the interests of members of one's own species and against those of members of other species."[12]

Singer's position is a "reformist" position because he argues that animals are morally considerable on the basis of their morally relevant likenesses to humans. It is a utilitarian ethic that includes animal suffering in the suffering that counts morally. Singer's consequentialist (and utilitarian) version of animal welfarism was instrumental in putting the issue of factory farming on the ethical map:

> Factory farm animals need liberation in the most literal sense. Veal calves are kept in stalls five feet by two feet. They are usually slaughtered when about four months old, and have been too big to turn in their stalls for at least a month. Intensive beef herds, kept in stalls only proportionately larger for much longer periods, account for a growing percentage of beef production. Sows are often similarly confined when pregnant, which, because of artificial methods of increasing fertility, can be most of the time. Animals confined in this way do not waste food by exercising, not do they develop unpalatable muscle.[13]

Singer's critique of factory farming documents all sorts of abuses of animals: forcing caged animals to stand and sleep on slatted floors without straw, because this makes cleaning their stalls easier for humans; feeding calves all-liquid diets until slaughter in order to produce the pale veal consumers prefer; overcrowded cages for poultry, which creates anti-social behaviors such as pecking each other to death; a combination of artificial lighting, temperature conditions, and drug injections to squeeze the maximum number of eggs out of hens.[14] While animal liberation will require great changes on the part of humans (e.g., ending factory farming, adopting moral vegetarianism, ceasing vivisection practices), Singer argues that animals deserve just that moral consideration.

The other main version of animal welfarism is the rights-based version defended by Tom Regan. Like Singer, Regan locates the moral considerability of nonhuman beings in their ethical proximity to humans. Unlike Singer, however, Regan argues that it is because animals are "subjects of a life" that they are morally considerable. Nonhuman beings resemble ("are kin to") humans "in quite the fundamental ways of being conscious, and thus to this extent [are] kin to us, have moral standing."[15] Regan writes:

> We are each of us the experiencing subject of a life; each of us a conscious creature having an individual welfare that has importance to us whatever our usefulness to others. We want and prefer things; believe and feel things; recall and expect things. And all these dimensions of our life, including our pleasure and pain, our enjoyment and suffering, our satisfaction and frustration, our continued existence or our untimely death—all make a difference to the quality of our life as lived, as experienced by us as individuals. As the same is true of those animals who concern us (those who are eaten and trapped, for example), they, too, must be viewed as the experiencing subjects of a life with inherent value of their own.[16]

Regan argues that all "subjects of a life" deserve moral consideration and respect. Since all subjects of a life are right-holders, animals are rights-holders deserving of moral consideration and respect:

> When it comes to the case for animal rights, then what we need to know is whether the animals who, in our culture are routinely eaten, hunted, and used in our laboratories, for example, are like us in being subjects of a life. And we *do* know this. We do *know* that many—literally, billions and billions—of these animals are the subjects of a life . . . and so have inherent value if we do. And since, in order to have the best theory of our duties to one another, we must recognize our equal inherent value, as individuals, reason—not sentiment, not emotion—reason compels us to recognize the equal inherent value of these animals. And, with this, their equal right to be treated with respect.[17]

In addition to these two versions of animal welfarism, there are other sorts of reformist positions in Western environmental ethics. I discuss four here.

Donald VanDeVeer defends a consequentialist ethic based on the kind of interests protected or promoted (rather than sentiency).[18] VanDeVeer distinguishes first between two kinds of interests: basic interests and nonbasic interests. For VanDeVeer, basic interests include interests in avoiding serious suffering and in having one's basic nutritional needs satisfied. Nonbasic interests include "serious" and "peripheral" interests. Serious interests are those that are difficult or costly to a thing's well-being to do without, though an entity can survive without such interests being met. For VanDeVeer, the interest of a lonely child to have a pet or of an eagle to be able to fly are examples of serious interests. Peripheral interests are those that remain (e.g., interests in wearing musk perfume or shooting a wolf for pleasure).

Using this distinction among three types of interests, VanDeVeer argues for an environmental ethic that adjudicates among conflicts of interests between humans and nonhuman animals (or simply "animals") on the basis of the kind of interests at stake and the psychological capacities of the parties whose interests conflict. He calls his position Two-Factor Egalitarianism. Two-Factor Egalitarianism weighs interests in such a way that some subordination of animal interests is justified, particularly in cases where the basic interests of humans and animals conflict (e.g., scientific experiments on animals where the promised utility for humans or other animals is very considerable), or where the basic interests of humans conflict with the peripheral interests of animals. According to VanDeVeer, Two-Factor Egalitarianism is a nonspeciesist principle that sides with critics who judge "much of the prevailing wholesale disregard of the basic interests of higher animals as unconscionable."[19] VanDeVeer argues that Two-Factor Egalitarianism avoids the extreme egalitarianism that is characteristic of some environmental ethics.

Paul Taylor defends a second type of reformist position, a Kantian-based "respect for nature" environmental ethic. According to Taylor, living things are "teleological centers of life" that have "inherent worth." As such, they are worthy of respect. Taylor describes his "respect for nature" environmental ethic as "biocentric" (or life-centered), rather than "anthropocentric" (or human-centered), since it universalizes the "attitude of respect" as deserving of all beings (and not simply humans) that have inherent worth. Taylor argues that humans must adopt an empathetic way of looking at the world by seeing "the natural order from its perspective"; otherwise, "we cannot see the point of taking the attitude of respect."[20]

Jay B. McDaniel defends a third sort of reformist position, a theologically based "stewardship ethic." Stewardship ethics typically rely on Judeo-Christian texts, which give humans "dominion over the fish of the sea and over the birds of the air and over every living thing that moves upon the earth" (Genesis 1:26–29). Here "dominion over" the earth is interpreted in the sense of stewardship, not domination, over the nonhuman natural environment. Advocates of stewardship ethics claim that, just as shepherds (as stewards) have moral responsibilities to tend to the well-being of their flocks and other living things, humans have stewardship responsibilities to nonhuman animals and nature.

McDaniel's stewardship ethic distinguishes between "kindly use" stewardship and "prudent management" stewardship.[21] McDaniel's claims that prudent management stewardship is an inadequate basis for a theology of nature, since "stewardship" here means no more than prudent management of nonhuman resources and a recognition of only the extrinsic (or instrumental) value of nature.[22] A spirituality of the earth must involve "not only a respect for the earth's intrinsic value, but a 'stewardly' approach to its usefulness":

It is very important to distinguish stewardship from a mere prudent management of nature. A healthy and biblically nourished idea of stewardship will not see nature as an alien substance from which we are detached and which we can manipulate at will. Rather—along with the first chapters of Genesis (2:4–4:16), various psalms (8, 19, 74, 104), passages from Isaiah (40:12–31, 45:9–13, 48:12–13) and Jeremiah (27:5 and 32:17), and themes from wisdom literature (Proverbs 3:19–20, 8:22–31)—it will recognize that humans are a part of, rather than apart from, nature. . . . An ecologically sensitive expression of stewardship will begin with the assumption shared by biblical perspectives and process theology; namely, that humans are united with their fellow creatures in being part of a single ontological order: an order named "the creation."[23]

McDaniel endorses a "kindly use" stewardship ethic that asserts that nature is a God-given gift to humans; we must "consciously choose to be the caretaker and shepherd of the soil."[24]

The fourth reformist environmental ethic discussed here is a modern version of ancient Greek "virtue ethics." Virtue ethics is an ethic of character, seeking to describe traits of morally good persons in terms of human dispositions and character traits, and not just their actions, consequences of their actions, or rights and rules governing their actions. One ought not be cruel to animals because cruelty is a vice, a bad character trait for an agent to possess. Although the prescription against cruelty to animals might be accepted by house theorists, nonvirtue-based ethics provide reasons based more on rules than on the character of moral agents.

One candidate for a virtue-based environmental ethic is Albert Schweitzer's "reverence for life" ethic. Schweitzer criticized all ethics hitherto that dealt "only with the relations of man to man," rather than also with plants and animals. Schweitzer argued that a human should extend to all life "the same reverence for life that he gives to his own."[25] For Schweitzer, this meant that the ethical person "shatters no ice crystal that sparkles in the sun, tears no leaf from its trees, breaks off no flower, and is careful not to crush any insect as he walks."[26]

Environmental ethicist Joseph Des Jardins argues that Schweitzer's ethic is a "virtue ethic" that heralds back to themes expressed by Plato, Aristotle, and Aquinas:

> Schweitzer's ethic focused not on the question "What should I do?" but on "What type of person should I be?" His was not an ethics solely on rules as much as it was an ethics of *character*, seeking first to describe morally good people in terms of their character and dispositions rather than in terms of their actions. . . . An *ethics of virtue* emphasizes moral character, or virtues, rather than rules or principles.[27]

Virtue ethics approaches questions of human responsibilities toward nature in terms of what morally good people will or ought to do. Discussing Schweitzer's views, Des Jardins argues:

> Schweitzer did not envision reverence for life merely as some rule that we could apply to specific situations and, as it were, simply read off the recommended decision. Reverence for life is more an attitude that determines who we are rather than a rule for determining what we should do. It describes a character trait, or a moral

virtue, rather than a rule of action. A morally good person stands in awe of the inherent worth of each life.[28]

So understood, Schweitzer's "reverence for life" ethic is a revised version of classical virtue ethics.[29]

The third type of position in Western environmental ethics is the category of *"mixed reform and radical"* positions. They utilize a combination of reformist and radical concepts in the formulation of an environmental ethic. I think Aldo Leopold's 1949 publication, "The Land Ethic," is such an ethic. To see why, consider just three brief passages from "The Land Ethic":

> (1) The land ethic simply enlarges the boundaries of the community to include soils, waters, plants, and animals, or collectively: the land. . . . In short, a land ethic changes the role of *Homo sapiens* from conqueror of the land-community to plain member and citizen of it. . . .
> (2) It is inconceivable to me that an ethical relation to land can exist without love, respect, and admiration for land, and a high regard for its value. By value, I of course mean something far broader that mere economic value; I mean value in the philosophical sense. . . .
> (3) A thing is right when it tends to preserve the integrity, stability, and beauty of the biotic community. It is wrong when it tends otherwise.[30]

These three simple but powerful passages constitute what many environmental ethicists claim are three fundamental presuppositions of any environmental ethic: humans are co-members of the ecological community; humans should love and respect the land; and, it is wrong to destroy the integrity, stability, and beauty of the biotic community. Indeed, as I argue in chapter 7, it is doubtful that any position that denies the sensibilities expressed in these three claims could be said to constitute a bona fide environmental ethic. So it isn't surprising that other theories (e.g., Taylor's "respect for nature" ethic and my version of ecofeminist philosophy) could be said to endorse these ethical sensibilities.

Why, then, do I describe Leopold's land ethic as a "mixed reform and radical" position? Claim 3 (above) is the famous Leopoldian principle that "a thing is right when it tends to preserve the integrity, stability, and beauty of a biotic community; it is wrong when it tends otherwise." Claim 3 suggests that Leopold's land ethic is a consequentialist position (a version of what might be called "ecoconsequentialism"). Indeed, if Leopold's land ethic were only that, it would be a "reformist" ethic. It would be properly interpreted as extending moral consideration to animals, trees, rocks, rivers, and whole ecosystems—what Leopold calls simply "the land"—on familiar, though revised, consequentialist, house grounds.

Yet viewing Leopold's land ethic in this way would be a serious historical and philosophical mistake. It is a historical mistake on any careful reading of Leopold's writings and life. Although Leopold's early career (roughly 1909–18) as a forester was influenced by Gifford Pinchot's defense of the "wise use" of forests—efficient, utilitarian-based forest management—Leopold came to rigorously reject such "economic determinism" and (by 1924) to advocate nationally for wilderness preservation. By 1930 Leopold began to explore the ecological value of predators, and by 1949, with the publication of "The Land Ethic," Leopold argued for the value of all species as contributing members of the "integrity, stability, and beauty" of the biotic community.

It also would be a philosophical mistake to suppose that Leopold's central ethical claim, (3), is simply some form of utilitarianism extended to ecological contexts for two reasons. The first reason is that, unlike reformist positions, Leopold's land ethic has an ecologically *holistic* cast: It emphasizes ecosystems as deserving of moral consideration.[31] In fact, Leopold was the first to suggest that ecological "wholes" (populations, communities, species, ecosystems) are morally considerable. This holistic approach is a departure from both house and reformist positions, which focus moral concern on discrete, separate, individual, particular entities. The second reason is that Leopold offers what he takes to be an equally pressing moral principle as constitutive of the land ethic—one ought to love and respect the land, claim 2. Leopold believed that both "the head and the heart," both ethical obligation and ecological conscience, are central to the land ethic. As he claims:

Obligations have no meaning without conscience, and the problem we face is the extension of the social conscience from people to land.
No important change in ethics was ever accomplished without an internal change in our intellectual emphasis, loyalties, affections, and convictions.[32]

When Leopold writes, "It is inconceivable to me that an ethical relation to land can exist without love, respect, and admiration for land, and a high regard for its value," he is expressing his deeply held conviction that "the evolution of a land ethic is an intellectual as well as emotional process."[33]

For these two reasons, Leopold's land ethic is best interpreted as a mixed reform and radical position—one that cannot sufficiently be unpacked simply by reforming *from within* the house. Rearranging the internal furniture or redecorating the house are not themselves sufficient to generate an adequate moral theory of the environment; some revolution *from without* is needed.

The fourth type of position in Western environmental ethics is sometimes referred to in texts on environmental ethics as "*radical.*" Radical positions are distinguished from the other three types of positions primarily in that they are much more comprehensive in scope (not limited to ethics per se) and they introduce nonhouse, sometimes non-Western, considerations. Texts on environmental ethics typically identify as "radical" positions deep ecology, bioregionalism, social (or political) ecology, and ecofeminism. Sometimes they also include non-European perspectives such as American Indian, Australian aborigine, and Asian positions.

Deep ecology is the name of a variety of positions. Drawing initially on the writings of Rachel Carson and Leopold, the term deep ecology was coined by Arne

Naess in his 1973 article "The Shallow and the Deep, Long-Range Ecology Movement."[34] Naess was attempting to move beyond a limited, resource-oriented, reformist environmentalism by articulating a comprehensive spiritual and philosophical worldview, an "ecological consciousness." Deep ecology is offered as an alternative to the dominant Western worldview of techno-industrial societies that regard "humans as isolated and essentially separate from the rest of nature."[35]

The main intuition of deep ecology is expressed by Australian philosopher Warwick Fox. He states: "It is the idea that we can make no firm ontological divide in the field of existence: That there is no bifurcation in reality between the human and the non-human realms . . . to the extent that we conceive boundaries, we fall short of deep ecological consciousness."[36] From this basic ontological intuition (i.e., intuition about what is real), Naess developed two norms that are themselves not derivable from other principles or intuitions: the norms of *self-realization* and *biocentric equality*. The norm of self-realization is intended to replace the Western notion of a self as an atomistic, isolated ego with the deep ecological notion of a self-in-Self: individual human selves (small s) are fully realized when they become "organically whole" ecological "Selves" (capital S). The notion of self-in-Self is expressed by such sayings as "No one is saved until we are all saved." The norm of biocentric equality is that all things in the biosphere have an equal right to live and blossom, to reach their own individual unfolding. The axiom of biocentric equality assumes that all entities in the ecosphere have equal intrinsic worth. It is related to the norm of self-realization in the sense that if we harm the rest of nature, we are harming ourselves. One implication of the norm of biocentric equality is that humans should live with minimum (rather than medium or maximum) impact on other species (e.g., by dramatically reducing human population levels). This norm generates what many call the guiding principle of deep ecology: "Simple in means, rich in ends."

A second "radical" position is bioregionalism ("bio" for life and "region" for territory). Bioregionalism centralizes the importance of place in environmental ethics. Here "place" refers both to geographic spaces and cultural contexts in which humans and nonhumans live. One goal of bioregionalism is that humans become simply "dwellers in the land," in part by quite literally understanding the places in which they live or dwell. As Kirkpatrick Sale explains,

> But to become dwellers in the land, . . . is to understand *place,* the immediate specific boundaries where we live. The kinds of soils and rocks under our feet; the sources of the water we drink; the meaning of the different kinds of winds; the common insects, birds, mammals, plants and trees; the particular cycles of the seasons; the times to plant and harvest—these are the things that are necessary to know. The limits of its resources; the carrying capacity of its lands and waters; the places where it must not be stressed; the places where its bounties can best be developed; the treasures that it holds and the treasures it withholds—these are the things that must be understood. And the cultures of the people, of the populations native to the land and of those who have grown up with it, the human social and economic arrangements

shaped by and adapted to the geomorphic ones, in both urban and rural settings — these are the things that must be appreciated. That, in essence, is bioregionalism.[37]

In order to come to know the land, one must "learn the lore." This means one must know the natural and human history of a place, and learn and develop a region's human and ecological possibilities in a sustainable manner over time.

A third "radical" position, social (or political) ecology claims that selfhood, reason, and freedom emerge *from* nature, not in sharp opposition *to* nature. Murray Bookchin, a leading social ecologist, eschews attempts to give a definition of social ecology. He states what distinguishes social ecology:

> It negates the harsh image we have traditionally created of the natural world and its evolution. And it does so not by dissolving the social into the natural, like sociobiology, or by imparting mystical properties to nature. . . . Instead . . . social ecology places the human mind, like humanity itself, within a natural context . . . so that the sharp cleavages between thought and nature, subject and object, mind and body and the social and natural are overcome, and the traditional dualisms of western culture are transcended by an evolutionary interpretation of consciousness. . . .[38]

There are six key features of social ecology: First, it is a philosophy of process and potentiality that views life as active, interactive, procreative, relational, and contextual. Nature is not a passive lump of "stuff" or "matter": it is self-directive in its evolutionary development. Second, social ecology is a biological way of thinking that views "nature" as a constellation of communities that are neither blind nor mute, cruel nor competitive, stingy nor necessitarian; "nature" is freed of all anthropocentric moral trappings. Third, social ecology is "social" in that it emphasizes the extent to which human society evolves out of nature: "Nature is always present in the human condition, and in the very ideological constructions that deny its presence in societal relationships."[39] Fourth, social ecology stresses that plant, animal, and human communities are properly viewed on a nature-society continuum, stressing the nonhierarchical continuities between nature and society. Social ecologists emphasize that there is no one true story of natural evolution in ecosystem relationships; this is just "a projection of our social relationships into the natural world." Fifth, social ecology asserts that there are no natural dominance-submission relationships. Hierarchies are socially constructed, institutional phenomena, not biological ones. The challenge is to experience the other ecologically, not hierarchically, as "the variety that enhances the unity of phenomena, enriches wholeness, and more closely resembles a food web than a pyramid."[40] Lastly, social ecology sees "otherness" in terms of complementarity rather than rivalry. Social ecologists object to any "natural" basis for an ideology of domination over nature. Nature is in some sense "willful" insofar as it seeks to preserve itself, to maintain its identity, to resist whatever threatens its integrity and complexity.

The fourth position often included in environmental ethics texts as a radical position is ecofeminism. Since this book is about ecofeminist philosophy and ethics and since I have provided an overview of ecofeminist positions in chapter 2, I do not provide a separate account of ecofeminist positions here.

In addition to these four textual examples of radical positions, "radical" Western environmental ethicists often appeal to non-Western traditions as a conceptual resource for environmental ethics, especially American Indian and Asian perspectives.[41] I discuss only American Indian views here.

Thomas W. Overholt and J. Baird Callicott identify four difficulties in discussing American Indian views toward the nonhuman natural environment.[42] First, there is no one American Indian belief system, though there are some common ideological threads. Second, historical and contemporary accounts of traditional American Indian views are united by the oral nature of the tradition and the inaccessibility of accounts of indigenous people to "outsiders" prior to contact with Europeans. Third, historical accounts are distorted by ethnocentrism and conflicting images of American Indians: some portray American Indians as "brutish savages," "violent beasts"; others portray American Indians as backward, gentle, receptive beings with whom amicable and profitable relations might be established. Fourth, there is always the tendency for outsiders (e.g., non-Indians) to impose their own cultural outlook on the selection and commentary of the narrative material.

Nonetheless, with these four caveats in place, Overholt and Callicott argue that traditional American Indian cultures provide an important source of knowledge about human–nature connections that contrast sharply with traditional Western, Anglo-American, and European views about the land and land use.[43] I summarize here some of the aspects of American Indian "ethnometaphysics" stressed by Overholt and Callicott.

Foremost among the many traditional American Indian views is the conception of land as borrowed or shared place; it is not property, not something owned. Land is conceived as not belonging to humans (e.g., as owners or masters of land). American Indian talk about selling or buying land (e.g., through treaties) or having land rights is a linguistic manifestation of colonial influences. Upon initial contact with Europeans, a treaty was innocently viewed within a traditional American Indian worldview as signifying a gift or willingness to share the land with Europeans, not as a contractual land arrangement by which Americans Indians "sold" the land to Europeans.

A second common theme is that land is sacred. Mother Earth was enspirited or ensouled. This is what Overholt and Callicott call a "metaphysic of nature," a sort of panpsychism whereby nature is viewed as alive, having power. Nonhuman natural objects (e.g., beaver, wolf, eagles, water, trees) are viewed as actors or agents endowed with specific capacities (e.g., volition, speech, emotion, reason, generosity, playfulness). These "powers" of the nonhuman world were accepted and respected as part of everyday experience. Prayer and dance are two familiar ways the powers of nonhuman natural beings were acknowledged and respected. This often involved ceremonies of "blessing the situation" (e.g., before a hunt or feast).

Third, the view of human nature was based on a kinship model of all creatures. All living things are brothers or sisters, uncles or mothers, grandfathers or other members of a family. "Mother Earth," "grandfather sky," and "brother deer" were viewed as kin. Among the Dakota, there were different sorts of persons: "four-legged persons," "two-legged persons," "wingeds" or "flying persons," and "swimmers." Differences between these beings—all identified as "persons"—were not differences in kind (as they are in the Western worldview). In fact, there is no word for animal in Dakota language. As a consequence, there cannot be a difference in kind and moral status between humans (as rational animals) and "animals."[44] Since human beings and nonhuman beings are viewed as kin, how one treats nonhuman natural beings is a matter of responsibilities owed to one's family members—a matter of kinship ethics.

Lastly, reciprocity and sharing are primary values among many traditional American Indian cultures. Reciprocal relationships between humans and nonhuman animals, for example, require appropriate offerings and a proper attitude of respect for all life forms, especially toward the less powerful. Appropriateness consists in a basic understanding of what is right in a given situation. Right action requires reciprocity on the part of humans toward their nonhuman kin (as occurs, for instance, when a Shoshone leaves a token gift such as a coin at the base of a pinon tree when taking pinon nuts from it).

This completes what I want to say here about these four types of positions in environmental ethics: house, reform, mixed reform and radical, and radical positions. Recognizing similarities and dissimilarities among these four types of positions has valuable practical ramifications. For example, one's views about capitalism and the role of market remedies for environmental destruction probably will (and logically should) differ depending on whether one views humans as individual, rational, self-interested pleasure maximizers, or as ecological selves who are co-members of an intrinsically valuable biotic community. Similarly, one's views about the role of ethical principles in environmental ethics will (and logically should) differ depending on whether one endorses the view that there is one absolute, cross-culturally valid, transcendent principle of morality, or whether one endorses the view that there are a plurality of equally plausible ethical principles and that one must appeal to the context to decide which is morally relevant in a particular case. One's views about moral vegetarianism probably will (and logically should) differ depending on whether one views animals as "biologically determined," as having no will of their own, as having only instrumental value, or whether one views animals as moral subjects that have equal rights to life as humans. One's views about human overpopulation will (and logically should) differ depending on whether one views human overpopulation in the Third World as a Third World problem (as Garrett Hardin's lifeboat ethic does), as a "women's problem," to be solved though birth control and reproductive technologies focused on women, or as an institutional equity problem requiring redistribution of wealth, land, and food. These differences will (and logically should) arise because the basic assumptions, values, attitudes, and beliefs—the conceptual frameworks—that underlie the various positions in environmental ethics differ and yield different practical implications for environmental practice and policy.

ECOFEMINIST PHILOSOPHICAL WORRIES ABOUT
COMMON ASSUMPTIONS IN ENVIRONMENTAL ETHICS

Both ecofeminist environmental ethicists and other environmental ethicists agree that "house" positions on the environment are problematic, because they assume that only humans are morally considerable. Such "human chauvinism" eliminates house positions from contention, at the outset, as viable environmental ethics.

But there are good ecofeminist philosophical reasons for also rejecting some of the other three types of positions in environmental ethics. These reasons concern four common assumptions made by many, sometimes all, of these positions: ethical absolutism, ethical monism, the objectivity of "the moral point of view," and conceptual essentialism (primarily with regard to the concepts of "persons" and "theory"). Although these assumptions are often associated with house and reformist positions, versions of them can be found in mixed and radical positions as well.

Ethical absolutism is the position that there are principles of morality that are binding on all moral agents; there are no contexts in which they can justifiably be overridden. Typically, ethical absolutism is coupled with claims about the nature of ethical principles, which are ahistorical, transcendent, objective, impersonal, impartial, and universal principles that are "valid" for all time. Defenders of ethical absolutism claim that it is only because ethical principles are absolute (nonoverridable) and universal (cross-culturally valid) that one can make legitimate ethical comparisons of different societies. For example, an appeal to an absolute and universal principle of equal human rights can help show why a society that forbids slavery is a better, morally preferred society to one that practices slavery. An appeal to the absolute and universal principle that right-holders deserve to be treated with respect can be used to show that a society that forbids and punishes cruelty to animals understood as right-holders is a better, morally preferred society to one that does not.

Ethical absolutism denies *ethical relativism*, the position that there are no absolute moral principles binding on all moral agents. Ethical absolutists deny the ethical relativist claim that ethics is simply about what is permitted by a particular society, culture, or social convention. (The spirit of ethical relativism is expressed in the familiar maxim, "When in Rome, do as the Romans do.") If one accepts ethical absolutism, then an important task of philosophical ethics is to determine what the absolute principles of morality are, to provide justification for these principles as absolute, and to clarify which actions (or kinds of actions) these principles prescribe or forbid.

The version of ecofeminist philosophy I defend challenges both ethical absolutism and ethical relativism. As I argue in chapter 5, the "absolutism versus relativism" debate in ethics presents the ethical options as an exclusivist either-or situation: Either one accepts that ethical principles are absolute (i.e., not context-dependent, not overridable), or one accepts that there are no cross-culturally valid ethical principles. But I argue that this is a false dichotomy. There is a viable alternative, what I call *ethical contextualism*. According to ethical contextualism, there may be absolute (i.e., nonoverridable) principles but, if there are, they are relatively few and not the ones typically given in traditional Western ethics. A moral injunction against torturing or oppressing morally relevant others would be among them.

Furthermore, according to ethical absolutism, the universality of ethical principles typically is that they are ahistorical principles that are binding on all moral agents, independent of context. While I defend the universality of moral principles (in chapter 5), I argue that their "universality" lies in their particularity—in their giving expression to morally significant values (e.g., rights, duties, utility, care, appropriate trust, friendship) whose meaning and application are themselves grounded in the particularities and contingencies of real people's lives, in real historical and material circumstances. They are not principles that are "carved in stone" and absolute or universal in the sense of never overridable.

Lastly, in the dominant philosophical traditions of Western ethics, ethical absolutism often masquerades as a gender-neutral stance when it is, in fact, often a male gender-biased (or other-biased) stance. By showing the gender (and other) biases of these principles, they are rejected as the absolute and universal principles of morality.

A second assumption of many positions in environmental ethics is *ethical monism* (in contrast to *ethical pluralism*). Ethical monism is the position that there is one and only one supreme principle of morality. What environmental ethicists who accept ethical monism disagree about is what that supreme principle is. Is it a reformist utilitarian principle that one ought to do whatever maximizes the good (preferences, utility) of some larger group than just the agent (e.g. society)? Is it a reformist Kantian principle that one ought to do those acts that are governed by a maxim that is valid for all rational agents, or a rights-based animal welfare principle that one ought to respect the rights of all subjects of a life? Is it a Leopoldian principle that a thing is right when it tends to preserve the integrity, stability, and beauty of the ecosystem, and that it is wrong when it ends otherwise?

The version of ecofeminist philosophy I defend denies ethical monism. In the Western tradition, ethical monism presumes a hierarchically ordered system of principles, rules, and rights, with one basic rule or right at the top of the hierarchy. The version of ecofeminist ethics I defend rejects ethical monism in favor of ethical pluralism. As I show (in chapter 5), an endorsement of ethical pluralism need not be a rejection of ethical principles, or a slide into ethical relativism, whereby it is difficult, if not impossible, to resolve intersocietal moral conflicts. But it is a rejection of the historically well-entrenched view in Western philosophy about the nature and role of ethical principles and theory in ethical decision-making.

The third assumption of many positions in environmental ethics is *the objectivity of the moral point of view*. This assumption captures the time-honored view that ethics ought to be conducted from the point of view of the disinterested, detached, impartial, rational observer. The claim is that the moral point of view must be objective in order to eliminate the interference of biased, partial, and contingent considerations in considerations of morality. These include such consid-

erations as the sex/gender, race/ethnicity, class, affectional orientation, geographic location, individual talent and psychological traits, social convention, or
historical time period of the agent. One is understood as taking the moral point of
view if one is doing things on principle and if, as a rational agent, one is able to
universalize one's principles—to make them binding on all moral agents. The
principles any rational and objective observer would choose under conditions of
free, uncoerced choice are universal, since any rational and objective observer
would end up choosing the same principles as binding.

The assumption of the objectivity of the moral point of view is problematic
from the perspective of ecofeminist philosophy I am defending. The moral point
of view I offer throughout this book is only a, not the, moral point of view. It
reflects the point of view of someone who is theorizing from a particular Euro-
American conceptual framework—who accepts certain values, holds certain
beliefs, endorses certain attitudes, and makes certain assumptions about humans,
nonhuman nature, ethics, and the like. As such, the moral point of view I offer is
not, and is not intended to be, objective in the sense of value-neutral, or detached,
or impartial. As a point of view that grows out of a particular conceptual framework, it is no better and no worse off *in this sense* than any human moral point of
view. No human moral point of view emerges ex nihilo; it emerges from within
some conceptual framework. But, as I argue in chapter 7, it is a better or preferred
moral point of view to ones that are sexist, racist, classist, colonialist, or naturist.

My rejection of an objective moral point of view (in the traditional philosophical sense) is also a rejection of *abstract individualism*, namely, the view that
selves are essentially solitary, separate, isolated, atomistic individuals, defined
apart from the social contexts and relationships in which they find themselves.[45]
My version of ecofeminist philosophy assumes that humans are socially embedded, *relational* (not abstract) selves. On this view, such features of our identities
as our gender, race/ethnic, class, affectional orientation, abilities, and geographic
location are not simply contingent, add-on features of the self. The human self is
not like an onion, where one can strip feature after feature until some core self
identified with ahistorical abilities to reason objectively and rationally, independent of any social context, is reached. Yet that is the view of the self that is presupposed by the classic notion of "the moral point of view" as the point of view
of the objective, rational observer.

The fourth assumption of many positions in environmental ethics is *conceptual
essentialism*. According to conceptual essentialism, such concepts as moral agent
and ethical theory are definable by a set of ahistorical, necessary, and sufficient
conditions. A moral agent is assumed to be a moral agent by virtue of having all
and only those properties that moral agents have. An ethical theory is assumed to
be an ethical theory by virtue of having all and only those properties that all and
only ethical theories have.

But, as I have argued in chapter 3 and continue to argue throughout the book,
conceptual essentialism is seriously problematic. First, conceptual essentialism

mistakenly assumes that there are some "essential" properties of moral agents or moral theories that can be given in terms of a set of necessary and sufficient conditions. The version of ecofeminist philosophy I defend rejects this assumption. I endorse *strategic essentialism*, the view that often it is practically (or strategically) useful to talk about moral persons, moral theories, even women and nature. Strategic essentialism permits, as a practical strategy, talk about commonalities among individuals and groups as moral persons, selves, women, and nature without thereby implying any biologically determined, socially unconstructed, conceptually essentialist account of moral persons, selves, women, and nature. Furthermore, the version of ecofeminist philosophy defended throughout this book rests on the notion of theory as quilting and selves as selves-in-relationship; in both cases, the role of context features prominently. Both notions reject a conceptually essentialist approach in terms of some set of necessary and sufficient conditions.

Since the version of ecofeminist philosophy I offer in this book challenges each of these four basic assumptions, it will not be theoretically compatible with other positions in environmental ethics that endorse any or all of these four assumptions. This provides yet another (a fourth) reason why I am uncomfortable with describing ecofeminist ethics as radical. Like most reform and mixed positions, some "radical" positions seem to endorse many of these assumptions.

ECOFEMINIST PHILOSOPHY AS A DISTINCTLY FEMINIST PERSPECTIVE IN ENVIRONMENTAL ETHICS

The version of ecofeminist philosophy I defend in this book does not fit neatly into any of the three types of positions in environmental ethics—reformist, radical, or mixed reform and radical positions. In fact, I think one of the distinctive strengths of the version of ecofeminist philosophy I defend in this book is that it generates a *transformative* environmental ethic—one that genuinely goes beyond the current positions in environmental ethics in ways that capture the strengths of these positions (reform, mixed, and radical) without inheriting their weaknesses.[46] How does it do that?

I argued (in chapter 3) that ecofeminist philosophy provides a distinctly feminist perspective in environmental ethics. My cursory treatment of leading positions in Western environmental ethics in this chapter reveals that gender is not a significant category of analysis for any of these positions other than ecofeminism. So ecofeminist philosophy adds an explicitly feminist perspective in environmental ethics that is missing from other accounts.

One might now ask, "Why does this matter? If the end result is the same—the development of an environmental ethic and practice that does not emerge out of, or reinforce, unjustified systems of human domination—what difference does it make whether an analysis of environmental issues is feminist or not?" This question is explicitly posed of ecofeminists like myself by deep ecologist Warwick Fox. Fox writes:

> It becomes difficult to see any essential difference between their [i.e., ecofeminists such as Warren] approach and that of deep ecology. As one ecofeminist-cum-deep ecologist said to me after reading Warren's article ["The Power and the Promise of Ecological Feminism"]: "Why doesn't she just call it [i.e., her vision of a transformative feminism] deep ecology? Why specifically attach the label *feminist* to it. . . ?"[47]

My argument here and throughout this book is that it really *does* matter that the analysis is feminist, that "the label *feminist*" is attached to my version of environmental philosophy and ethics.

There are three basic reasons for using "the label *feminist.*" First, there is the scholarly issue of accurately representing the historical and empirical realities of the interconnections among the dominations of women, other human Others, and nature. And those realities are that, at least in Western and Western-colonized societies, the feminization of nonhuman nature and the animalization and naturalization of women and men of color have been crucial to their "justified" dominations.

Second, according to ecofeminist philosophical analysis, the domination of women, other human Others, and the domination of nature are "justified" by an oppressive and, at least in Western societies, patriarchal conceptual framework characterized by a logic of domination. Failure to notice the nature of this connection leaves at best an incomplete, inaccurate, and partial account of what is required of a conceptually adequate environmental ethic. An ethic that does not acknowledge this simply is not the same as one that does, whatever else the similarities between them.

Third, the claim that, in contemporary culture, one could have an adequate environmental ethic that includes the data of interest to feminists but is not itself feminist assumes that, in contemporary patriarchal culture, the prefix "feminist" does *not* add anything crucial to the nature or description of "environmental ethics." But I have been arguing that this assumption is false: use of the prefix "feminist" currently helps to clarify just how the domination of nature is linked to patriarchy and the domination of women and other human subordinates. Where feminism is the movement to end all systems of unjustified domination (as I argued in chapter 3), use of the prefix feminist helps to clarify the ways in which ending the domination and exploitation of nature is linked to ending the domination and exploitation of women, people of color, the poor, and other subordinated human groups. As such, the prefix feminist has critical bite in contemporary culture: it serves as an important reminder that in contemporary sex-gendered, raced, classed, and naturist culture, an *unprefixed* position functions as a privileged and "unmarked" position. That is, without the prefix feminist, one presents "environmental ethics" as if it has no bias, including male-gender bias, which is just what ecofeminists deny: failure to notice the connections between the dominations of women, people of color, and nature *is* male-gender bias.

I assume that one of the goals of feminism is the eradication of all oppressive sex-gender (and oppressive race, class, age, affectional preference, colonialist) categories and the creation of a world in which difference does not breed domination—say, a world in 4001. In 4001, an adequate environmental ethic would be a feminist environmental ethic and the prefix "feminist" would be redundant and unnecessary. Similarly, the prefix environmental in "environmental ethics" would be unnecessary. But this is *not* 4001, and the current historical and conceptual reality is that the dominations of nature, women, and other subordinated humans are intimately connected. Failure to notice or make visible these interconnections in the present perpetuates the mistaken (and privileged) view that environmental ethics is *not* a feminist issue, and that the prefix *feminist* adds nothing to environmental ethics.

CONCLUSION

In this chapter I have attempted to do three things: to present an overview of the four types of positions in environmental ethics; to identify the nature of an ecofeminist philosophical critique of four basic assumptions that appear in many reformist, mixed, and radical positions in environmental ethics; and to clarify why I think the ecofeminist philosophical perspective I am defending provides for a transformative and distinctly feminist environmental ethic. I turn now in chapter 5 to a description and defense of my version of ecofeminist philosophical ethics.

NOTES

1. Some environmental ethicists do not view theories of animal welfarism as genuine environmental ethics because, it is argued, they do not view nonhuman nature (only nonhuman animals) as morally considerable. The account I offer here does not prejudge or resolve that dispute: By speaking of "nonhuman animals and/or nature," I acknowledge that dispute without getting bogged down here in it.

2. Joel Feinberg, *Social Philosophy* (Englewood Cliffs, N.J.: Prentice-Hall, 1973), 92.

3. Feinberg, *Social Philosophy,* 93.

4. Feinberg, *Social Philosophy,* 94.

5. If "respect for nature as morally considerable" is like "respect for humans as having equal moral worth" in that both are "groundless" (in Feinberg's sense), then it is not a defect of environmental ethics per se that it cannot justify the intrinsic worth or moral considerability of the nonhuman natural environment. An inability to justify such bottom-line claims is endemic to any philosophical ethic.

6. Feinberg, *Social Philosophy,* 94.

7. While some philosophers might describe three positions (consequentialist, deontological, and virtue theories), I am using the more traditional characterization in terms of consequentialist and nonconsequentialist positions, including virtue theories among the latter.

8. See Garrett Hardin, *Exploring New Ethics for Survival* (New York: Viking Press, 1972) and Garrett Hardin, "Living on a Lifeboat," *BioScience* 24 (October 1974): 561–68.

9. Some, myself included, would also claim that they are Euro-centric in what they take to be the nature of ethics, the nature of humans, and ways of assessing human conduct. My reasons for claiming this are laced throughout the book.

10. Peter Singer, "Animal Liberation," in *People, Penguins, and Plastic Trees: Basic Issues in Environmental Ethics,* ed. Christine Pierce and Donald VanDeVeer (Belmont, Calif.: Wadsworth, 1995), 52.

11. Singer, "Animal Liberation," 52. The quote by Bentham is from his *The Principles of Morals and Legislation,* Ch. 17, Sec. 1, footnote to paragraph 4.

12. Peter Singer, *Animal Liberationism: A New Ethics for Our Treatment of Animals* (New York: Avon Books, 1975), 7. Singer credits Richard Ryder with coining the term "speciesism."

13. Singer, "Animal Liberation," 57.

14. Singer, "Animal Liberation," 57.

15. Tom Regan, *All That Dwell Therein: Essays on Animal Rights and Environmental Ethics* (Berkeley: University of California Press, 1982), 87.

16. Tom Regan, "The Case for Animal Rights," in *People, Penguins, and Plastic Trees: Basic Issues in Environmental Ethics,* ed. Christine Pierce and Donald VanDeVeer (Belmont, Calif.: Wadsworth, 1995), 77.

17. Regan, "The Case," 78.

18. Donald VanDeVeer, "Interspecific Justice," in *People, Penguins, and Plastic Trees: Basic Issues in Environmental Ethics* ed. Christine Pierce and Donald Van DeVeer (Belmont, Calif.: Wadsworth, 1995), 85–98.

19. VanDeVeer, "Interspecific Justice," 97.

20. Paul Taylor, *Respect for Nature: A Theory of Environmental Ethics* (Princeton, N.J.: Princeton University Press, 1986), 99. Although Taylor calls his view "biocentric," the ontology he defends is (like Singer, VanDeVeer, and Regan) one of individual entities (e.g., plants and animals), not collective entities (e.g., ecosystems, species, and bioregions).

21. Jay B. McDaniel, *Earth, Sky, Gods and Mortals: Developing an Ecological Spirituality* (Mystic, Conn.: Twenty-Third Publications, 1990), 97.

22. Jay B. McDaniel, *Of God and Pelicans: A Theology of Reverence for Life* (Louisville, Ky.: Westminster/John Knox Press, 1989), 75.

23. McDaniel, *Earth, Sky,* 97–98.

24. McDaniel, *Earth, Sky,* 101.

25. Albert Schweitzer, *Out of My Life and Thought: An Autobiography* (New York: Holt, 1933), 185, 188.

26. Albert Schweitzer, *Philosophy of Civilization: Civilization and Ethics,* trans. John Naish (London: A. and C. Black, 1923), 254; cited in Roderick F. Nash, "Aldo Leopold's Intellectual Heritage," in *Companion to a Sand County Almanac: Interpretive and Critical Essays,* ed. J. Baird Callicott (Madison: University of Wisconsin Press, 1987), 73.

27. Joseph R. Des Jardins, *Environmental Ethics: An Introduction to Environmental Philosophy* (Belmont, Calif.: Wadsworth, 1993), 151.

28. Des Jardins, *Environmental Ethics,* 150.

29. Some might argue that Schweitzer's ethic, a sort of "mystical holism," is more radical than a revision of classical virtue ethics permits, since it extends moral consideration

to all living beings. So interpreted, Schweitzer's ethic would be a "mixed reform and radical position."

30. Aldo Leopold, "The Land Ethic," in *A Sand County Almanac and Sketches Here and There* (New York: Oxford University Press, 1977), 204, 223, 224–25.

31. I argue in chapter 7 that this is not an exclusivist holism. That is, Leopold's commitment to holism does not rule out the importance of individuals.

32. Leopold, "Land Ethic," 209–10.

33. Leopold, "Land Ethic," 223, 225.

34. Arne Naess, "The Shallow and the Deep, Long-Range Ecology Movement: A Summary," *Inquiry* 16, no. 1 (1973), 95–100.

35. Bill Devall and George Sessions, *Deep Ecology: Living as if Nature Mattered* (Salt Lake City: Peregrine Smith Books, 1985).

36. Quoted in Devall and Sessions, *Deep Ecology,* 66.

37. Kirkpatrick Sale, *Dwellers in the Land: Bioregional Vision* (San Francisco: Sierra Club Books, 1985), 42.

38. Murray Bookchin, *The Modern Crisis* (Philadelphia: New Society Publishers, 1986), 16, 55.

39. Bookchin, *Modern Crisis,* 68.

40. Bookchin, *Modern Crisis,* 67.

41. See, e.g., *Environmental Ethics*. Special Issue on Asian Traditions as a Conceptual Resource for Environmental Ethics 8, no. 4 (Winter 1986); Russell Goodman, "Taoism and Ecology," *Environmental Ethics* 2, no. 1 (Spring 1980): 73–80; Po-Keung Ip, "Taoism and the Foundation of Environmental Ethics,"*Environmental Ethics* 5, no. 4 (Winter 1983): 335–44.

42. Thomas W. Overholt and J. Baird Callicott, *Clothed-in-Fur and Other Tales: An Introduction to an Ojibwa World View* (Washington, D.C.: University Press of America, 1982).

43. For an overview of Anglo-American attitudes, see Eugene Hargrove, *Foundations for Environmental Ethics* (Englewood Cliffs, N.J.: Prentice-Hall, 1989), 48–75.

44. Remark made by Dr. Chris MatoNunpa at St. Olaf College, November 4, 1999.

45. This expression was first used by Alison M. Jaggar in her book *Feminist Politics and Human Nature* (Totowa, N.J.: Rowman & Littlefield, 1983), 42.

46. I do not argue in this book for a second claim, that the version of ecofeminist philosophy I defend in this book is a transformative *feminism*. While I think that claim is also true, I have argued for it elsewhere (Karen J. Warren, "Feminism and Ecology: Making Connections," *Environmental Ethics* 9, no. 1 [Spring 1987], 3–20).

47. Warwick Fox, "The Deep Ecology-Ecofeminism Debate and Its Parallels," in *Environmental Philosophy,* 2nd edition, ed. Michael E. Zimmerman, J. Baird Callicott, George Sessions, Karen J. Warren, and John Clark (Upper Saddle River, N.J.: Prentice-Hall, 1998), 242, n. 22. Fox refers to my article, "The Power and the Promise of Ecological Feminism," *Environmental Ethics* 12, no. 2 (Summer 1990), 125–46.

sion of ecofeminist ethics I defend is properly understood, a universal ethic. I and

Chapter Five

Ethics in a Fruit Bowl

Ecofeminist Ethics

Uppermost in my mind in writing this chapter on ecofeminist ethics were two sorts of challenges that surface in discussions of ecofeminist ethics. The first challenge is from those who believe that a universal ethic is both possible and desirable. They worry that insofar as an ecofeminist ethic centralizes issues of cultural diversity and context, it must deny the possibility and desirability of a universal ethic. The second challenge is from those who claim that ecofeminist philosophy is at best a set of loosely organized claims, but that it is not a theory. As such, it does not generate a bona fide ethic.

In this chapter I defend ecofeminist philosophy against both objections. I offer my version of ecofeminist ethics as "care-sensitive ethics." I argue that the version of ecofeminist ethics I defend is, properly understood, a universal ethic. I end by clarifying why the version of ecofeminist philosophy I defend is a genuinely theoretical position that can be helpful in understanding resolving ethical issues in environmental contexts.

FEMINIST AND ECOFEMINIST ETHICS

A feminist ethic involves a twofold commitment: to critique male bias in ethics wherever it occurs and to develop ethics that are not male-biased. A feminist ethic also involves articulation of values (e.g., care) often lost or underplayed in mainstream ethics. What makes the critiques of old ethical theories or conceptualizations of new ones "feminist" is that they are provided through a critical lens of gender analysis and include perspectives of what I have been calling "other Others."

Sometimes differences among feminist ethicists are cast in terms of reform or revolution. All feminists agree that the virtual exclusion of women from the domain of intellectual pursuits has resulted in male-gender bias, which must be eliminated.[1] What feminists disagree about is whether that bias can be eliminated by reform alone, or whether some form of conceptual revolution is necessary. If reform alone is sufficient, then feminists need only reapply old theories in new or different ways to remedy any male-gender bias. The main foundation and frame of the traditional Western ethical house would remain intact. However, if male-gender bias is in some sense structural—built into the theory (or house) itself—then some form of conceptual revolution is necessary; changes in the application of a theory will not be sufficient to remedy the bias. It will take more than inte-rior decorating to eliminate the bias.

The reform or revolution issue arises as well within ecofeminist ethics. Whether ecofeminist ethics is described as a reform, radical, or mixed reform and radical strategy (to use the terminology introduced in chapter 4) depends partly on the stan-dard of comparison being used and partly on the version of ecofeminist ethics being defended. All ecofeminist ethics currently is "radical" vis-à-vis other positions in environmental ethics insofar as they are explicitly and self-consciously feminist. They break with any and all positions in environmental ethics that do not make crit-ical gendered analyses central to their methodology and theoretical analysis. But, a particular ecofeminist ethic may be a mixed reform and radical position, perhaps even simply a reform position (e.g., some ecofeminist animal welfarist positions, discussed in chapter 6), insofar as it relies on concepts and positions found in reformist theories (e.g., concepts of autonomy, respect, virtue, liberty, justice, rights, utility, and democracy). The version of ecofeminist ethics I defend in this book is, in this sense, a mixed reform and revolution position.

As feminist ethicists, all Western ecofeminist ethicists agree that one must engage in theory-building without reintroducing male-biased categories (wherever and whenever they occur). In ecofeminist philosophy, this requires the development of ethical positions that do not replicate the sort of thinking characteristic of oppressive, including patriarchal, conceptual frameworks (discussed in chapter 3).

The stakes are high. If the claims of ecofeminist ethicists are plausible, then a feminist debate over environmental issues is much deeper and more basic to both the feminist and environmental movements than traditional conceptions of femi-nist ethics and environmental ethics might have us believe. By making nature a feminist issue and human oppression (by gender, race/ethnicity, class, geographic location, etc.) an environmental issue, the theoretical adequacy of feminism and environmental ethics themselves are at stake.

KEY FEATURES OF AN ECOFEMINIST ETHIC

The version of ecofeminist ethics I defend is based on what I take to be eight key features ("necessary" or "boundary" conditions) of an ecofeminist ethic. The first feature I argued for in chapter 3: ethical theory is conceived as theory-in-process that will change over time. Like all theory, an ecofeminist ethic is based on some generalizations. But the generalizations associated with it are a pattern of voices, a mosaic or tapestry within which the different voices that emerge out of concrete and alternative descriptions of ethical situations have meaning. The coherence of a feminist theory is given within historical and conceptual contexts and within a set of basic beliefs, values, attitudes, and assumptions about the world.

The second condition is that nothing is part of an ecofeminist ethic—part of an ecofeminist quilt—that promotes sexism, racism, classism, naturism, or any other "ism of social domination." Of course, people may disagree about what counts as a sexist act, racist attitude, classist behavior, or naturist policy. Still, the boundary conditions specify that an ecofeminist ethic must be anti-sexist, anti-racist, anti-classist, anti-naturist, and opposed to any "ism" that presupposes or advances a logic of domination.

Third, an ecofeminist ethic is a contextualist ethic—one that sees ethical discourse and practice as emerging from the "voices" of entities located in different historical circumstances. As Margaret Walker points out, contextualism has two dimensions: that of the individual, with her or his own history and identity, and that of relationships, with their own history and identity. An ecofeminist ethic is a kind of narrative about humans, human-human relationships, and human-non-human animal or nature relationships. Walker states that "The two [dimensions] are linked by the notion of a narrative, of the location of human beings' feelings, psychological states, needs, and understandings as nodes of a story (or of the intersection of stories) that has already begun, and will continue beyond a given juncture of moral urgency:"[2]

> This intertwining of selves and stories in narrative constructions which locate what is at stake, what is needed, and what is possible is at the heart of moral thinking for many women and feminist writers. As many forms of intelligence as the understanding of such stories requires are at work in the competent moral agent, on this view.[3]

Conceived as a sort of narrative, a contextualized ethic is a shift from a monist focus on absolute rights and rules to a pluralist focus on various values, principles, narrative constructions and forms of intelligence. It provides "a highly contextual attempt to see clearly what a human being is and what the nonhuman world might be, morally speaking, for human beings."[4] For ecofeminist ethicists, *how* a moral agent is in relationship to another—and not simply the nature of the agent or "other," or the rights, duties, and rules that apply to the agent or "other"—is of central significance.

Fourth, an ecofeminist ethic is an inclusivist ethic that grows out of and reflects the diversity of perspectives of women and other Others. It emerges from the voices of those who experience disproportionately the harmful destruction of nonhuman nature. An ecofeminist ethic, therefore, presupposes and maintains difference—difference among humans as well as between humans and nonhuman animals and nature—while also recognizing commonalities among these groups. Ecofeminist philosophy denies the "nature/culture" split and the claim that humans are totally separate and different from nonhuman nature: it recognizes that humans, as ecological selves, are *both* members of an ecological community (in some respects) and different from other members of that community (in other respects). Accordingly, the attention of ecofeminist ethics to relationships and community is not an erasure of difference but a respectful acknowledgment of it.

This condition of inclusiveness does two things: It ensures that the diverse voices of members of oppressed or dominated groups are given central legitimacy in ethical theory building; and, it helps to minimize empirical bias by ensuring that generalizations about humans and nonhuman nature are good generalizations. In this respect, they must pass what I call the 4-R test of a good generalization: The samples on which a generalization is based must be *r*epresentative, *r*andom, the *r*ight size, and *r*eplicable. Biased generalizations arise in ethics in much the same way they arise in science (or other fields), from skewed samples (e.g., by using only data on men or males), faulty stereotyping (e.g., of women and other Others), too small a sample size (e.g., because it is not diverse), or research outcomes that are not replicable (e.g., observations and analyses that are not obtained by feminist researchers and scientists). By being inclusive, ecofeminist ethics helps minimize such empirical bias by ensuring that any generalizations that are made about ethics and ethical decision-making include the voices of women and other Others.[5]

Fifth, an ecofeminist ethic makes no attempt to provide an "objective" point of view, since it assumes that in contemporary culture there really is no such point of view. As such, it does not claim to be "unbiased" in the sense of "value-neutral" or "objective." (The issues of "objectivity" and "bias" are discussed in chapter 7.) However, it does assume that whatever bias it has as an ethic that centralizes the voices of oppressed persons is a better bias—"better" because more inclusive and therefore less partial—than those that exclude those voices.

Sixth, an ecofeminist ethic provides a central place for values typically unnoticed, underplayed, or misrepresented in traditional ethics (e.g., values of care, love, friendship, and appropriate trust). These are values that presuppose that our relationships to others are central to an understanding of who we are.[6] It need not do this at the exclusion of considerations of rights, rules, or utility. There may be many contexts in which talk of rights or of utility is useful and appropriate. For instance, in contexts of contracts or property relationships, talk of rights may be useful and appropriate. In deciding what is cost-effective or advantageous to the most people, talk of utility may be useful and appropriate. But in an ecofeminist ethic, whether or not such talk is useful or appropriate will depend partly on the context; other values (e.g., values of care, trust, friendship) are *not* viewed as reducible to, or captured solely in terms of, such talk.

Seventh, an ecofeminist ethic involves a reconception of what it is to be human and to engage in ethical decision-making, since it rejects as either meaningless or currently untenable any gender-free or gender-neutral description of humans, ethics, and ethical decision-making. Like much of feminist ethics, an ecofeminist ethic rejects what Alison Jaggar calls "abstract individualism," the position that it is possible to identify a human essence or human nature that exists independently of any particular historical context.[7] Humans and human moral conduct are understood as given essentially (and not merely accidentally) in terms of networks or webs of historical and concrete relationships.

Lastly, as I will show, an ecofeminist ethic also reconceives the traditional Western philosophical concept of reason. In that tradition (called "the rationalist tradition"), reason typically is defined in terms of mental faculties that permit one to entertain abstract, objective principles, to choose among competing courses of action, to develop a life-plan, or to choose the best means to a desired end. Historically, it is this notion of reason that has been the hallmark of humanness and that has accounted for the superiority of humans over nonhuman animals and nature. The version of ecofeminist ethics I defend challenges this notion of reason and the rationalist tradition. I suggest that we make intelligence, not reason (as historically understood in the Western tradition), the umbrella category for the kind of thinking that humans and (some) nonhuman animals engage in. "Rational intelligence" and "emotional intelligence" are then seen as two aspects of intelligence; ethical motivation, reasoning, and practice require that the two operate in concert.

Of course, in contemporary societies, which are thoroughly structured by gender, race/ethnicity, class and other forms of domination, no one can maintain anything like perfect adherence to an ecofeminist ethic. Wherever current institutional structures are patriarchal (and white racist, classist, or naturist), it is not possible to lead an ecologically perfect lifestyle. To assume otherwise is to mistakenly assume that individual behavior is in no way constrained by the historical and material realities of "isms of domination"—institutions, structures, policies, roles, offices, positions. Furthermore, individuals may perpetuate "isms of domination" unknowingly, unconsciously, unintentionally, and covertly. In both institutional and individual cases, it is often very difficult to bring instances of domination to the surface. Nonetheless, we should sincerely aim at eliminating these "isms of domination."

In this context, I am reminded of Marilyn Frye's wonderful metaphor of a birdcage. When one myopically looks at just one wire in the cage or at one wire at a time, it is hard to see how a bird could be inhibited or harmed in any but the most accidental way. Frye claims:

> It is only when you step back, stop looking at the wires one by one, microscopically, that you can see why the bird does not go anywhere; and then you will see it in a moment. It will require no great subtlety of mental powers. It is perfectly *obvious* that the bird is surrounded by a network of systematically related barriers, no one of which would be the least hindrance to its flight, but which, by their relations to each other, are as confining as the solid walls of a dungeon.[8]

Just as the wires of the birdcage limit the freedom of those in the cage, "isms of domination" limit the freedoms of at least Others within those systems, whether they know it or not. A main project of ecofeminist ethics is to make visible the wires of the birdcage and to work to eliminate them.

Doing that in the here-and-now, with imperfect knowledge and institutional constraints, means that we will make mistakes, including mistakes about what is or is not an example of an "ism of domination." Current theories, like quilts, will have "patches" that have frayed, tattered, and need to be replaced. Where theorizing is conceptualized like quilting, as theory-in-process, it is not a death-knell problem with a given ecofeminist theory that an "ism of domination" unknowingly becomes part of the present ecofeminist quilt, to be removed and replaced at a later date when the mistake is revealed. Such "mistakes" are simply a lovely and welcome part of the process of theorizing.

CLIMBING FROM FEMINIST ETHICS TO ECOFEMINIST ETHICS

Many feminists (not just ecofeminists) have argued for the relevance of narrative as a way of raising philosophically germane issues in ethics. Unlike more traditional approaches to ethics, a narrative approach contextualizes ethical discourse in ways that make relationships and beings-in-relationships central to ethics. The use of narrative can be more than just a helpful literary device for describing ineffable experience or a methodology for documenting personal and social history; it can be an invaluable vehicle for revealing what is ethically significant in human interactions with humans and the nonhuman world.

So it is that I now turn to a personal narrative I wrote in 1980, after my first rock climbing experience. It was through this experience, and my narrative attempts to capture what was personally and ethically significant for me then, that I realized the need for a different language than the traditional philosophical language of rights, rules, and duties:

> On my first day of rock climbing I chose a somewhat private spot, away from other climbers and on-lookers. After studying "the chimney," I focused all my energy on making it to the top. I climbed with intense determination, using whatever strength and skills I had to accomplish this challenging feat. By midway I was exhausted and anxious. I couldn't see what to do next—where to put my hands or feet. Growing increasingly more weary as I clung somewhat desperately to the rock, I made a move. It didn't work. I fell. There I was, dangling midair above the rocky ground below, frightened but terribly relieved that the belay rope had held me. I knew I was safe. I took a look up at the climb that remained. I was determined to make it to the top. With renewed confidence and concentration, I finished the climb to the top.
>
> On my second day of climbing, I rappelled down about 200 feet from the top of the Palisades at Lake Superior to just a few feet above the water level. I could see no one—not my belayer, not the other climbers, no one. I unhooked slowly from the rappel rope and took a deep cleansing breath. I looked all around me—really looked—and listened. I heard a cacophony of voices—birds, trickles of water on the rock before me, waves lapping against the rocks below. I closed my eyes and began

to feel the rock with my hands—the cracks and crannies, the raised lichen and mosses, the almost imperceptible nubs that might provide a resting place for my fingers and toes when I began to climb. At that moment I was bathed in serenity. I began to talk to the rock in an almost inaudible, child-like way, as if the rock were my friend. I felt an overwhelming sense of gratitude for what it offered me—a chance to know myself and the rock differently, to appreciate unforeseen miracles like the tiny flowers growing in the even tinier cracks in the rock's surface. I came to know a sense of myself as *being in relationship* with the natural environment. It felt as if the rock and I were silent conversational partners in a longstanding friendship. I realized then that I had come to *care about* this cliff which was so different from me, so unmovable and invincible, independent and seemingly indifferent to my presence. I wanted to be *with the rock* as I climbed. Gone was the fierce determination to conquer the rock, to forcefully impose my will on it; I wanted simply to work respectfully with the rock as I climbed. And as I climbed, that is what I felt. I felt myself *caring* about this rock and feeling thankful that climbing provided the opportunity for me to know it and myself in this new way.[9]

This narrative reflects just one person's experience. But since it was through critical reflection on this narrative that I personally began to appreciate the philosophical and ethical significance of narrative, I want to describe now four features of narrative that, through this experience and narrative, I came to see as philosophically significant.

First, narrative can give voice to a felt sensitivity, an emotional disposition, or an attitude, too often lacking in traditional analytic ethical discourse—a sensitivity to conceiving of oneself as fundamentally being in relationships with others, including the nonhuman natural world. Narrative is a modality that *takes relationships seriously*. It thereby stands in contrast to a strictly reductionist modality that takes relationships seriously only or primarily because of the nature of the *relators* or parties to those relationships (e.g., relators conceived as moral agents, right-holders, interest-carriers, or sentient beings). A climber's relationship with the rock is itself a locus of value, in addition to and independent of whatever moral status she or the rock may have.[10]

Second, narrative often gives expression to a variety of ethical attitudes and behaviors overlooked or underplayed in mainstream Western ethics (e.g., a difference in attitudes and behaviors toward a rock when one is "making it to the top" and when one thinks of oneself as "friends with" or "caring about" the rock one climbs). These different attitudes and behaviors suggest an ethically germane contrast between types of relationships humans may have toward a rock (e.g., that of a conqueror imposing her will on the externalized Other and that of a carer working with the internalized other).

The ability to express felt differences between conquering and caring attitudes in relation to the nonhuman natural environment provides a third reason why the use of narrative is important to ecofeminist ethics. Narrative provides a way of conceiving of ethics and ethical meaning as *emerging out of* particular situations moral agents find themselves in, rather than as being *imposed* on those situations as a derivation from some predetermined, abstract rule or principle. This emergent feature of narrative centralizes the importance of *voice*. When a multiplicity of cross-cultural voices is centralized, narrative is able to give expression to a range of attitudes, values, beliefs, and behaviors that may be overlooked or silenced by imposed ethical meaning and theory.

Lastly, the use of narrative has argumentative significance by suggesting *what counts* as an appropriate conclusion to an ethical situation. Jim Cheney calls attention to this feature of narrative when he claims, "To contextualize ethical deliberation is, in some sense, to provide a narrative or a story, from which the solution to the ethical dilemma emerges as the fitting conclusion."[11] Since I experienced both, my own narrative helped me realize that my conqueror attitude and attendant feelings were at odds with my ethical attitude toward mountains and rocks as deserving of respect and care.

Again, Marilyn Frye's work helped me appreciate the ethical significance of these two attitudes. In her essay, "In and Out of Harm's Way: Arrogance and Love," Frye contrasts "the arrogant eye" ("arrogant perception") with "the loving eye" ("loving perception") as one way of getting at this distinction in the ethical attitudes of care and conquest:

> The loving eye is a contrary of the arrogant eye.
>
> The loving eye knows the independence of the other. It is the eye of a seer who knows that nature is indifferent. It is the eye of one who knows that to know the seen, one must consult something other than one's own will and interests and fears and imagination. One must look at the thing. One must look and listen and check and question.
>
> The loving eye is one that pays a certain sort of attention. This attention can require a discipline but not a self-denial. The discipline is one of self-knowledge, knowledge of the scope and boundary of the self. . . . In particular, it is a matter of being able to tell one's own interests from those of others and of knowing where one's self leaves off and another begins.[12]

According to Frye, the loving eye "knows the complexity of the other as something that will forever present new things to be known." It is not an invasive, coercive eye that annexes others to itself.

When one climbs a rock as a conqueror, one climbs with an arrogant eye. When one climbs with a loving eye, one constantly "must look and listen and check and question." One recognizes the rock as something very different, something perhaps totally indifferent to one's own presence, and finds in that difference joyous cause for celebration. One knows "the boundary of the self," where the self (the climber) leaves off and the rock begins. There is no fusion of two into one, but a complement of two acknowledged as separate, different, independent, yet in relationship if only because I, the climber, am perceiving it, responding to it, noticing it, attending to it.

The ecofeminist ethic I defend involves this shift in attitude of humans toward the nonhuman world from arrogant perception to loving perception (or what I sometimes call "caring perception"). Arrogant perception of others presupposes and maintains *sameness* in such a way that it expands the moral community only to those beings who are thought to resemble (be like, similar to, or the same as) "us" in some morally significant way. An ethic based on arrogant perception thereby builds a moral hierarchy of beings and assumes some common denominator of moral considerability by virtue of which like beings deserve similar treatment or moral consideration and unlike beings do not. Such an ethic generates a "unity in sameness" position.

In contrast, loving (or caring) perception presupposes and maintains difference—a distinction between the self and other, between human and at least some nonhumans and nature—in such a way that it is an expression of care about the other who/that is recognized at the outset as independent, dissimilar, different. As Maria Lugones says, in loving perception, "Love is seen not as fusion and erasure of difference but as incompatible with them."[13] "Unity in sameness" is an erasure of difference.

An attitude of loving perception of the nonhuman natural world raises issues about what it means for humans to care about the nonhuman world, a world acknowledged as being independent, different, perhaps even indifferent to humans. Humans *are* different from rocks in important ways, even if they are also both members of a shared or common ecological community. A moral community based on loving perception of oneself in relationship with a rock is one that acknowledges and respects difference, in addition to whatever sameness or commonality also exists.[14] The limits of loving perception are determined only by the limits of one's (e.g., a person's, a community's) ability to care—whether it is care about other humans or about the nonhuman world and elements of it.[15]

If what I have said so far is correct, then not only are there very different ways to climb a mountain; how one climbs it and how one narrates the experience of climbing it matter ethically. If one climbs with arrogant perception, with an attitude of "conquer and control," one keeps intact the very sorts of thinking that characterize a logic of domination and an oppressive conceptual framework. Since (as I argued in chapter 3) the oppressive conceptual framework that sanctions the domination of nature is a patriarchal one, one also thereby keeps intact, even if unwittingly, a patriarchal conceptual framework. Because the dismantling of patriarchal conceptual frameworks is a feminist issue, *how* one climbs a mountain and *how* one tells the story about the experience of climbing also are feminist issues.

THE "JUSTICE VERSUS CARE" DEBATE IN ETHICS

For me, the climbing narrative began my process of wondering whether appeals to traditional philosophical theories about absolute and universal rights, duties, rules, and principles are the best way to engage in ethics. Many ecofeminists, like many feminists, have expressed serious worries about the ability of traditional ethical theories to give expression to or capture the full range of relevant ethical issues. Such worries are at the core of the so-called justice versus care debate in feminist ethics.

Typically, the "justice versus care" debate has centered on two distinct perspectives in moral reasoning and practice, the "justice" and "care" perspectives. The justice perspective assesses moral conduct in terms of the basic rights and duties of relevant parties (e.g., right to life, duty to tell the truth or keep one's promises) or governing moral rules or principles (e.g., one ought to always treat persons with respect, one ought to do whatever maximizes utility). From a justice perspective, a moral agent is viewed as a rational, detached, disinterested, impartial, independent being; morality is viewed as a matter of relevant rights, rules, or principles; and moral conflict resolution is adjudicated by appeal to the most basic right, rule, or principle.[16] The ethical framework is essentially hierarchical or pyramidal, where the "authority" of a right, rule, or principle is given from the top of a hierarchy. Appeal to rights or duties, rules or principles provides a universalizable ethical decision-making procedure for resolving conflicts among individuals or groups of individuals. As a model of conflict resolution, it is primarily adversarial, based on a win-lose, zero sum model of conflict.

In contrast, the care perspective assesses moral conduct in terms of such values as care, friendship, and appropriate trust, which are not themselves reducible to a consideration of rights or rules. Selves are conceived as relational, embedded, partial, attached, interdependent, and historically situated. Morality is a matter of values, virtues, and vices, which are not unpacked in terms of hierarchically ordered, ahistorical principles of justice. Differences between these two ethical perspectives as methods of conflict resolution might be visualized as in diagram 5.1.

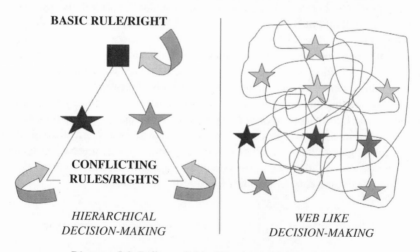

BASIC RULE/RIGHT

CONFLICTING RULES/RIGHTS

HIERARCHICAL DECISION-MAKING

WEB LIKE DECISION-MAKING

Diagram 5.1. Different Ethical Decision-Making Strategies

Feminist ethicists who offer a care perspective typically argue for an ethic of care. An ethic of care offers six types of criticisms of a traditional justice perspective (or ethic of justice): (1) it is based on a faulty conception of selves as atomistic individuals, rather than as beings-in-relationships; (2) it preserves a mistaken or limited concept of morality as fundamentally a matter of absolute and universal rights, rules, and principles; (3) it assumes that moral conflict resolution is always about adjudicating competing interests, rights, or rules of independent moral agents in a hierarchical, adversarial, winner-loser way; (4) it fails to appreciate the extent to which other values, particularly values of care, enter into actual decision-making of actual women (and others) confronted with genuinely morally ambiguous situations; (5) it misrepresents morality as nonambiguous, simplified, and abstract, when, for most of us, it is ambiguous, complex, and concrete; (6) its methodology tends to reproduce the status quo, entrenching existing power and authority relations by methodologically concealing those relations.

Consider the last point, (6), in more detail. Kathryn Pyne Addelson objects to the justice tradition on the grounds that it does not adequately address or remedy an important sort of bias that infects traditional ethics. Addelson argues that by representing the moral situation in a value-hierarchical way, the justice tradition conceals the fact that in contemporary society the point of view from the top of the hierarchy functions as an invisible, unmarked, and privileged point of view. A philosopher is a philosopher unless she is a feminist; then she is a feminist philosopher. Philosophy is philosophy, and ethics is ethics until critiqued by feminists (and others) who insist on marking each with an appropriate prefix; then philosophy is "dominant Western philosophy" and ethics is "dominant Western philosophical ethics." Neither is, as traditional philosophers have assumed, an ungendered, unraced, or unclassed tradition.

According to Addelson, the justice tradition maintains this historical bias by allowing "moral problems to be defined from the tops of various hierarchies of authority in such a way that the existence of the authority is concealed, and so the existence of alternative definitions that might challenge that authority and radically change our social organization is also concealed."[17] Addelson argues that the "authority" is given by the perspective of traditional academic philosophers who systematically ignore discussions of hierarchy, dominance, and subordination, which are so central to the point of view of those in subordinate positions in their moral decision-making. As such, relationships of power and subordination, so central to feminist discussions of morality, are invisible, go underground, or become a nonissue. The justice tradition does not adequately capture the point of view of those on the bottom of various Up-Down hierarchies.

CARE-SENSITIVE ETHICS

The scholarly literature on an ethic of care is extensive. While I do not discuss that literature here, the ecofeminist ethic I defend builds on it in key respects. In particular, it agrees with the six main criticisms care ethicists make of "the justice perspective" (identified by criticisms 1–6 above). Unlike most care ethicists, however, the care-sensitive ethics I defend in this chapter is *not* an "ethic of care."

I do *not* locate the moral significance of care in a separate ethic—an ethic of care—which (allegedly) contrasts or competes with, or is integrated with, an ethic of justice. Instead, I locate the moral significance of care in three features of what I call "care-sensitive ethics." First, an essential aspect of moral reasoning and moral motivation is the ability to care about oneself and others. I call this the "ability-to-care" condition. Second, the universality of ethical principles is as "situated universals," in contrast to the traditional notion of "universals" as ahistorical, transcendent, absolute universals. I call this the condition of "situated universalism." Third, the appropriateness or suitability of any ethical principle or practice in a given context is determined, at least in part, by considerations of care. I call this the "care practices" condition. I argue that care-sensitive ethics honors traditional values such as utility, self-interest, duty, and rights, as morally salient, even if not overriding, features of ethical situations.

To provide an image of what I am arguing, consider a fruit bowl full of lots of kinds of fruit (e.g., apples, oranges, bananas, mangoes, pineapples, tangerines, blueberries). All and only fruits (e.g., not books, shoes, vegetables) are appropriate candidates for the fruit bowl *as* fruit bowl. Which particular fruit is selected from the fruit bowl as the most appropriate or best suited fruit for a particular situation depends on that situation. If one is baking a banana cream pie, bananas are best-suited; if one is going backpacking or fixing an apple pie, apples are better. It is not that one fruit is better than the others in some abstract sense. It is just that one fruit (or several fruits) may be better than others in the circumstances.

The ecofeminist ethics I defend is like a fruit bowl with different kinds of fruit. Different ethical principles in Western philosophy (e.g., principles of self-

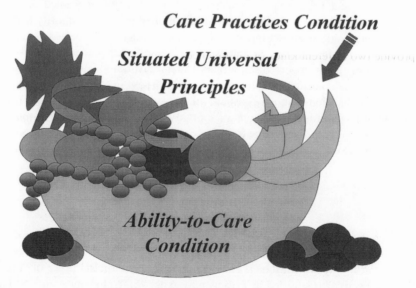

Diagram 5.2. Care-Sensitive Ethics

interest, utility, duty, rights, or virtue) are candidate fruits in the fruit bowl. Whether any candidate ethical principle really qualifies as a bona fide ethical position—gets into the fruit bowl—turns on whether it meets the first two conditions of care-sensitive ethics. As I will show, an ethical principle that does not make any room for emotional intelligence, particularly the importance of caring about oneself and others, in ethical reasoning and conduct will not qualify; it fails the ability to care condition. Nor would a traditional monist ethical principle that posits the primacy of one moral value and reduces all other moral values to this one primary value; it fails the condition of situated universalism. Whether any ethical principle in the fruit bowl is morally appropriate in a given context will depend on whether application of the principle satisfies the care practices condition.

I turn now to a consideration of each of these three features of care-sensitive ethics.

The Ability to Care

In his 1995 book *Emotional Intelligence,* psychologist Daniel Goleman presents scientific research to support a view of intelligence "in terms of what it takes to lead life successfully."[18] According to Goleman, there are two minds or brains, "one that thinks and one that feels": rational minds ("reason") and emotional minds ("emotion"). Goleman's thesis is not Cartesian mind-body dualism. Rather, Goleman is claiming that the anatomical centers for reason and emotion are located in different, though connected, parts of the brain. The neocortex is the seat of logic, reflection, and what is traditionally referred to as reason or rationality. The limbic system, comprised of the hippocampus and amygdala, is the seat of memory and emotions. According to Goleman, the rational mind and emotional mind provide very different, though intertwined, ways of knowing; they provide two different kinds of intelligences.

Goleman claims that "emotional intelligence"—both the sense in which there is intelligence *in* the emotions and the sense in which intelligence can be brought *to* the emotions—is what maintains an appropriate balance between the two "minds." Emotional intelligence recognizes that emotions matter for rationality. According to Goleman's research, "The intellect (rational mind) simply cannot work effectively without emotional intelligence"; what we do and ought to do in life is determined by both.[19]

Goleman's scientific case for the importance of emotional intelligence to ethics and ethical decision-making is illustrated clearly by the case of Elliot. Elliot underwent successful surgery for the removal of a brain tumor. However, afterward, those who knew him said he was no longer Elliot, that a drastic personality change had occurred. To use Goleman's language, after surgery Elliot's rational intelligence was as sharp as ever, but his emotional intelligence was seriously impaired. Elliot's neurologist, Dr. Antonio Damasio, wondered whether the severing of ties between the lower centers of Elliot's emotional brain, especially

the amygdala and related circuits, during the surgery could account for this personality change. Goleman states:

> [Dr. Damasio was] struck by one element missing from Elliot's mental repertoire:
> though nothing was wrong with his logic, memory, attention, or any other cognitive abil-
> ity, Elliot was virtually oblivious to his feelings about what had happened to him. . . .
> [His] thinking had become computerlike, able to make every step in the calculus of a
> decision, but unable to assign *values* to differing possibilities. Every option was neutral.
> And that overtly dispassionate reasoning . . . was the core of Elliot's problem: too little
> awareness of his own feeling about things made Elliot's reasoning faulty.[20]

Dr. Damasio found that Elliot remained capable of "dispassionate reasoning,"
since his rational mind was fully intact. That is, Elliot's rational intelligence
was fine. In fact, on many versions of classical liberal moral theory (e.g.,
Kantian), Elliot-after-surgery seems to instantiate the (Kantian) ideal of the
rational, impartial, detached observer! But Elliot's emotional intelligence was
seriously debilitated: Without the ability to feel or to care about any of the
options available to him, Elliot was incapable of moral reasoning. Elliot's case
suggests what Goleman explicitly argues for, namely, that the absence of emotional intelligence does not just produce bad or faulty moral reasoning; it pro-
duces no moral reasoning at all.

So, if the research of Goleman and others on human brain functioning is correct or even plausible, then reason without emotion—rational intelligence without emotional intelligence—is inadequate for ethics, ethical decision-making,
and ethical practice. What is necessary is emotional intelligence, of which the
ability to care about oneself and others is one of the basic skills.

The ability to care is not simply an amorphous feeling, a "*caring for*" something. One may or may not have any feelings for the one cared about ("the
cared-about")."*Caring about*" another is the expression of a cognitive capacity, an attitude toward the cared-about as deserving respectful treatment,
whether or not one has any particular positive feelings for the cared-about.
(More is said about the notion of care in chapters 6, 8, and 9.) Furthermore, the
ability to care about oneself or another is not simply an add-on feature of ethical deliberation; it is an element of emotional intelligence presupposed by it.
Without this ability—the case of Elliot—one is not motivated to act morally or
to engage in moral reasoning at all.

My basic argument for the ability-to-care condition as a necessary condition of
any care-sensitive ethic can now be stated formally as follows: (1) The ability to
care about oneself and others is (where the limbic system is intact) physically
possible, causally necessary, and in practice desirable for moral motivation and
reasoning. But, (2) if having a certain ability is physically possible, causally necessary, and in practice desirable for moral motivation and reasoning, then this
ability must be included as part of any adequate ethic. Thus, (3) the ability to care
must be included as part of any adequate ethic.

Implications of Emotional Intelligence for Ethics

The implications for ethics of research into emotional intelligence are significant. First, this research shows that the rationalist philosophical tradition that separates reason from emotion, elevates reason to a higher status than emotion, and predicates ethics, ethical knowledge, and ethical action on dictates of reason unencumbered by emotion is mistaken. Goleman himself makes this implication explicit:

> This [the interaction of rational and emotional intelligence] turns the old understanding of the tension between reason and feeling on its head: it is not that we want to do away with emotion and put reason in its place . . . but instead find the intelligent balance of the two. The old paradigm held an ideal of reason freed of the pull of emotion. The new paradigm urges us to harmonize head and heart.[21]

Both emotional intelligence and rational intelligence are needed for moral reasoning and decision-making. Goleman's work on emotional intelligence shows that empathy and care are crucial, at least psychologically, to effective moral reasoning. The requirement that any ethic be care-sensitive both acknowledges and ensures that an appropriate ethic is based in human psychology.

Second, Goleman's data provides scientific support for many of the claims of feminist care ethicists who insist on the importance of emotions, particularly care, to ethics. Care is no longer a "dumb emotion."[22] It is a moral emotion—an emotion crucially relevant to ethical motivation and decision-making. According to Goleman's research, the ability to empathize through care is part of what it *means* to have emotional intelligence.

Third, Goleman's work on emotional intelligence substantiates the claims of feminist care ethicists that an ethic must be based in human psychology.[23] As Rita Manning argues, "if an ethic is seen as providing guidance for living a good human life, then we must recognize important features of human psychology— the attachments of humans to other humans. . . . An ethic of care takes [human psychology] as central."[24] Emotions matter for rationality. What we psychologically can do and what we morally ought to do in life are both given by the interworkings of emotional and rational intelligence in concert. The case of Elliot is important because it shows what happens when emotional intelligence is lacking. One reason care is desirable, then, is that moral motivation for acting and ethical reasoning are not possible without it. The ability to care about oneself and others is a necessary (but not sufficient) condition of moral motivation and reasoning.

A time-honored philosophical issue that might arise at this point is whether one can derive the claim that one ought to care from the empirical claim that one can, in fact, care. This is the infamous "is-ought controversy" in traditional ethics: Can one derive ethical ("ought") claims from only factual ("is") premises? Does the is-ought controversy arise here?

I think the answer is no. Neither a defense of care-sensitive ethics generally nor a defense of the ability-to-care condition in particular is a defense of some supreme, absolute, moral principle of care. As such, neither is an attempt to derive an ethical principle, "One ought to care," from a factual claim, "One is able to care." Furthermore, neither is a defense of a separate "ethic of care." In fact, I am suggesting that attempts to capture the moral significance of care by defending a separate "ethic of care" (in contrast with an "ethics of justice") is the wrong way to proceed in valuing care. As such, the relevant questions are *not* (as they might be for an "ethic of care"): What are the ethical principles of care? Is an ethic of care compatible with an ethic of justice? Is an ethic of justice presupposed by an ethic of care? Rather, the relevant questions are about care as a crucial aspect of moral motivation, moral reasoning, and moral practices.

Whatever worries about the is-ought controversy arise do so because of a confusion about two distinct issues. One issue is about the ability to care as a necessary condition for moral motivation and moral reasoning. This issue concerns the ability-to-care condition. The other issue is about care as a criterion for assessing the appropriateness of any given ethical principle in a given context. This issue concerns the "care practices" condition. These are separate issues. No attempt is made here to logically derive one from the other.

This leads to a fourth point about the significance of the research Goleman documents: It suggests a unique answer to the question Why care? As a mistaken request for some more basic, foundational, principle in which to ground care, the question Why should I or anyone care? is somewhat like the question Why be moral? One can appeal to traditional ethical theories for any number of answers to both questions: One ought to care (or be moral) because self-interest requires it. Or, one ought to care (or be moral) because utility requires it, or duty requires it, or rights, justice, virtue, or the Golden Rule require it. But, as A. I. Melden pointed out with regard to the question Why should I be moral?,[25] none of these answers will satisfy one who does not accept moral reasons as bona fide reasons. So, if the question Why care? is understood as like the question Why be moral?—that is, as seeking some foundational principle in the traditional philosophical sense—there is no answer that will satisfy one who does not accept moral reasons as bona fide reasons.

But something else is going on with appeals to care—something quite different from the traditional Why be moral? question. This "something else" suggests that one should not treat Why should I (or anyone) care? as analogous to Why should I (or anyone) be moral? The ability to care (and emotional intelligence generally) is necessary (psychologically, physically, and causally) for moral reasoning. Without it, one would be like Elliot. So, unlike possible answers to the question Why be moral?, the question Why care? can be answered in a nonquestion begging way: One should care because one cannot reason morally, be motivated to act morally, choose to act morally, or value certain practices as moral and others as immoral or amoral—*unless one has emotional intelligence*—or, as I am expressing it, *unless one cares*. The ability and necessity of care are part of what it means to be a moral agent, moral reasoner, moral decision-maker that is not grounded in or derived from some more fundamental value (e.g., a value of utility, duty, rights, or virtue).[26]

As a fifth and last point, Goleman's research substantiates the claims of many feminists that care practices are gender-sensitive because of the historical association of care with females. The exclusion of the significance of care and care practices from traditional, canonical Western philosophy, then, is a serious omission. As Peta Bowden states:

> Currently the dominant tradition is focused primarily on the obligations owed universally and impartially in the kinds of relations that are typically associated with men. Given this focus, gender sensitivity requires an equal stress on the ethical implications of the special and 'partial' relations in which women are characteristically involved.[27]

Historically, practices of care have been associated with mothering, nursing, and friendship. Taking care and caring practices seriously for morality suggests "some promise of providing a gender-sensitive corrective to conventional moral theories."[28] Since all feminist ethicists (and not just care ethicists) want to expose male-gender bias in ethical theorizing and to offer, in their place, theories or positions which are not male-gender biased, taking care seriously as a moral value promises to provide such a corrective.

Situated Universalism

Why is it that one can watch a theatrical production of *Oedipus Rex*, *Hamlet*, or *Death of a Salesman*, plays written in historical time periods spanning roughly 2,000 years, and yet in some sense "identify" with the play? Or, listen to Australian aboriginal music played on a didgeridoo, a Celtic harp sonata, and a Louis Armstrong jazz composition and find personal meaning in each? Or, be moved to care about rainforests in Brazil, deforestation in India, or endangered condors in North America when one lives in Australia?

I think the prephilosophical answer is obvious and correct: There is something we bring to the situation that we have in common with others and something in the situation to which we, across cultures, resonate. This is sometimes put in ordinary language by saying that there are *universal* truths (themes, emotions, principles) expressed by these culturally specific practices.

Struck by the profound simplicity and truth of this prephilosophical answer, I have come to believe that there are universal ethical principles, but that this universality does not consist in their being abstract, ahistorical, transcendental, essentialist principles arrived at through reason alone. Rather, I think this *universality lies in particularity*—the guiding principle of "situated universalism." The common themes or emotions any of us experiences as audience participants to a Greek tragedy, Shakespearean drama, or Arthur Miller "common man" play arise out of, and are possible because of, our own particular contexts. It is in particular, concrete, felt, lived experiences and understandings of tragedy that "universal" themes (truths) are located, and it is through "universal" themes (truths) that we make sense of and understand particular situations and experiences. The underlying assumption of situated universalism is that every situation and every theory carries with it a social world.

The same can be said about care. To care about and understand the particular identities of persons who are struggling with race, gender, and class issues we must recognize and have some level of understanding of race, gender, and class as general features of contemporary social structures; similarly, to care about and understand such general issues as racism, sexism, and classism we must recognize and understand how they exist in particular people's lives and experiences. The particular and the general presuppose each other: We see the general in the particular, and we see the particular in the general. Again, this is the underlying assumption of situated universalism.

According to situated universalism, the "universality" of ethical principles like "One ought not cause unnecessary pain and suffering" lies in a social world where unnecessary pain and suffering are thought to be bad and avoidable, where notions of pain and suffering are accepted by a given community, where there is shared agreement among members of a given community about the domain in which the principle applies. Situated universalism thereby rejects the view that the universality of ethical principles is given in terms of some transcendental, abstract principles arrived at through reason alone, which captures some "essence" of right and wrong conduct that is binding on all people in all historical time periods under all socioeconomic conditions.

Furthermore, according to situated universalism, even if there are universal principles in this traditional sense (i.e., abstract, ahistorical, rational principles), predicating ethics on them would be viewed as missing much of the point of what ethics is and should be about. Ethics is not about what is rationally and morally permitted or required for any and all human beings in all contexts in accordance with some abstract principles. Ethics is not about what detached, impersonal, objective, rational agents engaged in grand theorizing deduce.[29] Rather, ethics is and should be about what imperfect human beings living in particular historical, socioeconomic contexts can and should do, given those contexts.

Having said all this, it does not follow from the claim that there are no, or no currently knowable, or no desirable, universal principles in the traditional sense of universal principles, that there are no universals and no ethical principles. Where "universal principles" are understood as guidelines—rules of thumb, useful generalizations, heuristic devices that are always morally relevant, even if not actually morally well suited to a given context—there are universal ethical principles. They are *situated universals*. They are "situated" in that they grow out of and reflect historically particular, real-life experiences and practices; they are "universal" in that they express generalizations common to and reflective of lives of diverse peoples situated in different historical circumstances.

If universal principles of ethics are situated, how is an ethic possible? An ethic in the traditional sense of a set of necessary and sufficient conditions for right conduct or a good life either is not possible or, if possible, not desirable. But this is as it should be: Real moral life situations, even the favored traditional philosophical situations involving truth-telling, promising, and contracts, are seldom, if ever, clear-cut. They are ambiguous and conflicting, and moral decision-making often involves equally strong, competing, and compelling values and reasons for acting one way or another. If a philosophical ethic is to be useful to and reflective of real-life decision-making, it must be flexible enough to account for the ethical ambiguities of real moral life, while providing guideline principles for resolving real moral conflicts. This is the underlying good sense of situated universalism.

In rejecting universal principles in the traditional sense, am I thereby rejecting principles of justice, or duty, or utility, or rights? No, not at all. What I am rejecting is ethical monism and its assumption of one and only one absolute (in the sense of nonoverridable) moral principle. Acceptance of situated universalism requires that traditional Western ethical principles of justice, duty, utility, or rights be understood as *situated* appeals and responses to the values named by those principles. Values of justice, duty, utility, or rights are still important in many moral contexts and deserve a key place in moral deliberations. But the principles these values find expression in are understood as situated universals—principles that are always relevant, even if not overriding, to understanding and resolving ethical disputes. They are like various fruits in a fruit bowl: They belong there; they have a place there; but none has priority as a principle over any other, independent of a given ethical context.

Care Practices

So far I have argued for two of the three features of care-sensitive ethics. I have argued for the ethical significance of the ability to care and for an understanding of ethical principles as situated universals. The last issue to address is how one chooses among competing ethical principles. I propose it is by determining which principle(s), when applied, reflects, creates, or maintains "care practices"—the third condition of care-sensitive ethics.

Care practices are practices that either maintain, promote, or enhance the health (well-being, flourishing) of relevant parties, or at least do not cause unnecessary harm to the health (well-being, flourishing) of relevant parties. The care-practices condition functions as a situated universal principle for choosing among ethical principles (in the fruit bowl) and for helping resolve moral conflicts.

Since situated universalism presupposes an intimate connection between the particular and the general, the care-practices condition, as a situated universal principle, also presupposes an intimate connection between the particular and the general. To care about and understand the particular identities of persons who, like the female characters in Ntozake Shange's *For Colored Girls Who Have Considered Suicide When the Rainbow Is Enuf,* struggle with race, gender, and class issues, we must recognize and have some level of understanding of race, gender, and class as general features of contemporary social structures. Conversely, to care about and understand general structural features of race, gender, and class with which these characters struggle, we must recognize and understand how they exist in particular people's lives and experiences. In this way, care practices "are possible and gain their meaning from social structures," and understanding social structures "requires recognizing their operation in particular situations and experiences."[30]

Consider another example. To care about condors in North America, rainforests in Brazil, and wild dolphins in Key West, Florida, we must have some level of understanding of the social meanings assigned to these "earth others" (even if, as is the case with children, this may be a limited, though developmentally appropriate, understanding). Conversely, to care about social meanings or structures that function to exploit or destroy natural environments we must have some level of understanding of their operation in particular cases of endangered species, deforestation, and harmful domestication of wild mammals. As a situated universal, the care-practices condition recognizes and evaluates the general through the particular and the particular through the general. In this way, the health (well-being, flourishing) of the particular is viewed as intimately connected with the health (well-being, flourishing) of the general. (This theme is threaded throughout the remaining chapters of the book.)

For now, I leave open what constitutes the care and health (well-being, flourishing) of selves and others. But the following are some examples of the sorts of concerns I have in mind: Those practices that oppress, torture, or exploit selves or morally relevant others are not genuine care practices. Those practices that violate the civil rights of selves and relevant others are not care practices. Those practices that cause unnecessary and avoidable harm to selves and relevant others (e.g., destruction of the stability, diversity, and sustainability of first peoples' cultures or natural ecosystems such as rainforests, oak savannahs, and fragile deserts) are not genuine care practices. Whether a principle of rights, utility, duty, or some other principle is the best or most appropriate principle for unpacking relevant moral prohibitions, obligations, or responsibilities in environmental situations will turn on the extent to which implementation of these situated universal principles promotes or reflects care practices.

Use of a practices condition for choosing among alternative, perhaps competing, principles and for assessing human conduct reinforces the view that the main function and serviceability of an ethical principle is to help guide the decision-making and actions of real people, in actual social and material realities, in the prefeminist present. Theory-making is not just an exercise in logic, and good theories are not just those that have logical consistency. By making the practices condition one of care, the importance of care to moral deliberation, action, and theory is highlighted.

But there are additional advantages of a care-practices condition that help clarify and resolve often overlooked characteristics of moral conflict. I cite six here.

First, some moral conflicts run contrary to general patterns.[31] As a general pattern, it may be that one should do what is just. But on traditional notions of justice, acting on the basis of care may not always be just. (I discuss this issue extensively in chapter 8.) For example, saving one's own child from drowning when another child is also drowning and where one cannot save both, on the basis of preferential care for one's own child, may conflict with a justice of fairness or impartiality or an equal right to life position. Nonetheless, it may be the right thing to do. The care-practices condition can accommodate both general patterns and specific exceptions (e.g., giving preference to one's own child rather than acting as a disinterested observer) without privileging either the general or specific to the exclusion of the other. This is because both care-sensitive ethics in general and the care-practices condition in particular do not predetermine which values are most appropriate in a given context.

Second, some conflicts can be understood and resolved by appeal to traditional principles *recast* as situated universals (e.g., nonreductionist principles of rights or utility that genuinely belong in the fruit bowl). A care-practices condition captures this. However, other conflicts cannot, and ought not, be so resolved. In cases where inclusive solutions cannot be found, conflict-resolution strategies of compromise, negotiation, and consensus must be used. The care-practices condition provides a way of deciding which strategy of conflict resolution to pursue in a given case: The most fitting strategy is one that either maintains, promotes, enhances the health (well-being, flourishing) of relevant parties, or at least does not cause unnecessary harm to their health (well-being, flourishing). Sometimes the most suitable conflict resolution strategy will be found by weighing alternative, situated universal principles in a hierarchical, adversarial, win-lose way; sometimes it will not.

Third, some conflicts are the result of symbolic and institutional structures. One reason a traditional monist principle may fail in a given case is that it may be ill-suited to moral conflicts that are the result of defective institutions and structures. Consider, for example, ethical decision-making structures that dichotomize lying and truth-telling, reason and emotion, care and justice. In such structures, conflicts are "*defined* in opposition to one another, and thus *necessarily* conflict."[32] Hierarchical conflict-resolution strategies may work well when a moral conflict *is* genuinely oppositional. But when it is not, one may need to challenge the decision-making *structures themselves*, and not simply the decisions and portrayals of moral conflict made *within* those structures (an issue addressed further in chapter 8).

Consider an example. The ethical dispute over old-growth forests is often presented (for example, in the media) as an exclusivist either-or issue of "loggers versus tree huggers." Such portrayals simplistically reduce a complex issue—the destruction of old-growth forests—to an exclusivist, oppositional, either-or dualism—"tree huggers" versus "loggers." The care-practices condition not only helps one understand and resolve both those conflicts that do, and those that do not, fit the oppositional, dualistic model; it also challenges the very models that construct ethical conflicts in terms of oppositional dualisms. In such cases, it may be the symbolic and structural features of the model itself that are at issue.

Fourth, some conflicts are gender sensitive. Since care practices historically have been associated with women, females, and "feminine" traits, the care-practices condition has the potential, in any given case, to honor both the contexts in which care is a primary value (e.g., friendship, parenting, nursing) and the lives, labor, and voices of women care-practitioners. It does so to the extent that it does not itself reinforce oppressive gender stereotypes and institutional structures.

Fifth, not all conflict is rationally resolvable without loss of value. Even resolution of those conflicts traditional Western philosophers focus on (e.g., truth-telling, promise-keeping, conflicts of rights) often involve a loss of important values (e.g., values involved in betraying a friend or grieving a loss). For example, sometimes "pro-choice" women who have abortions grieve their decisions, even though they believe the decision to be the right one and can provide rationally defensible justifications for abortion. This grieving is ethically (and not simply psychologically) important. It indicates that, for the woman, something deemed valuable or worthwhile is lost, forfeited, or otherwise not realized. Emotional intelligence is crucial to recognizing and understanding the importance of these lost, forfeited, or unrealized values. The care-practices condition provides a vehicle for doing this: it provides a way for looking at a range of issues relevant to understanding and resolving moral conflict, in a way that rational intelligence and traditional reason alone do not.

Lastly, as Clement argues, "it is a mistake to limit morality to conflict resolution."[33] The care-practices condition can be useful in preventing conflicts by necessitating that one look at local, historical realities relevant to a moral situation. Monistic and reductionist ethical principles, in effect, predetermine the morally basic considerations before actual moral situations arise. Before one knows any details about a moral situation or conflict, rights-based theories make a moral conflict an issue of rights, utilitarian theories make it an issue of utility, and so on. Such traditional monist ethical principles are often unhelpful in unpacking the moral dimensions of diverse moral situations, especially situations involving contextual consideration of care, *before* the situation or conflict arises. The care-practices condition permits flexibility about what the morally relevant variables in a potential conflict situation are, and requires familiarity with local situations in resolving moral conflicts.

ECOFEMINIST ETHICS AS A GENUINELY THEORETICAL POSITION

I end this chapter by addressing the second sort of worry about the nature and plausibility of ecofeminist moral philosophy with which I began this chapter: ecofeminist philosophy is not a theory. For example, J. Baird Callicott dismisses ecofeminist moral philosophy on the grounds that is not a theory and, hence, not an ethical theory. Callicott's view is that "ecofeminism necessarily eschews ethical theory."[34] Since this is a strong indictment of ecofeminist philosophy, it is important to consider his reasons. Callicott argues:

> There is no specific ecofeminist moral philosophy grounding a specific ecofeminist environmental ethic, identifiable as such through its particular theory of intrinsic value in or rights for nature, criterion of moral considerability, golden rule, set of commandments, or any of the other elements that we usually associate with ethics. . . .
>
> This is not because ecofeminism is so new that it has not yet attained theoretical maturity. This is rather because such elements are allegedly masculinist, not feminist, in essence. Feminist ethical writings, according to Warren, are irreducibly "contextual, . . . pluralistic, . . . not 'objective,'. . . particular, . . . and concrete." As a movement, ecofeminism is like a patchwork quilt ["Power and Promise," 139–41]. There is no governing design.[35]

According to Callicott, then, ecofeminism is not an ethical theory since it omits all necessary elements of an ethical theory: it lacks a "theory of intrinsic value in or rights for nature, criterion of moral considerability, golden rule, set of commandments, or any of the other elements that we usually associate with ethics." In fact, ecofeminism is anti-theory, since it views theory-building as a "masculinist" project. Callicott then goes beyond ethics to characterize ecofeminism as both anti-science and anti-reason.[36]

I think the views Callicott offers are mistaken. They are fundamentally at odds with what I have argued so far: I have argued (in chapter 3) for a conception of ecofeminist philosophy as a theoretical position. I have argued (also in chapter 3) for a conception of theorizing as quilting and a conception of theory as providing only necessary conditions—not both necessary and sufficient conditions—that give the quilt "an overall design." I have argued (in chapter 4) that an ecofeminist ethic is not grounded in either a notion of intrinsic value or a proof of moral considerability of nonhuman nature (of the sort Callicott requires for an ethical theory to be both an ethic and a theory). I did so because I think such a proof may not be possible, *not* because I think nonhuman nature is not morally considerable. I have argued (in this chapter and chapter 4) that ecofeminist ethics is a theoretical position based in a different conception of both ethics and theory than those endorsed by reformist, mixed reform and radical, and even some radical positions in environmental ethics. I have argued (in this chapter) for the ethical significance of narrative on the grounds that narrative is an important argumentative vehicle for ethical theorizing—not because, as Callicott states, according to ecofeminism "men typically construct theories, women typically tell stories."[37] I have argued (in this chapter) for the importance of care to ethical motivation, deliberation, and practice on both empirical and philosophical grounds. And I argue explicitly for the scientific grounding of ecofeminist philosophy in ecology in chapter 7 and for a more inclusive notion of justice in chapter 8.

As such, criticisms of ecofeminist philosophy as not theoretical, anti-theoretical, anti-science, and anti-reason simply are not an accurate portrayal of ecofeminist philosophy or ethics, either in 1993 (when Callicott's criticisms were published) or now. I encourage environmental ethicists who dismiss ecofeminist philosophy out of hand, to seriously engage themselves with the arguments presented by ecofeminist philosophers instead. Such engagement is at the heart of what ecofeminist philosophy is about.

CONCLUSION

I have argued in this chapter for "care-sensitive" ethics based on three conditions: an ability to care, situated universalism, and care practices. I have also argued against two sorts of criticisms of ecofeminism: Ecofeminism makes a universal ethic impossible or undesirable, and ecofeminist philosophy provides no ethic, no theory, and is, in fact, anti-theory. I want to end on a different note.

The importance of caring about others was profoundly brought home to me during the summer of 1997, when my daughter, Cortney, and I spent nearly one week swimming with wild bottlenose dolphins off the coast of Key West, Florida. What I learned through relating to these incredibly beautiful, sensitive, responsive, intelligent creatures changed how I think about myself, others, and ethics.

During the week, there were many occasions when I would encounter the dolphins under water; I would get to swim around them for ten or fifteen seconds at a time. But, unlike Cortney, throughout the week I had not experienced the joy of *swimming with them,* of being part of their community. As the last day of the swim approached, I began to think about my motivation for swimming with dolphins. I realized that although I knew better, I had pursued the dolphins with my own agenda and timetable: I wanted to swim with them, and I put all my energy into trying to make it happen. Never considering whether they wanted to swim with me, I exercised my will to try to control the outcome in much the same way I initially climbed mountains: by imposing my will on them, without genuine regard for their well-being. Despite good intentions, my perception and behavior were arrogant, not loving.

On the last day, that changed. On this day, I focused on what was genuinely within my control—using my will to change my motivation and attitudes about swimming with these dolphins. On this day when I entered the water, I did not swim anywhere. I just stayed still, by the boat. Although I could not see the dolphins in the murky ocean water, I closed my eyes and began speaking quietly to them, telling them that I would be grateful if they would permit me to swim with them, to join their community for a while.

Before I knew what was happening, several adult dolphins came and "took me" to their pod. At first I was breathless; I could hardly believe what was happening. But as I looked to each side, I saw that this was real: I was surrounded by wild dolphins—under me, in front of me, and on both sides—who had invited me to be part of their community for what turned out to be a timeless hour.

Reflecting later on that swim, it was profoundly clear to me that the dolphins had *chosen* to swim with me—to swim slowly so that I could be with them, to include me as they engaged in their ordinary activities of feeding, playing, being sexual, and touching each other. It was also clear to me that the dolphins had not changed over the course of the week; it was I who had changed. I had let go of my attempts to control the outcome. And I knew that the internal changes in me had made it possible for these intelligent and sensitive creatures to invite me to swim with them.

I also came to see things differently during that swim. At one point I turned to a calf swimming by my side and began voicing what was for me a profound realization. Looking directly in each other's eyes, I said to the calf, "Even if you are sentient, capable of language and communication, rational, a rights-holders, deserving of respect and protection—even if all this is true, which I believe it is— that's not what is morally basic. What is morally basic is that we *care about you.* Because if we don't care about you, there is no moral motivation for us to ponder whether rights, duties, utility, God's commands, or developing a virtuous character are the best avenues to pursue to secure your preservation."[38]

That swim was transformative for me. It helped me realize that despite myriad reasons to protect and honor these magnificent creatures, whether we do ultimately depends upon whether we humans do or learn how to care about them. Traditional principles of rights, duty, justice, utility, and self-interest may provide important philosophical avenues to secure protection of dolphins. But, they do not, by themselves, give expression to what is morally fundamental to human interaction with selves and others. To get at *that,* one must talk about and cultivate the ability to care about earth others, and to care about them as earth others— as dolphins, not simply as sources of enjoyment or other benefit for humans.

That swim brought home for me that one simply cannot fit the whole moral story about selves and others (humans and nonhumans) into the shoe of rights, or duty, or justice, or utility *without* loss of crucial moral value. To tell the proper moral story of the matter, attention to and cultivation of human capacities to care and to engage in care practices is needed. Providing that missing moral piece is what I think care-sensitive ethics is all about.

NOTES

1. For a general discussion of what feminists have meant when they claim that the Western philosophical tradition of rationalism has been male-biased, see my "Male-Gender Bias and Western Conceptions of Reason and Rationality," *American Philosophical Association on Feminism and Philosophy* 88, no. 2 (March 1989), 48–53.

2. Margaret Walker, "Moral Understandings: Alternative 'Epistemology' for a Feminist Ethics," *Hypatia: A Journal of Feminist Philosophy* 4, no. 2 (Summer 1989), 16.

3. Walker, "Moral Understandings," 7.

4. Jim Cheney, "Eco-Feminism and Deep Ecology," *Environmental Ethics* 9, no. 2 (Summer 1987), 144.

5. Notice that the standard of inclusiveness does not exclude the voices of men. It is just that the voices of women must be included, and any conflicts among voices must be accounted for in ways that do not promote gender, race, class, or other biases of domination.

6. The burgeoning literature on these values is noteworthy. See, e.g., Carol Gilligan, *In a Different Voice: Psychological Theories and Women's Development* (Cambridge: Harvard University Press, 1982); Nel Noddings, *Caring: A Feminine Approach to Ethics and Moral Education* (Berkeley: University of California Press, 1984); Maria Lugones and Elizabeth V. Spelman, "Have We Got a Theory for You! Feminist Theory, Cultural Imperialism, and the Women's Voice," *Women's Studies International Forum* 6 (1983), 573–81; Maria Lugones, "Playfulness, 'World-Travelling,' and Loving Perception," *Hypatia: A Journal of Feminist Philosophy* 2, no. 2 (1987), 3–19; Annette C. Baier, "What Do Women Want In A Moral Theory?" *Nous* 19 (1985), 53–63.

7. Alison M. Jaggar, *Feminist Politics and Human Nature* (Totowa, N.J.: Rowman & Littlefield, 1983), 42–44.

8. Marilyn Frye, *The Politics of Reality: Essays in Feminist Theory* (Trumansburg, N.Y.: Crossing Press, 1983), 5.

9. This narrative was first published in my "The Power and the Promise of Ecofeminism," *Environmental Ethics* 12, no. 2 (Summer 1990), 134–35.

10. Suppose, as I think is the case, that a necessary condition for the existence of a moral relationship is that at least one party to the relationship is a moral being (leaving open for our purposes what counts as a "moral being"). If this is so, then the Mona Lisa cannot properly be said to have or stand in a moral relationship with the wall on which she hangs, and a wolf cannot properly be said to have or stand in a moral relationship with a moose. Such a necessary condition account leaves open the question whether *both* parties to the relationship must be moral beings. My point here is simply that however one resolves *that* question, recognition of the relationships themselves as a locus of value is a recognition of a source of value that is different from and not reducible to the values of moral beings in those relationships.

11. Cheney, "Eco-Feminism and Deep Ecology," 144.

12. Marilyn Frye, "In and Out of Harm's Way: Arrogance and Love," in *Politics of Reality,* 75–76.

13. Lugones, "Playfulness," 3.

14. Cheney makes a similar point in "Eco-Feminism and Deep Ecology," 140.

15. Cheney, "Eco-Feminism and Deep Ecology," 138.

16. Notice the similarity between this notion of the self and the notion of *homo economicus* of liberal, market capitalist economics.

17. Kathryn Pine Addelson, "Moral Revolution," in *Women and Values: Readings in Recent Feminist Philosophy,* ed. Marilyn Pearsall (Belmont, Calif.: Wadsworth, 1986), 306.

18. Daniel Goleman, *Emotional Intelligence: Why It Can Matter More than I.Q.* (New York: Bantam Books, 1995), 43.

19. Goleman, *Emotional Intelligence,* 28.

20. Goleman, *Emotional Intelligence,* 52–53.

21. Goleman, *Emotional Intelligence,* 28–29.

22. Alison M. Jaggar, "Love and Knowledge," in *Gender/Body/Knowledge,* ed. Alison M. Jaggar and Susan R. Bordo (New Brunswick, N.J.: Rutgers University Press, 1989), 148–49.

23. In this respect, ethics must be based on an accurate notion of human capabilities. This is consistent with the position of ethical naturalism and moral realism.

24. Rita Manning, *Speaking from the Heart: A Feminist Perspective on Ethics* (Lanham, Md.: Rowman & Littlefield, 1992), 84.

25. A. I. Melden, "Why Be Moral?" *Journal of Philosophy* 45, no. 17 (1948), 449–56.

26. As a prerequisite of ethics, the ability to care also is not an ethical principle ("situated" or otherwise).

27. Peta Bowden, *Caring: Gender Sensitive Ethics* (London: Routledge, 1997), 5.

28. Bowden, *Caring,* 9.

29. Bowden, *Caring,* 3.

30. Alison M. Jaggar, "Caring as a Feminist Practice," in *Justice and Care: Essential Readings in Feminist Ethics,* ed. Virginia Held (Boulder, Colo.: Westview Press, 1995), 194–95. For a discussion of these features of a care perspective, see Lawrence Blum, "Moral Perception and Particularity," *Ethics* 101, no. 4 (July 1991), 701–25.

31. See Grace Clement, *Care, Autonomy, and Justice: Feminism and the Ethic of Care* (Boulder, Colo.: Westview, 1996), 46.

32. Clement, *Care, Autonomy,* 49.

33. Clement, *Care, Autonomy,* 82.

34. J. Baird Callicott, "The Search for an Environmental Ethic" (revised version), in *Matters of Life and Death,* 3rd edition, ed. Tom Regan (New York: McGraw-Hill, 1993), 336.

35. Callicott, "The Search for an Environmental Ethic," 333.

36. Callicott, "The Search for an Environmental Ethic," 335, 336–37.

37. Callicott, "The Search for an Environmental Ethic," 336.

38. Does "emotional intelligence" apply beyond the human species? I don't know. But, in one sense, it does not matter ethically if dolphins (or other nonhumans) are incapable of caring about themselves or others. All that matters is that human moral agents are carers; human relationships to nonhuman animals and nature are thereby morally assessable, whether or not the "other" is a moral agent or carer.

Chapter Six

Must Everyone Be Vegetarian?

Ecofeminist Philosophy and Animal Welfarism

Moral vegetarianism is the position that we should eat a vegetarian diet because it is morally the right thing to do, rather than for health, economic, or environmental reasons. The issue of moral vegetarianism is controversial, even among ecofeminists. Some ecofeminists argue that moral vegetarianism is a necessary condition of any ecofeminist practice and philosophy. Others either are not so sure or disagree.

Convinced that the issue of moral vegetarianism is one that ecofeminists should address, I do so here. I begin with a brief review of arguments for universal moral vegetarianism, followed by a presentation of five objections to those arguments. I then turn to a defense of my own position, what I call "contextual moral vegetarianism." Contextual moral vegetarianism is a care-sensitive position that rejects a "one size fits all" vegetarianism. I conclude that although universal moral vegetarianism is not required by ecofeminist philosophy as I understand it, ecofeminist philosophy does provide moral constraints on how earth others—nonhuman animals and the nonhuman natural environment—are conceptualized and treated.

ARGUMENTS FOR MORAL VEGETARIANISM

In chapter 4 I presented two main types of animal welfare arguments for universal moral vegetarianism: Peter Singer's consequentialist argument and Tom Regan's rights-based argument. Both are reformist, moral extensionist positions that base the moral considerability of nonhuman animals on traits they share with humans. For Singer, it is being sentient; for Regan, it is being the subject of a life. While all animal welfarists argue for universal moral vegetarianism, consequen-

125

tialist arguments (such as Singer's) are based on the unnecessary pain and suffering caused to animals by such practices as factory farming and hunting, while rights-based arguments (such as Regan's) are based on the rights of animals.

Ecofeminist animal welfarist arguments typically build on traditional animal welfare arguments. What makes them "ecofeminist" is that the analysis of oppression of nonhuman animals is based on a variety of women-animal connections: for example, sexist-naturist language, images of women and animals as consumable objects, pornographic representations of women as meat, male-perpetrated violence against women and nonhuman animals.[1] Ecofeminist animal welfarists argue that the unjustified dominations, objectification, and commodification of women and nonhuman animals occur in mutually reinforcing and conceptually inseparable ways. As such, any analysis of and solutions to unjustified Up-Down systems of domination must include recognition and elimination of harmful, historical women-animal connections. What ecofeminist arguments add to animal welfare arguments, then, is a critical gender analysis.

Ecofeminist animal welfare arguments typically include claims about animal rights. But what is not clear about those arguments is just what the alleged connection is between animal rights theory and a feminist vegetarian practice. For example, Carol Adams says that "not only is animal rights the theory and vegetarianism the practice, but feminism is the theory and vegetarianism is part of the practice. . . . Meat eating is an integral part of male dominance; vegetarianism acts as a sign of disease with patriarchal culture."[2] But, especially in light of her more recent work, there are good reasons for supposing that the essential connection Adams asserts between animal rights and ecofeminist moral practice is practical and strategic, not conceptual. The difference is important. As Deane Curtin claims, a practical connection is a political strategy of coalition building between feminism and the animal rights movement; it need not presuppose rights theory as its theoretical foundation.[3] A conceptual connection, on the other hand, places ecofeminist moral vegetarianism in the philosophical tradition of rights and obligations, as advocated by Regan. As we will see, there are important problems with Regan's rights-based view, which, presumably, any ecofeminist animal welfarism conceptually located in the Regan animal rights tradition inherits.

A similar case could be made for Marti Kheel's argument in support of universal moral vegetarianism. A founder of Feminists for Animal Rights, Kheel provides an ecofeminist defense of universal moral vegetarianism in terms of rights of animals. But she offers distinctly feminist criticisms of the animal rights views of Regan.[4] So, it is not clear to what extent Kheel's ecofeminist animal rights position is conceptually (and not just practically) based in the philosophical tradition of rights.

While it may not be clear from reading the work of ecofeminist animal rights activists whether their *theoretical* positions are based in a rights perspective, it is clear that their *practical* positions support a universal moral vegetarianism. I now turn to a consideration of five objections to animal welfare arguments for universal moral vegetarianism.

OBJECTIONS TO ARGUMENTS
FOR UNIVERSAL MORAL VEGETARIANISM

The first objection I call *the moral extensionist objection*. Animal welfarism reforms traditional ethics by extending moral consideration to nonhuman animals on the basis of some similarity they share with humans. Nonhuman animals get elevated to the status of full-fledged members of the moral club to which humans belong. The moral extensionist objection is that such club membership comes at an unacceptable price: a hierarchical, moral pecking order with humans at the apex is preserved; problematic value dualisms, such as culture versus nature, that place nonhuman animals with humans over and against the rest of nature (e.g., plants) are kept intact; and ecological "wholes" (such as populations, communities, species, and ecosystems) are inappropriately omitted from moral consideration. Because animal welfare arguments for a universal moral vegetarianism rest on such faulty moral extensionist premises, it is argued that animal welfarism fails as an environmental ethic and as a basis for a universal moral vegetarianism.

The importance of the moral extensionist objection is not only that it challenges traditional conceptions of ethics as hierarchically ordered, value-dualistic systems of rights and rules that govern the activities of moral agents or moral persons conceived as radically individualistic selves. It also challenges as anti-environmental and anti-ecological the view that the importance of earth others is their value as discrete individuals who are more like humans than the rest of nonhuman nature. Given the version of ecofeminist ethics I defended in chapter 5, and the view I defend in chapter 7 of earth others as both individuals and co-members of an ecological system, I endorse the moral extensionist objection. However, as I will show, this endorsement does not deny moral status to animals or give carte blanche acceptance to the consumption of animals.

A related, second objection to animal welfare arguments for universal moral vegetarianism is what I call *the relational selves objection*: Moral subjects are essentially relational selves, not atomistic individuals who, like the mythic Robinson Crusoe, supposedly exist independently of any historical, social, and material context. Animal welfarism fails because it mistakenly presumes otherwise. Whether one extends moral consideration to nonhuman animals on the basis of their sentiency or rights-holder status, animal welfare arguments succeed only if one accepts a mistaken view of moral subjects.

The relational selves objection challenges a conception of moral subjects as having an essence or essential nature independent of any historical, social, and material contexts and independent of any relationship to other moral subjects. The objection challenges, for example, the notion of self made popular by philosopher John Rawls: The self is a rational being whose very nature exists independent of historical and geographic location, gender, race, class, age, affectional orientation, abilities, talents, or religion. The Rawlsian self is able to reason morally and determine absolute and universal principles of morality "behind a veil of ignorance" about such things as the self's gender, race/ethnicity, class, talents, abilities, desires. In contrast, the view of selves as relational selves, as beings-in-relationships, makes context—historical and geographical location, gender, race/ethnicity, class, sexual orientation—and relationships to others an integral, and not dispensable or "add on" feature of one's nature and identity as a self.

The relational selves objection also challenges the conceptually essentialist view that there is some one set of necessary and sufficient condition properties—sentiency (Singer) or being the subject of a life (Regan)—which makes a being (whether human or nonhuman animal) morally considerable. Since I suggested in chapter 4 that there is or may be no such set of properties, and since I argue throughout this book for a view of selves-in-relation, I support the relational selves objection to animal welfare arguments for universal moral vegetarianism. This is not to deny the importance of selves as individuals and moral agents (a claim I also defend in chapter 7); it is to deny that one can define a self with no attention to social contexts and connections.

A third objection is what I call *the universalizing objection*. According to animal welfare arguments, there is a universal and absolute (that is, not overridable) moral prescription against eating animals. This is because the moral status of animals as sentient beings, subjects of a life, or moral rights-holders is not affected by their geographic location, the availability of alternative food sources, or the moral conventions of a particular culture in which animals live. The objection then proceeds as follows: If animal welfarism is true, then no human in any historical, social, or material context is ever justified in eating animals, not even those for whom alternatives to eating animals currently are often difficult to come by—not the Inuit and Ihalmiut, not Tibetans, not small family organic farmers, not poor rural women in the Southern Hemisphere. But this implication of animal welfarism is false; so, animal welfarism is unacceptable.

In the case of those for whom alternatives to eating animals currently are difficult or impossible to come by (e.g., the Inuit and Ihalmiut), the universalizing objection to animal welfarism rests on one of the most important principles of ethics, the so-called *"Ought" implies "can" principle*. This principle states that if one is morally obligated to do or forbear from doing a certain act (or kind of act) A (i.e., the "ought" condition), then one is capable of doing or not doing A (i.e., the "can" condition). This is sometimes stated as, one can only be held morally accountable for acts when one could have done otherwise. Genuine alternatives must be available to an agent for an agent's acts to be right or wrong and for an agent to be morally praiseworthy or blameworthy. According to the universalizing objection, animal welfare arguments violate the principle that "ought" implies "can": The eating of animals is morally wrong even in cases where there are no genuine alternatives. Since animal welfare arguments violate the "ought" implies "can" principle, animal welfare arguments are unacceptable.

Some who endorse the universalizing objection might be willing to concede that in a perfect world, where nonanimal food is abundant, available, and affordable for all humans living in all geographical, material contexts, it is morally preferable to not consume animals than to consume them. Some may even concede that in a perfect world, universal/moral vegetarianism would be morally required. But they insist that we do not now, or in the foreseeable future, live in a perfect world. In this world, animal welfarist's universal and absolute moral injunctions against eating animals is unjustified.

It will not do for an animal welfarist to respond to this objection by saying that, even though what such persons do is morally wrong, they are not morally blameworthy. Yet, when asked a question such as Are Inuit who consume animals doing something morally wrong? animal rights welfarists typically respond, "Yes: What they are doing is wrong, but they are morally excusable or forgivable."[5]

For three reasons, this response troubles me deeply. First, it, too, violates the principle that "ought" implies "can" by continuing to assert that what the Inuit do is wrong (i.e., they ought not eat animals) even though they cannot do otherwise. Second, this response reveals the moral arrogance and ethnocentrism of a position that leaves animal welfarists little choice but to maintain an "us-them" mentality that excuses the practices of others as forgivable moral failures. It does so by uncritically extending Western perspectives universally across all cultural contexts. When one exports a distinctively Western position or concept to cultural contexts where they do not fit, one risks engaging in a troublesome form of ethical colonialism. As Andrew Brennan states,

> What I do argue against is *ethical colonialism* whereby those situated in certain kinds of society, surrounded by certain kinds of goods and activities, declare that they have discovered universal ethical truths which do no more than reflect, in a suitably generalised way, their own local aspirations and ideals.[6]

As a related third point, this animal welfarist response keeps in tact a problematic win-lose, value-hierarchical, rights-based approach to ethics, where moral problems are defined and analyzed from the top of various moral hierarchies of power and privilege. It simply is not worth saving a moral system if all those who are not among the group at the top of various moral hierarchies of power and privilege end up being portrayed as moral simpletons, not fully rational moral agents, or moral beings incapable of choosing to do the right thing.

This issue of moral arrogance turns on an important philosophical distinction. It is the distinction between "a value judgment" and "being judgmental." A value judgment, such as "One ought not eat animals" or "Democracy is a good form of government," is an evaluation that can be supported (or justified) by appeal to reasons. Value judgments are open to the sort of philosophical criticisms given here, for example, in the form of objections to animal welfare arguments. It is part of the very business of philosophy to provide conceptually clear and well-supported arguments in support of value judgments. Being judgmental, on the other hand, is an undesirable trait of character; it is not about giving philosophical arguments for or against a position. Being judgmental is a kind of disrespectful, arrogant perception. It is one thing to provide and critique arguments for moral vegetarianism (i.e., to make value judgments); it is quite another to be morally judgmental of the eating practices of others.

A fourth objection to animal welfare arguments for universal moral vegetarianism is what Kathryn Paxton George calls the *male physiological norm objection*:[7] According to animal welfare arguments, the welfare interests of animals count as much as those of humans. This presumes that species equality, a mainstay of animal welfare arguments, is similar to and compatible with human equality; physiological differences among humans are not morally relevant to human equality. But these claims are false. They rest on a male physiological norm that is inappropriately blind to important empirical differences between healthy males and others—infants, children, adolescents, gestating and lactating women, some persons of ill health, some elderly, and many persons living in other cultural, racial/ethnic, class, and environmental contexts. One way these differences are apparent is that adult males can freely choose to practice vegetarianism (no consumption of animals) or veganism (no consumption of animal products) without significant risks to their health, whereas these other groups of humans often cannot. So, animal welfare arguments for universal moral vegetarianism ought to be rejected.

Notice that the male physiological norm objection is based on empirical claims (not provided here) intended to show an internal inconsistency in animal welfare arguments. That inconsistency allegedly arises because the male physiological norm violates the animal welfarist's own canons of impartiality, universality, and objectivity. For example, on the basis of this norm, animal welfarists mistakenly assume that, except in rare cases, everyone *could* be a vegetarian if only they chose to be. But this is not the case for many human groups (e.g., some infants, children, adolescents, gestating and lactating women, Inuit, primal peoples). Furthermore, if animal welfarists permit such routine exceptions to universal moral prohibitions against consuming animals or animal products, they concede the male-bias of traditional animal welfare arguments in a way that prevents the necessary universalizability and impartiality of those arguments.

The success of the male physiological norm objection depends on the truth of the empirical data on which it is based. Because the current evidence is sometimes conflicting, I do not know whether the empirical basis for the male physiological norm objection is correct. So I do not take a stand on the success of the objection. However, *if* the empirical claims are correct, then the male physiological norm objection has four key strengths: It reveals an allegedly impartial human norm in animal welfare arguments to be a gender-biased male norm; it acknowledges the relevance of such factors as gender, race/ethnicity, class, and geographic location to ethical theorizing; it recognizes differences among species and conflicts of interests between species, daring to ask the question "In whose interest is it that these differences not be acknowledged?"; and it challenges the ethical desirability of positions that excuse the nonvegetarian practices of others as moral weaknesses of will.

The fifth and last objection I consider here is *the predation objection*. It rests on an analogy between human hunting and wild predation. The objection is this: Since animal welfarists are opposed to human hunting (and the consumption of animals through human hunting), they must also be opposed to wild predation (and the consumption of nonhuman animals by nonhuman animals). After all, both acts have the same consequences (the unjustified killing of animals). Furthermore, since, according to animal welfarism, wild predation both causes suffering to prey and violates the rights of prey, animal welfarism implies that humans are morally obligated to intervene in wild predation. But this is false; humans are not obligated to intervene in wild predation. So, animal welfarism ought to be rejected. Animal welfare arguments do not establish that hunting and animal consumption through hunting are wrong.

The predation objection seems compelling against Regan's rights-based version of animal welfarism. This is because, according to that version, humans have moral duties to prevent or intervene in injustice. Since animals have rights, humans have a duty to intervene in and protect the violation of animal rights. Regan makes this explicit when he claims, "our duty regarding the respectful treatment of animals involves more than our taking care to treat them with respect. Since they have a valid claim to respectful treatment, we have a prima facie duty to assist them when others treat them in ways that violate their rights."[8] However, according to the predation objection, if humans have a duty to intervene to protect the rights of animals, then it seems humans have a duty to intervene to protect sheep from wolves. And this is an untenable position.

Regan's explicit defense of animal rights welfarism against this objection denies that humans have a duty to intervene to protect sheep from wolves, but *not* because sheep do not have rights in sheep-wolf cases. For Regan, animals (including wolf and sheep) have rights in *any* context they are in. So, sheep have rights even when attacked by wolves. Rather, Regan claims that the reason humans have no duty to intervene in wolf-sheep situations is that humans have a duty to intervene only in cases where rights are *violated*. And, according to Regan, no rights of the sheep are violated by wolves who attack them, because wolves are incapable of violating rights; only moral agents are capable of violating rights, and the wolf is not a moral agent.[9]

The main problem with this reasoning is that it relies on an odd and untenable notion of a right. Regan (and most rights theorists) claim that possession of a right to respectful treatment is not affected by context. So Regan must say, as he does, that sheep retain their rights, and wolves retain their rights, to respectful treatment in wolf-sheep (predator-prey) relationships, although neither is capable of *ever* violating or upholding or respecting the other's rights. Nor is any human duty-bound to protect either the rights of wolves or sheep in cases of predation.

But what could it mean to say that an animal has a right to respectful treatment though no one, anywhere, has any correlative duty to protect the right? Minimally, a right is a valid claim to something against someone. Rights correlate with duties in this respect: If A has a right to something (e.g., respectful treatment), then some other entity, B, has a duty to A (e.g., to provide respectful treatment). If, as Regan claims, sheep have a right, "a valid claim to respectful treatment," against whom does this right hold? Not the wolf, since the wolf has no duties to anyone. Not any human, since no humans have any duties to intervene in or prevent the killing of sheep by wolves. But this is implausible; it is not meaningful to talk of the rights of sheep in this context when no one anywhere or at any time has any duties to sheep.

I wholeheartedly agree with Regan that there is *no* violation of rights involved in predator-prey relationships. But, unlike Regan, I think this is because talk of rights in nonmoral contexts (such as nonhuman predator-prey contexts) does not arise, even if sheep have some rights in some *other* contexts. Talk of rights of sheep in nonhuman predator-prey contexts is the source of the problem.

An animal welfarist, even a rights-based animal welfarist (other than Regan), could defeat the predator objection by denying the analogy on which the predation critique rests. Animal welfarists could argue as follows: Human hunter-prey situations are different from nonhuman animal predator-prey situations. When human hunters kill, they perform an action (i.e., a willed event) that is one among several possible alternative acts available to them. When nonhuman hunters kill, they perform a behavior (not an "act" or "action") that is governed by instinct. As such, nonhuman animal predator-prey relationships, unlike human hunter-prey relationships, are not moral relationships. Since they are not moral relationships, the behaviors of nonhuman predators are not moral acts, the suffering of prey in those relationships is not a kind of moral (or morally relevant) suffering, and there is no meaningful talk of rights of nonhuman animals in nonhuman animal-animal relationships. Suffering and killings in nonhuman animal predator-prey relationships are neither right nor wrong, moral nor immoral, just nor unjust. Hence, issues about moral suffering and violation of rights do not arise. It is just that this is *not* a reply available on Regan's view.

Furthermore, the predation objection is not successful against consequentialist versions of animal welfarism. The issue about consequences is confused in the predation objection. For a consequentialist, the relevant issue is not whether two different acts (hunting and wild predation) have the same consequences, as the predation objection assumes. Rather, as Jennifer Everett argues, it is whether two acts available to the same agent (hunting or some other action available to the hunter; intervening in predation or some other action available to the would-be intervener) have the same consequences.[10] And a consequentialist such as Singer could argue that intervening in wild predation would bring about worse consequences than not intervening. One could argue, for example, that the overpopulation of deer herds, coupled with drastic reductions in wolf populations, exceeds both what the environment can sustain and results in unnecessary and painful death by starvation of deer in hard winters. Ironically, this could justify human hunting of deer under controlled conditions in order to manage deer populations.

In any case, consequentialist animal welfarism does not imply a duty to intervene in wild predation.

The discussion of these five objections completes what I want to say here about animal welfare arguments for universal moral vegetarianism. The rationale for including a discussion of these objections is twofold: It acquaints the reader with the sorts of issues at stake in debates about universal moral vegetarianism, including debates among ecofeminists; and it provides an important background for presenting my own position—a defense of contextual (not universal) moral vegetarianism.

CONTEXTUAL MORAL VEGETARIANISM

The position on vegetarianism I defend is critical of both ecologically holistic views that do not adequately respect the individual status of nonhuman animals as sentient, cognitive beings, and radically individualistic animal welfarist views that do not adequately respect the ecological status of animals (human and nonhuman) as members of an ecological community. I go between the horns of this "holism versus individualism" dilemma by defending a view of contextual moral vegetarianism that recognizes human and nonhuman animals as both discrete individuals and co-members of an ecological community.

As I am using the term, "contextual moral vegetarianism" asserts four claims: (1) Reasons for moral vegetarianism as a practice in a given circumstance will be affected by contexts of personal relations, gender, ethnicity, class, geographic location, and culture. (2) Moral vegetarianism is not a universally required practice in all contexts. (3) In principle, morally acceptable food-eating practices should not replicate or reinforce unjustified Up-Down systems of domination based on the power and privilege of Ups over Downs. (4) An ecologically informed care-sensitive ethics approach is helpful to unpacking the nature of our relations to nonhuman animals and to resolving contextual issues of moral vegetarianism. Consider now what is asserted by these claims.

Throughout the book I defend a version of ecofeminist philosophy according to which context *really* matters. Whether it is a visual image of ecofeminist philosophy as the intersection of three overlapping Venn circles, with "local or indigenous perspectives" one of the three circles (chapter 3); or, a metaphor of theorizing as quilting, where individual patches on the ecofeminist quilt are contributed by historically located quilters (chapter 3); or, a "fruit bowl" approach to ethics that honors traditional Western moral principles of rights, utility, self-interest, duty, or virtue as "situated universals" (chapter 5); or, a rejection of a single model of ecosystems in favor of an inclusive, observation-set dependent model as the ecological grounding of ecofeminist philosophy (chapter 7)—context is crucial for gathering information, theorizing, and making ethical judgments. So, it should not be surprising that I defend a contextual moral vegetarianism.

Contexts of personal relationships provide the most obvious sort of reason, claim 1 above, against a universal moral vegetarianism, claim 2 above. Deane Curtin describes such contexts when he says:

> Though I am committed to moral vegetarianism, I cannot say that I would never kill an animal for food. Would I not kill an animal to provide food for my son if he were starving? Would I not generally prefer the death of a bear to the death of a loved one? I am sure I would. The point of a contextualist ethic is that one need not treat all interests equally as if one had no relationship to any of the parties.[11]

Care-sensitive ethics permits that special relationships, particularly dependency relations, provide contextual reasons for not treating all interests equally. It does not do this carte blanche: It is not always moral to act on one's preferences, especially if so acting violates the care practices condition or keeps in place unjustified practices of domination. But care-sensitive ethics does let context matter morally. (I also discuss this position in chapter 8.)

Geographic contexts provide another sort of reason against universal moral vegetarianism, as we saw in the discussion of the universalizing objection. Curtin captures the importance of geographical context, especially in connection with cultural contexts, when he discusses the food practices of the Ihalmiut.

> The Ihalmiut, for example, whose frigid domain makes the growing of food impossible, do not have the option of a vegetarian cuisine. The economy of their food practices, however, and their tradition of "thanking" the deer for giving its life are reflective of a serious, focused, compassionate attitude toward the "gift" of a meal.

Curtin states that cultural context is also important among geographically "isolated" Tibetans:

> Tibetans, who as Buddhists have not generally been drawn to vegetarianism, nevertheless give their own bodies back to the animals in an ultimate act of thanks by having their corpses hacked into pieces as food for the birds. Cultures such as [this] have ways of expressing spiritually the idea "we are what we eat," even if they are not vegetarian.[12]

Cultural contexts may provide the most compelling sort of reasons against universal moral vegetarianism. Few, if any, primal cultures are vegetarian, even though many of them really believe that nonhuman nature is active, alive, enspirited, capable of willing, acting, and knowing. This is particularly interesting philosophically because, while such primal cultures seem to share a similar starting point as animal welfarism—a deeply held belief in nonhuman animals as subjects—they reach radically different conclusions than animal welfarists. How can one account for this difference?

According to Bruce Nordstrom-Loeb, probably the most basic explanation is that there *really* are basic differences in the worldviews of many primal cultures and animal welfarists.[13] Animal welfarists use distinctively Western ethical concepts and principles—consequences and rights—to argue against eating animals. Animal welfarist arguments make humans and nonhuman animals similar and morally equal—as well as different and morally superior to plants, rivers, mountains, and the rest of nature—by taking nonhuman animals out of nature and putting them in the moral club with humans. Animal welfarist arguments thereby keep in place the problematic value dualism "culture/nature."

Nordstrom-Loeb claims, in contrast, that many primal people really believe that humans are part of nature and that nature is a part of humans. There is no Western "culture/nature" value dualism. They also really believe that humans are both predator and prey, both eater and eaten. Given that one has to eat something, it is assumed that humans will eat plants and animals, and nonhuman animals will eat other nonhuman animals, plants, and humans. In many primal cultures, the belief was that if a hunter successfully killed a deer, it was because the deer "presented" or "offered" itself at that moment to be killed. Anthropologist Dorothy Lee, for example, describes the interconnection between language and cultural beliefs about hunting for the Wintu Indians of California. She argues that the Wintu believe in "a reality beyond his delimiting experience," a "timeless design" that, with "luck," can endow a hunter with effectiveness.

> He [the Wintu] believes in it [luck], and he taps it through his ritual acts and his magic, seeking "luck" to reinforce and validate his experiential skills and knowledge, to endow his acts with effectiveness. A hunter must have both skill and luck; but skill is the more limited. . . . Now knowledge and skill are phrased agentively and experientially; but luck is phrased passively or in terms of non-actualized reality. The hunter who has lost his luck does not say *I cannot kill deer any more*, but *deer don't want to die for me*.[14]

According to Lee, the passive linguistic construction "deer won't die for me" in the Wintu language reflects a cultural "attitude of humility and respect toward reality, toward nature" for which, she claims, there is no adequate English equivalent. She concludes:

> Our [Indo-European] attitude toward nature is colored by a desire to control and exploit. The Wintu relationship with nature is one of intimacy and mutual courtesy. He kills a deer only when he needs it for his livelihood, and utilizes every part of it, hoofs and marrow and hide and sinew and flesh. Waste is abhorrent to him, not because he believes in the intrinsic virtue of thrift, but because the deer had died for him.[15]

Primal views that humans are a part of nature, that humans are both eater and eaten, are neither a rationalization for hunting and consuming animals nor a romanticization of nature. They are expressions of deeply entrenched moral beliefs, often based on a worldview in which nonhuman animals and nature really are kin—brothers, sisters, grandfathers, grandmothers. Such primal views reinforce the point, discussed in chapters 5 and 7, that *how* a moral agent is in relationship to another—and not simply the nature of the agent or the "other"—is of central significance in a contextual ethic.

This culturally based understanding of human relationships to nonhuman animals is what I intended to convey when I ended my essay "The Power and the Promise of Ecological Feminism" with the following hunting story, told to me by a Lakota elder.

> The elder sent his son, then age seven, to live with his grandparents on a Lakota reservation so that his son would "learn the Indian ways." The grandparents taught the son how to hunt the four-leggeds of the forest. The boy was taught "to shoot your four-legged brother in his hind area, slowing it down but not killing it. Then, take the four-legged's head in your hands and look into his eyes. The eyes are where all the suffering is. Look into your brother's eyes and feel his pain. Then, take your knife and cut the four-legged under his chin, here, on his neck, so that he dies quickly. And as you do, ask your brother, the four-legged, for forgiveness for what you do. Offer also a prayer of thanks to your four-legged kin for offering his body to you just now, when you need food to eat and clothing to wear. And promise the four-legged that you will put yourself back into the earth when you die, to become nourishment for the earth, and for the sister flowers, and for the brother deer. It is appropriate that you should offer this blessing for the four-legged. When it is your time, you must give your body in this way, as the four-legged gives life to you for your survival."[16]

This story captures elements of a kinship (not consequentialist or rights-based) worldview, based on values of sharing, appropriate reciprocity, and respect for all life forms. Unlike animal welfarist views, it does not exclude the eating of any beings—human or nonhuman.

Two especially significant features of these cultural contexts emerge with regard to the issue of moral vegetarianism. First, in these cultural contexts, the eating of animals is permitted because the worldview really understands both humans and nonhumans ontologically as a part of nature, both eater and eaten. As Curtin says, "morality and ontology are closely connected here."[17] The view of humans, like their nonhuman animal kin, as both eater and eaten is an *ecological* view that puts humans where they belong ecologically—as part of nature and part of the food chain. This is the ecological piece sorely missing from animal welfarist accounts of humans. Second, in these cultural contexts, humans are present to the reality that the food they eat was once a live animal. To use Carol Adams's term, there is no "absent referent": there is no making of animals absent through language that reduces animals to "meat," no culturally encoded patriarchal message legitimating male control over inferior animals.[18] Animals are food, not meat.

This distinction between food and meat is central to ecofeminist philosopher Val Plumwood's rejection of universal moral vegetarianism. On February 5, 1985, she was attacked by a saltwater crocodile in Kakadu National Park, Australia. Plumwood is one of a handful of those who have experienced the crocodile's death roll (in fact, three death rolls!) and lived to describe it. In her aptly titled article, "Human Vulnerability and the Experience of Being Prey," Plumwood reflects on the experience that helped her realize fully, for the first time, "that I was prey." In an instant, her subject-centered framework ("from the inside") of an invincible, continuing self was forever shaken.

> I glimpsed the world for the first time "from the outside," as no longer *my* world, as raw necessity, an unrecognisably bleak order which would go on without me, indifferent to my will and struggle, to my life and to my death. This near-death knowledge, the knowledge of the survivor and of the prey, has some strange fruits, not all of them bitter.[19]

One of those "strange fruits" is that she really came to understand what it was to be part of the food chain—to be prey for crocodiles.

This realization is the cornerstone of Plumwood's argument for a contextual vegetarianism. She rejects what she calls "ontological vegetarianism," the position that nothing morally considerable should ever be ontologized as edible. According to Plumwood, ontological vegetarianism is an ethnocentric, universalizing, inadequately contextualized view of animals (both human and nonhuman) that "demonizes human (and animal) predation and predation identities" in ecologically problematic ways by failing to acknowledge that humans are both eater and eaten/edible.[20] When humans themselves are positioned in the food chain (not outside and above it), humans become conceptualized as edible. When humans are conceptualized as edible, then the animal welfare argument that, animals, like humans, can never be eaten breaks down.

Plumwood argues convincingly that what is needed is a contextual view of both animals and eating, which opposes the socially constructed view of animals as "meat." Adams's work successfully shows that "meat" is a culturally specific construction that, at least in Western cultures, involves reductionist, patriarchal, commodification of animals and women. What Plumwood adds to this analysis is that the notions "food" and "animals as edible food" do not necessarily have these features.[21] As edible food, animal food can be conceived either as meat or as food. The first is ethically problematic; the second is not. As Plumwood argues, animal food is ethically problematic only if one mistakenly ontologizes everything edible as "meat." In a telling analogy she claims:

> But saying that ontologising earth others as edible is responsible for their degraded treatment as "meat" is much like saying that ontologising human others as sexual beings is responsible for rape or sexual abuse. An ontologisation of the other in sexual terms may be a necessary condition for rape, but it can hardly be identified as the salient condition.[22]

With Plumwood's analysis in place, we are now poised to revisit the second significant feature of primal cultural views about nonhumans and food practices. In these culturally specific contexts, both human and nonhuman animals are conceptualized as edible, as food, not as meat. This partly explains why so often there are spiritual rituals around food gathering and eating: for example, hunting dances in which humans portray animals as powerful beings whose powers are to be honored and respected before a hunt; "prayers of the deer slayer," which are part of a tradition of "thanking" deer for the "gift" of giving its life and which express a promise to reciprocate, when it is time; American Indian ceremonies that ritually gather and thank plants before they may be generally consumed that season, or Asian Indian traditions of blessing seeds before planting and thanking Mother Nature for a harvest, or Shinto ceremonies which pay respect to the insects killed during rice planting.[23] These may be romantic (or romanticized) notions to Westerners when they are lifted out of their culturally specific contexts and uncritically added to otherwise unchanged Western frameworks. But they are not romantic notions to those for whom such practices are expressions of genuine, deeply held worldviews about kinship relationships between humans and nature. It is when food is reduced to meat that food-eating practices reinforce Up-Down thinking and relationships of domination toward nonhuman animals.

The movie *Babe* illustrates this point well. *Babe* problematicizes the concept of pigs as meat. Understood as a being with wants, needs, and an ability to communicate, Babe is not "just a pig"; that is, Babe is not just a consumable object, meat. Babe is an active subject, whom we come to care about. Babe captures why so many humans find it difficult, if not impossible, to conceive of killing and eating those animals who are their "pets" or who are named.[24]

Some animal welfarists may object at this point, claiming that it does not matter to the deer or to Babe whether they are killed humanely or violently by humans. What matters is that they are killed, and that such killing of them is wrong. They might also argue that no appeal to cultural contexts is relevant to the killing of deer and Babe from *their*—the deer's or Babe's—perspective.

This animal welfarist reply presumes that deer and pigs, for example, have "perspectives"—volitions, wants, needs, desires—that count morally in how humans treat them. Let's suppose this is true (as, indeed, I think it is): Does it follow that moral vegetarianism is universally required, independent of cultural contexts? I do not think so. Consider several analogies. For many chronically ill people seeking legalized euthanasia, it matters very much to them whether they are involuntarily killed by natural causes or voluntarily killed through the loving intervention of family members. From their perspective, it is preferable to die from the voluntary, even intentional, intervention of others. Persons seeking doctor-assisted suicide presumably would make even stronger claims. From their perspective, it is preferable to be killed than to die of natural causes. And I suspect that some humans would rather die from the paws of a bear or the jaws of a crocodile than from the hands of a Jeffrey Dahmer or a Hitler. So, *if* one is willing to talk about what matters to the deer and Babe "from their perspectives," and *if* one accepts the animal welfarist's analogy between humans and animals, then it is not clear to me that it does not or could not matter to them *how* and *why* they are killed. Babe does not want to just become bacon. From Babe's perspective, it may indeed matter how and when and where and why and by whom Babe dies; but it doesn't follow that, from Babe's perspective, no such death or killing is ever desirable or justified.

Reference to an animal's perspective is often part of some primal worldviews, as we have seen. Prayers of deer slayers and ceremonies of gratitude toward deer are not rationalizations for killing deer. Rather, they are a way of honoring an animal perceived to have chosen to offer its life at that moment as a gift. Furthermore, there is here no view about animals as commodities, "sacrificial lambs," meat, or beings who lack needs, wants, and interests or whose "perspectives" are not taken very seriously.

This brings me to the third feature of a contextual moral vegetarianism, (3): In principle, morally acceptable food-eating practices do not replicate or reinforce unjustified Up-Down systems of domination based on the power and privilege of Ups over Downs. There are noteworthy conceptual implications of this condition. Conceptually, when one conceives of animals or women as meat, one reinforces Up-Down hierarchical thinking and value dualisms (e.g., culture/nature), which reduce animals and women to inferior status as consumable objects. Eating meat, so understood, is a practice that violates this condition, (3).

There are also practical implications for those who eat animals if (3) is true. Those who eat animals should do so in ways that do not reinforce reductionist and patriarchal conceptions of animals as meat. They should avoid supporting practices that cause unnecessary and avoidable pain and suffering in the killing of animals; as such, they should avoid eating factory-farm produced food. When they are members of industrialized Western countries, those who eat animals should consider the effects of their eating practices on colonized countries—for example, on exploited labor markets in those countries, on the lifestyle and cultures of local peoples whose economies are taken over by "foreign" investors, on biodiversity and the destruction of rainforests incurred by raising animals (particularly cattle) for export to Western countries as meat. Those who consume animals and animal products should avoid these things because they replicate and reinforce unjustified systems of domination based on the power and privilege of Ups.

There also are practical implications for those who hunt if (3) is true. For example, many (perhaps all) contexts of recreational hunting, hunting for profit, and trade in wildlife will turn out to be unjustified. Consider relevant data: Hunting for sport and profit, especially so-called trophy hunting of "big-game animals," is a threat to the survival of many species of animals. Among the top-ten species of "trophy animals" are seven endangered species: the black rhino (3,000 remaining), Sumatran rhino (700 remaining), giant panda (100 remaining), Siberian tiger (500 remaining), Bengal tiger (4,000 remaining), Asiatic black bear, orangutan, Moluccan cockatoo, hawksbill sea turtle, and Orinoco crocodile.[25] Animals are killed illegally every year in several countries, including the Republic of Tanzania, where 700,000 are killed illegally annually. Turkmenistan permits open hunting, even of endangered species and animals in reserves, in order to attract foreign money. The world traffic in animals is a US $5 billion industry, with the United States and Western Europe the largest importers of live primates and live birds, respectively.[26]

Similar worries apply to recreational hunting as well. Recreational hunting is sometimes glorified, even by women and feminists, as a form of bonding with nature.[27] This may be true in individual cases, but, as Joni Seager claims, the data does not support this as a general defense of recreational hunting.

> Recreational hunters often defend their sport by saying it is a celebration of nature, but the record speaks otherwise. Around the world, recreational hunting has pushed hundreds of species to the brink of extinction, and in recent times, dozens more have been hunted out of existence. . . .
>
> Hunting is big business. Apart from the considerable sums of money sometimes paid for trophy hunting or rare mammals (or for trophy parts of those animals, such as a gorilla's paw or rhino's horn), the ordinary business of hunting generates considerable revenues: hunters in the U.S.A., for example, spend an estimated $16 billion annually on fees and equipment. In poor countries, such as Zimbabwe and Zambia, hunting is one of the major sources of revenue earned from rich foreigners. Everywhere, hunting is primarily a men's activity, and is often considered a rite of passage into manhood.[28]

This global "trophy" hunting and traffic in wildlife occurs in economic Up-Down contexts whereby rich buyers, typically from First World countries, provide the demand for animals supplied by a trafficking in wildlife by sellers in poor countries. It also occurs in ecological contexts where the actions of humans threaten both the survival of species of animals and the health (well-being, flourishing) of ecosystems. Since it is wrong to perpetuate these unjustified Up-Down systems, these practices in these contexts are wrong. Appeal to feature (3) with regard to hunting shows why these practices are wrong.

The last key claim of contextual moral vegetarianism is (4): A care-sensitive approach is helpful to unpacking the nature of our relations to nonhuman animals and to resolving contextual issues of moral vegetarianism. I end the chapter by discussing briefly what this means.

A CARE-SENSITIVE APPROACH TO CONTEXTUAL
MORAL VEGETARIANISM

In chapter 5 I argued for a care-sensitive ethics, which makes caring about oneself and others central to moral reasoning, deliberation, and action. What is this notion of care, and how does it relate to issues of moral vegetarianism?

According to Berenice Fisher and Joan Tronto, care is "*a species activity that includes everything that we do to maintain, continue, and repair our 'world' so that we can live in it as well as possible.* That world includes our bodies, our selves, and our environment, all of which we seek to interweave in a complex, life-sustaining web."[29] While I do not think the ability to care is limited to humans, I will assume here that, in other respects, Fischer and Tronto's characterization of care is plausible. When one cares about oneself or another, one is cognitively attentive to the needs, well-being, or flourishing of the cared-about.

Notice at the outset three other features of care. First, as we saw in chapter 5, "caring about" another may or may not also involve any feelings ("caring for") the other. Second, it is not a condition of "caring about" another that the other reciprocate the care. One can care about infants, wild animals, trees, forests, and ecosystems even if they do not or cannot reciprocate the care. Third, care and caring are processes, not events. As a process, care involves various "phases." Tronto identifies "four phases" of care, each with a concomitant virtue: "caring about, attentiveness; taking care of, responsibility; care-giving, a competence; and care-receiving, responsiveness."[30] Consider each of these phases in the context of human relationships to nonhuman nature.

The first phase, "caring about" the natural environment, involves a cognitive attentiveness to both its health, well-being, and flourishing and its status as morally considerable. Sometimes this may simply involve "loving perception"; other times it may involve actions and practices.

The second phase, "taking care of," involves having responsibilities toward the other, for example, the responsibilities of land-owners to take care of their land, of field ecologists to take care of prairies, or of lawmakers to take care of air and water pollution by enacting appropriate legislation and policies. These responsibilities do not necessarily entail any rights or duties on the part of the earth others; nonetheless, they are genuine responsibilities of the carer in prescribed contexts.

The third phase, "care giving," involves the exercise of competencies—skills, dispositions, capacities—which I argued (in chapter 5) Elliot-after-surgery lacked. Humans express "care giving" toward the natural environment when they engage in practices that contribute to its health, well-being, and flourishing—minimally, for example, through reuse, recycling, and reducing consumption of material goods.

Lastly, "care-receiving" is involved when and if the natural environment or its nonhuman members are capable of responding (or demonstrating a responsiveness) to human care practices. This response could be in terms of the ecological health of the land (a topic discussed in chapter 7) or the well-being of particular plants and animals.

Unless we are like Elliot-after-surgery, the human ability to care and to engage in care practices—basic features of care-sensitive ethics—are part of what it means for a human being to be a social and ecological self whose "nature" includes important relationships to earth others. With regard to contextual moral vegetarianism, a care-sensitive approach encourages humans to engage in the four phases of care: to learn to *care about* (be attentive to the needs and well-being of) nonhuman animals, individually and ecologically as a population, community, or species; to *take care of* (take responsibility for) animals by acting so as not to cause unnecessary suffering and avoidable pain to individual animals; to *give care to* (exhibit competencies regarding) animals by doing what is appropriate in a given context to support their health or well-being, either individually or as a population, community, or species; and, where relevant, to ensure that the animals *receive care* (are responsive) by understanding and respecting the needs of animals as both sentient beings and as members of a complex web of ecological relationships with other members (individuals, communities, and species) of the food chain.

Again, it is not possible to say ahead of time and independent of context, when and how these four phases of care actually occur. That is what makes contextual moral vegetarianism contextual rather than universal. On my understanding of ecofeminist philosophy, the best one can do regarding moral vegetarianism is to specify the necessary conditions of acceptable food practices concerning animals. These conditions are given, at least in part, by claims (1)–(4) above.

I think a care-sensitive approach to moral vegetarianism captures several features of ethics and ethical reasoning that are not adequately captured by animal welfarist approaches. First, care is *central to human life* in a way that rights and utility are not. Caring relations initiate human beings into the kind of interpersonal relationships and cultural awarenesses that full moral concern requires— both the commonalities and differences among humans, humans and nonhuman animals, and human cultures. Rather than focus moral discussion on the basic value of equality based on the sameness of humans and nonhuman animals, care focuses moral discussion on the basic value of care about others—others acknowledged as both similar and different. It affirms that human society should strive to enhance the quality of care in the world, including the nonhuman natural world,[31] rather than the quality of equality through sameness.

Second, a care-sensitive approach provides a *pluralist framework* for understanding that what is worth aiming at in our food practices involving animals is the well-being or flourishing of the cared-about—both individual animals (populations, species, ecosystems) and humans (communities, cultures). As a "fruit bowl approach" to moral vegetarianism, in some contexts this well-being or flourishing will be best captured and expressed in terms of the consequences, sentiency, or rights of animals; in other contexts it will not be.

Third, a care-sensitive approach to moral vegetarianism reflects an understanding of both human beings and nonhuman beings as *beings-in-relationships,* rather than atomistic individuals whose claims to respectful treatment exist independent of any social, historical, material, geographical, and cultural contexts. Included among the most important relationships human and nonhuman animals are in are *ecological* relationships as co-members of the food chain. It is only partially correct to focus on humans as individuals with rights and to consider animals as just like humans in this respect—the "species equality" assumption of animal welfarism.

Fourth, a care-sensitive approach is always *contextual*. As Joan Tronto claims, "judgments made about care arise out of the real, lived experiences of people in all of their variety. . . . [Care] is not necessarily privatized, individualized, or deinstitutionalized, but any thorough analysis of care requires that we be attentive to the complete context of care."[32] As we have seen, these include personal, gendered, geographical, and cultural contexts. Animal welfare arguments for universal moral vegetarianism conflict with the contextual nature of ethical theorizing and practice.

Fifth, a care-sensitive approach combines an *ethical* and *political* approach to moral vegetarianism that recognizes food-eating practices as socially constructed, culturally embedded, economically molded, politically reinforced practices. Unlike most animal welfarist approaches, a care-sensitive approach to contextual moral vegetarianism is attentive to differences in vulnerabilities, worldviews, and eating practices of humans in different social and material contexts. A politicized notion of care, unlike a "one size fits all" universal moral vegetarianism, reflects an understanding of the importance of differences in power and privilege of Ups and Downs with regard to the theory and practice of moral vegetarianism. A care-sensitive approach prohibits eating practices in contexts that maintain or perpetuate Up-Down relationships of unjustified domination, rather than prohibit the consumption of animals in context-independent, universal terms of animal rights. The bottom line for a contextual moral vegetarianism is that food practices regarding animals should not grow out of, reflect, or perpetuate oppressive conceptual frameworks and the behaviors such frameworks sanction.

Lastly, a care-sensitive approach to moral vegetarianism recognizes ethical theorizing and practice as *processes,* not events. To care about human and non-humans animals is to be engaged in a continually emerging process. It does not presuppose some fixed, morally hierarchical system of rights and rules by which ethical decisions are made and then applied from above. Because it is itself a process, a care-sensitive approach is well suited to understand and describe the health, well-being, or flourishing of human and nonhuman communities as processes that wax and wane over time.

As a process, care happens over time. One cannot care perfectly, in all morally relevant contexts, at all times. To assume otherwise is both to misunderstand what it is to be human and to treat care as an event. I think this is what universal animal welfarist prohibitions against hunting and animal consumption tend to do: They approach ethical issues about moral vegetarianism from a top-down, hierarchical structure by which rights of and consequences for animals "trump" all other considerations, at all times, in all contexts. For animal welfarists, moral vegetarianism is like an event everyone can and should practice always. To fail to do so is always to commit a moral wrong. This is not a view I share.

CONCLUSION

In this chapter I have defended contextual moral vegetarianism. I began with a consideration of objections to animal welfare arguments for universal moral vegetarianism. I then presented my view of contextual moral vegetarianism, ending with a discussion of contextual moral vegetarianism as a care-sensitive approach, which is preferable in key respects to universal animal welfarist approaches.

Two issues touched on in this chapter have yet to be addressed. The first concerns the ecological grounding of ecofeminist philosophy; the second concerns an understanding of justice from an ecofeminist philosophical perspective. I now turn to a discussion of these two issues in chapters 7 and 8, respectively.

NOTES

1. For examples of ecofeminist animal welfare positions, see Carol J. Adams and Josephine Donovan, eds., *Animals and Women: Feminist Theoretical Explorations* (Durham, N.C.: Duke University Press, 1995), and Greta Gaard, ed., *Ecofeminism: Women, Animals, Nature* (Philadelphia: Temple University Press, 1993).

2. Carol J. Adams, *The Sexual Politics of Meat: A Feminist-Vegetarian Critical Theory* (New York: Continuum, 1990), 167.

3. Deane Curtin, "Toward an Ecological Ethic of Care," in *Ecological Feminist Philosophies,* ed. Karen J. Warren (Bloomington: Indiana University Press, 1996), 67.

4. Marti Kheel, "The Liberation of Nature: A Circular Affair," *Environmental Ethics* 7, no. 2 (Summer 1985), 135–49.

5. I posed this question to Tom Regan in a question-answer period following his keynote address at the Global Ethics Conference on Environmental Justice, held at the University of Melbourne, October 15–18, 1997. The reply given here was Regan's reply.

6. Andrew Brennan, *Thinking About Nature: An Investigation of Nature, Value and Ecology* (Athens: University of Georgia Press, 1988), 176.

7. This is the substance of Kathryn Paxton George's article, "Should Feminists be Vegetarians? Viewpoint," *Signs* 19, no. 2 (1994), 405–34.

8. Tom Regan, *The Case for Animal Rights* (Berkeley: University of California Press, 1983), 282–83.

9. Regan, *Case for Animal Rights,* 285. As Bruce Nordstrom-Loeb commented to me, "So animals are close enough to humans to have the same and equal moral rights as humans, but not close enough to be moral agents."

10. This point is made by Jennifer Everett in "Environmental Ethics, Animal Welfarism, and the Problem of Predation: How Bambi Lovers Respect Nature," *Ethics and the Environment,* forthcoming, Spring 2000.

11. Curtin, "Toward an Ecological Ethic of Care," 75.

12. Curtin, "Toward an Ecological Ethic of Care," 75.

13. Personal conversation with Bruce Nordstrom-Loeb, June 6, 1999.

14. Dorothy D. Lee, *Freedom and Culture* (Englewood Cliffs, N.J.: Prentice-Hall, 1959), 128–89, italics in original.

15. Lee, *Freedom and Culture,* 129.

16. Karen J. Warren, "The Power and the Promise of Ecological Feminism," *Environmental Ethics* 12, no. 2 (Summer 1990), 145–6.

17. Curtin, "Toward an Ecological Ethic of Care," 76.

18. Adams, *Sexual Politics of Meat,* 40–63.

19. Val Plumwood, "Human Vulnerability and the Experience of Being Prey," *Quandrant* (March 1995), 30–31.

20. Val Plumwood, "Integrating Ethical Frameworks for Animals, Humans and Nature: A Critical Feminist Eco-Socialist Analysis," *Ethics and the Environment* (forthcoming, Spring 2000).

21. Plumwood, "Integrating Ethical Frameworks," 11.

22. Plumwood, "Integrating Ethical Frameworks," 10.

23. The Shinto example is from Curtin, "Toward an Ecological Ethic of Care," 75.

24. Commenting on an earlier draft, Bruce Nordstrom-Loeb added, "And perhaps this is why so many people believe their pets will go to heaven—an ultimate separation from nature available only to people in conventional Christian theology."

25. Joni Seager, *The New State of the Earth Atlas,* 2nd edition (New York: Simon and Schuster, 1995), 29–30.

26. Seager, *New State of the Earth Atlas,* 30–31.

27. See, e.g., Mary Zeiss Strange, *Woman the Hunter* (Boston: Beacon, 1997).

28. Seager, *New State of the Earth Atlas,* 124–25.

29. Berenice Fisher and Joan Tronto, "Toward a Feminist Theory of Caring," in *Circles of Care: Work and Identity in Women's Lives,* ed. Emily Abel and Margaret Nelson (Albany: State University of New York Press, 1990), 40, italics in original.

30. Joan C. Tronto, "Care as a Basis for Radical Political Judgments," *Hypatia* 10, no. 2 (Spring 1995), 142.

31. Tronto, "Care as a Basis," 143.

32. Tronto, "Care as a Basis," 142.

Chapter Seven

What Is Ecological about Ecofeminist Philosophy?

Ecofeminist Philosophy, Ecosystem Ecology, and Leopold's Land Ethic

This book is about the nature and significance of ecofeminist philosophy. This involves showing the ecological (and not merely environmental) good sense of ecofeminist philosophy. That is the primary goal of this chapter.

The distinction between "ecological" and "environmental" concerns is best viewed as a matter of emphasis (not as a difference in kind): "ecological" concerns tend to focus on interrelationships among nonhuman natural beings, species, and communities, while "environmental" concerns tend to focus on interrelationships between humans and nonhuman natural beings and substances, species, and communities. Establishing the ecological grounding of ecofeminist philosophy involves showing that ecofeminist philosophy is informed by and compatible with scientific, ecological views about nonhuman nature.

I establish the ecological good sense of ecofeminist philosophy in two distinct but related ways: First, I discuss what I take to be the leading theory to date in the discipline of ecosystem ecology, known among scientific ecologists as hierarchy theory.[1] I argue that there are six key features of hierarchy theory that make it a promising theoretical ecological grounding for ecofeminist philosophy. Second, I discuss what is the most widely known and popular text in environmental ethics among field ecologists (e.g., naturalists, foresters, fish and wildlife managers, parks and recreation ecologists)—the late Aldo Leopold's 1949 essay, "The Land Ethic." I argue for an updated interpretation of Leopold's land ethic that makes its basic ecological claims compatible with the perspective on ecosystem ecology provided by hierarchy theory, and many of its basic ethical claims compatible with the version of ecofeminist philosophy I am defending. Taken together, these two different ecological starting points—hierarchy theory and Leopoldian land ethics—provide good ecological grounds for calling ecofeminist philosophy an ecological position.

But the argument of this chapter does not stop here. I also argue that ecofeminist philosophy can make important contributions to both the discipline of ecology (particularly hierarchy theory) and Leopoldian land ethics. I end the chapter by arguing for the fruitfulness of ongoing dialogue and coalition-building among ecosystem ecologists (especially hierarchy theorists), Leopoldian land ethicists, and ecofeminist philosophers like myself. As Catherine Zabinski argues

> A dialogue between ecologists and ecofeminists would be beneficial for both groups, if for no other reason than to increase our understanding of each other's endeavors. But more important, there are definite contributions that an ecofeminist perspective could make in ecologists' thinking about nature and about the way nature is studied.[2]

Again, a visual representation of what I am doing in this chapter might be helpful.[3]

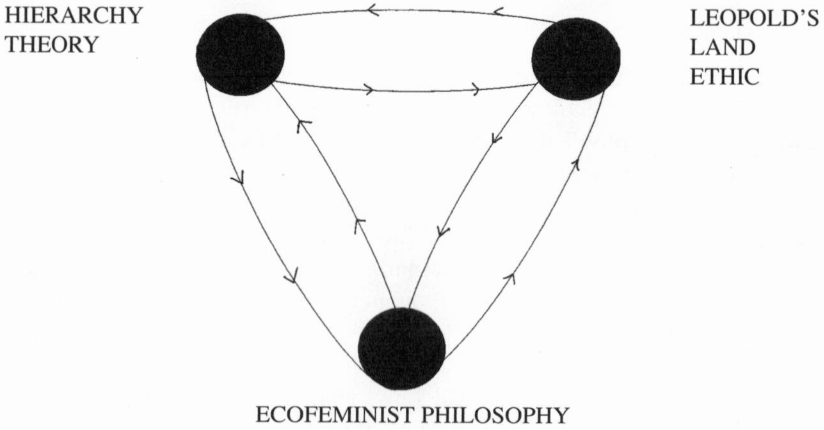

HIERARCHY
THEORY

LEOPOLD'S
LAND
ETHIC

ECOFEMINIST PHILOSOPHY

Diagram 7.1.   Common Bonds: Hierarchy Theory, Leopoldian Land Ethics, and Ecofeminist Philosophy

According to diagram 7.1, each of the three perspectives—hierarchy theory Leopoldian land ethics, and ecofeminist philosophy—makes some distinct contributions to the other two: Hierarchy theory provides an up-to-date scientific perspective about the nature of ecosystems and ecosystem health; Leopoldian land ethics provides an ecologically grounded ethical perspective on the importance of ecosystem health; and ecofeminist philosophy provides a feminist perspective on a range of issues relevant to both scientific ecology and ecologically informed ethics. What binds the three perspectives is not some single, unified theory or worldview that they all have in common, but a common nucleus—an ecological orientation to the world—around which they make distinct contributions and form distinct bonds. What I am exploring in this chapter are those distinct bonds.[4]

CONTEMPORARY ECOSYSTEM ECOLOGY:
"HIERARCHY THEORY"

Appeals to ecosystem ecology have figured importantly in the literature of environmental ethics. But environmental ethicists do not always agree about the nature of ecosystem ecology and what claims about ecosystem ecology imply, if anything, for environmental ethics. Given this disagreement, where should one begin in establishing the ecological good sense of ecofeminist philosophy?

A good starting place is with the nature of ecology. Ecology studies plants and animals, as individuals and together in populations and biological communities, in relation to their environments. Central to ecology is the notion of an ecosystem, often broadly conceived as all the interacting parts of the physical, chemical, and biological realms.

Historically, there have been two primary ways ecologists have viewed ecosystems. As ecologist Frank Golley describes them, "We can view nature either as a collection of objects or as process. Examples of objects are forest stands, lakes, and individual organisms. Process involves dynamic flow or change—for instance, the hydrolic cycle, evolutionary change, or the flow of energy."[5] These two approaches—the "objects" and "process" approaches—typically have been viewed as opposed approaches to the study of ecosystems. Each has vied as the correct or best approach to the study of ecosystems.

Recently, however, this oppositional, exclusivist way of viewing ecosystems has been challenged by ecologists known as hierarchy theorists. According to hierarchy theorists, there is not "one right way" of observing the natural world. Which approach—the "objects" or "process" approach—is best depends on one's "observation set" in a particular case. An *observation set*, according to hierarchy theorists, is "a particular way of viewing the natural world. It includes the phenomena of interest, the specific measurements taken, and the techniques used to analyze the data."[6] Hierarchy theorists argue that, at the level of particular observations (e.g., number of deer in a deer herd in a particular area, or the nutrients flowing into and out of a particular area of soil), specific problems call for particular observation sets and different observation sets explain different phenomena. At the level of theory, however, one must include multiple (not single) observation sets.

> One observation set might deal with the number of individuals in each species in an area and a contrasting observation set might contain only the total flux of nutrients into and out of the area. Each of these points of view emphasizes different phenomena and quite different measurements. But since neither encompasses all possible observations, neither can be considered to be more fundamental. When studying a specific problem, the scientists must always focus on a single observation set. However, when developing theory, many observation sets must be considered.[7]

Hierarchy theorists emphasize the importance of space-time (spatiotemporal) scale to an observation set for two reasons. The first reason concerns what is observed: Scale changes as an ecological problem changes. A spatiotemporal scale appropriate for studying glaciers will be different from a spatiotemporal scale appropriate for studying plants, fires, or photosynthesis. So, what counts as ecological "stability" or "instability," whether an ecological change is "temporary" or "enduring," and what it means to describe ecological change as "local" or "global," always must be understood relative to some particular scale. What is viewed as "stable" on a spatiotemporal scale of several million years may be very "unstable" on a spatiotemporal scale of nanoseconds. That is why "ecosystems have been seen as static or dynamic, as steady-state or as fluctuating, as integrated systems or as collections of individuals"[8]: the observations depend on different spatiotemporal scales. The importance of spatiotemporal scale to any description and evaluation of ecological phenomena explains why "ecological principles often do not translate well across these scales."[9]

The second reason spatiotemporal scale is important concerns the observer: How one views an ecosystem will depend on the spatiotemporal scale through which the observer is making observations, what phenomena are of interest, the specific measurements taken, and the techniques used to analyze the data. An ecosystem may be viewed differently as a constantly changing, dynamic entity, or as a constant, nondynamic background within which organisms operate, or as "inconsequential noise in major geomorphological processes."[10] Because an observer may correctly view ecological phenomena in either way, it is incorrect, in fact impossible, "to designate *the* components of *the* ecosystem."[11] Which designation is appropriate depends on the spatiotemporal scale though which the observer makes the observations and will change as that scale changes.

To summarize what has been said so far, hierarchy theory centralizes the importance of observation sets and spatiotemporal scale in studying ecosystems. Ecologists who study individual organisms (i.e., population-community ecologists) use space-time scales which result in viewing organisms as sturdy, endurable, well-defined, and separate entities. Ecologists who study energy flows (i.e., process-functional or energy flux ecologists) use space-time scales which result in viewing organisms as temporary reservoirs of energy, "momentary configurations," "local perturbations in an energy flux or field." These two different sets of observations depend on different observation sets, which, in turn, are dependent on different space-time scales. When one focuses exclusively on only one approach to studying ecosystems (as either objects or processes), one overlooks the complexity of natural systems. Such foci result in inadequate, because incomplete and one-sided, theories of ecosystems.

Taken by themselves, each approach has its limitations. The main limitation of the process approach lies in its tendency to view ecosystems as merely the sum of material and energy fluxes.[12] While understanding these fluxes is indispensable to an understanding of ecosystems, the limitation results whenever one

looks at fluxes of energy, material, and information as though they existed independently of the species involved in them. For many, this suggests an unacceptable form of holism that exaggerates the analogy between the organism and the ecosystem. Indeed, in the past, many authors have written as though the community or ecosystem *was* an organism.[13]

It is an "unacceptable form of holism" because ecosystems are not simply organisms (as if energy flows did not matter); nor are they simply energy flows (as if populations did not matter). They are both.

This limitation of the process approach arises clearly when dealing with effects of single populations on ecosystems. Where the loss or addition of key species (e.g., species of trees in a forest stand) significantly alters process rates—as is the case when one clear-cuts forests in the Brazilian rainforest—attention to species changes themselves, and not simply energy flows, must be directly considered. Dealing with ecosystems on the basis of flows and fluxes alone runs "the risk of ignoring essential features of biological organization,"[14] such as the existence and activities of discrete individuals (such as trees, plants, and animals in a forest stand). Furthermore, one cannot understand the "health" of an ecosystem that has lost or gained key species without attention to the species themselves.

There also are limitations to the objects approach. First, its population and species orientation makes the concept of a separate, abiotic environment problematic: abiotic components (e.g., nutrient atoms in soil and sediments) must be considered as part of an external environment rather than as part of the ecosystem itself. Second, the concept of a community in the objects (or population-community approach) is awkward. What counts as an "ecosystem community"? What are the boundaries of an ecosystem community? What counts as "members of the community"? The notion of a community is more reflective of a researcher's taxonomic background and sampling methodologies, than a theoretical requirement for explaining ecosystems. Third, the community concept is difficult to apply to belowground, functional processes. For example, the functional component known as the rhizosphere—the area immediately adjacent to the roots of terrestrial plants—does not fit easily into the community concept.[15] Similar problems occur in discussing aquatic ecosystems. Finally, it is difficult to infer ecosystem properties directly from species properties, since "ecosystem function may be insensitive to a range of variability in species [existence or] abundance."[16]

Given these limitations of each approach taken separately—the object and the process approaches—and given that natural entities such as deer, trees, and lakes can be looked at from either an organismic, object standpoint or an energy flow, nutrient cycling, process standpoint, hierarchy theorists conclude that there is not one "correct" concept of an ecosystem. The process (energy flux) approach is inconvenient and inappropriate for studying the loss of any single population of plants or animals, just as the objects (population-community) approach is inconvenient and inappropriate for studying nutrient retention in a clear-cut forest. The objects approach is good for studies of predation, competition, population growth, and migration, while the process approach is good for studying the rates at which some processes occur (e.g., oxygen-carbon dioxide cycles). Which approach is appropriate in a given context depends on what is being studied, the measurements taken, and how the data are analyzed.

According to hierarchy theorists, the failure to acknowledge the key role of observation sets accounts for the failure of current ecological theory to deal adequately with both ecological complexity and the conceptualization of ecosystems. Hierarchy theory claims that the future of ecological science lies in successfully integrating these two approaches into a single framework, one that goes between the horns of the dilemma (of choosing one approach or the other) by centralizing the importance of observation sets and spatiotemporal dimensions, and by locating an ecological approach in, or in relation to, a particular observation set. The overall health of an ecosystem will then be viewed from an *integrated* object and process perspective.

HIERARCHY THEORY—ECOFEMINIST PHILOSOPHY BONDS

To show how appeal to hierarchy theory helps establish the ecological good sense of ecofeminist philosophy, I discuss six areas of commonality—areas that establish a common ecological bond—between the two. This bonding occurs because, despite important differences between them, there are noteworthy theoretical compatibilities between my version of ecofeminist philosophy and hierarchy theory. To carry the molecular metaphor further, one could think of ecofeminist philosophy as having six key "receptor sites" for hierarchy theory.

The first area of commonality between hierarchy theory and ecofeminist philosophy (as I understand it) is that they offer highly *contextual* accounts of both theory and observations. Both are premised on the claim that there is no decontextualized, ahistorical, transcendental vantage point from which humans can make observations, take measurements, analyze data, draw conclusions, or view nature and human-nature interactions. This contextualization is built into each theory through the central notions of observation sets (in hierarchy theory) and conceptual frameworks (in ecofeminist philosophy).

This shared feature—the contextualized nature of theory and observations—is important for several reasons. First, both hierarchy theory and ecofeminist philosophy legitimate the importance of multiple vantage points to theory construction. For hierarchy theory, which particular vantage point is appropriate in a particular context will depend on such factors as spatiotemporal scale, the nature of the problem at hand, the explanatory and predictive power of the descriptions, how well founded the empirical generalizations are of the variety of interactions occurring with the phenomena under observation. The version of ecofeminist philosophy I defend agrees with this position about ecosystems and extends this view to ethics, as well. As I argued in chapter 5, ecofeminist ethics utilizes a "fruit bowl approach": Which ethical principle and which sort of conduct is appropriate in a particular context will depend on whether application of the principle in a particular case satisfies a "care practices" condition.

A second reason an attention to context is important for both hierarchy theory and ecofeminist philosophy is that *what* a thing (person, community, population, species, animal, river) is partly is a function of *where* it is—a function of the relationships in which it stands to other things and to its own history, including its evolutionary history and geographic location. For ecofeminist philosophy, the ecological context of human lives and conduct is ethically paramount. This is because, as Andrew Brennan claims,

> what ecology shows is not simply that the context makes a difference to the kind of action we engage in. It shows, rather, that what kinds of things we are, what sort of thing an individual person is, and what sorts of options for fulfillment and self-realisation are open, are themselves very much context-dependent.[17]

As I argued in chapter 3, this ecological context is not only a "natured" context; it is also a gendered, raced/ethnic, classed, geographic context.

A third reason context is important for both hierarchy theory and my version of ecofeminist philosophy is that both understand ecological discourse as always contextualized. Hierarchy theory contextualizes ecological discourse by making space-time dependent observation sets central to observations in ecology. Ecofeminist philosophy contextualizes both ecological and ethical discourse by making interrelationships central to both. In ethics, these relationships, including human relationships to the nonhuman world, in some sense define who we are.[18] This is why, in addition to whatever else we may be, human selves are ecological selves.

Turn now to a second area of commonality between hierarchy theory and ecofeminist philosophy. Both include interrelated *methodological* and *ontological* stances. As a methodological stance, hierarchy theory rejects the view that there is one right way to study ecosystems. As an ontological stance (about what is "real"), hierarchy theory claims there is no single, "correct," purely objective model (i.e., nonobservation set dependent model) of ecosystems. Any attempt by scientists to specify an "objective" account of what is "really" in the world—an ontology—is misguided. The "ontology" that emerges from any particular investigation is relative to the observation set that produced it.

This methodological and ontological aspect of hierarchy theory does not make it "relativist" or "subjective" in any pernicious sense. But it does mean that to accept a solution to a particular ecological problem is not to make any ontological commitments in any absolute (i.e., nonobservation set dependent or noncontextualized) sense. Any grand attempt to provide one correct point of view puts the ontological cart before the methodological horse.

Like hierarchy theory, ecofeminist philosophy denies that there is one right way to do philosophy or environmental ethics, and one purely objective model of humans and human-nonhuman interactions. But it, too, rejects a relativist, smorgasbord—anything goes—approach to theory. Like hierarchy theory, ecofeminist philosophy assumes that there are better and worse ways to study ecosystems—depending, in part, on whether they are based on appropriate observation sets and spatiotemporal scales—and better or worse ways to do philosophy. Just as hierarchy theory criticizes exclusivist either-or approaches to the study of ecosystems, ecofeminist philosophy, for example, criticizes any exclusivist, either-or approach to organizing and describing "reality" based on oppressive patriarchal conceptual frameworks. That is because such views serve to create, maintain, and reinforce male-biased worldviews and practices that justify the domination of the Other.

At this point one might ask, "Don't ecofeminist philosophers think that their position is the right or correct one?" Speaking for myself only, I see ecofeminist philosophy as a better philosophy—not the correct philosophy—than many of its Western philosophical alternatives. But my reasons for this are reasons, not prejudices, based on arguments for ecofeminist philosophy.

Not convinced, one might press the objection further by asking, "But isn't ecofeminist philosophy biased? After all, it is a feminist perspective, and any feminist perspective is biased." My answer is that whether ecofeminist philosophy is, indeed, "biased" and if it is biased, whether that bias is objectionable, depends on what counts as "bias." To see why this matters, consider three very different meanings of bias.

In one sense of "bias," what I call *empirical bias*, the charge of bias is about faulty or false generalizations. Empirical bias attaches to such items as assumptions, reasons, conclusions, and conceptual frameworks. In this empirical sense of bias, a feminist bias will arise in just the same sort of way that bias arises in generalizations in science: The generalizations will fail to pass the "4-R test" of a good generalization (discussed in chapter 5)—that a good generalization is based on *r*andom samples, *r*ight size samples, *r*epresentative samples, and *r*eplicable experiments or observations. Like science, ecofeminist philosophy assumes that empirical bias in any theory (including ecofeminist theory) can be minimized or eliminated by ensuring that generalizations pass the 4-R test. Thus, insofar as ecofeminist philosophy rejects *as* faulty generalizations about humans that fail to take into account relevant differences between men and women (for example, in the disproportionate harm of environmental costs to women), or which generate claims that are indeed false (for example, that women are genetically inferior or incapable of abstract reasoning), ecofeminist philosophy is not biased in this empirical sense. In fact, ecofeminist philosophy is a welcome corrective to such empirical biases wherever and whenever they occur in mainstream Western ethics.

There is a second sense of "bias," what I call *contextual bias*, in which all observations, all points of view, are biased: they are never context-free. This sort of bias is hard-wired into the nature of theorizing and observing. It is the sort of bias that comes with *any* and *all* observations, conceptual frameworks, theories. So, whatever contextual bias characterizes ecofeminist philosophy is no different *in kind* than the contextual bias of any theory, point of view, or observation set. There is nothing implicitly objectionable about it.

There is still a third sense of "bias," what I call *conceptual bias*, in which a given conceptual framework, point of view, or observation is biased: The claims, beliefs, values, attitudes, assumptions, concepts, and distinctions that characterize or emerge out of it are false or seriously problematic on conceptual (rather than empirical) grounds. According to ecofeminist philosophy, patriarchal conceptual frameworks are conceptually male-gender biased. The objectionable bias of a conceptual frameworks is attributable to the claims *it* makes, not to the ecofeminist analysis that reveals the bias of those claims. Thus, there is nothing inherently conceptually flawed about an ecofeminist philosophical perspective insofar as its claims, beliefs, values, and assumptions are true or plausible. That the starting point is feminist does not make the arguments given faulty. Showing an unacceptable conceptual bias (the third sense of "bias") of ecofeminist philosophy requires argumentation, not a knee-jerk dismissal of it "because it is feminist."

For me, one of the refreshing traits of ecofeminist philosophy is that it acknowledges up front its conceptual bias (i.e., its bias in this third sense of "bias"). The basic starting point of ecofeminist philosophy is that the dominations of women, other human Others, and nonhuman nature are interconnected, are wrong, and ought to be eliminated. The position I am defending in this book is that this conceptual bias is a *better bias* than a patriarchal or androcentric one that denies or overlooks the interconnections among systems of domination.

Return now to the discussion of commonalities (bonds) between hierarchy theory and ecofeminist philosophy. A third area of commonality is that both are, in theory, *anti-reductionist.* Each permits meaningful ecological talk of "individual" and "other," without the caveat that these notions are ultimately reducible to talk of processes or energy flows. Hierarchy theory rules out a view of individuals (e.g., animals) as ontologically reducible to something more basic (e.g., energy flows). There is no ontologically privileged (prior, fundamental) ecological description of nature. Hierarchy theory thereby challenges as mistaken the view expressed by Leopold scholar J. Baird Callicott that ecosystems ontologically subordinate objects to energy since "energy seems to be a more fundamental and primitive reality than material objects or discrete entities."[19] Both objects and energy are ontologically real. Even if (as physics reveals) all physical objects are made up of energy, physical objects are not ontologically reducible to energy.

This ecologically informed stance is a vital component of ecofeminist ethics. As an ecological and social position, ecofeminist philosophy describes both humans and nonhuman animals and nature as individuals (objects) and ecological "knots in webs of relationships" (energy flows). Ecofeminist philosophy's anti-reductionist ecological stance thereby agrees with hierarchy theorists that an "energy flux" approach to the study of ecosystems does not rule out an "objects" approach, and an ecologically informed ethic of discrete objects (e.g., trees, humans, rivers, animals) is both possible and desirable. An ecologically informed ecofeminist philosophy thereby disagrees with ecological holists, such as J. Baird Callicott, who claim that an ethic of objects is obsolete. According to Callicott, "ecology undermines the concept of a separable ego or social atom and thus renders obsolete any ethics which involves the concepts of 'self' and 'other' as primitive terms." [20] Callicott's view is true only if the "energy flux" view is the only and correct way to study ecosystems, which hierarchy theory shows it is not. Like hierarchy theory, an ecologically informed ecofeminist philosophy permits meaningful ecological talk of organisms as *both* "knots in a biospherical web of relationships" *and* discrete individuals, populations, and communities.

A fourth area of commonality between hierarchy theory and ecofeminist philosophy is *epistemological* (about knowledge, knowers, and objects of knowledge). The nature of an observation set links the observer with the observed in context-dependent ways. As such, both perspectives place our particular modes of access to the objects of our concern in the context of particular observation sets and conceptual frameworks. Whether our concern is ecological or ethical, theory is formulated against a background of epistemological relationships to the objects of concern. In this respect, knowledge is "situated"—it is always given within and relative to a particular set of observations, beliefs, values, attitudes, or assumptions.

A view of knowledge as "situated" does not imply epistemological relativism. As feminist biologist Donna Haraway argues, situated knowledges

> are as hostile to various forms of relativism as to the most explicitly totalizing versions of claims to scientific authority. But the alternative to relativism is not totalization and single vision. . . . The alternative to relativism is partial, locatable, critical knowledges sustaining the possibility of webs of connections called solidarity in politics and shared conversations in epistemology. Relativism is a way of being nowhere while claiming to be everywhere equally. . . . Relativism and totalization are both "god tricks" promising vision from everywhere and nowhere equally and fully.[21]

A view of knowledge as "situated" rejects both the absolutist position that one can be everywhere (by being nowhere in particular) and the relativist position that one can be everywhere equally (when one is really somewhere in particular). "Situated knowledges" attempt to find a larger vision by being "somewhere in particular."[22] We have encountered a similar view in ecofeminist ethics; it is the maxim of "situated universalism," that universality lies in particularity.

Does a view of knowledge as situated imply that there is no relevant or knowable scientific data? No, quite the contrary. Both hierarchy theory and ecofeminist philosophy make a central place for relevant scientific data (contextualized to a given observation set with particular scalar dimensions). In fact, so central to ecofeminist philosophy is relevant scientific information that "science" is part of one of the three main spheres of support in my visual representation of ecofeminist philosophy (given in chapter 3). What ecofeminist philosophers insist upon is that, where relevant, the perspectives and lives of women and other human Others with regard to nonhuman nature must be included as data.

A fifth area of commonality between hierarchy theory and ecofeminist philosophy is that they are *inclusivist, integrative frameworks* for mediating between historically opposed approaches. Hierarchy theory is an inclusivist framework that goes between the horns of the "object (population-community) versus energy flux (process)" dualism by valuing both approaches. Similarly, ecofeminist philosophy goes between the horns of the "culture versus nature" dualism by showing how humans are both "of culture" and "of nature," both concrete, discrete individuals and "biospherical knots in webs of relationships," both rational selves and ecological selves. But, as we saw in chapter 5, ecofeminist philosophy also is inclusivist in another respect. It offers an integrative ethical framework for mediating between two historically opposed approaches to environmental ethics: deontological (rights, virtue, and holistic) approaches and consequentialist approaches. An ecofeminist ethic may involve a commitment to rights in certain contexts and for certain purposes (e.g., in the protection of individual animals against unnecessary pain and suffering), and a commitment to utilitarian considerations in other contexts and for other purposes (e.g., in evaluating "costs" or harms to ecosystems or to nutrient cycling in an oak savannah).

The sixth commonality between hierarchy theory and ecofeminist philosophy is that each makes a central place for both *diversity* (or, difference) and *similarity.* Hierarchy theory is a framework that provides for both an ecology of differences and an ecology of similarities, depending on the context and the observation set. For example, biodiversity, as a feature of ecosystems, is not reducible to talk of the sameness of organisms or the oneness of energy flows. That would be the case only if one approach to ecosystems or nature had ontological priority over the other.

In fact, one of the most philosophically interesting features of hierarchy theory is that it privileges the notion of diversity (or, difference) when studying interactions *between* different subsystems ("holons") of ecosystems, and it privileges the notion of similarities *among* members of the same subsystem. Hierarchy theory thereby challenges the truth of the popular slogan, "Everything is interconnected," that a tug on any part of the ecosystem has an effect on every other part of the system. As hierarchy theorists insist, "if all parts of a complex system interact directly and symmetrically, then there is a low probability that the system will endure [*precisely because*] . . . a disturbance anywhere in the system tends to affect all other parts of the system."[23] For this reason, hierarchy theorists argue that "the old imagery of the natural world as having everything connected to everything else is shortsighted. It is the relative disconnection that constitutes the organization of the system."[24]

Critical to the stability of an ecosystem is the relative *dis*connection of subsystems ("holons") from one another. If this were not the case, then when elm trees die from Dutch elm disease, other neighboring species of trees (e.g., oak, pine, maple, ash) would also be vulnerable to the disease and die. The stability of multispecies forests depends in part on the disconnection of different species of trees. So, everything may be tied to everything else in *some* sense, but it is not in any ontologically reductionist or holistic way.

Similarly, ecofeminist philosophy also values diversity, both ecological diversity and cultural diversity, and offers insights into their interconnections. Typically, where biodiversity is preserved (e.g., where indigenous forests in India are kept intact, or rainforests in Brazil are not clear-cut), so is cultural diversity (there is a flourishing of a diversity of native languages, rituals, art, lifestyles); where biodiversity is threatened or destroyed, so is cultural diversity (e.g., through loss of land, languages, tribal bonds, kinship communities, rituals, sustainable relationships to the land). The health (flourishing, well-being) of the one tends to assist the health (flourishing, well-being) of the other. An ecofeminist philosophical commitment to diversity is a commitment to *both* cultural and biological diversity, without that ruling out considerations of similarities among humans or between humans and nonhuman animals and nature.

These six "bonds" between hierarchy theory and ecofeminist philosophy show how hierarchy theory provides ecological grounding for ecofeminist philosophy. But, the "bonds" go the other way, too: Ecofeminist philosophy can also make contributions to hierarchy theory and ecosystem ecology. I mention just a few such contributions here.

One contribution ecofeminist philosophy can make is its understanding of the roles played by socially constructed values in the practice and theory of science. As ecofeminist philosopher Patsy Hallen shows, values and interests shape science in many ways: the selection of goals for science; the choice of problems and research projects; the methodologies used; the choice of experimental design; the behavior shown toward research subjects; the language used; the content of theoretical formulations in science; and the evaluation and interpretation of scientific results.[25] When those values, attitudes, assumptions, and beliefs reinforce or maintain socially constructed views of females and males in ways that inferiorize female behavior, they are "male-biased" (both empirically biased and conceptually biased by their faulty claims to objectivity and universality).

Perhaps an example of male-bias in science may be helpful here. Feminist primatologists such as Donna Haraway and Sarah Blaffer Hrdy have challenged traditional observational and explanatory models for primate social organization as androcentric.[26] The assumption of such models was that primate social organization was structured around male dominance hierarchies. If any attention was focused on observing female primate behavior, females were cast in passive and primarily nurturing roles, while males were cast in culturally stereotyped and sanctioned active, courting, and promiscuous roles. Assumptions of male dominance hierarchies prevented traditional primatologists from seeing "the full extent of female choice, initiative and aggressivity or its polyandrous expression," and from seeing that dominance hierarchies are neither universal nor always male.[27] It prevented traditional researchers from seeing, for example, that it is usually estrous females that select mating partners, that in some species (e.g., Japanese macaques, rhesus macaques, and vervets) species dominance is matrilineal, and that no evidence supports the view that dominant males have more frequent access to females than less dominant males in baboon troops.[28] The patriarchal conceptual framework of traditional primatologists, based on socially constructed notions of female and male behavior, not only blinded these researchers from raising and correcting crucially relevant assumptions about female primate behavior and male dominance hierarchies; conceptually, it did not permit such issues to get raised at all. The "observation set" based on faulty but hitherto (that is, before the work of feminist primatologists) unchallenged assumptions affected both the observer and the observations made. They were empirically and conceptually biased in ways that systemically privileged and reinforced assumptions of male superiority: They were "male-biased."

Ecofeminist philosophy can also contribute to the theory and practice of science by revealing how power and privilege function in the social construction of scientific knowledge, for example, by reinforcing faulty notions of science as value-neutral and by portraying "the object"of knowledge (nature) as passive and inert. As a corrective to such tendencies, Haraway recommends that we view nature as an active agent or participant in the construction of knowledge. Again, drawing on her notion of "situated knowledges," Haraway argues that "situated knowledges require that the object of knowledge be pictured as an actor and agent, not as a screen or a ground or a resource, never finally as slave to the master that closes off the dialectic in his unique agency and his authorship of 'objective' knowledge." Haraway credits ecofeminists as having "perhaps been most insistent on some version of the world as active subject." She encourages us all to revision the world "as [a] coding trickster with whom we must learn to converse."[29]

Nobel Prize-winning cytogeneticist Barbara McClintock is an example of a scientist who exemplifies Haraway's view of relating to nature as active subject or agent. Reflecting on her research on the maize plant, McClintock describes how she became "friends" with each kernel of corn over her twenty years of research with the maize plant. She viewed each maize plant as an active agent or participate in what she came to know about the maize plant. McClintock encourages scientists to "let the material [in her case, the corn plant] speak to you" by developing a "feeling for the organism."[30] McClintock meant this literally, not figuratively or poetically.

To summarize, six areas of commonality between ecofeminist philosophy and hierarchy theory provide theoretical ecological grounding for ecofeminist philosophy. There also are important contributions about women–other human Others–nature connections, power and privilege, and the social construction of science that ecofeminist philosophy can offer ecological science. I now turn to the question whether Leopold's land ethic and ecofeminist philosophy share common ground.

LEOPOLD'S LAND ETHIC

In chapter 4 I identified three cornerstone claims of Leopold's land ethic: (1) Humans are co-members of the ecological community. (2) Humans should love and respect the land. (3) It is wrong to destroy the integrity, stability, and beauty of the biotic community. I stated that any position that denies the sensibilities expressed in these three claims would not constitute a genuine environmental ethic. So, one would expect ecofeminist philosophy to be Leopoldian in this respect. And, as I will show, it is.

But to endorse these three "sensibilities" as central to any environmental ethic is not necessarily to endorse, verbatim, the language, arguments, or applications Leopold offers. My interest in Leopold's land ethic, like my interest in hierarchy theory and ecological science, is in theoretical and practical coalition-building: I want to establish common ground between ecofeminist philosophy, ecosystem ecology, and Leopold's land ethic in order to promote ongoing dialogue and coalition-building among the three.

Recall that the first area of commonality between hierarchy theory and ecofeminist philosophy was that both emphasize the contextual nature of observations, explanations, and theory. A crucial aspect of this attention to context is the recognition that *what* a thing is is partly a function of *where* it is. Leopold's land ethic is a marvelous example of ecological and ethical sensitivity to context. First, the lasting impact of Leopold's writings is partly due to their ability to show how ecology contributes to the contextualization of moral thought. Leopold writes:

> That man is, in fact, only a member of a biotic team is shown by an ecological interpretation of history. Many historical events, hitherto explained solely in terms of human enterprise, were actually biotic interactions between people and land. The characteristics of the land determined the facts quite as potently as the characteristics of the men who lived on it.[31]

Leopold's discussion of the origins of bluegrass in Kentucky and the development of the landscape of the Southwest reinforce his point that these historical events are "biotic interactions" between people and land. They illustrate beautifully how *what* something is partly is a function of *where* it is.

Second, Leopold's "ecological interpretation of history" is central to his development of the concept of land as a community, and to his "extension of ethics" to the land as "a process in ecological evolution."[32] He writes, "all ethics so far evolved rest upon a single premise: that the individual is a member of a community of interdependent parts. . . . The land ethic simply enlarges the boundaries of the community to include soils, waters, plants, and animals, or collectively: the land."[33] This is, I think, the most important contribution of Leopold's "land ethic." It provides an explicitly ecological context for rethinking who humans are and what ethics implies. "In short, a land ethic changes the role of *Homo sapiens* from conqueror of the land-community to plain member and citizen of it. It implies respect for his fellow-members, and also respect for the community as such."[34]

Third, Leopold contextualizes his ecological and ethical claims by explicitly utilizing spatiotemporal scales as a norm for evaluating direct human impact on nonhuman nature ("anthropogenic change").[35] For example, Leopold contrasts evolutionary changes, which are "usually slow and local," with human-imposed changes, which are much faster and "of unprecedented violence, rapidity, and scope."[36] His ethical censure of what he saw as destructive land use is based on the spatiotemporal scale of anthropogenic change. Callicott states this Leopoldian point simply and well.

> Volcanoes bury the biota of whole mountains with lava and ash. Tornados rip through forests, leveling trees. Hurricanes erode beaches. Wild fires sweep through forests as well as savannas. Rivers drown floodplains. Droughts dry up lakes and streams. . . . The problem with anthropogenic perturbations—such as industrial forestry and agriculture, exurban development, drift net fishing, and such—is that they are far more frequent, widespread, and regularly occurring than are nonanthropogenic perturbations.[37]

In similar fashion, Leopold's contextualization of his ethical claims about human conduct toward nonhuman nature draws on his sensitivity to spatiotemporal scale. Again I cite Callicott:

> Among the abnormally frequent and widespread anthropogenic perturbations that Leopold himself censures in "The Land Ethic" are the continent-wide elimination of large predators from biotic communities; the ubiquitous substitution of domestic species for wild ones; the ecological homogenization of the planet resulting from the anthropogenic "world-wide pooling of faunas and floras," the ubiquitous "polluting of waters or obstructing them with dams."[38]

So, Leopold's land ethic complements the focus on the contextual nature of observation sets, the importance of spatiotemporal scale, and the context-dependent nature of what we see, know, believe, and value. In this way, his project converges with those of hierarchy theory and ecofeminist philosophy.

The second and third areas of commonality between hierarchy theory and ecofeminist philosophy are their insistence that there is no one right way to study ecosystems (a methodological stance) and no ontologically privileged view of ecosystems (an ontological stance). Each resists reductionist strategies that reduce individuals to energy flows. Does or would Leopold agree?

Since Leopold's ecological views predate hierarchy theory by several decades, it may seem somewhat disingenuous to critique Leopold by determining whether his views are compatible with a theory that did not exist at the time he wrote. This is clearly a worry here—when considering whether Leopold assumed an ontologically privileged view of ecosystems, or whether he assumed that individuals were reducible to energy flows.

Nonetheless, I address the question here since I think Leopold is often misconstrued by scholars in a way that makes his views seem incompatible with hierarchy theory. And because they need not be so construed, Leopold's views are more compatible with an ecofeminist philosophy informed by hierarchy theory than Leopoldians might suppose. Consider why.

Sometimes Leopold describes organisms as discrete individuals. This is the case when, in *A Sand County Almanac,* he writes about geese, woodcocks,

grouse, partridge, skunk, chickadees, warblers, pigeons, egrets, cranes, field spar-
rows, the prairie chicken, tamaracks, a meadow mouse, a rough-legged hawk,
deer, rabbits, wolf, coyotes, prairie plants, marsh, river, fish, pine, birch, oak and
aspen trees, wilderness. Sometimes Leopold writes about organisms—indeed,
"the land" collectively—as energy flows. For example, after Leopold introduces
"the biotic pyramid" as "a symbol of land," he writes:

> Land, then, is not merely soil; it is a fountain of energy flowing through a circuit of
> soils, plants, and animals. Food chains are the living channels which conduct energy
> upward; death and decay return it to the soil. The circuit is not closed; some energy
> is dissipated in decay, some is added by absorption from the air, some is stored in
> soils, peats, and long-lived forests; but it is a sustained circuit, like a slowly aug-
> mented revolving fund of life.[39]

And in an earlier set of essays ("Wildlife in American Culture"), Leopold writes
that "there is value in any experience that reminds us of our dependency on the
soil-plant-animal-man food chain, and of the fundamental organization of the
biota."[40] The food chain is about discrete populations of individuals as individual
consumers, producers, and decomposers; but it also is about the energy flow patterns within biotic communities. So, Leopold seems to give attention to both individuals and energy flows without reducing the former to the latter—a main precept of hierarchy theory.

Yet environmental philosophers and Leopold scholars such as Callicott routinely
describe Leopold's land ethic as "holistic" (neither "individualistic" nor individualistic in some respects and holistic in others). For example, Callicott claims:

> Indeed, as "The Land Ethic" develops, the focus of moral concern shifts gradually
> away from plants, animals, soils, and waters severally to the biotic community col-
> lectively. . . . Leopold invokes the "biotic rights" of *species*—as the context indi-
> cates—of wildflowers, songbirds, and predators. In The Outlook, the climatic section
> of "The Land Ethic," nonhuman natural entities, first appearing as fellow members,
> then considered in profile as species, are not so much as mentioned in what might be
> called the "summary moral maxim" of the land ethic: "A thing is right when it tends
> to preserve the integrity, stability, and beauty of the biotic community. It is wrong
> when it tends otherwise."[41]

On this interpretation, Leopold's attention to individuals is best described either
as a feature of his earlier writings or as ultimately reducible to talk of energy
flows. On this interpretation, Leopold's land ethic makes an "object ontology"
obsolete. The land ethic is not only holistic; it is, as Callicott claims, "holistic
with a vengeance."

> The Land Ethic not only provides moral considerability for the biotic community per
> se, but ethical consideration of its individual members is preempted by concern for
> the preservation of the integrity, stability, and beauty of the biotic community. The
> land ethic, thus, not only has a holistic aspect; it is holistic with a vengeance.[42]

Which is a more accurate or generous way to interpret Leopold's land ethic — as "holistic with a vengeance" or as granting both individualistic and holistic aspects to the objects of ecology? While Leopold's "summary moral maxim" may be holistic, I think it is a mistake to interpret Leopold's overall ecological and ethical positions as "holistic with a vengeance" by making individuals just conduits of energy. I have three worries about such a characterization, each of which involves undervaluing much of what is so important and lovely about Leopold and his writings.

My first worry is that the "holistic with a vengeance" characterization of Leopold undervalues Leopold's ethical motivation for writing *A Sand County Almanac*. In the foreword to that book, Leopold's opening words are "there are some who can live without wild things, and some who cannot. These essays are the delights and dilemmas of one who cannot."[43] Leopold describes his own essays as "the delights and dilemmas" of one who cannot live without "wild things" — presumably referring to individuals, populations, and communities of deer, birds, trees, forests, rivers, not to nutrient cycles and energy flows.

My second worry concerns what a "holistic with a vengeance" interpretation of Leopold's land ethic does to the ethical backbone of Leopold's land ethic. It reduces Leopold's land ethic to the "summary moral maxim" that what is right "tends to preserve the integrity, stability, and beauty of the biotic community," and then interprets that principle as applying to processes and energy flows (rather than to particular, nonreducible objects). But Leopold's land ethic is not reducible in this way, since it also involves the crucial moral claims that humans ought to cultivate love for the land and to treat the land with respect. And it involves these additional moral claims in ways that make them fundamental components of the land ethic, not features of it that are reducible to the principle that "what is right tends to preserve the integrity, stability, and beauty of the biotic community." It just is not Leopoldian to interpret Leopold's claims that we ought to love and respect the land as meaning that one ought to love energy flows — as if that is all the land really is. Even if this were in some sense true, its truth would not capture what Leopold *means* when he talks of loving the land.

This brings me to my third worry. It is a disservice to Leopold to suggest that his often passionate descriptions of nature are not about discrete objects, in all their glory as discrete objects. One has only to read "Thinking Like a Mountain" to appreciate the profound change that overcame Leopold after killing a wolf.

> We reached the old wolf in time to watch a fierce green fire dying in her eyes. I realized then, and have known ever since, that there was something new to me in those eyes — something known only to her and to the mountain. I was young then, and full of trigger-itch. I thought that because fewer wolves meant more deer, that no wolves would mean hunter's paradise. But after seeing the green fire die, I sensed that neither the wolf nor the mountain agreed with such a view.[44]

Or, to read his description of the return of the banded chickadee and its fear of windy places in his essay "65290": "To the chickadee, winter wind is the boundary of the habitable world. If the chickadee had an office, the maxim over his desk would say: 'Keep calm.' "[45] Or, to read his lament in "The Marshland Elegy" over the loss of cranes and marshes by "an epidemic of ditch digging and land-booming":

> Thus always does history, whether of marsh or market place, end in paradox. The ultimate value in these marshes is wildness, and the crane is wildness incarnate. But all conservation of wildness is self-defeating, for to cherish we must see and fondle, and when enough have seen and fondled, there is no wilderness left to cherish.[46]

Even a random selection among Leopold's essays would show that, for Leopold, the ethical treatment of "the land" includes the ethical treatment of individuals as individuals (and not simply as energy flows or "process" over substance).

For these reasons, I think the most faithful reading of Leopold is that he thought both individuals and energy flows were real. While Leopold indeed made "wholes" morally considerable, he did not thereby make individuals morally inconsiderable, ontologically unimportant, or reducible to energy flows. The "holism with a vengeance" interpretation of Leopold's ecological views is precisely the "unacceptable form of holism that exaggerates the analogy between the organism and the ecosystem" that hierarchy theorists reject. Since there are good reasons, found in Leopold writings, *not* to interpret either Leopold's ecological views or his ethical views as committed to this sort of "holism," I suggest philosophers and ethicists resist doing so.

The fourth commonality between hierarchy theory and ecofeminist philosophy is epistemological: there is no context-independent knowledge. This epistemological stance stresses the importance of our particular, context-dependent relationships to the objects of our concern. Such views are laced throughout Leopold's *A Sand County Almanac* and his essay "The Land Ethic." For example, Leopold's discussion of "land health" expresses such epistemological commitments. Leopold argues that land health is fundamental to preserving the "integrity, stability, and beauty of the biotic community,"[47] and claims that "the most important characteristic of an organism is that capacity for internal self-renewal known as health."[48]

Leopold insists, rightly, that data from ecology are crucial to determining land health. "A science of land health needs, first of all, a base datum of normality, a picture of how healthy land maintains itself as an organism."[49] But, for Leopold, knowing what counts as "land health" in any particular case depends on knowing such contextual features as the spatiotemporal scale of the observation set in which data about land health and land sickness are collected (something hierarchy theorists insist upon).

> The disappearance of plants and animal species without visible cause, despite efforts to protect them, and the irruption of others as pests despite efforts to control them, must, in the absence of simpler explanations, be regarded as symptoms of sickness in the land organism. Both are occurring too frequently to be dismissed as normal evolutionary events.[50]

Leopold introduces "the biotic pyramid" in his discussion of land health because, he claims, a land ethic "presupposes the existence of some mental image of land as a biotic mechanism."[51]

Furthermore, for Leopold, an ethical relationship to the land requires both head and heart. He writes that "we can be ethical only in relation to something we can see, feel, understand, love or otherwise have faith in."[52] Leopold's epistemological views resonate strongly with an ecofeminist ethic that integrates rational intelligence and emotional intelligence (chapter 5). This is nowhere more important than in his description of what is involved in adopting a land ethic. "The evolution of a land ethic is an intellectual as well as an emotional process."[53] "It is inconceivable to me that an ethical relation to land can exist without love, respect, and admiration for land."[54] Like ecofeminist philosophical ethics, Leopold's land ethic calls for changes in both our intellectual and emotional understanding about the land and the human-land relationship. "No important change in ethics was ever accomplished without an internal change in our intellectual emphasis, loyalties, affections, and convictions."[55] As Andrew Brennan states so well, "The intimate knowledge of organisms in their natural state, and understanding of their physiology, their role in biological communities, their capacity for flourishing . . . is a way of providing a context within which an attitude of care about natural things makes sense."[56]

A fifth area of commonality between hierarchy theory and ecofeminist philosophy is that they are inclusivist, integrative frameworks for mediating between dualistic, historically opposed approaches to nature and human-nature relationships. Does Leopold's land ethic provide this sort of inclusivist, integrative framework as well? Leopold certainly is aware of the role of dualisms in forestry, wildlife ecology, and agriculture between those who regard the land as soil, and its function as commodity-production, and those who regard the lands as a biota, and its function as something broader.[57] Leopold sees in these dualisms "the same basic paradoxes: man the conqueror *versus* man the biotic citizen; science the sharpener of his sword *versus* science the searchlight of his universe; land the slave and servant *versus* land the collective organism."[58] However, rather than challenging the problematic nature of the dualisms themselves (as ecofeminist philosophers do), Leopold argues for one member of the dualistic pair: "man the biotic citizen," "science the searchlight of his universe," "land the collective organism."

Is this a sufficiently large rift between Leopold and ecofeminist philosophy to prevent a theoretically promising common ground between them? I do not think so. Looked at in the larger context of all his writings, Leopold clearly rejected some of the problematic dualisms at the heart of an ecofeminist philosophical critique: culture/nature, human/nonhuman Other, conqueror/conquered, master/slave. Leopold also clearly recognizes humans as both "plain members of the biotic community" and yet also different from rocks, mountains, and ecosystems in our abilities to reason, to understand, to formulate a land ethic, to recognize value and confer rights, to show respect and love for the natural world. Seen in this way, the land ethic can be interpreted in a way that includes all humans, nonhuman earth others, and the land, collectively, in "the moral community" without adoption of an exclusivist "either-or" value dualism. And this interpretation captures what, in fact, has made Leopold's land ethic so significant from a historical and philosophical point of view: It was the first ethic in the Western philosophical ethical tradition to systematically include nonhumans—whether populations, species, and communities of plants and animals taken individually or as wholes—within the range of moral consideration. In these respects, Leopold's land ethic is an inclusivist framework.

The sixth and last area of commonality between hierarchy theory and ecofeminist philosophy is that they centralize both diversity and similarity in and across ecological and human social contexts. Does Leopold's land ethic also do this? In some ways it does. First, Leopold explicitly links cultural diversity with biodiversity.

> Wilderness was never a homogenous raw material. It was very diverse, and the resulting artifacts are very diverse. These differences in the end-product are known as cultures. The rich diversity of the world's cultures reflects a corresponding diversity in the wilds that gave them birth.

Leopold goes on to describe two impending changes: "One is the exhaustion of wilderness in the more habitable portions of the globe. The other is the world-wide hybridization of cultures through modern transport and industrialization."[59] Leopold laments the "exhaustion of wilderness" and "world-wide hybridization of cultures" as the destruction of both ecological and cultural diversity. For Leopold, the "wild roots" of cultures and the importance of our ecological heritage are part of human cultural heritage that should be preserved. He makes this view explicit in "Wildlife in American Culture" when he writes, "The culture of primitive [*sic*] peoples is often based on wildlife. Thus the plains Indian not only ate buffalo, but buffalo largely determined his architecture, dress, language, arts, and religion."[60] For Leopold, the value and loss of cultural diversity is intimately connected with the value and loss of biodiversity. Like ecofeminist philosophers, Leopold sees biotic diversity and "land health" as intimately connected with cultural diversity.

A second reason for supposing Leopold centralizes both diversity and similarity in and across ecological and human social contexts is that embryonic forms of social justice and gender issues also can be found in Leopold's writings. In fact, the opening lines of "The Land Ethic" read:

> When Odysseus returned from the wars in Troy, he hanged all on one rope a dozen slave-girls of his household whom he suspected of misbehavior during his absence. This hanging involved no question of propriety. The girls were property. The disposal of property was then, as now, a matter of expediency, not of right and wrong.[61]

Leopold's rare reference to gender here is significant, not only because it occurs in 1949 as the opening lines of "The Land Ethic," but because it explicitly makes an analogy between conceptions and treatment of "land" as mere property and conceptions and treatment of "girls" as mere property—both of which are unacceptable for Leopold. Leopold continues with the analogy in the next few pages of "The Land Ethic": "There is as yet no ethic dealing with man's relation to land and to the animals and plants which grow on it. Land, like Odysseus's slave girls, is still property. The land-relation is still strictly economic, entailing privileges but no obligations."[62] So fundamental to Leopold's view of the land and the land ethic is a worry about the mere economic value of land as property, like Odysseus's slave girls, that he writes in the foreword to *A Sand County Almanac,*

> We abuse land because we regard it as a commodity belonging to us. When we see land as a community to which we belong, we may begin to use it with love and respect. There is no other way for land to survive the impact of mechanized man, nor for us to reap from it the esthetic harvest it is capable, under science, of contributing to culture.
>
> That land is a community is the basic concept of ecology, but that land is to be loved and respected is an extension of ethics.[63]

Leopold's point is that although humans may use the land and other humans as means to some ends, humans ought never *merely* use land or humans as means to some end. Both land and humans have value independent of their use-value to humans. Nonhuman nature, like Odysseus's "slave girls," has more than economic or instrumental value. It is morally considerable.

A third reason for supposing that Leopold centralizes both diversity and similarity is that he is concerned with issues in urban ecology and with preserving the epistemic value of what those who work the land often know about the land. For Leopold, ecological science "has wrought a change in the mental eye"; it has changed our perceptions of what we see. It has enabled us to see the beauty and "incredible intricacies of the plant and animal community."[64] He then claims (in "The Conservation Esthetic") that one need not have a Ph.D. in ecology in order to "see" one's country:

> On the contrary, the Ph.D. may become as callous as an undertaker to the mysteries at which he officiates. . . . The weeds in a city lot convey the same lesson as the redwoods; the farmer may see in his cow-pasture what may not be vouchsafed to the scientist adventuring the South Seas. Perception, in short, cannot be purchased with either learned degrees or dollars.[65]

Here Leopold not only acknowledges occasions when those who work close to the land may have important knowledge about it that is unavailable to the professionally trained ecologist; he also acknowledges the importance of urban ecology, that "the weeds in a city lot convey the same lesson as the redwoods."

We have seen throughout this book that concerns for urban ecology and the environmental plights of cities are key organizing themes for ecofeminist activism. Naturalist and city dweller Mike Weilbacher defines and defends urban environmental education (EE) this way:

> For me, urban EE is not *who* you teach, but *what* you teach. It's about the complex interworkings of the urban environment—where garbage goes on collection day, where electricity flow from, where tap water originates, and where it goes when it is flushed. It's about shade trees reducing summer temperatures. It's discussing why Pittsburgh's air and the Delaware River's water are cleaner now than fifty years ago.
>
> Yes, of course it's about green spaces and the opossums, skunks, raccoons, bats, bees, and birds that live there, but it's so much *more* than tired studies of weeds, trees, and backyard bugs. It's about the systems that keep you *alive!*
>
> Urban environmental education is, simply, teaching about the urban environment. Weeds, bugs, and pond life are a low priority. The residents of cities like Philadelphia, Erie, Scranton must first understand their relationships within the urban environment, must first understand their connections to the larger world through the life support systems that keep them alive–energy, food, water, transportation.[66]

The epistemological significance of urban environmental education, contextualized to the material realities of life in a city, can be found in Leopold's conviction that "the weeds in a city lot convey the same lesson as the redwoods." While Weilbacher's views may be more human-centered than Leopold would like, Weilbacher's ecological approach to urban environmental education meets city people where they are—in cities with city environmental problems.

Like Weilbacher, Leopold has deeply felt worries about a lack of ecological literacy among the general population (at least, in the United States). In a frequently quoted passage, Leopold writes,

> There are two spiritual dangers in not owning a farm. One is the danger of supposing that breakfast comes from the grocery, and the other that heat comes from the furnace.
>
> To avoid the first danger, one should plant a garden, preferably where there is no grocer to confuse the issue.
>
> To avoid the second, he should lay a split of good oak on the andirons, preferably where there is no furnace, and let it warm his shins while a February blizzard tosses the trees outside.[67]

For Leopold, there is no substitute for direct, personal experience of "nature." But, like Weilbacher, Leopold recognizes that one doesn't need to leave the city to have such experiences.

But, in other ways, Leopold's land ethic is *not* sufficiently sensitive to issues of gender and environmental justice to satisfy an ecofeminist philosopher. An ecofeminist philosophical perspective is important to an updated and revised Leopoldian land ethic in at least six ways.

First, ecofeminist philosophy can contribute an analysis of the pitfalls of value dualistic thinking within dominance-subordination contexts and a sensitivity to the ways considerations of gender, race, and class contribute to the observations, analyses, and theories of environmental ethics. The ecofeminist focus on the interconnections among social systems of domination would broaden and deepen a Leopoldian critique of contemporary land-use attitudes and behaviors.

Second, ecofeminist philosophy would recast issues of environmental education in inclusive terms, rejecting the "either-or" issue of choosing between the "educating about nature in nature" approach (e.g., by exporting inner city kids to nature centers in rural areas) or "educating about nature in cities" (e.g., Weilbacher's) approach. It would argue for the advantages and limitations of each, depending on the context.

Third, ecofeminist philosophy would draw attention to the institutional nature of much of contemporary environmental destruction. For Leopold, the philosophical (not economic) value of the land will be realized only through significant efforts of landowners. While Leopold appreciates the role government plays in the management of forests, fisheries, migratory birds, soil and watersheds, parks and wilderness areas, he argues that ultimately a system of conservation depends on assigning "more obligations to the private landowner."[68] An ecofeminist philosophical perspective can add a critical dimension to that analysis by reminding Leopoldians that a lot of citizens (in the United States and around the globe) are not "private landowners," and that the disproportionate burdens they suffer from environmental degradation are often due to the activities of private landowners and multinational corporations. Furthermore (as I argue in chapter 8), there are institutional (and not merely "personal" or "private" landowner) issues about both the distribution and conception of environmental justice that an ecofeminist philosophical perspective is well poised to provide.

As a related fourth point, an ecofeminist perspective can be used to highlight the ways in which ecosystem health (well-being, flourishing) is intimately connected to the "health" of human social systems. In fact, this latter point is so important to my understanding of ecofeminist philosophy that it is discussed extensively in chapters 8 and 9.

Fifth, an ecofeminist philosophical perspective would challenge the tendency of Leopoldians to speak of a Leopoldian land ethic as the best environmental ethic, especially given cross-cultural differences in the plight and status of women, other human Others, and nature. For example, conservation efforts, so dear to Leopold's land ethic, must include women (and not just generic "citizens") in the decision-making, policy formation, and implementation processes. As we saw in chapter 1, this is especially true in the Third World, where women, as both users and managers of the natural resources base, have extensive knowledge of the environment.[69]

Lastly, an ecofeminist philosophical perspective would promote a view about nonhuman animals that places significant constraints on the hunting and consuming of animals as food. Leopoldians like Callicott tend to view Leopold's land ethic as an extreme form of ecological holism. One drawback of ecological holism is its tendency to view animals *solely* as members of an ecological "net of biospherical relationships." They forget that animals are *also* individuals, with sentiency, interests, desires, and needs. Leopold knew this. It would be a seriously disingenuous reading of, for example, the famous wolf passage, to assume otherwise.

Of course, pointing out that Leopold saw wolves as "individuals" will not make Leopold's views any friendlier to ecofeminists who argue against all hunting and consumption of animals. Leopold was a recreational hunter who consumed animals. Nothing an ecofeminist says about the land ethic will or could change that. Leopold also did not associate the objectification of women with the objectification of animals as "meat," which is central to many ecofeminist arguments concerning hunting and meat-eating. Leopold's limited gender analysis only went so far as to recognize that "land, like Odysseus' slave-girls, was property." Leopold's land ethic is not, and cannot possibly be interpreted as, the basis for any ethic (ecofeminist or otherwise) against all forms of hunting or animal consumption. Insofar as an ecofeminist ethic prohibits the sort of hunting and consuming of animals that Leopold supports, there cannot be a Leopoldian-based ecofeminist ethic.

But I am not arguing for a Leopoldian-based ecofeminist ethic, or an ecofeminist-based Leopoldian land ethic. I am simply arguing that there are grounds of commonality between a Leopoldian land ethic and an *ecologically* informed ecofeminist philosophy, and that there are important contributions ecofeminist philosophy can make to a Leopoldian land ethic. That Leopold's land ethic is not, by itself and unrevised, an ecofeminist ethic is part of what makes the contributions of an ecofeminist ethic distinct and significant.

CONCLUSION

In this chapter I have argued that there is sufficient common ecological ground among ecofeminist philosophy, ecosystem ecology (as given by hierarchy theory), and Leopoldian land ethics to warrant describing ecofeminist philosophy as an ecologically informed position. I also have argued that ecofeminist philosophy can make important contributions to both hierarchy theory and Leopoldian land ethics.

It is a two-way street: Just as ecofeminist philosophy gains an important ecological perspective from hierarchy theory and Leopold's discussion of the land ethic, so, too, hierarchy theory and Leopoldian land ethicists can learn from and benefit by an ecofeminist philosophical perspective. The considerable common ground among the three suggests that they could, and I think should, be engaged in mutually beneficial, theoretically productive, and practically useful dialogue and coalition-building.

NOTES

I dedicate this chapter to Nina Bradley, the third child and first daughter of Aldo and Estella Leopold. I met Nina in 1991 at her home on the Leopold Reserve in Baraboo, Wisconsin. She is a remarkable human being: loving, insightful, and passionate about the land.

Her embrace of me and responsiveness to my views has made a remarkable difference in my life. The motivation for writing this chapter occurred while Nina and I were together at a conference celebrating the fiftieth anniversary of publication of her father's book, *A Sand County Almanac* ("Aldo Leopold's Land Ethic: A Legacy for Public Land Managers," May 13–16, 1999, at the National Conservation Training Center, in Shepherdsville, Virginia). It was because of that conference that I knew I wanted to write a chapter in this book on Leopold. Nina was the person for whom I wanted to write it.

1. For an in-depth description of hierarchy theory, see R. V. O'Neill, D. L. DeAngelis, J. B. Waide, and T. F. Allen, *A Hierarchical Concept of Ecosystems* (Princeton, N.J.: Princeton University Press, 1986). For a more detailed description of hierarchy theory and defense of the links between hierarchy theory and ecofeminist philosophy, see Karen J. Warren and Jim Cheney, "Ecological Feminism and Ecosystem Ecology," in *Ecological Feminist Philosophies*, ed. Karen J. Warren (Bloomington: Indiana University Press, 1996), 224–62.

2. Catherine Zabinski, "Scientific Ecology and Ecological Feminism: The Potential for Dialogue," in *Ecofeminism: Women, Culture, Nature,* ed. Karen J. Warren (Bloomington: Indiana University Press, 1997), 319.

3. This diagram emerged from a personal conversation with Bruce Nordstrom-Loeb.

4. Notice that I am not defending a Leopoldian land ethic, a Leopoldian-based ecofeminism, or an ecofeminist land ethic. Nor am I defending how a Leopoldian land ethic could contribute to hierarchy theory—another leg of the hierarchy theory–Leopoldian land ethic bond. I am only discussing bonds that link ecofeminist philosophy with hierarchy theory, hierarchy theory with Leopoldian land ethics, and Leopoldian land ethics with ecofeminist philosophy.

5. Frank B. Golley, *A Primer for Environmental Literacy* (New Haven, Conn: Yale University Press, 1998), 1.

6. O'Neill et al., *Hierarchical Concept,* 7.

7. O'Neill et al., *Hierarchical Concept,* 7.

8. O'Neill et al., *Hierarchical Concept,* 86.

9. O'Neill et al., *Hierarchical Concept,* 20.

10. O'Neill et al., *Hierarchical Concept,* 83.

11. O'Neill et al., *Hierarchical Concept,* 83.

12. O'Neill et al., *Hierarchical Concept,* 15–16.

13. O'Neill et al., *Hierarchical Concept,* 14.

14. O'Neill et al., *Hierarchical Concept,* 16.

15. O'Neill et al., *Hierarchical Concept,* 18.

16. O'Neill et al., *Hierarchical Concept,* 18.

17. Andrew Brennan, *Thinking About Nature: An Investigation of Nature, Value and Ecology* (Athens: University of Georgia Press, 1988), 162.

18. Jim Cheney, "Eco-Feminism and Deep Ecology," *Environmental Ethics* 9, no. 2 (Summer 1987), 144.

19. J. Baird Callicott, "The Metaphysical Implications of Ecology," *Environmental Ethics* 8, no. 4 (Winter 1968), 310.

20. Callicott, "Metaphysical Implications," 301.

21. Donna Haraway, "Situated Knowledges: The Science Question in Feminism and the Privilege of Partial Perspective," *Feminist Studies* 14, no. 3 (Fall 1988), 584.

22. Haraway, "Situated Knowledges," 590.

23. O'Neill et al., *Hierarchical Concept,* 94.

24. O'Neill et al., *Hierarchical Concept,* 86.

25. Patsy Hallen, "Careful of Science: A Feminist Critique of Science," *The Trumpeter* 6, no. 1 (Winter, 1989), 3–8.

26. Donna Haraway, "Primatology is Politics by Other Means," in *Feminist Approaches to Science,* ed. Ruth Bleier (New York: Pergamon, 1984), 77–118; Sarah Blaffer Hrdy, "Empathy, Polyandry, and the Myth of the Coy Female," loc. cit., 119–46.

27. Ruth Bleier, "Introduction," *Feminist Approaches to Science* (New York: Pergamon, 1986), 8.

28. Ruth Bleier, *Science and Gender: A Critique of Biology and Its Theories on Women* (New York: Pergamon, 1984), 29.

29. Haraway, "Situated Knowledges," 592–93, 593–94, 596.

30. Evelyn Fox Keller, "Women, Science, and Popular Mythology," in *Machina Ex Dea: Feminist Perspectives on Technology,* ed. Joan Rothschild (New York: Pergamon, 1983), 141. For a complete treatment of Keller's treatment of McClintock's work, see Keller, *A Feeling for the Organism: The Life and Work of Barbara McClintock* (San Francisco: W. H. Freeman, 1983).

31. Leopold, "The Land Ethic," in *Sand County,* 205.

32. Leopold, "Land Ethic," 202. Leopold also claims, "The extension of ethics [to the land] is an evolutionary possibility and an ecological necessity" (203).

33. Leopold, "Land Ethic," 203–4.

34. Leopold, "Land Ethic," 204.

35. J. Baird Callicott, "Do Deconstructive Ecology and Sociobiology Undermine Leopold's Land Ethic?" in *Environmental Philosophy,* 2nd edition, ed. Michael E. Zimmerman, J. Baird Callicott, George Sessions, Karen J. Warren, and John Clark (Upper Saddle River, N.J.: Prentice-Hall, 1998), 158.

36. Leopold, "Land Ethic," 217.

37. Callicott, "Deconstructive Ecology?", 159.

38. Callicott, "Deconstructive Ecology?", 217.

39. Leopold, "Land Ethic," 216.

40. Leopold, "Wildlife in American Culture," *Sand County,* 178.

41. Leopold, "Land Ethic," 224–45, cited in J. Baird Callicott, "The Conceptual Foundations of the Land Ethic," in *Companion to* A Sand County Almanac: *Interpretive and Critical Essays* (Madison: University of Wisconsin Press, 1987), 196.

42. Callicott, "Conceptual Foundations," 196.

43. Leopold, "Foreword," *Sand County,* vii.

44. Leopold, "Thinking Like a Mountain," *Sand County,* 130.

45. Leopold, "65290," *Sand County,* 91.

46. Leopold, "Marshland Elegy," *Sand County,* 100, 101.

47. Leopold, "Land Ethic," 224–45.

48. Leopold, "Wilderness," *Sand County,* 194.

49. Leopold, "Wilderness," 196. Correctly or incorrectly, Leopold thought two norms were available for such study: northeastern Europe and wilderness.

50. Leopold, "Wilderness," 194.

51. Leopold, "Land Ethic," 214.

52. Leopold, "Wilderness," 200.

53. Leopold, "Land Ethic," 225.

54. Leopold, "Land Ethic," 223.

55. Leopold, "Land Ethic," 209–10.

56. Brennan, *Thinking About Nature,* 138.

57. Leopold, "Land Ethic," 221.

58. Leopold, "Land Ethic," 223.

59. Leopold, "Wilderness," 188.

60. Leopold, "Wildlife in American Culture," 177.

61. Leopold, "Land Ethic," 201.

62. Leopold, "Land Ethic," 203.

63. Leopold, "Foreword," *Sand County,* viii–ix.

64. Leopold, "The Conservation Esthetic," *Sand County,* 174.

65. Leopold, "Conservation Aesthetic," 174.

66. Mike Weilbacher, "In City Is the Preservation of the World," *Pennsylvania Alliance for Environmental Ethics (PAEE) Newsletter* 15, no. 4 (Fall 1991), 4.

67. Leopold, "Good Oak," *Sand County,* 6.

68. Leopold, "Land Ethic," 213.

69. M. Vollers, "Healing the Ravaged Land: Third World Women and Conservation," *International Wildlife* 18, no. 1 (1988), 4–9.

Chapter Eight

With Justice for All

Ecofeminist Philosophy and Social Justice

In this chapter I focus on the topic of social justice. I begin with a description of a contemporary model of social justice, the "distributive model." I argue that, by itself, this model of justice is incomplete as a model of social justice. I then argue for a more inclusive concept of social justice, one which incorporates nondistributive issues. I conclude by sketching what is included in an inclusive concept of social justice—one which is needed to incorporate important issues of environmental justice.

SOCIAL JUSTICE AS DISTRIBUTION

In contemporary Western philosophy, the main model of social justice is a "distributive model." A distributive model focuses on one central question: *Who ought to receive what benefits and burdens, and on what grounds ought they receive them?* I take some time here to discuss this model, both because of its central significance to considerations of social justice and because features of this model bear on what I want to argue about the need for a more inclusive notion of social justice.

In distributively just societies, it is assumed that *one ought to treat equals equally and treat unequals unequally in direct proportion to their equality or inequality* (Aristotle's principle of equality of treatment). According to Aristotle's principle, injustice occurs when equals are treated unequally and unequals are treated equally. For example, *if* all humans are moral equals with regard to their having certain rights, and *if* rights are distributed on the basis of humanness, then it is unjust to treat women or people of color in ways that violate their rights. This injustice can be explained on a distributive model of justice, since what is being

175

distributed here (rights) can be shown to be distributed on the wrong basis (gender or race/ethnicity), rather than on the correct basis (humanness). Equals were
treated unequally, which violates Aristotle's principle of equal treatment.

To know how to apply Aristotle's principle in a given case, one needs to know
two things: *what* is being distributed, and what is the *basis* of distribution. Aristotle's principle does not specify either. It just says that when humans are equal
in the relevant respects, treat them equally; when humans are unequal in the relevant respects, treat them unequally. It does not say what counts as a case of
"treating equals equally" or "treating unequals unequally."

The sorts of things that get distributed (the "what" issue) are rights, taxes, jobs,
admission places in schools, salaries, welfare, charitable aid, food, "natural
resources," and legal penalties and punishments. The basis of distribution (the
"basis" issue) is given by different material principles of justice. These principles
identify different criteria for distributing goods and services. The task is then to
connect up *what* is being distributed with the appropriate *basis* for distributing it.

Traditionally, there are seven *bases* of distribution, so-called material principles of social justice. They are distinguished by whether there are morally relevant differences among beings (traditionally, humans) when distributing certain
goods and burdens. The two egalitarian principles treat beings (traditionally,
humans) as morally equal in certain distributive situations, and the five nonegalitarian principles treat beings (traditionally, humans) as morally unequal in certain distributive situations. What, then, are these seven principles of justice?

The two egalitarian principles are the principles of *basic equality* and of *basic
need*. According to the principle of basic equality, some benefits are distributed
in accordance with the relevant sameness of beings. Appeal to this principle has
been used to justify the ascription of basic rights to all humans: All humans, by
virtue of being humans, deserve rights to life and liberty. According to the principle of basic needs, some benefits are distributed in accordance with the relevant
sameness of basic needs of beings. Appeal to this principle has been used to justify the ascription of other rights to all human beings: All humans, by virtue of
their basic needs, have a right to adequate food, clothing, and shelter. In both
examples, the underlying assumption is that there are no morally relevant differences among humans that warrant differences in human entitlement to goods
based on human equality and basic need.

In contrast, the five nonegalitarian principles recognize differences among
beings as morally relevant to the distribution of some benefits and burdens. The
principle of *merit* distributes a benefit or burden (e.g., a job, a grade, a salary)
according to some set of qualifications (or merit); the principle of *compensation*
distributes a benefit or burden (e.g., money, land, court-appointed community
service work) according to some criteria of reparation for harm incurred; the principle of *ability* distributes a benefit or burden (e.g., shares in a corporation, taxes)
according to one's native, learned, or earned capacity to provide (as in the Marxist dictum, "From each according to his ability; to each according to his need");

the principle of *utility* distributes a benefit or burden (e.g., location of a shopping mall or a hazardous waste site) according to the net benefit to some group (e.g., society), typically measured in economic terms through "cost-benefit analysis"; and, the principle of *effort* distributes a benefit or burden (e.g., entitlement to discounts for participating members in a food cooperative) according to the amount of work (or other kinds of input) an individual or group has contributed toward a given project.

On a distributive model of social justice, justice occurs when one distributes something on the correct basis. The task, then, is to determine which of these seven principles of justice is the correct principle to use in a given case. In cases of ethical disagreement about what is just, people tend to disagree about both what is being distributed and which principle is the appropriate basis for the distribution.

THE NEED FOR ENVIRONMENTAL JUSTICE

Recently, ethical disagreements have surfaced with regard to the distribution of environmental harms. This has prompted grassroots activism and philosophical theorizing about "environmental justice." We encountered some of these issues in chapter 1. They were issues about the disproportionate harm suffered by women, people of color, the poor, and children around a variety of environmental ills. We saw that whether it is trees, forests and forestry, unsanitary water, food production and agriculture, or training in environmental technologies, it is often poor women and children, particularly women and children of color in the Southern Hemisphere (the South), who suffer disproportionately the effects of environmental degradation. Poor rural women and children throughout the South walk farther for fuel wood and fodder, experience disproportionately higher health risks in the presence of unsanitary water, and grow food on depleted soils. It is women who experience the burdens of a gender division of labor, which gives women unequal access to cash, crops, and credit, and it is women who experience the inappropriateness of technologies developed without a basic understanding of women's daily lives and needs.

We also saw in chapter 1 that sometimes environmental justice issues are about race and socioeconomic status (e.g., in the location of hazardous waste in the United States). Poor women and children of color face disproportionate health risks in the United States because of the presence of toxic substances in poor communities of color.

Not surprisingly, then, environmental activists and theorists have appealed to a distributive model of social justice to show why these environmental harms are matters of justice. In fact, appeals to the distributive model of justice in environmental cases has been so important that most theorists *define* environmental justice as "distributive justice." For example, Peter Wenz claims that environmental justice focuses "on the distribution of benefits and burdens among all of those

affected by environmentally related decisions and actions." Similarly, Troy Hartley, defending a Kantian-based view, claims that environmental justice is "the fair
distribution of environmental quality."And Daniel Wigley and Kristin Shrader-
Frechette claim, "Environmental justice is mainly concerned with distributive
equity and is based on the principle of equal treatment for equal beings."[1] In
short, environmental justice has been assumed to be about the fair or equitable
distribution of environmental goods, services, and "resources." On these views,
the environment is a commodity whose distribution is governed by traditional
principles of distributive justice.

That environmental justice issues have been seen as distributive issues makes
sense. Social justice as distributive justice has been virtually the only model of
social justice to date. Its strengths make it friendly to both grassroots environmental activists and environmental theorists seeking relief from environmental
injustices. Consider four notable strengths.

First, a distributive model permits the extension of important ethical concerns
about social justice to environmental issues. In this way, many environmental
issues become social justice issues. For example, ecofeminists and others can
appeal to a distributive model of justice to show why the disproportionate harms
suffered by women, people of color, and the poor are a case of injustice: They
violate Aristotle's formal principle of equality by inequitably distributing environmental burdens to persons or groups on morally irrelevant bases (e.g., gender,
race, class). Animal welfarists argue that a distributive model provides a vehicle
for arguing that factory farming practices involve unnecessary cruelty to animals,
which either violates the rights of animals (Tom Regan's view) or is unacceptable
on utilitarian grounds (Peter Singer's view). As such, factory farming practices
are not only morally unacceptable; they are unjust.

As a related second point, a distributive model of social justice can help link
concerns of the environmental movement with the concerns of the civil rights and
women's movements as all social justice movements. Appeals to principles of
distributive justice not only show why disproportionate costs of environmental
degradation suffered by women, people of color, children, and the Third World
are wrong; they also capture the political reality that women, people of color,
poor people, and children are among a new core of radical environmentalists
around the globe fighting to protect their families, homes, and communities from
environmental toxins.

A third strength of a distributive model of social justice for environmental contexts is that it is amenable to uses of popular cost-benefit analyses for resolving conflicting claims about just outcomes. This is especially important in economic, political, and legal contexts where assigning quantifiable "costs" and "benefits" is
strategically crucial in ascertaining and resolving environmental conflicts. For
example, when the interests of humans conflict about such things as whether and
where to locate a highway, city park, or garbage incinerator, cost-benefit analyses
have played a crucial role in determining outcomes. Cost-benefit analyses also can

be useful in assessing damages, allocating benefits and burdens, or determining remuneration or compensation for environmental harms to injured parties.[2]

In his groundbreaking 1974 book, *Should Trees Have Standing: Toward a Theory of Legal Rights for Natural Objects,* Christopher Stone used familiar cost-benefit analyses to defend what was then a strikingly novel idea: awarding legal rights to nonhuman "natural objects." According to Stone, to say that an entity has a legal right means that three criteria are satisfied: "They are, first, that the thing can institute legal action *at its behest*; second, that in determining the granting of legal relief, the court must take *injury to it* into account; and, third, that relief must run to the *benefit of it.*"[3]

Stone appeals to welfare economics for calculating both costs to natural objects for injuries to it and compensatory damages for loss of important "environmental values." Stone suggests that one way to measure costs and damages is to calculate the amount of money it would take to make the natural object whole. He uses an analogy to human injury cases:

> When a man is injured in an automobile accident, we impose upon the responsible party the injured man's medical expenses. Comparable expenses to a polluted river would be the costs of dredging, restocking with fish, and so forth. It is on the basis of such costs as these, I assume, that we get the figure of $1 billion as the cost of saving Lake Erie.[4]

Although computing damages on the basis of making the environment whole is hard and not without difficulties, Stone shows that it is possible. The awarding of compensatory damages would make natural objects genuine beneficiaries of monetary awards. Where "repairing the natural object" by making it whole is not a feasible option, Stone suggests that monetary awards "could be put into a trust fund to be administered by the object's [legal] guardian."[5] In any case, Stone's proposal uses a traditional distributive model of social justice to provide a way of making natural objects beneficiaries of court awards for damages to them. What is distributed is money; the amount of the monetary distribution is determined through cost-benefit analyses; and the basis of the distribution is the principle of compensation. Damage to "earth others" themselves, and not just to humans whose interests are affected by damage to earth others, is made possible and justified on grounds of distributive justice.

A fourth strength of a distributive model of justice is that appeals to it can reveal and help to overcome important deficiencies in economic markets. These market deficiencies arise where the outcomes recommended by economic analyses conflict with considerations of justice, generating what some economists call "the justice-efficiency quandary" in economics. The "quandary" is this: How can one reconcile economic market efficiency in the allocation of resources necessary to produce desired goods and services, with justice in the distribution of the wealth necessary to purchase those goods and services?

Consider how the efficiency/equity quandary arises. According to environmental economists, "*Efficiency* is defined as maximum consumption of goods and services given the available amount of resources. . . . *Equity* refers to a just distribution of total goods and services among all consumer units."[6] On this definition, efficiency is determined by the preferences of the consumer, which typically is expressed in what economists call "a willingness to pay." But efficient outcomes may be distributively unjust outcomes. This is likely in cases where market forces consistently and disproportionately locate hazardous waste in communities of color. It is likely in cases where values other than those a market can price are relevant (an issue I discuss later). It is likely to arise in cases where nonhuman beings (e.g., animals) are presumed to have some claims against humans even though they are not "consumers" who can themselves express their preferences through a market system. And it is likely to arise where the appropriate issue is not one of market efficiency at all. Appeal to a distributive model of social justice can show why mechanisms of free-market capitalism alone (e.g., without governmental interference through social regulation) may produce efficient but socially unjust outcomes: Markets may distribute burdens and benefits efficiently but inequitably.

Mark Sagoff offers a different reason why efficiency and "willingness to pay" are problematic for measuring environmental quality or determining environmental outcomes:

> Willingness to pay? What is wrong with that? The rub is this. Not all of us think of ourselves primarily as consumers. Many of us regard ourselves as citizens as well. As consumers, we act to acquire what we want for ourselves individually; each of us follows his or her conception of *the good life*. As citizens, however, we may deliberate over and then seek to achieve together a conception of the good society.[7]

Our dual human roles as consumer and citizen may conflict. For any number of reasons, we may buy gas-guzzling automobiles yet vote for laws that prohibit the production of gas-guzzling automobiles. We may vacation in remote forested areas while we vote for laws that declare those very areas as "wilderness areas" that prohibit human recreation. We may buy houses in predominately white communities, free of hazardous waste contamination, but vote for more equitable policies that distribute environmental toxins equitably among all communities (not just in communities of color). In such cases, consumer interests may be met by considerations of efficiency and willingness to pay, but citizen interests often are not. When they are not, it is often because those interests are about issues of justice—what a good society is—rather than efficiency—what a good life (for the individual consumer) is. Somewhat paradoxically, appeal to a distributive model of social justice can help reveal and provide justification for nonmarket remedies to deficiencies in market mechanisms.

These four strengths of a distributive model are important and real. Increased global awareness of environmental injustices has been heightened because appeal to a distributive model makes clear just why the disproportionate harms experienced by women, people of color, the poor, and children are cases of injustice. Why would anyone be critical of a distributive model?

LIMITATIONS OF THE DISTRIBUTIVE
MODEL OF SOCIAL JUSTICE

Despite its unassailable strengths, I think there are good reasons to be concerned about a distributive model of social justice as *the only* model of social justice. These reasons concern both cases where social justice is, and cases where social justice is not, about distribution. Consider, now, some of these reasons.

In her book *Justice and the Politics of Difference,* Iris Marion Young critiques the distributive model of social justice for its tendency to do two things: First, "it tends to focus thinking about social justice on the allocation of material goods such as things, resources, income, and wealth, or on the distribution of social positions, especially jobs." Second, even when the distributive paradigm is widened to include nonmaterial social goods (e.g., power, opportunity, self-respect), it continues to treat them as static things, rather than as functions of social relations and processes.[8] According to Young, neither material nor nonmaterial goods are always "things." Consequently, they are not always distributable things. Insofar as they are not distributable things, the distributive model of social justice does not do them justice.

What are some of these material and nonmaterial goods that, according to Young, a distributive model fails to accommodate? Young identifies three categories of goods. These three categories, and the social justice issues raised in connection with each, provide the launching point for my remarks about limitations of a distributive model of social justice as the only (or even as always the best) model of environmental justice.[9]

The first type of good Young identifies is *social decision-making structures of power and privilege*. These are "structures" that help determine patterns of distribution, for example, political, legal, and economic institutions, *within which* decisions are made, rather than the decisions themselves.[10]

I have provided an ecofeminist critique of oppressive patriarchal conceptual frameworks and the structures and institutional contexts to which they give rise. (More is said about this in chapter 9.) From an ecofeminist philosophical perspective, social justice is not adequately served by critiquing distributional patterns *within* oppressive institutional structures and contexts; one also must explicitly challenge the oppressive conceptual frameworks and the institutions *themselves*. One must challenge patriarchal decision-making structures that hierarchically organize power and privilege of Ups over Downs and justify a logic of domination, not just the decisions made and distributions enacted within those structures.

The hundreds of grassroots environmental organizations and actions initiated by women and low-income minorities throughout the world are doing exactly that. They are not simply challenging the distribution of toxins within communities of color, or the distribution of water collection and distribution tasks among women and children, or the inequitable and disproportionate effect of deforestation on women as managers of domestic households and subsistence economies in the South—though they certainly are challenging all of these. They are also challenging the injustice of oppressive (e.g., patriarchal, racist, classist, ethno-centric, colonialist) *institutions themselves.* They are challenging economic, political, legal and colonial decision-making structures that give unjustified power, privilege, and authority to Ups over Downs in such matters as determin-ing where to locate hazardous waste landfills or deciding on the rules and proce-dures that will be used to permit such decisions to be made. So, it is not just the distribution of sexist, racist, classist, or other oppressive institutions that is prob-lematic; it is also the nature of those institutions themselves (within which the decisions are made) that is problematic. They are problematic because they are structured such that those at the top of various hierarchies are imbued with the power and privilege to define reality, determine decision-making procedures, or otherwise systematically advantage Ups over Downs.

The second type of good Young describes as not accommodated by a distribu-tive model of justice is the *definition (not distribution) of labor.* According to Young, a distributive model certainly can help one see the injustice of unjust gen-der and race distributions of labor. For example, it can show why a gendered divi-sion of labor in the household is unfair, or why paying women less for compara-ble work is unjust. On a distributive model, both are unjust because they use a morally irrelevant trait—gender—as the basis for distributing household labor and salaries. But a distributive model does not and cannot address problematic biases in the very meaning of various categories of labor (occupations, jobs). For example, it does not and cannot address the gender and race biases in the job cat-egories "domestic servant" and "grape picker." Where race, gender, class, and colonial status are built into the meaning of labor and various job categories, nondistributive issues arise. These issues are not reducible to distributive issues about how a type of labor (occupations, jobs) is allocated.

Young's critique of a distributive model for its inability to address social jus-tice issues involved in the meaning of "labor," "job," or "occupation" is relevant to ecofeminism. Many environment-related jobs are imbued with derogatory race, gender, class, colonialist, and age overtones. For example, current meanings of the job categories weeding, water collection, and wood gathering, uranium mining, and grape picking are associated with Downs (viz., women, American Indians, and "migrant workers") and the inferior status of contributions of Downs (e.g., work understood as "women's work" or menial, physical, bodily, blue-collar labor). These occupations are associated with Downs in such a way that one could fail to notice the injustice of the gendered, raced, classed, colonial meanings (or definitions) of the job categories *themselves* if one focused only on how these jobs are disproportionately distributed among women, people of color, immigrants, colonized peoples, or the poor.

This latter point deserves further elaboration. Historically, some philosophers (e.g., Plato, Marx, and Mill) argued against the unjust distribution of educational and legal opportunities on the basis of "sex." The distribution of jobs (offices, opportunities, positions) on the basis of "sex" is clearly an important issue of distributive justice. But that is not enough. Without a notion of the gendered definition of jobs themselves, one cannot explain why it is, for example, that it is women who do "women's work." Appeal to women's biology may explain why women bear children, but it does not explain why women raise them. To explain this, one needs to understand that the job category "child rearing" (historically) is defined as "women's work." The very definition of labor as "women's work" functions in such a way that one could fail to notice the injustice of the gendered meaning of the job category *itself*—separate from and in addition to the various ways "women's work" is unjustly distributed among women. To notice this is to reinforce the point (made explicit in chapter 5) that just as particular situations gain meaning from social structures (e.g., gender, race, and class), so, too, such social structures gain meaning through particular situations.

The third category of goods Young claims is not adequately addressed by a distributive model of social justice is *culture*. Culture includes the imagery, symbols, meanings, habits, and stories through which people express themselves and communicate with one another. In addition to specific cultural artifacts, which are themselves distributable, Young claims that there are important nondistributive features of cultures themselves (e.g., cultural integrity) that are important social justice issues.

Issues of cultural justice are key to ecofeminist ethics and philosophy. Throughout this book I have argued that the cultures and cultural contexts *themselves*—the contexts in which environmental costs and benefits are analyzed, calculated, and distributed—are among the most important issues any adequate environmental ethic must address. The loss of Amazonian rainforest is not just about the loss of forests and biodiversity. It is also about the loss of indigenous Amazonian culture and tribal attachments—symbolic, experiential, ideological— to the Brazilian rainforest. Similarly, the loss of traditional American Indian ways of life—oral traditions, ritual, creation myths, a kinship connection with "Mother Earth and Grandfather Sky," and values of sharing and appropriate reciprocity that grow out of that lifestyle—is not reducible to the loss of surface land mass or jobs or treaty rights, though it certainly is also that. Similar claims could be made about the loss of Australian aboriginal art, music, "dreamtime" stories, "walkabout" experiences of the bush, tribal self-sufficiency, and integrity among Australian aboriginal peoples. These cultural losses are *themselves* issues of environmental justice, in addition to whatever distributive issues are raised by violation of rights, diminishing of individual liberties, or economic disutilities created by the destruction of biodiversity, cultural diversity, and sovereign statehood.

This latter point is important for "outsiders" attempting to understand and resolve conflicts between indigenous (or primal) peoples and nonindigenous "others." When American Indians in Minnesota and Wisconsin argue for their "right to spearfish" at times, in places, and in ways their white neighbors are forbidden to fish, distributive issues are clearly at issue. In the rights-based litigious system of the United States, legal resolution of conflicts between American Indians and their white fisher neighbors will involve determining which parties have which rights in which circumstances, and the basis on which those parties have those rights. But if "outsiders" mistakenly think that only distributive issues of rights and economic costs/benefits are at stake in such conflicts, they will have missed something ethically basic (especially from the point of view of many "insiders"). What is *also* at issue is the respectful treatment of cultures themselves—the cultural values, integrity, history, lifestyle, sustainability, and identities of the parties to the conflict. Not all issues of "culture" are reducible to distributive issues about rights (utility, merit, compensation, basic human needs). Even a "right to have one's culture treated respectfully," if there is such a right, does not reduce, simply, to issues about how one does or does not distribute cultural artifacts. Cultures are not reducible to the items or "things" in them.

A caveat is in order here. To say that respecting cultures is, at least in part, a nondistributive issue of social justice is not to say that it is always morally appropriate or just to preserve cultures (or a particular culture). Nor is it to deny that distributive issues (e.g., land claims, treaty rights) are important issues of social justice. It is to say that preservation of cultures and cultural diversity (e.g., different languages, customs, traditions, rituals, symbols, stories, myths, attachments, world views) is an issue of social justice that is not always reducible to distributive issues *without loss of significant value*. Even when talk of rights (e.g., American Indian spear-fishing rights, Brazilian property rights to indigenous flora and fauna in the Brazilian rainforest, Aboriginal Australian land rights) is morally relevant and significant to justice considerations, the whole of the moral story cannot be adequately captured by talk of rights. To reduce all issues of cultural diversity, integrity, and identity to issues of distribution is to misunderstand the meaning and structure of cultures. As I claimed in chapter 5, this is why grieving is ethically significant. Those who grieve the loss of a sacred burial ground, language, culture, or species are mourning the loss (misplacement, absence) of something of significant value to the bereaved; redistributing what there is does not capture the moral significance of what has been lost.

According to Young, what these three categories of goods—institutional contexts, definitions of labor and occupations, and culture—have in common is that they are neither primarily nor exclusively "things"; hence, they are neither primarily nor exclusively distributable "things." They cannot neatly be divided up into discrete parts—parts that then do or do not get distributed. Rather, according to Young, these three types of goods are (or also are) *processes, functions, structures, and relations, which themselves produce distributions, rather than the distributions produced.*[11] Patriarchal Up-Down decision-making structures and institutions of domination function to replicate Up-Down hierarchies of power and privilege. They thereby create and reinforce Up-Down relationships of domination and subordination. These structures, relationships, and functions produce "things" that get unfairly distributed in ways that reinforce and maintain these structures. To describe and critique these structures and relationships, one needs to do more than simply describe and critique the inequitable distributions that occur within them. One must also critique the structures themselves that produce the inequitable distributions. And *that* critique involves looking at such things as conceptions and relationships of power and privilege, how gender, race, and class structure social meanings and practices, how hierarchical Up-Down structures of power and privilege function to produce inequitable distributions of goods and services, and the how invisibility of bias prejudices accounts of reason, ethics, and knowledge—the sorts of things addressed in this book. And these are, or involve, nondistributive issues of justice. A nondistributive model of social justice is needed to give them their appropriate due in any adequate model of social and environmental justice.

In addition to its failure to adequately address the three sorts of goods—institutional contexts, definitions of labor and occupations, and culture—initially described by Iris Young, I have three additional worries about a distributive model of social justice. First, most distributive models presuppose a view about humans as radically individualistic, equally situated, moral agents. So conceived, a focus on individual rights and social utility is well suited to distributive contexts: Rights attach to individuals, and utility calculations are based, in part, on preferences of individuals as consumers. But there are contexts in which this view of humans is less well suited. For example, they are less well suited to contexts where humans are viewed as communal beings, in kinship relationships to others, and where the good of the community is the important, overriding value. These are also contexts in which gift economies, not market economies, are the basis of human exchange of goods and services. These are contexts in which talk of social groups and communities, not individuals, is important. Because, as Young claims, a distributive model rests on an ontology which pays too little attention to social groups and social situations, it tends to pay insufficient attention to these other contexts.[12]

This insufficient attention to group similarities and differences is important to an ecofeminist philosophical critique. Insofar as a distributive model of social justice "pays too little attention to social groups and social situations," as Young claims, it also will be insufficiently attentive to ecological groups—species, populations, communities, ecosystems, and natural habitats. Attending to ecological groups *themselves* (and not just to their individual members), as well as to important differences among them (e.g., differences among prairies, marshes, dunes, rainforests, deserts, oceans), is, from an ecofeminist perspective, crucial to any ecologically informed ethic. So, if the survival of ecosystems is an issue of environmental justice, then a distributive model of social justice which pays too little attention to social groups is not well poised to accommodate this issue.

My second and related worry concerns the conception of a human being that underlies many distributive models of social justice. This is a conceptually essentialist notion of a human (e.g., humans as rational animals or as rational self-interested pleasure maximizers). The version of ecofeminist philosophy I have defended relies on a view of humans as selves-in-relations (or relational selves).

As both individuals and members of social and ecological communities, a human is who she or he is in large part by virtue of the relationships she or he is in. If this view of relational selves is correct, then a distributive model alone will be inadequate as the model of environmental justice insofar as it relies on an inaccurate conception of humans as individuals whose "essence" does not include reference to social or ecological contexts.

My third worry is that a distributive model alone cannot adequately capture or give expression to considerations of care in those contexts in which care is about nondistributive issues of social justice. This is not to say that justice does not involve care; it does. Being just is one way of caring about others. Rather, it is to suggest that sometimes care-sensitive ethics will countenance as "just" practices and relationships that may be deemed "unjust" on a distributive model. This is especially likely in cases of special relationships (e.g. relationships between friends) and dependency relationships (e.g., relationships between a mother and her child, a nurse and his patient, humans and pets). As Anthony Weston argues:

> A perspective that honors relationship may acknowledge that an ethic of care and of special relationship is not entirely fair. But from this perspective fairness is not the overriding and ultimate ethical concern. Impartial fairness is instead only one strand in a much richer fabric. The demands of love and relationship go beyond and may even go against justice. [One] may even be obliged to do what is unjust to save his wife.[13]

Recasting Weston's point, fairness often is given as the ultimate norm on a distributive model of social justice. But in real-life situations of care that honor special or dependency relationships, the carer may be morally justified, even obliged, to treat the cared-about in ways that conflict with the demands of distributive justice concerns about fairness. In contrast, a nondistributive model of social justice that values care in contexts of special relationships may deem such conduct as not only just, but in some sense morally obligatory. In environmental contexts, care-sensitive ethics may involve overriding distributive principles of justice in some contexts of special or dependency relationships between humans and "earth others" (e.g., a pod of dolphins, pets, a rock, a wilderness area).

Even for distributive models based on an egalitarian ideal of social cooperation between moral equals, care is important to justice. As Weston claims:

> respect for the importance of caring [about] one another and the value of receiving care and giving care. It then becomes a matter of political justice for basic institutions to make provisions for and facilitate satisfactory dependency relations. . . . For a well-ordered society, therefore, to instill in its citizens a sense of justice and a sense of what is right, it must also be sensitive to our vulnerability to dependency and to the vulnerability of those who attend to dependents.[14]

To the extent that such a priority of care does not yet exist, part of the ecofeminist social justice agenda is "to help fashion it."[15]

What does it mean to care about "earth others"? As I argued in chapter 6, just as an answer to the question of what one's responsibilities are to one's friend is a highly contextual matter, so an answer to what constitutes care about others is a highly contextual matter. It involves both a complex understanding of what it is to be a human being—a carer—and an understanding of how those complex webs of relationships that constitute the human moral community might include "earth others" as cared-about. A transformation of our understanding of the moral community to include nonhumans is *not* moral extensionism: It is not the extension of moral privilege to (some) nonhuman creatures just because they happen to resemble us in desirable ways (for example, because they are rational, sensitive, or alive). Rather, it is a matter of trying to come to an understanding of what it might mean to respond to something in the nonhuman environment as a member of one's moral community. In trying to come to such an understanding, one is engaged in reconceiving oneself as an ecological self and one's community as including the ecological community. Caring about "earth others" is, in this reflexive and nonanthropocentric way, caring about oneself.

AN INCLUSIVE NOTION OF SOCIAL JUSTICE

I have argued so far that a distributive notion of social justice is, by itself, incomplete as a notion of social and environmental justice. I have suggested that a more inclusive notion of social justice is needed, one that captures the morally significant features of both distributive and nondistributive issues of justice. What would such an expanded and reconceived notion of justice look like? Culling from the preceding remarks, I end by suggesting six features of an inclusive conception of social justice.

First and foremost, an inclusive concept of social justice incorporates both distributive and nondistributive issues of justice. At least six sorts of issues are included among relevant nondistributive issues of justice: social decision-making and institutional structures (e.g., patriarchy as a structural feature of society); definitions of labor and occupations (e.g., conceptions of child rearing as "women's work"); cultures (e.g., cultural integrity, identity); social groups and situations (including ecological groups and situations); special relationships (e.g., between friends) and dependency relationships (e.g., between parent and child); and the nature of human and "earth others" as beings-in-relation. These six raise issues of justice that are not reducible to a conception of justice solely in terms of distribution.

Second, an inclusive concept of social justice recognizes that justice is always "situated": It can only be understood through the particular situations and social structures that give them meaning in a dynamic, integrative, interactive way. To the extent that a distributive model of justice assumes an egalitarian ideal of social cooperation among moral equals, without reference to actual social contexts and structures, it rests on a faulty premise. In Eva Feder Kittay's words, it "falsely assumes individuals to be equally situated and equally empowered."[16]

Third, an inclusive concept of social justice is not based exclusively on a notion of equality as sameness. Equality based on sameness does not adequately address the issues of difference, dominance, and dependency at the center of feminist critiques of many models of social justice. As Kittay summarizes:

> Their [feminist] difference critiques of equality have pointed to the implicit use of men—more specifically, white middle-class men—as the standard against which equality is assessed. These feminists have argued that this norm is unfit for incorporating all whose identity is marked by their gender, race, class, and other socially salient difference. Other feminists, elaborating a dominance critique, have underscored the power difference between men and women. Men's entrenched dominance over women means that gender-neutral, equality-based policies either fail to address issues that specially affect women or merely preserve the relations of dominance that are already in effect . . . the dependency critique maintains that by construing society as an association of equals, conceived as individuals with equal powers, equally situated in the competition for the benefits of social cooperation, one disregards the inevitable dependencies of the human condition, thereby neglecting the condition both of dependents and those who care for dependents.[17]

In cases where difference, dominance, and dependency create unequal powers and privileges among morally equal adults, an attention to those three—difference, dominance, and dependency—is necessary to remedy resulting injustices.

In rejecting a notion of "justice as sameness," one is not thereby denying important commonalities among humans (or humans and earth others). Rather, it is a recognition that, in contemporary society, it is only by acknowledging, respecting, and working through differences that any meaningful notion of community, commonality, or social cooperation can be achieved.[18] This point is stated eloquently by Audre Lorde:

> It is not the differences between us that are separating us. It is rather our refusal to recognize those differences and to examine the distortions which result from our misnaming them and their effects upon human behavior and expectations. . . . Too often we pour the energy needed for recognizing and exploring differences into pretending those differences are insurmountable barriers, or that they do not exist at all. This results in a voluntary isolation or false and treacherous connections. Either way, we do not develop tools for using human differences as a spring board for creative change within our lives.[19]

Fourth, social justice fundamentally requires the elimination of institutional domination and oppression.[20] Societies structured by "isms of domination" are unjust, not simply by virtue of the ways in which benefits and burdens are distributed, but also by virtue of the nature of the nondistributive features of social structures that give rise to these distributions. These structures produce distributions but are not themselves the distributions produced. Oppressive conceptual frameworks and "isms of dominations" are morally unacceptable structures used to "justify" the power and privilege of Ups over Downs. Solutions to injustice (including environmental injustice) require more than just ensuring that social distributions are equitable. They also require altering the systematic, structural, and institutional relations and practices of oppression and domination.

Fifth, an inclusive concept of social justice recognizes the important role played by care in motivating and sustaining justice. I assume that both justice and care inform the value system of ecofeminist philosophy. Both are important moral ideals. As such, I assume that care and justice are compatible. As Alison Jaggar succinctly states:

> If care and justice are construed as values or ideals, there seems no reason to doubt that both may be part of the same value system and compatibility in this sense is not threatened by occasional uncertainty over which ideal should take precedence, just as liberty and equality may both be part of a single value system even though there may be occasional tension between them.[21]

Since an inclusive concept of justice includes issues of distributive justice, it includes Aristotle's principle of equal treatment, as well as the additional seven principles of distributive justice. But these principle must be supplemented by nondistributive considerations, such as the care-practices condition of care-sensitive ethics (discussed in chapter 5).

Lastly, an inclusive concept of social justice rests on a theory of individuals (whether human or nonhuman earth others) as both discrete objects and beings-in-relation. In the case of humans as both social and ecological selves, it insists that considerations of justice must involve attention to both social and ecological contexts.

A theory of social justice based on an inclusive concept of justice (and not just a distributive concept of justice) recognizes that, in contemporary social reality, either there is not one set of necessary and sufficient conditions for the realization of justice, or, if there were, it is not currently (if ever) possible to know what these conditions are. An inclusive theory of social justice will require, as a necessary condition of justice, the absence of both particular practices and social structures of oppression and unjustified domination. This necessary condition applies in both distributive and nondistributive contexts. But any sufficient conditions of social justice must be filled out in historically and socially sensitive ways, paying attention to the six features of "inclusive justice" (identified above). Otherwise, one has no way to give special recognition to the significance of historically located social structures, institutions, cultures, group differences, and special relationships of care and dependency that the model is intended to honor. A main contribution of ecofeminist philosophy is to show why nondistributive issues are important issues of environmental and social justice.

CONCLUSION

In this chapter I have argued that, despite the significant strengths of a distributive model of social justice, by itself such a model is inadequate or incomplete.

After discussing limitations of a distributive model, I concluded that an inclusive concept of social justice is needed—one that captures both distributive and nondistributive features of justice. I end this chapter with an illustrative quote from Native Hawaiian attorney Mililani Trask:

> Our people know that the Akua puts us here on this earth to be guardians of these sacred lands. It is a God-given responsibility and trust that a sovereign nation must assume if it is to have an integrity. And so we in Ka Lahui have undertaken this struggle. Environmental racism is the enemy. The question is, What is our response? That really is environmental justice? I'll tell you one thing I learned in law school at Santa Clara. Do you know how they perceive and teach justice, the white schools of this country? A blind white woman with her eyes covered up by cloth, holding the scales of justice. . . .
>
> Well, environmental justice is not a blindfolded white woman. When I saw the woman with the scales of justice in law school, I thought to myself, "You know, if you blindfold yourself, the only thing you're going to do is walk into walls."[22]

To avoid simply "walking into walls," to creatively resolve environmental justice issues, one certainly needs the support of those who are working on environmental cases in legal and distributive contexts. But, Trask cautions us, that is not enough: "Do not put your eggs in the basket of the blind white lady. We must try other approaches."[23] I am suggesting that recognizing and caring about nondistributive issues of environmental and social justice are among the other approaches we must try.

NOTES

1. Peter Wenz, *Environmental Justice* (Albany: State University of New York Press, 1988), 4; Troy W. Hartley, "Environmental Justice: An Environmental Civil Rights Value Acceptable to All World Views," *Environmental Ethics* 17, no. 3 (Fall 1995), 287; Daniel C. Wigley and Kristin Shrader-Frechette, "Consent, Equity, and Environmental Justice," in *Faces of Environmental Racism: Confronting Issues of Global Justice,* ed. Laura Westra and Peter S. Wenz (Lanham, Md.: Rowman & Littlefield, 1995), 137.

2. See Christopher Stone, *Should Trees Have Standing? Toward a Theory of Legal Rights for Natural Objects* (Los Altos, Calif.: William Kaufmann, 1974).

3. Stone, *Should Trees Have Standing?*, 11, italics in original.

4. Stone, *Should Trees Have Standing?*, 29.

5. Stone, *Should Trees Have Standing?*, 33.

6. Joseph Seneca and Michael Taussig, *Environmental Economics,* 2nd edition (Englewood Cliffs, N.J.: Prentice-Hall, 1979), 6.

7. Mark Sagoff, *The Economy of the Earth: Philosophy, Law, and the Environment* (New York: Cambridge University Press, 1988), 27, italics in original.

8. Iris Marion Young, *Justice and the Politics of Difference* (Princeton, N.J.: Princeton University Press, 1990), 14, 16.

9. It is not my intent to defend Young. My intent is to use relevant features of Young's critique to sketch both the limitations of such a model for environmental issues and the reasons for saying that what is needed is a more inclusive concept of justice.

10. Young argues that a distributive model "tends to ignore, at the same time that it often presupposes, the institutional context that determines material distributions" (*Justice and the Politics of Difference,* 18).

11. Young, *Justice and the Politics of Difference,* 18.

12. Young, *Justice and the Politics of Difference,* 4

13. Anthony Weston, *Toward Better Problems: New Perspectives on Abortion, Animal Rights, the Environment, and Justice* (Philadelphia: Temple University Press, 1992), 141.

14. Weston, *Toward Better Problems,* 24–25.

15. Weston, *Toward Better Problems,* 25.

16. Eva Feder Kittay, "Taking Dependency Seriously: The Family and Medical Leave Act Considered in Light of the Social Organization of Dependency Work and Gender Equality," *Hypatia* 10, no. 1 (Spring 1995), 11.

17. Kittay, "Taking Dependency Seriously," 10–11.

18. Audre Lorde, "Age, Race, Class, and Sex: Women Redefining Difference," in *Sister Outsider: Essays & Speeches by Audre Lorde* (Trumansburg, N.Y.: Crossing Press, 1984), 115–16.

19. Audre Lorde, "The Master's Tools Will Never Dismantle the Master's House," in *This Bridge Called My Back: Writings by Radical Women of Color,* 2nd edition, ed. Cherrie Moraga and Gloria Anzaldua (New York: Kitchen Table, Women of Color Press, 1983), 110–13.

20. See Young, *Justice and the Politics of Difference,* 15.

21. Alison M. Jaggar, "Caring as a Feminist Practice," in *Justice and Care: Essential Readings in Feminist Ethics,* ed. Virginia Held (Boulder, Colo.: Westview, 1995), 184.

22. Mililani Trask, "Native Hawaiian Historical and Cultural Perspectives on Environmental Justice," *Race, Poverty and the Environment* 3, no. 1 (Spring 1992), 6.

23. Trask, "Native Hawaiian," 6.

Chapter Nine

Surviving Patriarchy

Ecofeminist Philosophy and Spirituality

Ecofeminists disagree about the nature and place of spirituality in ecofeminist politics and practice. As we have seen (in chapter 2) "spiritual ecofeminists" defend spirituality as a necessary part of any ecofeminist politics or philosophy. Other ecofeminists claim that spiritual ecofeminism, at least as conceptualized and practiced in contemporary Western cultures, reinforces harmful gender stereotypes about women as "closer to nature than men," less rational and more emotional than men. Still others like myself claim that ecofeminist spiritualities occupy an important place in ecofeminism, even if they are not necessary to ecofeminist theory and practice. In this chapter I say why I think this is so.

The debate about the significance of ecofeminist spiritualities is very controversial, especially among ecofeminist philosophers. There are two main reasons for this. The first reason is not specific to ecofeminism, though it is specific to Western models of philosophy. It is that spirituality is presumed to fall within the province of religion or theology, but not philosophy. The crucial distinction here is between "spirituality" and "philosophy of religion." Philosophy of religion has always had an important place in Western philosophy. But that is because philosophy of religion is concerned with the sort of publically debatable issues philosophy proper is concerned with: for example, arguments for the existence of God (How can one prove God exists?); the problem of evil (How could an all good, all knowing, all powerful God permit evil?); the free will/determinism problem (How does one reconcile free will with scientific conceptions of nature as "determined" or "in principle, predictable"?); or, the nature of religious faith (What is religious faith and how is it like or unlike rational belief?). By contrast, concerns about spirituality are presumed to rest on basically "private," personal, and ineffable experiences that are not open to argumentation and debate. So they, unlike issues in philosophy of religion, belong outside the domain of philosophy. Insofar as some ecofeminist philosophers agree with this view of spirituality, they join their philosophical colleagues in placing ecofeminist spirituality outside the realm of philosophy.

The second reason is specific to ecofeminism. Some ecofeminist philosophers criticize conceptions of ecofeminist spirituality, especially those offered by "spiritual ecofeminists" (discussed in chapter 2), as unacceptably essentialist and universalist. They are rejected insofar as they rest on claims about women as naturally more caring, more nurturing, and closer to nature than men.

I agree with ecofeminists who reject such essentialist and universalizing assumptions about women. But I have also come to believe that the subsequent inattention to ecofeminist spiritualities by feminist philosophers is a mistake. Ecofeminist spiritualities deserve serious ecofeminist philosophical attention for a number of reasons: *Historically,* ecofeminist spiritualities have played a vital, grassroots role in the emergence of ecofeminism as a political movement. Historical accuracy in how ecofeminism is described or represented, then, requires that ecofeminist philosophers grapple with the claims made by those who defend various ecofeminist spiritualities. *Politically,* the sorts of protest actions ecofeminists often cite as examples of ecofeminist activism (e.g., the Chipko movement in India or Women of All Red Nations [WARN] in the United States organizing against environmental racism) often grow out of, and gain their strength from, spiritual traditions (e.g., Gandhian "satyagraha" nonviolence actions or spirituality-based kinship cultures). Honoring the spiritual dimensions of such ecofeminist activism involves a recognition of their spiritual roots.[1] *Ethically,* ecofeminist spiritualities raise issues about the relevance of ritual, symbol systems, and values (e.g., values of care, appropriate reciprocity, trust, love, kinship, community) to ecofeminist ethical theory and practice. Ecofeminist philosophers can learn something important about these values from a serious look at the ways they arise and function in different cultural contexts. *Theoretically,* ecofeminist spiritualities challenge ecofeminist philosophers to consider the relevance of a "politics of women's spirituality" to ecofeminist philosophy, and *conceptually,* they raise important issues about women–other human Others–nature connections, which are at the heart of ecofeminist philosophy.

In addition, ecofeminist spiritualities are important *epistemologically,* since practitioners often base their spirituality on claims about the importance of immediate, concrete, felt experiences of women-nature connections. Since ecofeminist philosophy is interested in "situated knowledges" and "standpoint epistemologies" (see chapter 2), it needs to address the role spiritualities do or could play in the generation, articulation, and understanding of such knowledge claims. *Methodologically,* ecofeminist spiritualities require ecofeminist theorists who are "outsiders" (i.e., nonmembers of an oppressed group) to come to terms with what Uma Narayan calls "methodological caution" and "methodological humility" when engaging in criticism of spiritual practitioners who are "insiders" (i.e., members of oppressed groups).[2] Methodological caution requires that outsiders conduct themselves under the assumption that, as outsiders, they may be missing something important about insider experience and knowledge, that what appears to outsiders to be a mistake on the part of the insider may make more sense if the outsiders had a fuller understanding of the context.[3] Methodological humility requires that outsiders sincerely attempt to carry out their criticisms of the insider's perceptions in ways that do not amount to, or even seem to amount to, attempts to denigrate or dismiss entirely the validity of the insider's point of view. Since many women in various cultures claim that spirituality is important to their ability to live under conditions of oppression, ecofeminist philosophers need to take such claims seriously on methodological grounds.

For these reasons, then, I think ecofeminist spiritualities are philosophically important. My primary goal in this chapter is to explore the potential of ecofeminist spiritualities to intervene in and creatively change patriarchal (and other) systems of oppression.[4]

The chapter is divided into two sections. In the first section, I discuss what I understand to be the nature of spirituality and ecofeminist spirituality, showing connections between ecofeminist spirituality and power, nonviolence, and care. In the second section, I present a model of patriarchy as an unhealthy social system.[5] I illustrate how the model works by using examples concerning rape and militarism. Although many of the examples of patriarchal domination discussed in previous chapters would suffice, I chose these examples for two reasons: They are important topics in ecofeminism that are not previously discussed in this book, and they fit well with the discussion of spirituality and ecofeminist spirituality provided in the first section. I conclude by showing how ecofeminist spiritualities do (or could) play important interventionist and creative roles in dismantling patriarchy as a social system.

The placement of this discussion of ecofeminist spiritualities at the end of this book is deliberate. Spirituality begins, so to speak, where the limits of philosophical proof (i.e., logical argumentation) leave off. So I have placed the discussion of spirituality at the end, after completing my discussion of the nature and importance of ecofeminist philosophy. It also just seems fitting to end this book by naming as "spiritual" that which I think is spiritual and which motivates so many environmental ethicists and activists to do what we do.

SPIRITUALITY

Existential philosopher Søren Kierkegaard argued that humans must face the inescapability of an existential truth: As "rational" beings with mental capacities, our reason and will seem free and limitless, capable of soaring with the gods and achieving immortality. As "animals" bound by a physical body, humans are hopelessly mortal, physical, limited beings whose lives are just "ashes to ashes, dust to dust." The "existential truth" is that humans are both radically free (by virtue of our power of reason) and radically determined (by virtue of our animality and physicality). Humans are thereby a union of opposites—self-consciousness and a physical body.[6] The deeply anxiety-producing "existential dilemma" is how to be both.

Notice that Kierkegaard's views are steeped in rationalist assumptions about what it is to be human. According to rationalism, humans are who we are because we are rational; because humans are rational, we are morally superior to nonhuman animals. Unlike other animals, humans can reason, will actions and outcomes, entertain abstract principles of morality, choose among alternative acts, do right and wrong. For Kierkegaard, only a "leap of faith" provides a resolution to the human existential dilemma.[7]

The existential dilemma is a real dilemma—a problem—only if one falsely believes that "where there's a will, there's a way." That is, the dilemma arises only if one assumes that there are no limits to what humans can successfully will. For those like myself who accept the very real, felt, concrete, daily limits of human reason and what humans can successfully will, there is no dilemma. The dilemma dissolves because the crucial underlying assumption needed to generate the dilemma—that human reason and the human will's ability to determine outcomes is limitless—is false. The "existential dilemma" is based on a faulty conception of what it is to be human. As I will now argue, spirituality still involves a Kierkegaardian "leap of faith," but this leap is not taken in order to resolve the "existential dilemma" (as Kierkegaard thought). It is taken in order to enter into the spiritual dimensions of human life.

What Is Spirituality?

Visualize a person poised between two doors. Behind her is the door to the familiar, to the known, to the past. In front of her is the door to the unfamiliar, to the unknown, to the future. She is holding on to the door behind her, reaching out unsuccessfully to open the door ahead of her. As hard as she tries, she cannot reach the door ahead of her. It is there, within reach, but only if she lets go of the door behind her. She knows that if she lets go of the door behind her, there will be a time, however brief or long, perhaps quite frightening, when she will be suspended between the two, attached to neither.

This image conveys much of what I want to say here about spirituality. The movement from the known door to the unknown door is what I mean by a "spiritual movement." One experiences a spiritual movement when one is willing to let go of the door, to be suspended between doors. It is in "letting go" of the door that one experiences living in the moment, being "in the present." One chooses to seek and embrace such moments to the extent that one is willing to let go of the door. To choose to let go, one must trust—have faith—that either one can reach the other door or, at least, one will land on one's feet trying.

Kierkegaard describes this choosing to let go of the door as taking "a leap of faith." What makes this leap of faith "spiritual" (rather than, say, "cognitive" or even "behavioral") is that it expresses a belief (or willingness to believe) that there exists some power or presence (some energy, force, being, deity or deities, God or Goddess) other than and in addition to any individual ego that will nourish or sustain one when one lets go of the door.

What enables one to let go of the door? I do not know, exactly. But I believe it involves a willingness to accept the limitations on what humans can successfully will.[8] Ernest Kurtz captures what I intend by the distinction between what any individual ego can and cannot will when he claims, "I can will knowledge, but not wisdom; submission, but not humility; self-assertion, but not courage; congratulations, but not admiration; religiosity, but not faith; reading, but not understanding; physical nearness, but not emotional closeness; dryness, but not sobriety."[9] Knowledge, submission, self-assertion, congratulations, religiosity, reading, physical nearness, dryness—all of these can be willed. Wisdom, humility, courage, admiration, faith, understanding, emotional closeness, sobriety— these cannot be willed. The latter fall outside the realm of what humans can successfully will.

When I think of the distinction between what can and what cannot successfully be willed, I am reminded of the Cowardly Lion in *The Wizard of Oz* who so desperately wanted courage. The Lion willed to act bravely and to believe his friends when they told him he was brave. The Lion even acted bravely by taking steps along the yellow brick road to meet the Wizard. But, as the Lion found out, neither his friends nor the Wizard could give him courage. Courage is, as Dorothy says, "in us all along." Courage cannot be achieved through an individual's attempts to will it. Courage "asks for a serious effort while it can only be received as a gift."[10] Paradoxically, to find courage the Cowardly Lion needed to give up the willful attempt to get it.

The Cowardly Lion's movement from bravery to courage is, for me, a spiritual movement. It comes simply, but not easily, only when he gives up trying to control or will what cannot be controlled or willed. It is only in relinquishing one's attempt to will something that, in fact, one is powerless to will, that courage, humility, wisdom, and emotional intimacy can blossom. Like the love one has for one's child, courage, humility, wisdom, and emotional intimacy cannot be willed, earned, or won by good deeds. Cognitive understanding and acceptance of the limitations on what one can successfully will are a start; the rest requires a spiritual plunging in.

If Kierkegaard's "leap of faith" expresses a willingness to let go of the door, then the spiritual plunge expresses a willingness to accept "*grace*." Without appropriate faith, one gets paralyzed in place, holding on to the door, unable to let go. When one chooses to let go of what one cannot, in fact, control, win, earn, or make happen— when one is willing to be suspended between doors—one also is or becomes willing to receive grace. Whatever else grace is, it is always latently within us. Grace is a gift we give ourselves when we let go of the door. In Ntozake Shange's *For Colored Girls Who Have Considered Suicide When the Rainbow Is Enuf,* grace is what the

character "lady in red" is talking about when she says, "i found god in myself & i
loved her—i loved her fiercely."[11] Paradoxically, like courage and faith, one must
give up attempts to will grace in order to receive it.

Since an understanding of spirituality, faith, and grace turns on a distinction
between what humans can and cannot successfully will, it is no surprise that
Western philosophy often places spirituality outside the province of Western philosophy. Discussions of spirituality are placed outside Western philosophy not
only because they are not amenable to philosophical proof; they are placed outside also because such claims challenge the rationalist foundation of much of
Western philosophy. Talk of spirituality as a fundamental part of "human nature"
is at odds with these rationalist assumptions.

What Are Ecofeminist Spiritualities?

My understanding of ecofeminist spiritualities reflects and builds upon my understanding of spirituality (provided in the preceding section). First, ecofeminist
spiritualities are *feminist:* They express a commitment to the elimination of male-
gender privilege and power over women in their myths, rituals, symbols, language, and value systems. Second, ecofeminist spiritualities are *spiritualities:*
They express faith in a life-affirming (rather than life-denying) power or presence
(energy, force, being, deity or deities, God or Goddess) other than and in addition
to one's own individual ego. They affirm that this power or presence is "greater
than the individual ego, greater than their name, their family, their special attributes as individuals."[12] Ecofeminist spiritualities have what I understand to be
basic features of spirituality (described above). Third, ecofeminist spiritualities
are *ecofeminist:* They express a twofold commitment to challenge harmful
women–other human Others–nature interconnections and to develop earth-
respectful, care-sensitive practices toward humans and earth others. Just as
ecofeminist ethics makes caring about oneself and others central to ethical theory
and practice, ecofeminist spiritualities make caring about oneself and others,
including earth others, central to conceptions and practices of spirituality.

At the heart of ecofeminist spiritualities is a movement toward healthy, life-
enhancing, nourishing, restorative values, beliefs, practices, and systems. Having
said this, there is room for significant disagreement about what ecofeminist spiritualities look like. From my perspective, minimally, an ecofeminist spirituality
must meet the "border conditions" of an ecofeminist philosophical quilt. That is,
it should not contribute to the maintenance of "isms of domination." A white
supremacist conception or practice of spirituality, for example, would not meet
these conditions. Furthermore, ecofeminist spiritualities are not simply "personal" or "private" spiritualities. Because they are feminist, they also have a
"public" and political context. Ruether cautions Northern (Northern Hemisphere)
spiritual ecofeminists about the need for a political component to their understanding and practice of ecofeminist spiritualities:

Psycho-spiritual reconnecting with women's bodies and nature can become a recreational self-indulgence for a privileged counter-cultural Northern elite if these are the *only* ideas and practices of ecofeminism; if the healing of our bodies and our imaginations as Euro-Americans is not connected concretely with the following realities of over-consumption and wealth: the top 20 percent of the world's human population enjoys 82 percent of the wealth while the other 80 percent scrapes along with 18 percent; and the poorest 20 percent of the world's people, over a *billion* people—disproportionately women and children—starve and die early from poisoned waters, soil, and air.[13]

Since the contexts in which women, other human Others, and nonhuman nature have been dominated by patriarchal structures are very different, ecofeminist spiritualities must "examine and take responsibility for their actual social context." This includes an examination of the ways Northern peoples have been heirs and beneficiaries of colonial conquest.[14] Such examination is involved in "the politics of ecofeminist spiritualities."

Ecofeminist Spiritualities and Power

Ecofeminist spiritualities, like all spiritualities, embody a kind of power, including the personal power ("empowerment") experienced by one who chooses to let go of the door. But ecofeminist spiritualities also do express interpersonal, political power. So an examination of the nature of power is relevant to a discussion of ecofeminist spiritualities.

Rosabeth Moss Kanter defines power as "the ability to mobilize resources to achieve self-determined ends."[15] On this view of power, power is neither inherently positive nor inherently negative. Minimally, the use of human power is inappropriate or morally impermissible from the ecofeminist point of view I am defending when its exercise creates or maintains (or is intended to create or maintain) unjustified relationships of domination and subordination. Minimally, it is appropriate or morally permissible when it does not. Since patriarchy sanctions, perpetuates, and justifies oppressive *power-over* relationships of domination and subordination, patriarchy involves the illegitimate uses of power.

I think there are five types of power. The first, *"power-over* power," presupposes Up-Down relationships. But (as we saw in chapter 3) not all Up-Down relationships are inherently bad. For example, Up-Down power exercised by a parent (an Up) over an infant (a Down) in such a way that it prevents an infant from injuring herself or himself without causing unnecessary or avoidable pain to the infant is an appropriate use of "power-over power." It is inappropriately exercised when used by leaders (Ups) to keep those in subdominant positions (Downs) from realizing or exercising their civil rights. This was the sort of morally indefensible power exercised by the white minority government over black South Africans during Apartheid.

A second type of power is *"power-with* power"—coalitionary, solidarity, or other relatively equalizing power relations with others. It, too, can be appropriately or inappropriately exercised. Coalitionary power between the Ku Klux Klan and John Birch Society in the United States, intended to deprive African Americans and others of their civil rights, is an illegitimate exercise of white supremacist power-with power. Coalitionary power-with power among the women's, peace, and environmental movements that does not perpetuate any unjustified systems of domination would be an appropriate exercise of power.

A third type of power is *"power-within* power"—power mobilized around one's "inner resources." It can be positive and empowering, as it often is for rape survivors who think and act as survivors rather than as (mere) victims. Or it can be negative and self-destructive, as it often is for women suffering from anorexia nervosa who use their inner resources to restrict what they eat, sometimes to the point of death.

A fourth type of power is *"power-against* power"—a distinctive type of power exercised by Downs against Ups within oppressive Up-Down contexts. During the civil rights movement of the 1960s in the United States, African Americans exercised power-against power through sit-ins, public strikes, voting alternatives, and sometimes violent action. When, why, which, and whether such acts are appropriate uses of power-against will depend on one's views, for example, about the justification of acts of civil disobedience.

Lastly, there is *"power-toward* power"—a process or movement from one habit, lifestyle, set of behaviors, or belief system to another. When it is positive, it is a movement away from unhealthy, life-denying systems and relationships to healthy, life-affirming systems and relationships; when it is negative, it is a movement from one unhealthy relationship or system to another.

Ecofeminist spiritualities do (or could) involve any or all of these types of power. The type of power involved will vary according to the context. Whether the use of power is justified will depend, minimally, on whether it reproduces beliefs, values, attitudes, and behaviors of unjustified domination.

Ecofeminist Spiritualities and Nonviolence

It is not always easy to tell which exercises of power are morally appropriate or legitimate. This is true even when exercises of power are linked with violence. Consider several scenarios offered by Jo Vellacott.

> I am a member of an oppressed minority; I have no way of making you listen to me; I turn to terrorism. I am a dictator, yet I cannot force you to think as I want you to. I fling you in jail, starve your children, torture you. I am a woman in a conventional authoritarian marriage situation; I feel helpless and inferior and powerless against my husband's constant undermining; so I in turn undermine him, make him look foolish in the eyes of his children. Or I am a child unable to prevent her parents' constant quarreling and to defend herself against her mother's sudden outbursts of rage. I smash something

precious and run away, or I take to thieving or I may even kill myself. Or I am the President of the United States; with all the force at my command I know of no way to make sure that the developing nations—especially the oil-rich nations—will dance to my tune; so I turn to the use of food as a political weapon, as well as building ever more armaments. Violence is resourcelessness.[16]

Vellacott's conclusion is that "violence is resourcelessness." This suggests that violence is a lack of power. But this conclusion seems contrary to fact, as well as contrary to Vellacott's own examples: Her own examples show that members of oppressed minorities, women in oppressive marriages, and children—not just dictators and presidents—have significant power. What, then, is Vellacott's point about the connection between violence and resourcelessness?

I think Vellacott's point is that one is, in some sense, "resourceless" when one fails to use power in positive, morally acceptable, or appropriate ways. Both people in dominant positions (e.g., dictators and presidents) and in subordinate positions (e.g., racial minorities, women in authoritarian marriages, children) may turn to violence when they feel powerless. However, some ecofeminists (and others, such as pacifists) argue that at least for Ups, there are *always* alternatives to the use of violence and that spirituality provides a basis for such nonviolent action. Gandhi, Martin Luther King Jr., the Chipko women, and hundreds of grassroots activists globally are examples of people who, unlike those in Vellacott's scenarios, perform spiritually based, nonviolent protest actions as Downs in unjustified Up-Down systems. Ecofeminist spiritual practices, too, have involved nonviolent exercises of power to "mobilize resources to achieve desired ends." They have been defended on grounds that they fight systems of domination without using strategies of domination. To borrow from Audre Lorde, they refuse "to dismantle the master's house with the master's tools."[17]

Does a commitment to nonviolence require relinquishing one's anger or refraining from making moral judgments? Certainly not. Anger is a "moral emotion." It has an important cognitive dimension—namely, the felt conviction that one has been unduly or unfairly harmed in some way. Persons who refuse to feel or express anger when it is in their best interest to do so, or who choose not to take a stand against injustice that they can influence, are accountable for their failure to recognize, or to act on the recognition, that they or others deserve better. As Aristotle observed over 2,000 years ago,

Those who are not angry at the things they should be angry at are thought to be fools, and so are those who are not angry in the right way, at the right time, or with the right persons; for such a man is thought not to feel things nor to be pained by them, and, since he does not get angry, he is thought unlikely to defend himself; and to endure being insulted and put up with insult to one's friends is slavish.[18]

Perhaps it is not so surprising, then, that the notion of the appropriate use of anger is at the root of some feminist conceptions of nonviolence. For example,

Pam McAllister claims that feminist nonviolence involves the merging of "rage with compassion:"

> The peculiar strength of nonviolence comes from the dual nature of its approach—
> the offering of respect and concern on the one hand and of defiance and stubborn
> noncooperation with injustice on the other. Put into the feminist perspective, nonvi-
> olence is the merging of our uncompromising rage at the patriarchy's brutal destruc-
> tiveness with a refusal to adopt its ways . . . to focus on rage alone will exhaust our
> strength . . . force us to concede allegiance to the path of violence and destruction.
> On the other hand, compassion without rage renders us impotent, seduces us into
> watered-down humanism, stifles our good energy. . . . By combining our rage with
> compassion, we live the revolution every day.[19]

This notion of nonviolence as "rage with compassion" is helpful to understanding the spiritual dimension of care and care-based communities. Consider now
why this is so.

Ecofeminist Spiritualities and Care

In my defenses of ecofeminist ethics (chapter 5) and contextual vegetarianism
(chapter 6), I offered three personally meaningful stories to illustrate the importance to ethical practice and theory of "loving (or caring) perception" and of
"being present to another": stories about rock climbing, swimming with wild dolphins, and a conversation with a Lakota elder. I now want to show why for me
these stories, and the notions of care-sensitive ethics, loving perception, and
being present to another that they invoke, also have a spiritual dimension.

To care about another is to be present to the other—to be actively attentive to
the other, to listen, to learn, to receive from the other—where the other is
acknowledged and valued as different from ourselves. Without the ability to see
the other as different from ourselves, one risks experiencing the other only in
terms of one's own needs, wants, desires, and expectations. One risks perceiving
the other—whether humans, dolphins, or rocks—arrogantly rather than lovingly.

How does one develop the capacity to care? As we saw in chapters 5 and 6,
care has a cognitive component. It is difficult, if not impossible, to care about
another whom one perceives as not deserving respect or moral consideration. We
also saw that the ability to care in particular situations is affected by social structures. Caring about a woman who has been raped or a dolphin that has been
bludgeoned to death are possible and take on meaning, in part, because of social
structures of sexism and naturism. In this respect, care has both a particular and
a social component.

For me, the ability to care also has a spiritual component. Henri Nouwen provides a wonderful illustration of what I think is involved spiritually in caring
about another in the following Zen story.

There is a story about a university professor who came to a Zen master to ask him about Zen. Nan-in, the Zen master, served him tea. He poured his visitor's cup full, and then kept pouring. The professor watched the overflow until he could no longer restrain himself. "It is over full. No more will go in!" "Like this cup," Nan-in said, "you are full of your own opinions and speculations. How can I teach you Zen unless you first empty your cup?"[20]

As Nouwen says, "To care means first of all to empty our own cup."[21] It is not possible to care—to be present to another, to be attentive to the other, to actively listen to the other—if our cup is full. That is because there is no room left, no free space, to listen for and receive what the other provides.

But, to care about ourselves and others also involves something much more profound and difficult. It involves daring to see our commonalities with "the other" who is so different from us, often by painfully having our most cherished beliefs about ourselves and others challenged. Again, I quote Nouwen.

When we dare to care, then we discover that nothing human is foreign to us, but that all the hatred and love, cruelty and compassion, fear and joy can be found in our own hearts. When we dare to care, we have to confess that when others kill, I could have killed too. When others torture, I could have done the same. When others heal, I could have healed too. And when others give life, I could have done the same. Then we experience that we can be present to the soldier who kills, to the guard who pesters, to the young man who plays as if life has no end, and to the old man who stopped playing out of fear of death. . . . Through this participation we can open our hearts to each other and form a new community.[22]

In a spiritual sense, developing the capacity to care involves having the courage to see in ourselves "the bad person"—the tyrant who kills, the rapist who rapes, the parent who abuses. If we are to heal the wounds of oppressive systems, if our presence to another is to be a healing presence, we may need to develop this capacity to see the "humanity" in other humans and to care about earth others. This is more than a psychological ability to empathize, since the courage involved is, as the Cowardly Lion learned, a combination of willing and letting go, being receptive to and receiving grace.

This spiritual dimension of the capacity to care was poignantly brought home to me seventeen years ago on February 6, 1983, when a segment entitled "The Gentleman Was a Devil" aired on the CBS television show *60 Minutes*.[23] The segment includes an excerpt of film footage from 1961 when Yehiel Dinur, a survivor of the Holocaust who had personally been selected by Adolf Eichmann to be sent to the concentration camps at Auschwitz, testified at Eichmann's trial. In the 1961 film footage, we (the television viewing audience) see Dinur faint in the middle of his testimony, as several medics in white coats hastily enter the courtroom and carry him away. Years later, in the 1983 interview with Mike Wallace for *60 Minutes,* Wallace asks Dinur "What happened?" Here is their exchange:

> WALLACE: Why did Yahiel Dinur collapse? He says it was the realization that the Eichmann who stood before him at the trial was not the godlike army officer who had sent millions to their death. This Eichmann, he said, was an ordinary man, an unremarkable man. And if this Eichmann was so ordinary, so human, says Dinur, then he realized that what Eichmann had done, any man could be capable of doing—even Yahiel Dinur.

> DINUR: Then came—came everything. Then I saw that I am capable to do this. I am exactly like he—not god. It's not a god, it's not a Hitler, it's not a Heidrich, it's not, it's not Adolf Eichmann.

> WALLACE: It's me. It's you.

> DINUR: It's me.

> WALLACE: Yahiel Dinur says Eichmann is in all of us—in you, in me, in him, Dinur.[24]

I doubt I will ever forget this interview. It is, for me, the living testimony of a person who has all the justification philosophy can provide for both hating another human being, Adolf Eichmann, and for radically distancing himself, as a human being, from Eichmann, as a "monster." But Yahiel Dinur did not do that; he could not do that. When Dinur realized that Eichmann was just "an ordinary human being" like himself, he collapsed, unable to continue his testimony. Nothing had changed about his moral approbation of Eichmann as a person or about his moral judgment of the heinous nature of Eichmann's crimes. What had changed was Dinur's understanding of himself and his willingness to accept that the capacity for evil—horrible, unspeakable evil—is latent in every human being, himself included.[25]

If we dare to care, if we dare to enter into community with others through an honest recognition of our commonalities and differences, we will be poised to create genuinely respectful, nonviolent, care-based, intentional communities where commonalities and differences are just that—commonalities and differences. In such communities, the interaction among individuals and groups is ordered from within those relationships and is based on mutual agreement. Such intentional communities are a creative alternative to violence-prone communities where order is imposed from outside through unjustified domination.[26]

PATRIARCHY AS AN UNHEALTHY SOCIAL SYSTEM

In this section, I turn to what may seem like a very different, unrelated topic: the nature of patriarchy as an unhealthy social system. But I do so for a very specific reason. Having discussed the nature of ecofeminist spirituality, I now want to show the interventionist and creative roles ecofeminist spiritualities do or could play in patriarchal (and other oppressive) contexts. I do so by beginning with a discussion of patriarchal systems of domination as unhealthy systems.

A "system" is a group or network of interacting elements regarded as constituting a larger whole or unit. The human body is a system of interactive units, including subsystems such as the digestive, neurological, and muscular systems. Ecosystems are systems that consist in interactions among cells, organisms, populations, and communities. Family systems consist of the members, their roles and behaviors, and the rules that govern how the family members operate. Belief systems consist of interconnected values, attitudes, assumptions, myths, judgments, beliefs, and facts that characterize a group, culture, or society. Social systems consist of the dynamic interaction of individuals and institutions (including roles, rules, offices, positions, and practices).[27] Workplaces, colleges and universities, governmental agencies, sports organizations, and families are examples of social systems.

Systems can be described in terms of degrees of health or lack of health. Minimally, a healthy ecosystem has the capacity for self-renewal, as Aldo Leopold states.[28] Minimally, a healthy belief system consists in true beliefs (rather than, say, beliefs steeped in denial, rationalization, and minimization) which do not create, maintain, or reinforce unjustified domination. Minimally, a healthy social system is one in which individual members and groups get their basic needs met.

Notice that the health of a social system is not about the stability or longevity of a system. Long-standing systems such as patriarchy, European feudalism, or Southern slavery in the United States were relatively stable systems that, nonetheless, were unhealthy; the well-being, interests, and needs of members of the system (women, peasants, African Americans) were undermined, denied, and disregarded. Furthermore, the health of a system is a richly contextual notion. In the case of human social systems, human needs and capacities are contingent upon social and environmental contexts. What makes a social system in Western urban contexts healthy may not be what makes a social system in non-Western rural contexts healthy. In the case of ecological systems, what counts as the health of an ecosystem will depend on such factors as the spatiotemporal scale of one's observations, the measurements taken, and the sort of data deemed relevant (as hierarchy theorists in ecology make clear).

Since the health of a system is highly contextual, it makes sense to view health along a continuum. At one end, unhealthy social systems tend to be highly rigid, closed systems. Rules and roles tend to be nonnegotiable and to be determined by Ups in Up-Down, power-over hierarchies. A high value is placed on control and exaggerated concepts of rationality (even though, ironically, the system's survival may depend on irrational ideologies of denial and rationalization). On the other end, relatively healthy social systems tend to be highly flexible, open systems characterized by an absence of Up-Down relationships of domination and subordination. Problems are openly acknowledged and resolved. Relationships tend to be egalitarian, mutual, appropriate, and reciprocal. The well-being of all members of the system is highly valued.

Since the health of a social system involves the ability of individual members and groups to get their basic needs met, health has a lot to do with power.[29] This is because, as we have seen, power involves the ability to mobilize resources to achieve self-determined ends. To the extent that Downs in Up-Down systems of power relationships have limited access to the type of power necessary to mobilize resources to achieve self-determined ends, due to the inappropriate, inequitable, or illegitimate exercise of power by Ups over Downs, the systems themselves (and not just the system's members) may be characterized as unhealthy.

Although it is not possible to pinpoint what counts as health, one can still talk about healthy and unhealthy systems and make intersocietal comparisons. For example, a society without slavery is healthier in that respect than one with slavery. A society without patriarchal domination is healthier in that respect than one with patriarchal domination. A society that does not involve unnecessary exploitation of the earth is healthier in that respect than one that does. When Lake Erie burned more than two decades ago, that was good evidence that the lake was relatively unhealthy, since not only is it not a property of water to be flammable, but the survival needs of individual component members of flora and fauna could not be met under those conditions.[30]

In evaluating the health of a social system, ecological, and not merely social and material, conditions are important. This is because human members of social systems are both ecological and social selves. As ecological selves, humans need such things as adequate nutrition, sunshine, and shelter, potable water, clean air, and nontoxic living areas. As social selves, humans need love, friendship, meaningful work, and relationships (as Abraham Maslow, Ashley Montague, and others have shown). These sets of needs are interconnected: Not only will the health of a social system be determined, in part, by how well it meets the needs of humans as social and ecological selves; it must also be determined, in part, by how well it provides for the flourishing or well-being of the natural environment (on which vital human social and ecological needs depend).

I now turn to a consideration of patriarchy as an unhealthy social system. The claim that patriarchy is a social system locates patriarchy within historical, socioeconomic, cultural, and political contexts thoroughly structured by such factors as gender, race/ethnicity, class, age, ability, religion, national and geographic location. The claim that patriarchy is an unhealthy social system describes and evaluates patriarchy as a system of Up-Down relationships of domination and subordination in which Downs, and, in many respects, Ups, have difficulty getting their basic needs met. The Downs in unhealthy patriarchal systems include women, other human Others, and nonhuman animals and nature.

One way to visualize patriarchy as an unhealthy social systems is shown in diagram 9.1.[31]

(a)
Faulty Beliefs
(Patriarchal Conceptual Framework)

(d)
Unmanageability
of Life

(b)
Impaired Thinking &
Language of Domination

(c)
Behaviors of Domination

Diagram 9.1. Patriarchy as an Unhealthy Social System

This model portrays an unhealthy social system as a *closed circle* of individual and institutional ways of thinking, speaking, and behaving that is rooted in a faulty belief system.

To illustrate how the "circle" perpetuates itself, I use the examples of militarism and rape.

Let's start with patriarchal belief systems, (a), and patriarchal thinking and language, (b). Journalist Amanda Smith reports that at the Naval Academy, woman-hating is deliberately taught through marching songs and punishment for unsoldierlike behavior. She cites as "one of the milder examples" that is "not too foul to put in a public newspaper," a marching song that states:

> "My girl is a vegetable . . . my girl ain't got no eyes,
> Just sockets full of flies."

The song continues to boast of "cutting a woman in two with a chain saw or ramming an ice pick through her ears, then using the pick as a handlebar to ride her like a Harley motorcycle."[32] Men keep "Hog Logs" of female visitors to the academy reception office whom they deem unattractive, and "male midshipmen wear Chiquita and Dole banana stickers in their hats to mark each time they have sex with a date on the academy grounds."[33] Such patriarchal thinking is supported by sexist language, which reinforces a view of women as a foul and lowly class. Recruits and soldiers who fail to perform are addressed as faggot, girl, sissy, cunt, pussy, prissy, wimp, lays. The ultimate insult is to be womanlike; insulting men as womanlike has been used throughout history against the vanquished.[34]

Patriarchal thinking and sexist-naturist language also pervades Western nuclear weaponry parlance.[35] Nuclear missiles are on "farms," "in silos." That part of the Trident submarine where twenty-four multiple warhead nuclear missiles are lined up, ready for launching, is called "the Christmas tree farm." BAMBI is the acronym developed for an early version of an anti-ballistic missile system (for Ballistic Missile Boost Intercept). In her article, "Sex and Death in the Rational World of Defense Intellectuals," Carol Cohn describes her one-year immersion in a university's center on defense technology and arms control. She relates a professor's explanation of why the MX missile is to be placed in the silos of the new Minuteman missiles, instead of replacing the older, less accurate ones: "Because they're in the nicest hole—you're not going to take the nicest missile you have and put it in a crummy hole." Cohn describes a linguistic world of vertical erector launchers, thrust-to-weight ratios, soft lay downs, deep penetration, penetration aids (devices that help bombers of missiles get past the "enemy's" defensive system, also known as "penaids"), the comparative advantages of protracted versus spasm attacks—or what one military adviser to the National Security Council has called "releasing 70 to 80 percent of our megatonnage in one orgasmic whump"—where India's explosion of a nuclear bomb is spoken of as "losing her virginity" and New Zealand's refusal to allow nuclear-arms or nuclear-powered warships into its ports is described as "nuclear virginity."[36] Such language and imagery creates, reinforces, and justifies nuclear weapons as a kind of sexual dominance.

Such patriarchal thinking and language in military contexts, (b), is manifested in patriarchal behaviors of domination, (c). Probably no behavior of domination is more symptomatic and symbolic of patriarchy than rape.

> Women everywhere are terrorized by rape and the ever present threat of rape in their ordinary lives. . . . Almost everywhere, rape is exercised as a "privilege" of power, and institutional rape is a widespread problem: of prisoners and female detainees by jail guards and police, of patients by orderlies in hospitals, of refugees by authorities in refugee camps. In several countries [e.g., Mexico, India, Pakistan] . . . police rape is epidemic—and in some cases, is even acknowledged to be so by judicial authorities.[37]

Given the global prevalence of rape, it should not be surprising that military war rapes (e.g., gang rape by soldiers, beatings, and sexual enslavement) are not uncommon. Rape is routinely viewed as a privilege of victors in war, a way of showing who won. For example, during the mid- to late 1990s, mass military rapes of women and children in war-ravaged Rwanda, Somalia, Croatia, Bosnia-Herzegovina, and Kosovo were common knowledge. This is true even though it is extremely difficult to quantify wartime rape. As the United Nations reports,

> Estimates of the number of women raped in the former Yugoslavia vary widely. In its January 1993 report, the European Community investigative mission cited 20,000 rapes. The United Nations Commission of Experts was able to identify 800 victims from Bosnia-Herzogovina by name. Based on the number of pregnancies resulting

from rape and a formula for predicting a woman's chance of becoming pregnant through one act of intercourse, a team of physicians estimated the number of rapes at 11,900.[38]

Military rapes during war continue, even though rape was recognized as a prosecutable war crime in 1995.[39]

This account of the global phenomena of rape, including military rape, as a patriarchal behavior of domination, (c), brings us to feature (d) of patriarchy as an unhealthy system: life becomes "unmanageable" for women rape survivors, other humans, and earth others. Military action makes life unmanageable for both human and ecological communities by releasing toxins, pollutants, and radioactive materials into the air, water, and food.[40] Long-term environmental damage from the 1991 Persian Gulf War, for example, includes destruction of urban water and sewage systems, massive air pollution, and oil "lakes" caused by oil fires, damage to marine wildlife, coral reefs, and coastal wetland caused by oil spills at sea, and damage to deserts by land mines.[41] Similar military environmental damage occurred in Serbia as a result of NATO bombings in 1999.[42]

Even during peacetime, military activity contributes to the unmanageability of life, (d). The U.S. military, for example, is a major contributor to the national and global proliferation of toxic wastes. In his book *The Threat at Home: Confronting the Toxic Legacy of the U.S. Military,* Seth Shulman documents a history of neglect and "national sacrifice zones," polluted beyond any possible future cleanup, from Lakehurst, New Jersey, to Denver, Colorado, to Jacksonville, Florida, Tucson, Arizona, and Sacramento, California. The shore of 100-acre, human-made Basin F, "a phosphorescent toxic lake on the outskirts of Denver, Colorado," is believed by many to be "the earth's most toxic square mile."[43] It contains toxic sludge, including nearly 11 million gallons worth of wastes, "including byproducts of the manufacture of nerve gas and mustard gas—chemical weapons whose lethality is normally measured in minute quantities such as milligrams."[44]

The toxic legacy of the U.S. military is something many (white) North Americans seem to be ignorant of. As Shulman puts it:

> As I used to do, most people associate the problem of toxic waste only with corporate industrial giants like Union Carbide, Exxon, or DuPont. In fact, the Pentagon's vast enterprise produces well over a ton of toxic wastes every minute, a yearly output that some contend is greater than that of the top five U.S. chemical companies combined. To make matters considerably worse, the military branch of the federal government has for decades operated entirely unrestricted by environmental law. . . . Billions of toxic wastes—a virtual ocean—have been dumped by the U.S. military directly into the grounds at thousands of sites across the country over the past several decades . . . The Rocky Mountain Arsenal stands as a tragic symbol of the nation's military toxic waste problem.[45]

Shulman concludes that "the toxic legacy left by our nation's military infrastructure may well constitute the largest and most serious environmental threat this country faces."[46]

The U.S. military's toxic legacy is not confined to the United States. As Shulman shows, nuclear testing and dumping by the United States, as well as by France and the United Kingdom, have made "some formerly idyllic islands radioactive for thousands of years, and turned their inhabitants into refugees."[47] Life has become unmanageable for these people. Joni Seager agrees:

> In 1982, the U.S.A. dumped contaminated topsoil from Eniwetok on Runit, covering it with a 375-foot wide concrete dome. By the early 1990s the dome was already cracked. Tunit will be radioactive for some 25,000 years . . . Since 1982, U.S.A. missile launchers have used Kwajalein—the world's largest coral atoll—for target practice. The atoll's 8,500 inhabitants now live in barracks on a tiny island nearby . . . The Marshall Islands were the major nuclear test zone of the U.S.A. The rate of thyroid cancer there is now rising steeply . . .[48]

So, we have come full circle—from (a), to (b), to (c), to (d) and back again to (a). In the context of militarism, we have seen how patriarchal conceptual frameworks, (a), give rise to sexist/naturist thinking and language, (b), which is manifested in behaviors of domination, (c), which, in turn, make life on earth unmanageable for many of the earth's inhabitants, (d). Where do ecofeminist spiritualities fit in?

ECOFEMINIST SPIRITUALITIES AND PATRIARCHY AS AN UNHEALTHY SOCIAL SYSTEM

Around the globe, ecofeminists have been actively involved in women's nonviolent, anti-militarism actions, protesting the unmanageability of life under patriarchal and military domination. The Seneca Falls and Greenham Commons Peace Camps, the 1981 Women's Pentagon Action, the Puget Sound Women's Peace Camp, FANG (a small all-women's Feminist Anti-Nuclear Action Group), and Women's Strike for Peace (WSP) are just a few of the grassroots feminist peace groups that have included ecofeminists. "The Mothers of Plaza de Mayo," women who march every Thursday in the main square in Buenos Aires, Argentina, to commemorate the lives of "the disappeared" in the "Dirty War" (the "guerra sucia" between 1976–1983) when the country was ruled by military generals, certainly illustrates the courageous peace politics of women. Week-in and week-out they protest the lives of victims, mostly between the ages of seventeen and twenty-five, who have been imprisoned, tortured, often shot. Some estimate that over 30,000 have simply disappeared without a trace. Charlene Spretnak expresses the view of many ecofeminists.

> Militarism and warfare are continual features of a patriarchal society because they reflect and instill patriarchal values and fulfill needs of such a system. Acknowledging the context of patriarchal conceptualizations that feed militarism is a first step toward reducing their impact and preserving life on Earth.[49]

Appeal to the model of patriarchy as an unhealthy social system shows the unmanageability of life under patriarchy, (d), for what it is—a predictable, "logical," even "normal" consequence of patriarchal beliefs, values, attitudes, language, and behaviors. This element of predictability explains the appropriateness of what I call the "Of course" response: "Of course, you feel crazy when men say it's your fault that you were raped, or that you could have prevented it." "Of course, your life has become unmanageable. You are a female in a country where male military personnel think rape of women is a right of the victor." "Of course, you feel frightened. By standing up for yourself, you're breaking all the rules, rocking the boat." The "Of course" response affirms that those who feel crazy, powerless, alone, confused, angry, or frustrated within unhealthy systems such as patriarchy are experiencing just what one would expect of them.

What the model of patriarchy as an unhealthy social system reveals is that no matter where one starts on the circle, (a)–(d), one eventually comes round to one's starting point. The circle operates as an insulated, closed system that, unchecked and unchallenged, continues uninterrupted. It becomes, quite literally, an unhealthy, vicious circle.[50]

How does one break out of this unhealthy system? Getting the right beliefs by rearranging one's thinking is an important part of the process, but it is not enough. One can have the right beliefs about the prevalence of rape, one's lack of culpability as a rape victim, and the institutional nature of rape and still be raped. One can understand connections among faulty beliefs systems, sexist/naturist language, and military behaviors of control and domination and still witness one's home, one's culture, and the natural environment destroyed by patriarchal and military aggression. So, even if one must start with oneself and one's belief system, one cannot end there. Since the problem is *systemic*, the system itself must be intervened upon and changed—by political, economic, social, and other means.

This is where I think ecofeminist spiritualities come in. I think ecofeminist spiritualities are properly included among those possible "other means" of intervening upon and creatively changing patriarchal systems. Most obviously, they do (or could) challenge patriarchy by replacing faulty patriarchal beliefs, impaired language, and dominating behavior with nondominating values, beliefs, language, rituals, behaviors, and practices. By intervening in this way on one of the basic legs of the scaffolding that holds patriarchal structures in place, (a), ecofeminist spiritualities have the potential to make significant systemic changes.

But if ecofeminist spiritualities did only this, if they focused only on conceptual frameworks, (a), they would be like other ecofeminist approaches which focus on cognitive and behavioral changes. While this is crucial and necessary, there is nothing distinctly spiritual about this response. What is distinctive about ecofeminist spiritualities is their spiritual power to help heal the wounds of patriarchy where cognitive and behavioral strategies alone are not enough.

How do ecofeminist spiritualities do this? Returning now to the account of spirituality offered at the beginning of this chapter, ecofeminist spiritualities provide survival and empowerment strategies in the prefeminist, patriarchal present to anyone willing to "let go of the door" to destructive, patriarchal beliefs and behaviors, and to "dare to care" about themselves and others in nondominating ways. They provide opportunities for like-spirited people to be genuinely present to each other—to dare to listen, to grieve, to feel, to share, to give, to receive. By simply being present to each other—without fixing or curing or solving or recommending or teaching or evaluating—ecofeminist spiritualities provide the space, the "empty cup," within which healing can occur.

This healing will sometimes involve nonviolent "rage with compassion." And that compassion is not something one can cognitively will. It is a spiritual gift of "daring to care" in Nouwen's sense of being present to oneself and others. This healing will also involve a spiritual movement away from unhealthy, life-denying communities based on unjustified power-over domination, control, manipulation, and violence, toward healthy, life-affirming, intentional communities based on nondominating interaction and cooperation. They will be respectful communities of commonalities and differences that do not breed domination. They will be communities of hope.

Daring to care involves more than getting the right beliefs. It involves a willingness to be present to ourselves, others, and the realities of domination and oppression. This is *spiritual care*. To quote Tronto again (from chapter 6), spiritual care is part of what we can do, "*to maintain, continue, and repair our 'world' so that we can live in it as well as possible.* That world includes our bodies, our selves, and our environment, all of which we seek to interweave in a complex, life-sustaining web."[51]

CONCLUSION

I began this chapter by citing reasons ecofeminist spiritualities deserve serious ecofeminist philosophical attention. I then offered my understanding of ecofeminist spiritualities, and their connections to power, nonviolence, and care. With these notions in place, I turned to a discussion of a model of patriarchy as an unhealthy social system, using militarism to illustrate the model. I concluded that ecofeminist spiritualities do (or could) play important interventionist and creative roles in changing patriarchy as a social system. At the level of intervention, ecofeminist spiritualities do (or could) challenge and disrupt the core beliefs, thinking, and behaviors on which the systems' survival depends. At the level of creativity, ecofeminist spiritualities do (or could) help create healthier, life-affirming, cooperative, care-based, nonviolent, intentional communities, organized in nondominating ways to ensure that the basic needs of individual and group members are met.

Failure to acknowledge the potential roles care-based ecofeminist spiritualities do or could play in changing patriarchal systems perpetuates the mistaken view that spirituality is not or cannot be a legitimate feminist political concern. Hopefully, the perspective offered in this chapter suggests how and why such a view would be both a philosophical mistake and a disservice to the lives and testimonies of practitioners of ecofeminist spiritualities.

In the chapter "Dreaming Ecology" from her book *Nourishing Terrains,* Deborah Rose Bird describes the kinship relationships between Australian aboriginal peoples and their land—"country"—as "intense, intimate, and full of responsibilities." She then says:

> I occasionally succumb to the temptation to sort these relationships into categories— there are ecological relationships of care, social relationships of care, and spiritual relationships of care. But Aboriginal people are talking about a holistic system, and the people with whom I have discussed these matters say that if you are doing the right thing ecologically, the results will be social and spiritual as well as ecological. If you are doing the right spiritual things, there will be social and ecological results.[52]

Not unlike Deborah Bird Rose, throughout this book I have talked about the importance of care in contexts of ecological, ethical, and spiritual relationships. But I am struck by the realization, unanticipated at the outset of the writing process, that by closing this book on ecofeminist philosophy from a Western perspective with a discussion of ecofeminist spiritualities, I have ended the book where, for most Australian aboriginal peoples, the story really begins:

> If you are doing the right thing ecologically, the results will be social and spiritual as well as ecological. If you are doing the right spiritual things, there will be social and ecological results.

NOTES

1. In a personal conversation, Bruce Nordstrom-Loeb pointed out that such movements often describe themselves as religious—not spiritual—movements, suggesting that "spiritual" may be an outsider's label applied to insider phenomena.

2. Uma Narayan, "Working Across Differences: Some Considerations on Emption and Political Practice," *Hypatia: A Journal of Feminist Philosophy* 3, no. 2 (Summer 1988), 37–38.

3. This does not mean or imply that whatever the insider claims to know is true, any more than whatever the outsider claims to know is false. Both insiders and outsiders can be mistaken; both insiders and outsiders can have their views coopted. But it is a "methodological caution" to outsiders—often the purveyors of educational degrees and licenses— to remember that what they "know" as outsiders may not be true or correct or applicable.

4. In some respects, my goal is modest. I do not discuss particular positions that have been advanced in the Western ecofeminist debate over spirituality. (Some of these positions are presented in chapter 2.) Nor do I discuss the varieties of ecofeminist spiritualities that have emerged within Buddhist, Hindu, Taoist, Jewish, Christian, American Indian, Pagan, or Wiccan frameworks. In other respects, my goal is ambitious, since I have self-

consciously chosen to explore a topic, spirituality, which is typically considered outside the realm of Western philosophical discourse.

5. In my essay "A Feminist Philosophical Perspective on Ecofeminist Spiritualities," in *Ecofeminism and the Sacred,* ed. Carol J. Adams (New York: Continuum Press, 1993, 119–32), I describe the model in terms of "functionality" and "dysfunctionality," not "health" and "unhealth." In a personal conversation, Bruce Nordstrom-Loeb pointed out the confusion caused by the language of functionality/dysfunctionality: In therapeutic contexts, it is associated with rules, roles, behaviors of healthy and unhealthy social systems. But in social science contexts, a custom or practice or role is functional for the system if it contributes to the survival of the system as a whole, even if it also involves domination, inequality, and injustice. As such, I have chosen to eliminate talk of "functionality" and "dysfunctionality" here.

6. These views of Kierkegaard's are discussed by Ernest Becker in *The Denial of Death* (New York: Free Press, 1973), 68–69.

7. See Søren Kierkegaard (trans. Walter Lowrie), *The Concept of Dread*, 1844 (Princeton, N.J.: Princeton University Press, 1957), 141–42.

8. Bruce Nordstrom-Loeb commented on an earlier draft: "It may also involve our 'animal nature'—our embodied experience at being able to do things, like run, which are beyond our rational description. We experience 'miracles' we cannot understand or explain. It may also involve our emotions: when we are loved and cared for, we can more readily believe that we will be sustained when we take a foolish chance."

9. Ernest Kurtz, *Shame and Guilt: Characteristics of the Dependency Cycle* (Minneapolis: Hazelden Foundation, 1981), 25.

10. Nouwen says this about the paradox of prayer, in *Reaching Out: The Three Movements of the Spiritual Life* (Garden City, N.Y.: Doubleday, 1975), 89.

11. Ntozake Shange's *For Colored Girls Who Have Considered Suicide When the Rainbow Is Enuf* (New York: Bantam, 1977), 67. I thank Charme Davidson for suggesting this quote to me.

12. From Stephan Bodian, "Simple in Means, Rich in Ends: An Interview with Arne Naess." In *Environmental Philosophy,* ed. Michael E. Zimmerman, J. Baird Callicott, George Sessions, Karen J. Warren, and John Clark (Englewood Cliffs, N.J.: Prentice- Hall, 1998), 185–86.

13. Rosemary Radford Ruether, *Women Healing Earth: Third World Women on Ecology, Feminism, and Religion* (Maryknoll, N.Y.: Orbis, 1996), 5.

14. Ruether, *Women Healing Earth,* 5.

15. Rosabeth Moss Kanter, *Men and Women of the Corporation* (New York: Basic, 1977), 116.

16. Jo Vellacott, "Women, Peace and Power," in *Reweaving the Web of Life: Feminism and Non-Violence,* ed. Pam McAllister (Philadelphia: New Society Publishers, 1982), 32.

17. Audre Lorde, "The Master's Tools Will Never Dismantle the Master's House," in *This Bridge Called My Back: Writings by Radical Women of Color,* 2nd edition, ed. Cherrie Moraga and Gloria Anzald`a (New York: Kitchen Table, Women of Color Press, 1983), 98–101.

18. Aristotle, "Nichomachean Ethics," Book 4, Section 5, in *The Basic Works of Aristotle* (New York: Random House, 1941), 996.

19. Pam McAllister, "Introduction," *Reweaving the Web of Life: Feminism and Non-Violence* (Philadelphia: New Society Publishers, 1982), iii–iv.

20. Henri J. M. Nouwen, *Out of Solitude: Three Meditations of the Christian Life* (Notre Dame, Ind.: Ave Maria Press, 1974), 42.

21. Nouwen, *Out of Solitude,* 42–43.

22. Nouwen, *Out of Solitude,* 42–43.

23. "The Gentleman Is a Devil," produced and broadcast by CBS television's *60 Minutes* on February 6, 1983. Transcript of the broadcast provided by Burrell Transcripts (Box 7, Livingston, NJ 07039-0007), Vol. 15, no. 21: 1–20.

24. *60 Minutes,* Burrell's Transcripts, 17.

25. It is the link between a capacity to care and grace that I think the sober alcoholic expresses when he or she nonjudgmentally beholds a drunken alcoholic and says to himself or herself, "But for the grace of God, there go I."

26. Duane L. Cady, *From Warism to Pacifism: A Moral Continuum* (Philadelphia: Temple University Press, 1989),79–82.

27. I assume here that social systems are human systems.

28. Aldo Leopold, "Wilderness," in *A Sand County Almanac and Sketches Here and There* (New York: Oxford University Press, 1977), 194.

29. Although I think it is appropriate to speak of the power of cells, organisms, populations, energy circuits, fluxes, and flows, I restrict my discussion here to human uses of power. With only slight modification on the notion of power, a cell's power (for example) would be its ability to mobilize resources to achieve determined ends—ends "determined" mainly by its genetically programmed structure and environment.

30. Whether the lake had the internal capacity for self-renewal was not determined before humans intervened to clean up the lake.

31. My ideas for this model emerged after reading Patrick Carnes's book, *Out of the Shadows: Understanding Sexual Addiction* (Minneapolis: CompCare, 1983), 15.

32. Amanda Smith, "At Naval Academy, Hatred toward Women Is Part of Life," *Minneapolis Star/Tribune,* 13 November 1992: 19A.

33. Smith, "At Naval Academy," 19A. For an interesting account of the symbolic significance of Chiquita and Dole bananas, see Cynthia Enloe, *Bananas, Beaches, and Bases* (Berkeley: University of California Press, 1990).

34. Charlene Spretnak, "Naming the Cultural Forces that Push Us Toward War," in *Exposing Nuclear Phallacies,* ed. Diana E. H. Russell (New York: Pergamon, 1989), 57. See also Brian Easlea's *Fathering the Unthinkable: Masculinity, Scientists, and the Nuclear Arms Race* (London: Pluto Press, 1983), and Jane Caputi, "Unthinkable Fathering: Connecting Incest and Nuclearism," in *Bringing Peace Home: Feminism, Violence, and Nature,* ed. Karen J. Warren and Duane L. Cady (Bloomington: Indiana University Press, 1996), 133–51. It is interesting to note that even references to stereotypically female-gendered traits of childbearing and mothering are not free from patriarchal coopting in military contexts. In December 1942, Ernest Lawrence's telegraph to the physicists at Chicago concerning the new "baby," the atom bomb, read, "Congratulations to the new parents. Can hardly wait to see the new arrival." As Carol Cohn argues in her work, "Sex and Death in the Rational World of Defense Intellectuals" (in *Exposing Nuclear Phallacies,* ed. Diana E. H. Russell [New York: Pergamon, 1989]), the idea of male birth, with its accompanying belittling of maternity, gets incorporated into the nuclear mentality. The "motherhood role" becomes that of "telemetry, tracking, and control." Once the sexism of the co-opted imagery is revealed, the naming of the bombs that destroyed Hiroshima and Nagasaki—"Little Boy" and "Fat Man"—seems only logical, even if perverse. As Cohn claims, "these ultimate destroyers were . . . not just any progeny but male progeny.

In early tests, before they were certain that the bombs would work, the scientists expressed their concern by saying that they hoped the baby was a boy, not a girl—that is, not a dud" (Cohn, 141).

35. See also Penny Strange, "It'll Make a Man Out of You: A Feminist View of the Arms Race," in *Exposing Nuclear Phallacies,* ed. Diana E. H. Russell (New York: Pergamon, 1989), 104–26.

36. Cohn, "Sex and Death," 133–37.

37. Joni Seager, *The New State of the Earth Atlas,* 2nd edition (New York: Simon and Schuster, 1995), 116.

38. *The World's Women, 1995: Trends and Statistics* (New York: United Nations, 1995), 164.

39. Seager, *New State of the Earth Atlas,* 116.

40. It is interesting to note that many ecofeminists draw an analogy between rape of women and "rape of the earth."

41. Seager, *New State of the Earth,* 64.

42. For example, see "Airstrikes Leave Legacy of Poisoned Land," in *USA Today,* July 21, 1999, 6A.

43. Seth Shulman, *The Threat at Home: Confronting the Toxic Legacy of the U.S. Military* (Boston: Beacon, 1992), xi.

44. Shulman, *Threat at Home,* xi.

45. Shulman, *Threat at Home,* xiii.

46. Shulman, *Threat at Home,* 7.

47. Seager, *New State of the Earth,* 63.

48. Seager, *New State of the Earth,* 62.

49. Spretnak, "Naming the Cultural," 54.

50. The insulated, viciously reinforcing and circular nature of unhealthy social systems has led some to comment on their "addictive" nature. For example, in their work *Indefensible Weapons: The Political and Psychological Case Against Nuclearism* (New York: Basic, 1982), Robert Jay Lifton and Richard Falk describe a phenomenon they call "nuclearism." Nuclearism is the "psychological, political, and military dependence on nuclear weapons as a solution to a variety of human dilemmas, most ironically that of 'security' " (ix). They argue that nuclearism has the quality of an addiction, one that can be ended only through "nuclear awareness" (112).

51. Joan C. Tronto, "Care as a Basis for Radical Political Judgments," *Hypatia* 10, no. 2 (Spring 1995), 142.

52. Deborah Bird Rose, *Nourishing Terrains: Australian Aboriginal Views of Landscape and Wilderness* (Canberra: Australian Heritage Commission, 1996), 49.

Bibliography

Adams, Carol J. "Ecofeminism and the Eating of Animals." In *Ecological Feminist Philosophies,* ed. Karen J. Warren. Bloomington: Indiana University Press, 1996: 114–36.

——. *Neither Man Nor Beast: Feminism and the Defense of Animals.* New York: Continuum, 1994.

——. *The Sexual Politics of Meat: A Feminist-Vegetarian Critical Theory.* New York: Continuum, 1990.

——, ed. *Ecofeminism and the Sacred.* New York: Continuum, 1993.

Adams, Carol, and Josephine Donovan, ed. *Animals and Women: Feminist Theoretical Explorations.* Durham, N.C.: Duke University Press, 1995.

Adams, Carol, and Karen J. Warren. "Feminism and the Environment: A Selected Bibliography." *American Philosophical Association Newsletter on Feminism and Philosophy* 90, no. 3 (1991): 148–57.

Addelson, Kathryn Pine. "Moral Revolution." In *Women and Values: Readings in Recent Feminist Philosophy,* ed. Marilyn Pearsall. Belmont, Calif.: Wadsworth, 1986: 291–309.

Adorno, Theodor, and Max Horkheimer. *The Dialectic of Enlightenment.* New York: Continuum, 1993.

Agarwal, Bina. *Engendering the Environment Debate: Lessons Learnt from the Indian Subcontinent.* East Lansing: Center for Advanced Study of International Development, Michigan State University, 1991.

——. "The Gender and Environment Debate: Lessons from India." *Feminist Studies* 18, no. 1 (1992): 119–58.

"Airstrikes Leave Legacy of Poisoned Land." *USA Today,* 21 July 1999: 6A.

Alaimo, Stacy. "Cyborg and Ecofeminist Interventions: Challenges for an Environmental Feminism." *Feminist Studies* 20, no. 1 (Spring 1994): 133–52.

Alcoff, Linda, and Elizabeth Potter. *Feminist Epistemologies.* New York: Routledge, 1993.

Allen, Paula Gunn. "Kopis´taya (A Gathering of Spirits)." In *Sisters of the Earth: Women's*

217

Prose and Poetry about Nature, ed. Lorraine Anderson. New York: Vintage, 1991: 336–37.

——. *The Sacred Hoop: Recovering the Feminine in American Indian Tradition.* Boston: Beacon, 1986.

——. "The Woman I Love Is a Planet; The Planet I Love Is a Tree." In *Reweaving the World: The Emergence of Ecofeminism,* ed. Irene Diamond and Gloria Feman Orenstein. San Francisco: Sierra Club, 1990: 52–57.

Ames, Roger T. "Taoism and the Nature of Nature." *Environmental Ethics* 8, no. 4 (Winter 1986): 317–50.

Anderson, Lorraine, ed. *Sisters of the Earth: Women's Prose and Poetry About Nature.* New York: Vintage, 1991.

"Another Tailhook Pilot Flies." *Time,* 4 October 1993: 18.

Anzald'a, Gloria. *Borderlands: The New Mestiza/La Frontera.* San Francisco: Spinsters/ Aunt Lute, 1987.

Aristotle. "Nichomachean Ethics." In *The Basic Works of Aristotle.* (New York: Random House, 1941): 928–1112.

Atwood, Margaret. *The Handmaid's Tale.* New York: Seabury Press, 1985.

Bagby, Rachel L. "Daughters of Growing Things." In *Reweaving the World: The Emergence of Ecofeminism,* ed. Irene Diamond and Gloria Feman Orenstein. San Francisco: Sierra Club, 1990: 231–48.

Baier, Annette C. "What Do Women Want In A Moral Theory?" *Nous* 19 (1985): 53–63.

Balbus, Isaac. *Marxism and Domination: A Neo-Hegelian, Feminist, Psychoanalytical Theory of Sexual, Political and Technological Liberation.* Princeton, N.J.: Princeton University Press, 1982.

Bandyopadhyay, Jayanta, and Vandana Shiva. "Chipko: Rekindling India's Forest Culture." *The Ecologist* 17, no. 1 (1987): 26–34.

Bar-On, Bat Ami. "Why Terrorism Is Morally Problematic." In *Feminist Ethics,* ed. Claudia Card. Lawrence: University of Kansas Press, 1991: 107–25.

Becker, Ernest. *The Denial of Death.* New York: Free Press, 1973.

Benhabib, Seyla. *Situating the Self: Gender, Community, and Postmodernism in Contemporary Ethics.* New York: Routledge, 1992.

Biehl, Janet. *Rethinking Ecofeminist Politics.* Boston: South End Press, 1991.

Bigwood, Carol. *Earth Muse: Feminism, Nature, and Art.* Philadelphia: Temple University Press, 1993.

Birke, Lynda. *Feminism, Animals, Science: The Naming of the Shrew.* Bristol, Pa.: Open University Press, 1994.

Bleier, Ruth. *Science and Gender: A Critique of Biology and its Theories on Women.* New York: Pergamon, 1984.

——, ed. *Feminist Approaches to Science.* New York: Pergamon, 1986.

Blum, Lawrence. "Moral Perception and Particularity." *Ethics* 101, no. 4 (July 1991): 70–25.

Bodian, Stephan. "Simple in Means, Rich in Ends: An Interview with Arne Naess." In *Environmental Philosophy,* 1st edition, ed. Michael E. Zimmerman, J. Baird Callicott, George Sessions, Karen J. Warren, and John Clark. Englewood Cliffs, N.J.: Prentice-Hall, 1998: 182–92.

Bookchin, Murray. *The Ecology of Freedom: The Emergence and Dissolution of Hierarchy.* New York: Black Rose Books, 1991.

———. *The Modern Crisis.* Philadelphia: New Society Publishers, 1986.

———. *The Philosophy of Social Ecology: Essays on Dialectical Naturalism.* New York: Black Rose Books, 1990.

———. *Remaking Society.* Boston: South End Books, 1990.

———. *Toward an Ecological Society.* Montreal: Black Rose Books, 1980.

Bowden, Peta. *Caring: Gender Sensitive Ethics.* London: Routledge, 1997.

Braidotti, Rosi, Ewa Charliewicz, Sabine Hävscher, and Saskia Wieringa. *Women, the Environment and Sustainable Development: Toward a Theoretical Synthesis.* Atlantic Highlands, N.J.: Zed Books, 1994.

Brandt, Barbara, and Anne Wilson Schaef. *Whole Life Economics: Revaluing Daily Life.* Philadelphia: New Society Publishers, 1995.

Brennan, Andrew. *Thinking About Nature: An Investigation of Nature, Value and Ecology.* Athens: University of Georgia Press, 1988.

Budapest, Zsuzsanna E. *The Goddess in the Office: A Personal Energy Guide for the Spiritual Warrior at Work.* San Francisco: Harper San Francisco, 1993.

Buege, Douglas. "Epistemic Responsibility to the Nature: Toward a Feminist Epistemology for Environmental Ethics." *American Philosophical Association Newsletter on Feminism and Philosophy* 91 (Spring 1992): 73–78.

Burtt, Edwin. "Philosophers as Warriors." In *The Critique of War,* ed. Robert Ginsberg. Chicago: Henry Regnery, 1969.

Buvinic, Mayra, and Sally W. Yudelman. *Women, Poverty, and Progress in the Third World.* New York: Foreign Policy Association, 1989.

Cady, Duane L. *From Warism to Pacifism: A Moral Continuum.* Philadelphia: Temple University Press, 1989.

Caldecott, Leonie, and Stephanie Leland, ed. *Reclaim the Earth: Women Speak Out for Life on Earth.* London: Women's Press, 1983.

Callicott, J. Baird. "The Conceptual Foundations of the Land Ethic." In *Companion to A Sand County Almanac: Interpretive and Critical Essays,* ed. J. Baird Callicott. Madison: University of Wisconsin Press, 1987: 186–217.

———. "Do Deconstructive Ecology and Sociobiology Undermine Leopold's Land Ethic?" In *Environmental Philosophy,* 2nd edition, ed. Michael E. Zimmerman, J. Baird Callicott, George Sessions, Karen J. Warren, and John Clark. Upper Saddle River, N.J.: Prentice-Hall, 1998: 145–64.

———. *Earth's Insights: A Survey of Ecological Ethics from the Mediterranean Basin to the Australian Outback.* Berkeley: University of California Press, 1994.

———. *In Defense of the Land Ethic: Essays in Environmental Philosophy.* Albany: State University of New York Press, 1989.

———. "The Metaphysical Implications of Ecology" *Environmental Ethics* 8, no. 4 (Winter 1986): 301–16.

———. "The Search for an Environmental Ethic" (revised version). In *Matters of Life and Death,* 3rd edition, ed. Tom Regan. New York: McGraw Hill, 1993: 332–82.

Capra, Fritjof, and Charlene Spretnak. *Green Politics.* New York: Dutton, 1984.

Caputi, Jane. *Gossips, Gorgons and Crones: The Fates of the Earth.* Santa Fe, N.M.: Bear and Company, 1993.

———. "Unthinkable Fathering: Connecting Incest and Nuclearism." In *Bringing Peace Home: Feminism, Violence, and Nature,* ed. Karen J. Warren and Duane L. Cady. Bloomington: Indiana University Press, 1996: 133–51.

Card, Claudia, *The Natural Lottery: Character and Moral Luck.* Philadelphia: Temple University Press, 1996.

———, ed. *Feminist Ethics.* Lawrence: University of Kansas Press, 1991.

Carnes, Patrick. *Out of the Shadows: Understanding Sexual Addiction.* Minneapolis: CompCare, 1983.

Carson, Rachel. *Silent Spring.* Boston: Houghton Mifflin, 1962.

Charnas, Susy McKee. *Motherlines.* New York: Berkley, 1979.

———. *Walk to the End of the World.* New York: Ballantine, 1974.

Chatwin, Bruce. *The Songlines.* New York: Penguin, 1987.

Cheney, Jim. "Eco-Feminism and Deep Ecology." *Environmental Ethics* 9, no. 2 (Summer 1987): 115–45.

———. "Nature/Theory/Difference: Ecofeminism and the Reconstruction of Environmental Ethics." *Contemporary Philosophy* 13 (January/February 1990): 1–14.

———. "The Neo-Stoicism of Radical Environmentalism." *Environmental Ethics* 11, no. 4 (Winter 1989): 293–325.

———. "Postmodern Environmental Ethics: Ethics as Bioregional Narrative." *Environmental Ethics* 11, no. 2 (Summer 1989): 117–34.

Cheng, Chung-Ying. "On the Environmental Ethics of the *Tao* and the *Ch'i.*" *Environmental Ethics* 8, no. 4 (Winter 1986): 351–70.

Chodorow, Nancy. *The Reproduction of Mothering: Psychoanalysis and the Sociology of Gender.* Berkeley: University of California Press, 1978.

Christ, Carol. "Rethinking Theology and Nature." In *Reweaving the World: The Emergence of Ecofeminism,* ed. Irene Diamond and Gloria Feman Orenstein. San Francisco: Sierra Club Books, 1990: 58–69.

———. "Why Women Need the Goddess: Phenomenological, Psychological, and Political Reflections." In *Womanspirit Rising,* ed. Judith Plaskow and Carol Christ. New York: Harper and Row, 1979: 273–87.

Clark, J. Michael. *An Unbroken Circle: Ecotheology, Theodicy, and Ethics.* Irving, Texas: Monument, 1996.

Clement, Grace. *Care, Autonomy, and Justice: Feminism and the Ethic of Care.* Boulder, Colo.: Westview, 1996.

Code, Lorraine. *What Can She Know?: Feminist Theory and the Construction of Knowledge.* Ithaca, N.Y.: Cornell University Press, 1991.

Cohn, Carol. "Sex and Death in the Rational World of Defense Intellectuals." In *Exposing Nuclear Phallacies,* ed. Diana E. H. Russell. New York: Pergamon, 1989: 127–59.

Collard, Andree, with Joyce Contrucci. *Rape of the Wild: Man's Violence Against Animals and the Earth.* Bloomington: Indiana University Press, 1988.

Collins, Patricia Hill. *Black Feminist Thought: Knowledge, Consciousness, and the Politics of Empowerment.* New York: Routledge, 1991.

Cook, Julie. "The Philosophical Colonization of Ecofeminism." *Environmental Ethics* 20, no. 3 (Fall 1998): 227–46.

Cope-Kasten, Vance. "A Portrait of Dominating Rationality." *American Philosophical Association Newsletter on Feminism and Philosophy* 88, no. 2 (March 1989): 29–34.

Corrigan, Theresa, and Stephanie Hoppe. *And a Deer's Ear, Eagle's Song and Bear's Grace.* San Francisco: Cleis, 1990.

———. "Lives on Earth: Developing Animal Rights Consciousness." *woman of power: a magazine of feminism, spirituality, and politics,* 20 (Spring 1991): 59–63.

——. *With a Fly's Eye, Whale's Wit, and Woman's Heart: Animals and Women.* San Francisco: Cleis, 1989.

Crittenden, Chris. "Subordinate and Oppressive Conceptual Frameworks: A Defense of Ecofeminist Perspectives." *Environmental Ethics* 20, no. 3 (Fall 1998): 247–63.

Cuomo, Christine. "Ecofeminism, Deep Ecology, and Human Population." In *Ecological Feminism,* ed. Karen J. Warren. New York: Routledge, 1994: 88–105.

——. *Feminism and Ecological Communities: An Ethic of Flourishing.* London: Routledge, 1998.

——. "Toward Thoughtful Ecofeminist Activism." In *Ecological Feminist Philosophies,* ed. Karen J. Warren. Bloomington: Indiana University Press, 1996: 42–51.

——. "Unravelling the Problems in Ecofeminism." *Environmental Ethics* 14, no. 4 (Winter 1992): 351–63.

——. "Why War Is Not Merely an Event." *Hypatia: A Journal of Feminist Philosophy* 11, no. 4 (1997): 30–45.

Cuomo, Christine, and Lori Gruen. "On Puppies and Pussies: Animals, Intimacy, and Moral Distance." In *Daring to Be Good: Feminist Ethico-Politics,* ed. Bat Ami Bar-On and Anne Ferguson. New York: Routledge, 1997: 129–43.

Curtin, Deane. "Toward an Ecological Ethic of Care." In *Ecological Feminist Philosophies,* ed. Karen J. Warren. Bloomington: Indiana University Press, 1996: 66–81.

Daly, Mary. *Gyn/Ecology: The Metaethics of Radical Feminism.* Boston: Beacon Press, 1978.

——. *Outercourse: The Be-Dazzling Voyage.* San Francisco: HarperCollins, 1992.

Daly, Mary, and Helene Atwan, ed. *Quintessence... Realizing the Archaic Future: A Radical Elemental Feminist Manifesto.* Boston: Beacon, 1998.

Daschle, Thomas A., "Dances with Garbage," *Christian Science Monitor,* 14 February 1991, 18.

Davion, Victoria. "Integrity and Radical Change." In *Feminist Ethics,* ed. Claudia Card. Lawrence: University of Kansas Press, 1991: 180–92.

——. "Is Ecofeminism Feminist?" In *Ecological Feminism,* ed. Karen J. Warren. New York: Routledge, 1994: 8–28.

d'Eaubonne, Françoise. *Le Feminisme ou La Mort.* Paris: Pierre Horay, 1974.

Des Jardins, Joseph R. *Environmental Ethics: An Introduction to Environmental Philosophy.* Belmont, Calif.: Wadsworth, 1993.

Devall, Bill, and George Sessions. *Deep Ecology: Living as if Nature Mattered.* Salt Lake City: Peregrine Smith, 1985.

Diamond, Irene. "Babies, Heroic Experts, and a Poisoned Earth." In *Reweaving the World: The Emergence of Ecofeminism,* ed. Irene Diamond and Gloria Feman Orenstein. San Francisco: Sierra Club Books, 1990: 201–10.

——. *Fertile Ground: Women, Earth, and the Limits of Control.* Boston: Beacon Press, 1994.

——. *Fertility as a Sound of Nature: Echos of Anger and Celebration.* Eugene, Ore.: Department of Political Science, University of Oregon (unpublished manuscript).

Diamond, Irene, and Gloria Feman Orenstein, ed. *Reweaving the World: The Emergence of Ecofeminism.* San Francisco: Sierra Club, 1990.

Dillard, Annie. *Teaching a Stone to Talk.* New York: Harper and Row, 1982.

Doubiago, Sharon. "Deeper Than Deep Ecology: Men Must Become Feminists." *New Catalyst Quarterly* 10 (Winter 1987–88): 10–11.

Du Bois, W. E. B. *The Souls of Black Folk.* New York: Random House, 1990.

Dunayer, Joan. "Sexist Words, Speciesist Roots." In *Animals and Women: Feminist Theoretical Explorations,* ed. Carol J. Adams and Josephine Donovan. Durham, N.C.: Duke University Press, 1995: 11–31.

Dunbar, Dirk. *The Balance of Nature's Polarities in New-Paradigm Theory.* New York: Peter Lang, 1994.

Easlea, Brian. *Fathering the Unthinkable: Masculinity, Scientists, and the Nuclear Arms Race.* London: Pluto Press, 1983.

———. *Science and Sexual Oppression: Patriarchy's Confrontation with Woman and Nature.* London: Weidenfeld and Nicolson, 1981.

Eisler, Riane. *The Chalice and the Blade: Our History, Our Future.* San Francisco: Harper and Row, 1988.

———. "The Gaia Tradition and the Partnership Future." In *Reweaving the World: The Emergence of Ecofeminism,* ed. Irene Diamond and Gloria Feman Orenstein. San Francisco: Sierra Club, 1990: 23–34.

Everett, Jennifer. "Environmental Ethics, Animal Welfarism, and the Problem of Predation: How Bambi Lovers Respect Nature." *Ethics and the Environment,* forthcoming, Spring 2000.

Feinberg, Joel. *Social Philosophy.* Englewood Cliffs, N.J.: Prentice-Hall, 1973.

Ferry, Luc (trans. Carol Volk). *The New Ecological Order.* Chicago: University of Chicago Press, 1995.

Fisher, Berenice, and Joan C. Tronto. "Toward a Feminist Theory of Caring." In *Circles of Care: Work and Identity in Women's Lives,* ed. Emily Abel and Margaret Nelson. Albany: State University of New York Press, 1990: 35–62.

Fortmann, Louise P., and John Bruce. *You've Got to Know Who Controls the Land and Trees People Use: Gender, Tenure and the Environment.* Harare: Centre for Applied Social Science, University of Zimbabwe, 1991.

Fortmann, Louise P., and Sally K. Fairfax. "American Forestry Professionalism in the Third World: Some Preliminary Observations on Effects." In *Women Creating Wealth: Transforming Economic Development,* Selected Papers and Speeches from the Association of Women in Development Conference (Washington, D.C., 1988): 105–8.

Fortmann, Louise P., and Dianne Rocheleau. "Women and Agroforestry: Four Myths and Three Case Studies." *Agroforestry Systems* 9, no. 2 (1985): 253–72.

Fox, Warwick. "The Deep Ecology-Ecofeminism Debate and Its Parallels." In *Environmental Philosophy,* 2nd edition, ed. Michael E. Zimmerman, J. Baird Callicott, George Sessions, Karen J. Warren, and John Clark. Upper Saddle River, N.J.: Prentice Hall, 1998: 227–44.

Freudenberg, Nicholas, and Ellen Zaltzberg. "From Grassroots Activism to Political Power: Women Organizing Against Environmental Hazards." In *Double Exposure: Women's Health Hazards on the Job and at Home,* ed. Wendy Chavkin. New York: Monthly Review, 1984: 246–72.

Friedl, Ernestine. *Women and Men: An Anthropologist's View.* New York: Holt, Reinhart and Winston, 1975.

Friedman, Marilyn. "The Social Self and the Partiality Debates." In *Feminist Ethics,* ed. Claudia Card. Lawrence: University of Kansas Press, 1991:161–79.

From Sun Up. Video. Maryknoll, N.Y.: Maryknoll World Productions, 1987.

Frye, Marilyn. *The Politics of Reality: Essays in Feminist Theory.* Trumansburg, N.Y.: Crossing Press, 1983.

Gaard, Greta. *Ecological Politics: Ecofeminists and the Greens.* Philadelphia: Temple University Press, 1998.

——. ed. *Ecofeminism: Women, Animals, Nature.* Philadelphia: Temple University Press, 1993.

Gauna, Jeanne. "Unsafe for Women, Children and Other Living Things." Albuquerque, N.M.: South West Organizing Project (October 1991).

Gearhart, Sally Miller. *The Wanderground: Stories of the Hill Women.* Boston: Alyson Publications, 1984.

"The Gentleman Was A Devil." *60 Minutes* television show; broadcast date 6 February 1983.

George, Kathryn Paxton. "Should Feminists be Vegetarians? Viewpoint." *Signs* 19, no. 2 (1994): 405–34.

Gilligan, Carol. *In a Different Voice: Psychological Theories and Women's Development.* Cambridge: Harvard University Press, 1982.

Gilligan, Carol, J. V. Ward, and J. McLean Taylor with B. Baridge, ed. *Mapping the Moral Domain: A Contribution of Women's Thinking to Psychological Theory and Education.* Cambridge, Mass.: Harvard University Press, 1988.

Goleman, Daniel. *Emotional Intelligence: Why It Can Matter More than I.Q.* New York: Bantam Books, 1995.

Golley, Frank B. *A Primer for Environmental Literacy.* New Haven, Conn.: Yale University Press, 1998.

Goodman, Russell. "Taoism and Ecology." *Environmental Ethics* 2, no. 1 (Spring 1980): 73–80.

Gottlieb, Roger S., ed. *This Sacred Earth: Religion, Nature, Environment.* New York: Routledge, 1995.

Gray, Elizabeth Dodson. *Green Paradise Lost.* Wellesley, Mass.: Roundtable Press, 1981.

Green, Elizabeth, and Mary Grey, ed. *Ecofeminism and Theology: Yearbook of the Society of Women in Theological Research.* Kampen, Netherlands: Kok Pharos, 1994.

Griffin, Susan. *Pornography and Science: Culture's Revenge Against Nature.* New York: Harper and Row, 1981.

——. *Woman and Nature: The Roaring Inside Her.* New York: Harper and Row, 1978.

Grimshaw, Jean. *Philosophy and Feminist Thinking.* Minneapolis: University of Minnesota Press, 1986.

Gruen, Lori. "Dismantling Oppression: An Analysis of the Connection Between Women and Animals." In *Ecofeminism: Women, Animals, Nature,* ed. Greta Gaard. Philadelphia: Temple University Press, 1993: 60–90.

——. "On the Oppression of Women and Animals." *Environmental Ethics* 18, no. 4 (Winter 1996): 441–44.

——. "Toward an Ecofeminist Moral Epistemology." In *Ecological Feminism,* ed. Karen J. Warren. New York: Routledge, 1994: 120–38.

Hallen, Patsy. "Careful of Science: A Feminist Critique of Science." *The Trumpeter* 6, no. 1 (Winter 1989): 3–8.

Hamilton, Cynthia. "Women, Home, and Community." *woman of power: a magazine of feminism, spirituality, and politics,* 20 (Spring 1991): 42–53.

Haraway, Donna. *Primate Visions: Gender, Race and Nature in the World of Modern Science.* New York: Routledge, 1989.

———. "Primatology Is Politics by Other Means." In *Feminist Approaches to Science,* ed. Ruth Bleier. New York: Pergamon, 1984: 77–118.

———. *Simians, Cyborgs, and Women: The Reinvention of Nature.* New York: Routledge, 1991.

———. "Situated Knowledges: The Science Question in Feminism and the Privilege of Partial Perspective." *Feminist Studies* 14, no. 3 (Fall 1988): 575–99.

Hardin, Garrett. *Exploring New Ethics for Survival.* New York: Viking, 1972.

———. "Living on a Lifeboat." *BioScience* 24 (October 1974): 561–68.

Harding, Sandra. "Rethinking Standpoint Epistemology: What is 'Strong Objectivity'?" In *Feminist Epistemologies,* ed. Linda Alcoff and Elizabeth Potter. New York: Routledge, 1993: 49–82.

———. *The Science Question in Feminism.* Ithaca, N.Y.: Cornell University Press, 1986.

———. *Whose Science? Whose Knowledge?: Thinking from Women's Lives.* Ithaca, N.Y.: Cornell University Press, 1991.

Harding, Sandra, and Merrill Hintikka, ed. *Discovering Reality: Feminist Perspectives on Epistemology, Metaphysics, Methodology and the Philosophy of Science.* Dordrecht: Reidel, 1983.

Hargrove, Eugene. *Foundations for Environmental Ethics.* Englewood Cliffs, N.J.: Prentice-Hall, 1989.

Harjo, Joy. *In Mad Love and War.* Middleton, Conn.: Wesleyan University Press, 1990.

———. *She Had Some Horses.* New York: Thunder's Mouth, 1983.

———. *What Moon Drove Me to This?* New York: I. Reed Books, 1979.

Harris, Adrienne, and Ynestra King. *Rocking the Ship of State: Towards a Feminist Peace Politics.* Boulder, Colo.: Westview, 1989.

Hartley, Troy W. "Environmental Justice: An Environmental Civil Rights Value Acceptable to All World Views." *Environmental Ethics* 17, no. 3 (Fall 1995): 277–89.

Held, Virginia. *Feminist Morality: Transforming Culture, Society, and Politics.* Chicago: University of Chicago Press, 1993.

Hofrichter, Richard, ed. *Toxic Struggles: The Theory and Practice of Environmental Justice.* Philadelphia: New Society Publishers, 1993.

Hogan, Linda. *Daughters, I Love You.* Denver: Loretto Heights College Publications, 1981.

Hoskins, Marilyn. "Observations on Indigenous and Modern Agroforestry Activities in West Africa." In *Problems of Agroforestry.* Freiburg: University of Freiburg, 1982.

Hrdy, Sarah Blaffer. "Empathy, Polyandry, and the Myth of the Coy Female." In *Feminist Approaches to Science,* ed. Ruth Bleier. New York: Pergamon, 1984: 119–46.

Hughes, Dana. "What's Gotten Into Our Children." Los Angeles: Children Now, 1990.

"The Indian and Toxic Waste," *Minneapolis Star/Tribune,* 4 July 1990, 7A.

Ip, Po-Keung. "Taoism and the Foundation of Environmental Ethics." *Environmental Ethics* 5, no. 4 (Winter 1983): 335–44.

Irigaray, Luce. *Thinking the Difference: For a Peaceful Revolution.* New York: Routledge, 1989.

Jaggar, Alison M. "Caring as a Feminist Practice." In *Justice and Care: Essential Readings in Feminist Ethics,* ed. Virginia Held. Boulder, Colo.: Westview Press, 1995: 179–202.

———. *Feminist Politics and Human Nature.* Totowa, N.J.: Rowman & Littlefield, 1983.

———. "Love and Knowledge." In *Gender/Body,/Knowledge,* ed. Alison M. Jaggar and Susan R. Bordo. New Brunswick, N.J.: Rutgers University Press, 1989: 145–71.

Jasso, Sonia, and Maria Mazorra. "Following the Harvest: The Health Hazards of Migrant and Seasonal Farmworking Women" In *Double Exposure: Women's Health Hazards On the Job and At Home,* ed. Wendy Chavkin. New York: Monthly Review Press, 1984: 86–99.

Kanter, Rosabeth Moss. *Men and Women of the Corporation.* New York: Basic, 1977.

Keller, Evelyn Fox. *A Feeling for the Organism: The Life and Work of Barbara McClintock.* San Francisco: W. H. Freeman, 1983.

———. "Women, Science, and Popular Mythology." In *Machina Ex Dea: Feminist Perspectives on Technology,* ed. Joan Rothschild. New York: Pergamon, 1983: 130–50.

Kelly, Petra. *Thinking Green! Essays on Environmentalism, Feminism, and Nonviolence.* Berkeley, Calif.: Parallax, 1994.

Kheel, Marti. "Animal Liberation is a Feminist Issue." *The New Catalyst Quarterly* 10 (1987–88): 8–9.

———. "From Healing Herbs to Deadly Drugs: Western Medicine's War Against the Natural World." In *Healing the Wounds: The Promise of Ecofeminism*, ed. Judith Plant. Philadelphia: New Society Publishers, 1989: 96–114.

———. "The Liberation of Nature: A Circular Affair." *Environmental Ethics* 7, no. 2 (Summer 1985): 135–49.

Kierkegaard, Søren (trans. Walter Lowrie). *The Concept of Dread*, 1844. Princeton, N.J.: Princeton University Press, 1957.

King, Roger J. H. "Caring About Nature: Feminist Ethics and the Environment." In *Ecological Feminist Philosophies,* ed. Karen J. Warren. Bloomington: Indiana University Press, 1996: 82–96.

King, Ynestra. "The Eco-Feminist Imperative." In *Reclaim the Earth: Women Speak Out for Life on Earth,* ed. Leonie Caldecott and Stephanie Leland. London: The Women's Press, 1983: 9–14.

———. "Ecological Feminism." *Zeta Magazine* (July/August 1988): 124–27.

———. "The Ecology of Feminism and the Feminism of Ecology." In *Healing the Wounds: The Promise of Ecofeminism*, ed. Judith Plant. Philadelphia: New Society Publishers, 1989: 18–28.

———. "Feminism and the Revolt of Nature." *Heresies #13: Feminism and Ecology* 4, no. 1 (1981): 12–16.

———. "Healing the Wounds: Feminism, Ecology, and the Nature/Culture Dualism." In *Reweaving the World: The Emergence of Ecofeminism,* ed. Irene Diamond and Gloria Feman Orenstein. San Francisco: Sierra Club, 1990: 106–21.

Kittay, Eva Feder. "Taking Dependency Seriously: The Family and Medical Leave Act Considered in Light of the Social Organization of Dependency Work and Gender Equality." *Hypatia* 10, no. 1 (Spring 1995): 8–29.

Kittay, Eva Feder, and Diana T. Meyers, ed. *Women and Moral Theory.* Savage, Md.: Rowman & Littlefield, 1987.

Koberstein, Paul. "Exxon Oil Spill Taints Lives of Aleut Indian Villagers." *Sunday Oregonian,* 24 September 1989, A2.

Kolodny, Annette. *The Lay of the Land: Metaphor as Experience and History in American Life and Letters.* Chapel Hill: University of North Carolina Press, 1975.

Kurtz, Ernest. *Shame and Guilt: Characteristics of the Dependency Cycle.* Minneapolis: The Hazelden Foundation, 1981.

Lahar, Stephanie. "Ecofeminist Theory and Grassroots Politics." In *Ecological Feminist Philosophies,* ed. Karen J. Warren. Bloomington: Indiana University Press, 1996: 1–18.

——. "Roots: Rejoining Natural and Social History." In *Ecofeminism: Women, Animals, Nature,* ed. Greta Gaard. Philadelphia: Temple University Press, 1993: 91–117.

Lakoff, George, and Mark Johnson. *Metaphors We Live By.* Chicago: University of Chicago Press, 1980.

Lawson, Nicholas. "Where Whitemen Come to Play." *Cultural Survival Quarterly,* 13, no. 2 (1989): 54–56.

Lee, Dorothy D. *Freedom and Culture.* Englewood Cliffs, N.J.: Prentice-Hall, 1959.

LeGuin, Ursula. *Always Coming Home.* New York: Bantam, 1985.

——. *At The Edge of the World: Thoughts of Words, Women, Places.* New York: Harper and Row, 1989.

——. *Buffalo Gals and Other Animal Presences.* Santa Barbara, Calif.: Capra, 1987.

——. *Wild Oats and Fireweed.* New York: Harper and Row, 1988.

Leland, Stephanie. "Feminism and Ecology: Theoretical Connections." In *Reclaim the Earth: Women Speak Out for Life on Earth,* ed. Leonie Caldecott and Stephanie Leland. London: Women's Press, 1983: 67–72.

Leopold, Aldo. *A Sand County Almanac and Sketches Here and There.* New York: Oxford University Press, 1949, 1977.

Lifton, Robert Jay, and Richard Falk. *Indefensible Weapons: The Political and Psychological Case Against Nuclearism.* New York: Basic, 1982.

Linking Energy with Survival: A Guide to Energy, Environment, and Rural Women's Work. Geneva: International Labour Office, 1987.

Lorde, Audre. "Age, Race, Class, and Sex: Women Redefining Difference." In *Sister Outsider: Essays and Speeches by Audre Lorde.* Trumansburg, N.Y.: Crossing Press, 1984: 114–23.

——. "The Master's Tools Will Never Dismantle the Master's House." In *This Bridge Called My Back: Writings by Radical Women of Color,* 2nd edition, ed. Cherrie Moraga and Gloria Anzald´a. New York: Kitchen Table, Women of Color Press, 1983: 98–101.

Lugones, Maria. "On the Logic of Pluralist Feminism." In *Feminist Ethics,* ed. Claudia Card. Lawrence: University of Kansas Press, 1991: 35–44.

——. "Playfulness, 'World-Travelling,' and Loving Perception." *Hypatia: A Journal of Feminist Philosophy* 2, no. 2 (1987): 3–19.

Lugones, Maria, and Elizabeth V. Spelman. "Have We Got A Theory For You! Feminist Theory, Cultural Imperialism, and The Women's Voice." *Women's Studies International Forum* 6 (1983): 573–81.

Lyons, Alana. *Now It's Our Turn: How Women Can Transform Their Lives and Save the Planet.* Malibu, Calif.: Jaguar 1998.

MacIntyre, Alasdair C. *After Virtue: A Study in Moral Theory.* Notre Dame, Ind.: University of Notre Dame Press, 1984.

Macy, Joanna. "Awakening to the Ecological Self." In *Healing the Wounds: The Promise of Ecological Feminism,* ed. Judith Plant. Santa Cruz, Calif.: New Society Publishers, 1989: 201–11.

Macy, Joanna, John Seed, Pat Fleming, and Arne Naess. *Thinking Like a Mountain: Towards a Council of All Beings.* Philadelphia: New Society Publishers, 1988.

Manning, Rita. *Speaking from the Heart: A Feminist Perspective on Ethics.* Lanham, Md.: Rowman & Littlefield, 1992.

McAllister, Pam, ed. *Reweaving the Web of Life: Feminism and Non-Violence.* Philadelphia: New Society Publishers, 1982.

McDaniel, Jay B. *Earth, Sky, Gods and Mortals: Developing an Ecological Spirituality.* Mystic, Conn.: Twenty-Third Publications, 1990.

——. *Of God and Pelicans: A Theology of Reverence for Life.* Louisville, Ky.: Westminster/John Knox, 1989.

Meine, Curt. *Aldo Leopold.* Madison: University of Wisconsin Press, 1988.

Melden, A. I. "Why Be Moral?" *Journal of Philosophy* 45, no. 17 (1948): 449–56.

Mellor, Mary. *Breaking the Boundaries: Towards a Feminist Green Socialism.* London: Virago, 1992.

——. *Feminism and Ecology.* New York: New York University Press, 1997.

Merchant, Carolyn. *The Death of Nature: Women, Ecology and the Scientific Revolution.* San Francisco: Harper and Row, 1980.

——. *Earthcare: Women and the Environment.* New York: Routledge, 1995.

——. "Ecofeminism and Feminist Theory." In *Reweaving the World: The Emergence of Ecofeminism,* ed. Irene Diamond and Gloria Feman Orenstein. San Francisco: Sierra Club Books, 1990: 100–05.

——. *Radical Ecology: The Search for a Livable World.* New York: Routledge, 1992.

Midgley, Mary. *Animals and Why They Matter.* Athens: University of Georgia Press, 1983.

Mies, Maria. *Patriarchy and Accumulation on a World Scale: Women in the International Division of Labor.* Atlantic Highlands, N.J.: Zed Books, 1986.

Mies, Maria, and Vandana Shiva. *Ecofeminism.* Atlantic Highlands, N.J.: Zed Books, 1993.

Mills, Patricia Jagentowicz. "Feminism and Ecology: On the Domination of Nature." In *Ecological Feminist Philosophies,* ed. Karen J. Warren. Bloomington: Indiana University Press, 1996: 211–27.

Minnick, Elizabeth. *Conceptual Errors Across the Curriculum: Toward a Transformation of the Curriculum.* Memphis: Research Clearinghouse and Curriculum Integration Project, at the Center for Research on Women, Memphis State University, 1986.

Moberg, David. "In the Amazon, An Epidemic of Greed." *In These Times,* 1–7 (May 1991): 3.

"Mothers of Prevention," *Time,* 10 June 1991, 25.

Muir, John. *The Wilderness World of John Muir,* ed. Edwin Way Teale. Boston: Houghton Mifflin, 1954.

Muir, Tom, and Anne Sudar. "Toxic Chemicals in the Great Lakes Basin Ecosystem: Some Observations." Burlington, Ont.: Environment Canada, 1988 (unpublished).

Murphy, Patrick D. "Ground, Pivot, Motion: Ecofeminist Theory, Dialogics, and Literary Practice." In *Ecological Feminist Philosophies,* ed. Karen J. Warren. Bloomington: Indiana University Press, 1996: 228–43.

——. "Introduction: Feminism, Ecology, and the Future of the Humanities." *Studies in the Humanities* (Special Issue on Feminism, Ecology, and the Future of the Humanities, ed. Patrick D. Murphy) 15, no. 2 (1988): 85–89.

——. *Literature, Nature, and Other: Ecofeminist Critiques.* Albany: State University of New York Press, 1995.

Murphy, Raymond. *Rationality and Nature: A Sociological Inquiry into a Changing Relationship.* Boulder, Colo.: Westview, 1994.

Naess, Arne. "The Deep Ecological Movement: Some Philosophical Aspects." *Philosophical Inquiry* 8 (1986): 10–31.

——. *Ecology, Community, and Lifestyle: Outline of an Ecosophy,* trans. and ed. David Rothenberg. Cambridge: Cambridge University Press, 1989.

——. "The Shallow and the Deep, Long-Range Ecology Movement: A Summary." *Inquiry* 16, no. 1 (1973): 95–100.

Narayan, Uma. "Working Across Differences: Some Considerations on Emotions and Political Practice." *Hypatia: A Journal of Feminist Philosophy* 3, no. 2 (Summer 1988): 31–48.

Nash, Roderick F. "Aldo Leopold's Intellectual Heritage." In *Companion to* A Sand County Almanac: *Interpretive and Critical Essays,* ed. J. Baird Callicott. Madison: University of Wisconsin Press, 1987: 62–88.

——. *American Environmentalism: Readings in Conservation History.* New York: McGraw-Hill, 1990.

Noddings, Nel. *Caring: A Feminine Approach to Ethics and Moral Education.* Berkeley: University of California Press, 1984.

Nordquist, Joan. *Ecofeminist Theory: A Bibliography* (Social Theory: A Bibliographic Series, No. 36). Santa Cruz, Calif.: Reference and Research Services, 1994.

Norwood, Vera. *Made from This Earth: American Women and Nature.* Chapel Hill: University of North Carolina Press, 1993.

Nouwen, Henri J. M. *Out of Solitude: Three Meditations of the Christian Life.* Notre Dame, Ind.: Ave Maria Press, 1974.

——. *Reaching Out: The Three Movements of the Spiritual Life.* Garden City, N.J.: Doubleday, 1975.

Nussbaum, Martha C. *Love's Knowledge: Essays on Philosophy and Literature.* New York: Oxford University Press, 1990.

Oliver, Mary. *American Primitive.* Boston: Little, Brown, 1983.

Olson, Ann, and Joni Seager. *Women in the World: An International Atlas.* New York: Simon and Schuster, 1986.

O'Neill, R. V., D. L. DeAngelis, J. B. Waide, and T. F. Allen. *A Hierarchical Concept of Ecosystems.* Princeton, N.J.: Princeton University Press, 1986.

Orenstein, Gloria. *The Reflowing of the Goddess.* New York: Pergamon, 1990.

Ortner, Sherry B. "Is Female to Male As Nature Is to Culture?" In *Women, Culture, and Society,* ed. M. Z. Rosaldo and L. Lamphere. Stanford, Calif.: Stanford University Press, 1974: 67–87.

Overholt, Thomas W., and J. Baird Callicott. *Clothed-in-Fur and Other Tales: An Introduction to an Ojibwa World View.* Washington, D.C.: University Press of America, 1982.

Pearsall, Marilyn, ed. *Women and Values: Readings in Recent Feminist Philosophy.* Belmont, Calif.: Wadsworth, 1986.

Perlez, Jane. "Inequalities Plague African Women." *Minneapolis Star/Tribune,* 4 March 1991, 4A.

Philipose, Pamela. "Women Act: Women and Environmental Protection in India." In *Healing the Wounds: The Promise of Ecofeminism,* ed. Judith Plant. Philadelphia: New Society Publishers, 1989: 67–75.

Piercy, Marge. *Women on the Edge of Time.* New York: Fawcett Crest, 1976.

Pietilä, Hilkka. *Making Women Matter.* London: Zed Books, 1990.

Pinchot, Gifford. "The Birth of 'Conservation.'" In *American Environmentalism: Readings in Conservation History,* ed. Roderick F. Nash. New York: McGraw-Hill, 1990.

Plant, Judith, ed. *Healing the Wounds: The Promise of Ecofeminism.* Philadelphia: New Society Publishers, 1989.

——. "Searching for Common Ground: Ecofeminism and Bioregionalism." In *Reweaving the World: The Emergence of Ecofeminism,* ed. Irene Diamond and Gloria Feman Orenstein. San Francisco: Sierra Club, 1990: 155–61.

Plumwood, Val. "Ecofeminism: An Overview and Discussion of Positions and Arguments." *Australasian Journal of Philosophy* 64, Supplement on Women and Philosophy (June 1986): 120–39.

———. "Ethics and Instrumentalism: A Response to Janna Thompson." *Environmental Ethics* 13, no. 2 (Summer 1991): 139–50.

———. *Feminism and the Mastery of Nature.* New York: Routledge, 1993.

———. "Human Vulnerability and the Experience of Being Prey." *Quandrant* (March 1995): 29–34.

——— . "Integrating Ethical Frameworks for Animals, Humans and Nature: A Critical Feminist Eco-Socialist Analysis," *Ethics and the Environment* (forthcoming, Spring 2000).

———. "Nature, Self, and Gender: Feminism, Environmental Philosophy, and the Critique of Rationalism." In *Ecological Feminist Philosophies,* ed. Karen J. Warren. Bloomington: Indiana University Press, 1996: 155–80.

Primavesi, Anne. *From Apocalypse to Genesis: Ecology, Feminism, and Christianity.* Minneapolis: Fortress, 1991.

Rae, Eleanor. *Women, the Earth, the Divine (Ecology and Justice).* Maryknoll, N.Y.: Orbis Books, 1994.

Regan, Tom. *All That Dwell Therein: Essays on Animal Rights and Environmental Ethics.* Berkeley: University of California Press, 1982.

———. *The Case for Animal Rights.* Berkeley: University of California Press, 1983.

———. "The Case for Animal Rights." In *People, Penguins, and Plastic Trees,* ed. Christine Pierce and Donald VanDeVeer. Belmont, Calif.: Wadsworth, 1995: 32–39.

———, ed. *Earthbound: New Introductory Essays in Environmental Ethics.* Philadelphia: Temple University Press, 1984.

Regan, Tom, and Peter Singer, ed. *Animal Rights and Human Obligations.* Englewood Cliffs, N.J.: Prentice-Hall, 1976.

Restoring the Balance: Women and Forest Resources. Rome: Food and Culture Organization and Swedish International Development Authority, 1987.

Rich, Adrienne. *Your Native Land, Your Life.* New York: Norton, 1986.

Roach, Catherine. "Loving Your Mother: On the Woman-Nature Connection." In *Ecological Feminist Philosophies,* ed. Karen J. Warren. Bloomington: Indiana University Press, 1996: 52–65.

Rocheleau, Dianne, Barbara Thomas-Slayter, and Esther Wangari, eds. *Feminist Political Ecology: Global Issues and Local Experiences.* New York: Routledge, 1996.

Rose, Deborah Bird. *Nourishing Terrains: Australian Aboriginal Views of Landscape and Wilderness.* Canberra: Australian Heritage Commission, 1996.

Rosenberg, Harriet S. "The Home Is the Workplace: Hazards, Stress, and Pollutants in the Household." In *Double Exposure: Women's Health Hazards on the Job and at Home,* ed. Wendy Chavkin. New York: Monthly Review, 1984: 219–45.

Ruddick, Sara. *Maternal Thinking: Toward a Politics of Peace.* Boston: Beacon, 1989.

Ruether, Rosemary Radford. *Ecofeminism: Symbolic and Social Connections Between the Oppression of Women and the Domination of Nature.* Charlotte: University of North Carolina, 1991.

———. *Gaia and God: An Ecofeminist Theology of Earth Healing.* San Francisco: Harper San Francisco, 1992.

———. *New Woman, New Earth: Sexist Ideologies and Human Liberation.* New York: Seabury, 1975.

———, ed. *Women Healing Earth: Third World Women on Ecology, Feminism, and Religion.* Maryknoll, N.Y.: Orbis, 1996.

Russell, Dick. "Environmental Racism." *The Amicus Journal* (Spring 1989): 22–32.

Sachs, Carolyn E., ed. *Women Working in the Environment.* Bristol, Penn.: Taylor and Francis, 1997.

Sagoff, Mark. *The Economy of the Earth: Philosophy, Law, and the Environment.* New York: Cambridge University Press, 1988.

Sale, Kirkpatrick. *Dwellers in the Land: Bioregional Vision.* San Francisco: Sierra Club, 1985.

Salleh, Ariel Kay. "Deeper than Deep Ecology: The Eco-Feminist Connection." *Environmental Ethics* 6, no. 4 (Winter 1984): 339–45.

———. *Ecofeminism as Politics: Nature, Marx and the Postmodern.* New York: Zed Books, 1997.

———. "The Ecofeminism/Deep Ecology Debate." *Environmental Ethics* 14, no. 3 (Fall 1993): 195–216.

———. "Epistemology and the Metaphors of Production: An Eco-Feminist Reading of Critical Theory." *Studies in the Humanities* (Special issue on Feminism, Ecology, and the Future of the Humanities, ed. Patrick D. Murphy), 15, no. 2 (1988): 130–39.

———. "Working with Nature: Reciprocity or Control?" In *Environmental Philosophy: From Animal Rights to Radical Ecology,* 2nd edition, ed. Michael E. Zimmerman, J. Baird Callicott, George Sessions, Karen J. Warren, and John Clark (Upper Saddle River, N.J.: Prentice-Hall, 1998): 315–24.

Sanday, Peggy. *Female Power and Male Dominance: On the Origins of Sexual Inequality.* New York: Cambridge University Press, 1981.

Sandilands, Catriona. *The Good-Natured Feminist: Ecofeminism and the Quest for Democracy.* Minneapolis: University of Minnesota Press, 1999.

Schweitzer, Albert. *Out of My Life and Thought: An Autobiography.* New York: Holt, 1933.

———. *Philosophy of Civilization: Civilization and Ethics,* trans. John Naish. London: A. and C. Black, 1923.

Seager, Joni. *Earth Follies: Coming to Feminist Terms with the Global Environmental Crisis.* New York: Routledge, 1993.

———. *The New State of the Earth Atlas,* 2nd edition. New York: Simon and Schuster, 1995.

———. *The State of Women in the World Atlas.* London: Penguin, 1997.

Sen, Gita, and Caren Grown. *Development, Crises and Alternative Visions: Third World Women's Perspectives.* New York: Monthly Review, 1987.

Seneca, Joseph, and Michael Taussig. *Environmental Economics,* 2nd edition. Englewood Cliffs, N.J.: Prentice-Hall, 1979.

Shange, Ntozake. *For Colored Girls Who Have Considered Suicide When the Rainbow Is Enuf.* New York: Bantam, 1977.

Shiva, Vandana. *Close to Home: Women Reconnect Ecology, Health and Development Worldwide.* Philadelphia: New Society Publishers, 1994.

———. *Staying Alive: Women, Ecology and Development.* London: Zed Books, 1988.

Shulman, Seth. *The Threat at Home: Confronting the Toxic Legacy of the U.S. Military.* Boston: Beacon, 1992.

Silko, Leslie Marmon. *Almanac of the Dead: A Novel.* New York: Penguin, 1991.

——. *Ceremony.* New York: New American Library, 1977.

——. "Landscape, History and the Pueblo Imagination." In *On Nature: Nature, Landscape, and Natural History,* ed. Daniel Halpern. San Francisco: North Point, 1987, 83–94.

Singer, Peter. "Animal Liberation." In *People, Penguins, and Plastic Trees: Basic Issues in Environmental Ethics,* ed. Christine Pierce and Donald VanDeVeer. Belmont, Calif.: Wadsworth Publishing Company, 1995: 23–31.

——. *Animal Liberationism: A New Ethics for Our Treatment of Animals.* New York: Avon Books, 1975.

Slicer, Deborah. "Your Daughter or Your Dog? A Feminist Assessment of the Animal Research Issue." In *Ecological Feminist Philosophies,* ed. Karen J. Warren. Bloomington: Indiana University Press, 1996: 97–113.

Smith, Amanda. "At Naval Academy, Hatred toward Women Is Part of Life." *Minneapolis Star/Tribune,* 13 November 1992: 19A.

Smith, Barbara, ed. *Home Girls: A Black Feminist Anthology.* New York: Kitchen Table, Women of Color Press, 1983.

Snyder, Howard A. *Earthcurrents: The Struggle for the World's Soul.* Nashville: Abingdon, 1995.

Spelman, Elizabeth V. *Inessential Woman: Problems of Exclusion in Feminist Thought.* Boston: Beacon, 1988.

Spencer, Daniel T. "Ecological and Social Transformations and the Construction of Race and Place: A View From Iowa." Unpublished paper, n.d.

Spretnak, Charlene. "Ecofeminism: Our Roots and Flowering." In *Reweaving the World: The Emergence of Ecofeminism,* ed. Irene Diamond and Gloria Feman Orenstein. San Francisco: Sierra Club Books, 1990: 3–14.

——. "Naming the Cultural Forces that Push Us Toward War." In *Exposing Nuclear Phallacies,* ed. Diana E. H. Russell. New York: Pergamon, 1989: 53–62.

——. *The Spiritual Dimension of Green Politics.* Santa Fe, N.M.: Bear and Company, 1985.

——. *States of Grace: The Recovery of Meaning in the Postmodern Age.* New York: Harper Collins, 1991.

——. "States of Grace." In *Environmental Ethics: Convergence and Divergence,* eds. Susan J. Armstrong and Richard G. Botzler. New York: McGraw Hill, 1993: 466–74.

——. "Toward an Ecofeminist Spirituality." In *Healing the Wounds: The Promise of Ecological Feminism,* ed. Judith Plant. Philadelphia: New Society Publishers, 1989: 127–32.

——, ed. *The Politics of Women's Spirituality: Essays on the Rise of Spiritual Power Within the Feminist Movement.* Garden City, N.Y.: Anchor, 1982.

Starhawk. "Feminist, Earth-Based Spirituality and Ecofeminism." In *Healing the Wounds: The Promise of Ecological Feminism,* ed. Judith Plant. Philadelphia: New Society Publishers, 1989.

——. *The Spiral Dance: A Rebirth of the Ancient Religion of the Great Goddess.* New York: Harper and Row, 1979.

——. *Truth or Dare: Encounters with Power, Authority, and Mystery.* San Francisco: Harper and Row, 1989.

The State of India's Environment, 1984–85: The Second Citizen's Report. New Delhi: Center for Science and Environment, 1985.

Sterba, James P. *Earth Ethics: Environmental Ethics, Animal Rights, and Practical Appli-*

cations. Englewood Cliffs, N.J.: Prentice-Hall, 1995.

——. *Justice for Here and Now.* New York: Cambridge University Press, 1998.

Stone, Christopher D. *Should Trees Have Standing? Toward a Theory of Legal Rights for Natural Objects.* Los Altos, Calif.: William Kaufmann, 1974.

Strange, Mary Zeiss. *Woman the Hunter.* Boston: Beacon, 1997.

Strange, Penny. "It'll Make a Man Out of You: A Feminist View of the Arms Race." In *Exposing Nuclear Phallacies,* ed. Diana E. H. Russell. New York: Pergamon, 1989: 104–26.

Sturgeon, Noël. *Ecofeminist Natures: Race, Gender, Feminist Theory and Political Action.* New York: Routledge, 1997.

Tapahonso, Luci. *A Breeze Swept Through.* Albuquerque, N.M.: West End Press, 1987.

Taylor, Paul. *Respect for Nature: A Theory of Environmental Ethics.* Princeton, N.J.: Princeton University Press, 1986.

Teish, Luisa. "Women's Spirituality: A Household Act." In *Home Girls: A Black Feminist Anthology,* ed. Barbara Smith. New York: Kitchen Table, Women of Color Press, 1983: 331–51.

Tepper, Sheri. *The Gate to Women's Country.* New York: Bantam, 1989.

Thompson, Patricia J., ed. *Environmental Education for the 21st Century: International and Interdiscplinary Perspectives.* New York: Peter Lang, 1997.

Timberlake, Lloyd. *Africa in Crisis: The Causes, the Cures of Environmental Bankruptcy.* Philadelphia: New Society Publishers, 1986.

Tinker, Irene. "Women and Energy: Program Implications." Washington, D.C.: Equity Policy Center, 1980.

Tong, Rosemarie. *Feminist Thought: A Comprehensive Introduction.* Boulder, Colo.: Westview, 1989.

"Toxic Waste and Race in the United States: A National Report on the Racial and Socioeconomic Characteristics of Communities with Hazardous Waste Sites," 1987, Commission for Racial justice, United Church of Christ, 105 Madison Avenue, New York, NY 10016.

Trask, Mililani. "Native Hawaiian Historical and Cultural Perspectives on Environmental Justice." *Race, Poverty and the Environment* 3, no. 1 (Spring 1992): 6–8.

Tronto, Joan C. "Care as a Basis for Radical Political Judgments." *Hypatia* 10, no. 2 (Spring 1995): 141–49.

Tuana, Nancy, and Karen J. Warren, ed. Special issues on Feminism and the Environment, *American Philosophical Association Newsletter on Feminism and Philosophy* 90, no. 3 (Fall 1991) and 91, no. 1 (Winter 1992).

Turpin, Jennifer E., and Lois Ann Lorentzen, ed. *The Gendered New World Order: Militarism, Development, and the Environment.* New York: Routledge, 1996.

United Nations. Conference on Environment and Development. *Women, Children and Environment: Implications for Sustainable Development.* Geneva: UNCED, 1991.

——. Development Fund for Women. *Women, Environment, Development: Action for Agenda 21.* New York: The Fund, 1991.

——. Economic Commission for Africa. *Handbook on Women in Africa.* 1975.

VanDeVeer, Donald. "Interspecific Justice." In *People, Penguins and Plastic Trees: Basic Issues in Environmental Ethics,* ed. Christine Pierce and Donald VanDeVeer. Belmont, Calif.: Wadsworth, 1995: 51–64.

Van Gogh, Anna. *Promise Me Love: A Preview of a Brighter Tomorrow.* Grand Junction,

Colo.: Lucy Mary Books, 1993.

Vellacott, Jo. "Women, Peace and Power." In *Reweaving the Web of Life: Feminism and Non- Violence,* ed. Pam McAllister. Philadelphia: New Society Publishers, 1982: 30–41.

Vollers, M. "Healing the Ravaged Land: Third World Women and Conservation." *International Wildlife* 18, no. 1 (1988): 4–9.

Walker, Alice. *Living by the Word: Selected Writings 1973–1987.* New York: Harcourt Brace Jovanovich, 1988.

———. "Only Justice Can Stop a Curse." In *Reweaving the Web of Life: Feminism and Non-Violence,* ed. Pam McAllister. Philadelphia: New Society Publishers, 1982: 262–65.

———. *The Temple of My Familiar.* New York: Pocket Books, 1990.

Walker, Margaret. "Moral Understandings: Alternative 'Epistemology' for a Feminist Ethics." *Hypatia: A Journal of Feminist Philosophy* 4, no. 2 (Summer 1989): 15–28.

Waring, Marilyn. "Your Economic Theory Makes No Sense." In *If Women Counted: A New Feminist Economics.* New York: Harper and Row, 1988.

Warren, Karen J. "Care-Sensitive Ethics and Situated Universalism." *Global Environmental Ethics,* ed. Nicholas Low. London: Routledge, 1999: 131–45.

———. "Critical Thinking and Feminism." *Informal Logic* 10, no. 1 (Winter 1988): 31–42.

———. "Deep Ecology and Ecofeminism." In *Philosophical Dialogues: Arne Naess and the Progress of Ecophilosophy,* ed. Nina Witoszek and Andrew Brennan. Lanham, Md.: Rowman & Littlefield, 1999: 255–69.

———. "Environmental Justice: Some Ecofeminist Worries About a Distributive Model." *Environmental Ethics* 21, no. 2 (Summer 1999): 151–61.

———. "Feminism and Ecology: Making Connections." *Environmental Ethics* 9, no. 1 (Spring 1987): 3–20.

———. "Feminism and the Environment: An Overview of the Issues." *American Philosophical Association Newsletter on Feminism and Philosophy* 90, no. 3 (Fall 1991): 108–16.

———. "A Feminist Philosophical Perspective on Ecofeminist Spiritualities." In *Ecofeminism and the Sacred,* ed. Carol Adams. New York: Continuum, 1993: 119–32.

———. "Male-Gender Bias and Western Conceptions of Reason and Rationality." *American Philosophical Association Newsletter on Feminism and Philosophy* 88, no. 2 (March 1989): 48–53.

———. "The Power and the Promise of Ecological Feminism." *Environmental Ethics* 12, no. 2 (Summer 1990): 125–46.

———. "Re-Writing the Future: The Feminist Challenge to the Malestream Curriculum." *Feminist Teacher* 4, no. 2/3 (Fall 1989): 46–52.

———. "Taking Empirical Data Seriously: An Ecofeminist Philosophical Perspective." In *Ecofeminism: Women, Culture, Nature,* ed. Karen J. Warren. Bloomington: Indiana University Press, 1997: 3–20.

———. "Toward an Ecofeminist Peace Politics." In *Ecological Feminism,* ed. Karen J. Warren. New York: Routledge, 1994: 179–99.

———, ed. *Ecofeminism: Women, Culture, Nature.* Bloomington: Indiana University Press, 1997.

———, ed. *Ecological Feminism.* New York: Routledge, 1994.

———, ed. *Ecological Feminist Philosophies.* Bloomington: Indiana University Press, 1996.

Warren, Karen J., and Duane L. Cady. "Feminism and Peace: Seeing Connections." In *Bringing Peace Home: Feminism, Violence, and Nature,* ed. Karen J. Warren and Duane

L. Cady. Bloomington: Indiana University Press, 1996: 1–15.

――, ed. *Bringing Peace Home: Feminism, Violence, and Nature.* Bloomington: Indiana University Press, 1996.

Warren, Karen J., and Jim Cheney. "Ecological Feminism and Ecosystem Ecology." In *Ecological Feminist Philosophies,* ed. Karen J. Warren. Bloomington: Indiana University Press, 1996: 244–62.

――. "Ecosystem Ecology and Metaphysical Ecology: A Case Study." In *Environmental Ethics* 15, no. 2 (Summer 1993): 99–116.

Weilbacher, Mike. "In City Is the Preservation of the World." *Pennsylvania Alliance for Environmental Ethics (PAEE) Newsletter* 15, no. 4 (Fall 1991): 4–5, 14.

Wenz, Peter. *Environmental Justice.* Albany: State University of New York Press, 1988.

Weston, Anthony. *Toward Better Problems: New Perspectives on Abortion, Animal Rights, the Environment, and Justice.* Philadelphia: Temple University Press, 1992.

White, Beverly. "Environmental Equity Justice Centers: A Response to Inequity." In *Environmental Justice: Issues, Policies, and Solutions,* ed. Bunyan Bryant. Washington, D.C.: Island Press, 1995: 57–65.

Wigley, Daniel C., and Kristin Shrader-Frechette. "Consent, Equity, and Environmental Justice." In *Faces of Environmental Racism: Confronting Issues of Global Justice,* ed. Laura Westra and Peter S. Wenz. Lanham, Md.: Rowman & Littlefield, 1995: 135–59.

Wijkman, Anders, and Lloyd Timberlake. *Natural Disasters: Acts of God or Acts of Man?* Philadelphia: New Society Publishers, 1988.

Wilhelm, Kate. *Juniper Time.* New York: Pocket Books, 1980.

Williams, Terry Tempest. "The Wild Card." *Wilderness* (Summer 1993): 26–29.

Women and the World Conservation Strategy. Gland: International Union for the Conservancy of Nature, 1987.

The World's Women, 1970–1990: Trends and Statistics. New York: United Nations, 1990.

The World's Women, 1995: Trends and Statistics. New York: United Nations, 1995.

Young, Iris Marion. *Justice and the Politics of Difference.* Princeton, N.J.: Princeton University Press, 1990.

Zabinski, Catherine. "Scientific Ecology and Ecological Feminism: The Potential for Dialogue." In *Ecofeminism: Women, Culture, Nature,* ed. Karen J. Warren. Bloomington, Ind.: Indiana University Press, 1997: 314–24.

Zahava, Irene. *Through Other Eyes: Animal Stories by Women.* Freedom, Calif.: Crossing Press, 1988.

Zimmerman, Michael E. *Contesting Earth's Future: Radical Ecology and Postmodernity.* Berkeley: University of California Press, 1994.

――. "Feminism, Deep Ecology and Environmental Ethics." *Environmental Ethics* 9, no. 1 (Spring 1987): 21–44.

Index

235

About the Author

Karen J. Warren is professor of philosophy at Macalester College in St. Paul, Minnesota. Her primary areas of scholarly interest are feminist and environmental philosophy. In addition to her college and university teaching, she has taught philosophy in a prison and, for more than twenty-five years, to primary and secondary school children. She has spoken on ecofeminist philosophy in Argentina, Australia, Brazil, Canada, Finland, Norway, Russia, and Sweden, as well as throughout the United States. She is the author of more than forty-five refereed articles, editor or co-editor of five books, and recipient of a first place award for the video "Thinking Out Loud: Teaching Critical Thinking Skills." Her scholarly passion is ecofeminist philosophy.